SOCIAL CHOICE AND WELFARE

CONTRIBUTIONS
TO
ECONOMIC ANALYSIS

145

Honorary Editor

J. TINBERGEN

Editors

D.W. JORGENSON
J. WAELBROECK

NORTH-HOLLAND PUBLISHING COMPANY
AMSTERDAM · NEW YORK · OXFORD

SOCIAL CHOICE
AND
WELFARE

Edited by

PRASANTA K. PATTANAIK

University of Birmingham

MAURICE SALLES

Université de Caen

1983

NORTH-HOLLAND PUBLISHING COMPANY

AMSTERDAM · NEW YORK · OXFORD

ISBN 0444 86487 3

Publishers:

NORTH-HOLLAND PUBLISHING COMPANY
AMSTERDAM · NEW YORK · OXFORD

Sole distributors for the U.S.A. and Canada:

ELSEVIER SCIENCE PUBLISHING COMPANY, INC.
52 VANDERBILT AVENUE
NEW YORK, N.Y. 10017

Library of Congress Cataloging in Publication Data

Main entry under title:

Social choice and welfare.

    (Contributions to economic analysis ; 145)
    "Papers presented at the symposium on collective choice, which was held in Caen, from September 4-9, 1980"--Pref.
    1. Social choice--Congresses. 2. Welfare economics--Congresses. I. Pattanaik, Prasanta K. II. Salles, Maurice. III. Series.
HB846.8.S6 1983   302'.13   83-2397
ISBN 0-444-86487-3

PRINTED IN THE NETHERLANDS

Introduction to the series

This series consists of a number of hitherto unpublished studies, which are introduced by the editors in the belief that they represent fresh contributions to economic science.

The term "economic analysis" as used in the title of the series has been adopted because it covers both the activities of the theoretical economist and the research worker.

Although the analytical methods used by the various contributors are not the same, they are nevertheless conditioned by the common origin of their studies, namely theoretical problems encountered in practical research. Since for this reason, business cycle research and national accounting, research work on behalf of economic policy, and problems of planning are the main sources of the subjects dealt with, they necessarily determine the manner of approach adopted by the authors. Their methods tend to be "practical" in the sense of not being too far remote from application to actual economic conditions. In addition they are quantitative rather than qualitative.

It is the hope of the editors that the publication of these studies will help to stimulate the exchange of scientific information and to reinforce international cooperation in the field of economics.

The Editors

Preface

This volume comprises papers presented at the Symposium on Collective Choice which was held in Caen from 4 September to 9 September 1980; the papers have been refereed and revised following the discussions which took place during the Symposium.

The Symposium was hosted by the Centre d'Etudes et de Recherches d'Economie Mathématique (now Institut des Sciences de la Décision) of the Université de Caen. Its organization would not have been possible without the generous and constant support of Professor Robert Le Duff, Director of the Département de Préparation aux Affaires. We gratefully acknowledge a grant from the Université de Caen.

In view of the phenomenal expansion of social choice theory and welfare economics over the last two decades, we felt that such a symposium was appropriate. We chose the particular date because we expected that the possibility of attending both this meeting and the World Congress of the Econometric Society at Aix-en-Provence would be an incentive for specialists in social choice and welfare economics to travel to France.

We would like to thank all the participants for their co-operation and help which made the task of organizing the Symposium easy and pleasant. In particular, we would like to thank Wulf Gaertner, Paul Grout, Peter Hammond, Steve Matthews, Hervé Moulin, Yew-Kwang Ng, Amartya Sen and Kotaro Suzumura for having given generously their time for refereeing the papers. We are extremely grateful to Drs. Ellen M. van Koten, the Economics Editor of North-Holland Publishing Company, for her encouragement and advice, and for her patience with delays in our preparing the manuscript. Finally, we would like to thank Academic Press, Inc. and North-Holland Publishing Company for their kind permission to reproduce respectively the paper by Peter Coughlin and Shmuel Nitzan (published in the *Journal of Economic Theory*, 1981) and the paper by Jean-Pierre Barthélémy (published in *Mathematical Social Sciences*, 1982).

P.K. PATTANAIK

M. SALLES

Contents

List of participants

Alain Albizatti, Université de Paris IX, France
Joseph Abdou, Université de Paris IX, France
Nick Baigent, University of Swansea, Wales
Taradas Bandyopadhyay, University of Hull, England
Salvador Barberá, University of Bilbao, Spain
Jean-Pierre Barthélémy, Ecole Nationale Supérieure des Télécommunications, Paris, France
Pierre Batteau, Université d'Aix-Marseille III, France
Thom Bezembinder, Catholic University of Nijmegen, Holland
Georges Bordes, Université de Bordeaux, France
Donald Campbell, University of Toronto, Canada
Graciela Chichilnisky, University of Essex, England
Eva Colorni, City of London Polytechnic, England
Peter Coughlin, Stanford University, U.S.A.
Christian Dave, Centre Universitaire de la Réunion, France
Rajat Deb, Southern Methodist University, Dallas, U.S.A.
Gabrielle Demange, Université de Paris IX, France
Bhaskar Dutta, Indian Statistical Institute, Calcutta, India
Xavier Freixas, Université de Toulouse, France
Wulf Gaertner, University of Osnabruck, Germany
Roy Gardner, Iowa State University, U.S.A.
Julio Grafe, University of Bilbao, Spain
Paul Grout, University of Birmingham, England
Peter Hammond, Stanford University, U.S.A.
Geoffrey Heal, University of Essex, England
Gilbert Laffond, Université de Paris IX, France
Ian McIntyre, University of Birmingham, England
Richard McKelvey, California Institute of Technology, U.S.A.
Maurice McManus, University of New South Wales, Australia
Eric Maskin, Massachussetts Institute of Technology, U.S.A.
Steve Matthews, Northwestern University, U.S.A.

Bernard Monjardet, Ecole des Hautes Etudes en Sciences Sociales, France
Hervé Moulin, Université de Paris IX, France
Shmuel Nitzan, Hebrew University of Jerusalem, Israel
Yew-Kwang Ng, Monash University, Australia
Marcel Ovide-Etienne, Université de Caen, France
Prasanta Pattanaik, University of Birmingham, England
Bezalel Peleg, Hebrew University of Jerusalem, Israel
Zvi Ritz, University of Illinois, U.S.A.
Jean-Charles Rocher, Université de Paris IX, France
Ariel Rubinstein, Hebrew University of Jerusalem, Israel
Maurice Salles, Université de Caen, France
Amartya Sen, Oxford University, England
Norman Schofield, University of Essex, England
Kotaro Suzumura, Kyoto University, Japan
H. Peyton Young, International Institute of Applied Systems Analysis, Austria

Introduction

P.K. PATTANAIK
University of Birmingham

and

M. SALLES
Université de Caen

Twenty-five years ago, in a rather surprising conclusion to his book *Theoretical Welfare Economics* (1975), Graaff wrote:

> I do feel very strongly that the greatest contribution economics is likely to make to human welfare, broadly conceived, is through positive studies — through contributing to our understanding of how the economic system actually works in practice — rather than through normative welfare theory itself... .
>
> In my view the job of the economist is not to try to reach welfare conclusions for others, but rather to make available the positive knowledge — the information and the understanding — on the basis of which laymen (and economists themselves, out of office hours) can pass judgment.

The phenomenal expansion of the theory of social choice and welfare since 1957 is the proof that a large number of economists and other social scientists did not agree with Graaff. In this context, can we suggest that Graaff's opinion was based on a strong belief that the study of social welfare was welfare *economics* and as such a research subject for economists only? But the current theory of social welfare encompasses within its domain not only most of welfare economics but also social choice theory, voting theory, and significant parts of moral, political, and social philosophy (ethics) as well as large parts of game theory. We can trace the origin of our subject back to the eighteenth century, the so-called Age of Enlightenment in France, through the works of Borda (1781) and Condorcet (1785) (for important and detailed historical comments see Black,

Social Choice and Welfare, edited by P.K. Pattanaik and M. Salles
© *North-Holland Publishing Company, 1983*

1958, and Rashed, 1974; Rashed stressing the influence of John Locke's thought on the philosophy of Condorcet). Despite the interesting contributions of Dodgson (Lewis Carroll) and of American scholars trying to solve the difficult apportionment problems, voting theory almost disappeared from the scientific scene when welfare economics started its development mainly owing to Pigou's magnum opus, *The Economics of Welfare* (1932), of which the first edition was published in 1912 under the title *Wealth and Welfare*. At last, in the late 1940s and the 1950s, the papers and books of Arrow, Black, Downs, and Farquharson endowed social choice and voting theory with sure foundations. In the introduction to his book *Social Choice and Individual Values* (1963) Arrow clearly related the problem of building collective preference from individual preferences to Bergson and Samuelson social welfare function. (Later Samuelson, 1967, wrote: "Indeed, I shall argue again here the thesis that the Arrow result is much more a contribution to the infant discipline of mathematical politics than to the traditional mathematical theory of welfare economics." We can agree because Samuelson used the adjective *traditional*, but again what is and what should be the mathematical theory of welfare economics?)

In some sense, Arrow's negative central theorem is purely ethical. It shows essentially that certain value judgements which we might find fair to incorporate in a social choice mechanism are logically inconsistent. It can also be viewed as a generalization and axiomatization of the Condorcet paradox. More precisely, let N be the finite set of individuals (voters) of cardinality n, and X the set of alternatives. Each individual i is endowed with a preference ordering (a common assumption in economics) R_i over X. An Arrovian social welfare function f associates to an n-tuple $(R_1, ..., R_n)$ of individual preference orderings over X a collective preference ordering over X. This function must satisfy four conditions which can be considered as minimal requirements. The first asserts that the domain of the function is unrestricted: all n-tuples are permissible. The second excludes aggregation methods such as Borda's rule: if for two n-tuples $(R_1, ..., R_n)$ and $(R_1', ..., R_n')$, and two alternatives a and b, the restrictions to $\{a, b\}$ of R_i and R_i' are identical for each individual, the restrictions to $\{a, b\}$ of $f(R_1, ..., R_n)$ and $f(R_1', ..., R_n')$ are also identical. This condition, which Arrow called independence of irrelevant alternatives, and defined here in the restricted way it is used in the proof of the impossibility theorem, strongly emphasizes the ordinal aspects of the social welfare function (see Murakami, 1968).

The third condition is a Pareto-type condition: given two alternatives, a and b, if every individual strictly prefers a to b, then the collectivity also strictly prefers a to b. Finally, dictatorship is made impossible by the last condition: there is no individual whose strict preferences emerge as the social strict preferences irrespective of the others' preferences. These four conditions for a social welfare function are inconsistent given that there are at least two individuals and three alternatives. To avoid this negative result different writers have followed alternative routes.

The first was to enlarge the set where the aggregation function takes its values, i.e. to weaken the rationality requirements (particularly, transitivity) for collective preferences, or to study aggregation processes taking choice functions as values (which, in the literature on existence theorems, is essentially similar). Despite some possibility theorems due to Sen (1969, 1970a), one must remember the minimality of Arrow's conditions. Replacing transitivity of the collective weak preference by transitivity or acyclicity of the strict preference relation does not take us very far. It suffices then to modify the conditions (for example, by replacing the no-dictator condition by a no-vetoer condition, or to add a monotonicity condition) to get again negative results (see, for instance, Mas-Colell and Sonnenschein, 1972; Blau and Deb, 1977; Blair, Bordes, Kelly and Suzamura, 1976; and Kelly, 1978; see also Sen's surveys, 1977, 1982, for brilliant explanations and a complete bibliography). One should also note that the full force of Arrow's result is retained when the collective preference is a semi-order (Blair and Pollack, 1979; Blau, 1979).

The second escape route stems from Black's contributions (1948, 1958). Black showed that if the domains of specific aggregation rules were restricted by excluding some configurations of individual preference orderings, rationality of the collective preference could be preserved. Of course, the unrestricted domain condition of Arrow's theorem is violated and the practical meaning of the restriction should be discussed. The first restricted preference condition introduced in the case of the majority rule is single-peakedness. Afterwards the majority rule, or majority-type rules, have been intensively studied, leading to characterization theorems for different rationality conditions, mainly by Inada, Sen, Pattanaik, and Fishburn. Other rules, such as simple games, have also been considered by Dummett and Farquharson, Nakamura, and Salles. Finally, Kalai and Muller provided such conditions for the existence of social welfare functions in general. (For this literature see Pattanaik, 1971, Fishburn, 1973, and the survey by Gaertner and Salles, 1981.)

Positive results have also been obtained when the restriction is number-dependent, i.e. when the distribution of individuals over the preferences is constrained. The main contributors in this area have been Saposnik, Bowman and Colantoni, Kaneko, Gaertner and Slutsky (see Gaertner and Salles, 1981, for references).

Finally we must mention the very important and somewhat neglected possibility results obtained by relating the nature of the aggregation procedure to the number of alternatives (Craven, 1971; Ferejohn and Grether 1974), or in the case of simple games by relating some number calculated from the structure of the considered game to the cardinality of the set of alternatives (Nakamura, 1979). (See also the relationship between this question and the dimension of the policy space problem in the contributions of Greenberg and Schofield to which we refer below.)

Arrow's analysis confined itself to a framework which derived the social ordering solely on the basis of individual orderings over the set of alternatives. Therefore it ruled out the use of any cardinal information about individual preferences, and also any possibility of interpersonal comparison of utilities. This has been widely recognized to be a highly restrictive feature ever since the publication of Arrow's result. While, in positive economics, the framework of cardinal preferences may be adequate in explaining certain types of consumer behaviour, this in itself does not constitute sufficient justification for eschewing in the normative theory of social choice, notions of cardinal and interpersonally comparable utility if these notions otherwise make intuitive sense and can be given empirical as well as analytical basis. Note that the introduction of cardinal utilities, by itself, does little to alleviate Arrow's problem if one continues to rule out interpersonal comparisons of utilities (see Sen, 1970a); a richer theory in this context is possible only when one is prepared to admit interpersonal comparisons of utility. A number of writers have developed alternative formal structures incorporating different assumptions about measurability and interpersonal comparability of utilities. This investigation has provided a large number of important results which, among other things, have greatly clarified the structure of social welfare rules such as utilitarianism (see, for example, Harsanyi, 1953, 1955, 1977; Ng, 1975; Blackorby and Donaldson, 1977, 1979; Maskin, 1978b; Deschamps and Gevers, 1978) and the lexicographic version of Rawls' (1971) maximin principle (see, among others, Hammond, 1976; d'Aspremont and Gevers, 1977; Maskin, 1978b; Deschamps and Gevers, 1978; Roberts, 1980a, 1980b; Arrow, 1977; and Sen, 1974, 1976a). An important question which arises in this context is whether the individual preferences refer to the individuals' interests in some sense or to their ethical judgements about what is good for the society. Sen (1979a) points out that "in judgement aggregation exercises ... it may be very difficult to have room for anything other than mechanically recording people's preference rankings ... There the exercise may have to make do with the n-tuple of individual orderings only". However, the case for the ordinal framework in the context of aggregation of ethical judgements is perhaps stronger than the one suggested by Sen. Even when cardinal information about individual preferences is readily available (so that the aggregation exercise does not have to make do with individual orderings only), the intuitive justification for using the cardinal content of such information is far from obvious when the preferences under consideration represent people's judgements about what is good for society.

While the general framework adopted by Arrow explicitly rules out the use of information relating to cardinal and interpersonally comparable utilities, the specific assumptions used by Arrow generate a type of neutrality (i.e. symmetric treatment of alternatives) which, in general, makes it impossible to take into account information about the specific nature of alternatives. Much of the thinking in welfare economics and the theory of social choice resembles Arrow's analysis in this respect: the normative problem of social choice is posed in a fashion which directly or indirectly leads to the exclusion of information about the nature of social alternatives as distinguished from information about individual preferences over the alternatives. Yet some of our deep intuitive conceptions of the rights of individuals and groups are based precisely on specific characteristics of the alternatives involved. Thus, while we may be prepared to accept the majority decision rule for deciding between two alternative foreign policies, we may find it thoroughly unacceptable that the majority opinion should override an individual's preference for practising a particular religion. The point has been forcefully argued in a series of papers by Sen (1970b, 1976b, 1979b) whose justly famous paradox of the Paretian liberal has inspired a large literature (see Gibbard, 1974; Blau, 1975; Kelly, 1976; Hammond, 1979; and Gaertner and Kruger, 1979, for a sample of this literature; an elegant survey is to be found in Sen, 1976b).

Instead of first laying down specific ethical criteria for social choice and then examining whether any group decision procedures satisfy these criteria (this is the pattern followed by the well known impossibility theorems), one could start with specific decision rules (used in real life or otherwise) and try to analyse their ethical properties. The pioneering study of this type was by May (1952, 1953) who established a set of necessary and sufficient conditions for the simple majority decision rule. This was followed by Murakami (1968), Fine (1972), and Fishburn (1973, chs. 3 and 4) who explored the structure of representative democracy or multi-stage majority decisions. The axiomatic structure of the Borda rule and variants of it has also been analysed in several contributions including Gardenfors (1973), Smith (1973), Young (1974), and Fine and Fine (1974). Clearly, such exercises are valuable in so far as they clarify the exact structure of familiar decision rules.

In trying to give a brief outline of some of the major developments in social choice theory we have so far concentrated on the ethical aspects. However, even a brief sketch such as this would be grossly incomplete unless we commented on some of the important aspects of the positive theory of social choice. Whether ethically acceptable or not, in real life group decisions are being arrived at all the time. The positive theory of social choice seeks to construct descriptive and predictive models of such decision-making processes (of course, such models may also have implications for the normative problem of designing an ethically acceptable rule for aggregating individual preferences). The literature here is as large and as diverse as the literature on the normative social choice theory. We touch upon only a few major problems in this area; most of these emphasize the link between game theory and the theory of social choice.[1]

That Arrow's analysis has a strong game-theoretic flavour was realized fairly early. Referring to his impossibility theorem, Arrow (1963, p. 59) himself observed: "The negative outcome expressed in this theorem is strongly reminiscent of the intransitivity of the concept of domination in the theory of multi-person games." However, it was the important paper of Wilson (1972) which first demonstrated that some of Arrow's conditions were sufficient to generate a class of strong, simple games. Such links between classes of group decision procedures in social choice theory and familiar classes of games were explored in much greater detail in Bloomfield's (1971) unpublished dissertation which deserves to be better known. This important line of investigation has recently been continued by Peleg and Moulin. (In addition to Peleg's chapter in this volume, see the important, detailed studies of Peleg, 1980, and Moulin, 1981.)

Much of the normative theory of social choice is concerned with aggregation of individual preferences assuming that the true preferences of the individuals are known. However, rational individuals pursuing their own interests may choose not to reveal their true preferences; they may resort to strategic voting or deliberate misrevelation of preferences. The phenomenon of strategic voting was explored in Farquharson (1969), but it was the seminal work of Gibbard (1973) and Satterthwaite (1975) which brought the problem to the centre of social choice theory. The fundamental result proved by Gibbard (1973) demonstrates that every non-dictatorial game form with at least three possible outcomes will lead to the non-existence of a dominant strategy for some individual, and for some preference ordering over outcomes, which that individual may have. A straight corollary of this result is the Gibbard—Satterthwaite result on manipulability of voting schemes which shows that under every non-dictatorial voting procedure which specifies exactly one outcome for every preference profile, some individual sometimes will find it profitable to misreveal his preferences. The importance of this for normative theory is obvious. If one cannot devise a "reasonable" decision

---

[1]   Game-theoretic concepts are used in all areas of the theory of social choice and welfare economics, and *n*-person game theory is closely related to many of these areas. As a matter of fact, Riker and Ordeshook (1973) and Abrams (1980) devote a large number of pages to game theory in their books on political theory; conversely, Luce and Raiffa (1957) present Arrow's theorems in their book on games and decisions. Readers unfamiliar with the basic concepts of game theory may start with the excellent survey of Shubik (1981).

procedure which can elicit people's true preferences from them, then we do not even have the basic raw material for the normative exercise of aggregating individual preferences.

Attempts have been made to modify the framework of the Gibbard—Satterthwaite manipulability theorem by replacing the mechanisms of voting schemes (or decision rules which for every preference profile defines a unique outcome) by decision rules which permit ties among outcomes (see, for example, Barbera, 1977; Gibbard, 1977; Kelly, 1978; Gardenfors, 1976; and McIntyre and Pattanaik, 1981), and also by introducing alternative equilibrium concepts of varying stringency (see Pattanaik, 1978). The negative manipulability result remains essentially intact despite such modifications. Perhaps the most important conceptual development since the Gibbard—Satterthwaite result in this general area came from Peleg (1978) and Maskin (1978b, 1979). The basic idea is as follows. Suppose we have a given ethically desirable social decision function. Then the problem is visualized as one of devising a game form $\mathscr{G}$ (the permissible strategies in $\mathscr{G}$ may or may not be orderings over alternatives) such that for every profile of true preferences of individuals one can find under $\mathscr{G}$ an equilibrium (in some relevant sense of the term) in which the outcome will coincide with the outcome yielded by the ethically desirable social decision function for the profile of true preferences under consideration. While the problem was formulated in this general form by Maskin (1978a, 1979), Peleg (1978) considered the special case where the strategies in $\mathscr{G}$ are preference orderings and the outcome function figuring in $\mathscr{G}$ is the ethically desirable social decision function. This line of analysis has been pursued by a number of writers, sometimes with encouraging positive results (for systematic exposition and expansion of much of this literature see Moulin, 1981, and Peleg, 1980; see also Gibbard, 1978, for an important negative result).

Another important aspect of voting theory which has been worked out mainly by political scientists is the theory of electoral competition. This theory stems from Downs' *Economic Theory of Democracy* (1957). It presents two main features. The first is about the electoral process itself, and the second deals with the existence of equilibrium points.

Each decision-maker (voter) is endowed with a utility function defined on a policy space and an ideal point in this space where his utility is maximized. Candidates (parties) express their programme as a point of the policy space. A rational voter will then choose the candidate whose programme is the "nearest" to his ideal point, since the utility for him of a programme will be a decreasing function of the distance between this point and his ideal point. Of course, this implies that the policy space is endowed with a metric structure. In general such a structure is given by considering an Euclidean space. If the voters' utility function is supposed to be given once and for all, the candidates' programmes are not. Thus, candidates will try to adopt a policy position that will attract a majority of the voters. A great variety of assumptions can be made on such a model. The reader is referred for interesting and competent surveys to Riker and Ordeshook (1973) and Abrams (1980).

The analysis of the conditions which guarantee the existence of equilibrium solutions in spatial models is significantly different from the one evoked above as an escape route to Arrow's impossibility theorem. We still may consider specific aggregation rules but, as Kramer (1973) has shown, the restriction conditions of the Black–Fishburn–Inada–Pattanaik–Sen variety have virtually no meaning in a multi-dimensional setting. An entirely new approach to these problems has been devised. The vast literature in this area stems from a seminal paper by Plott (1967). (For a brief survey see Gaertner and Salles, 1981; for interesting developments relating the aggregation procedure (quota-games) to the dimension of the policy space see Greenberg, 1979; and for further elegant results and extensions see Schofield's, 1981, monograph.)

From the brief outline that we have given above it is clear that the theory of social choice and welfare has acquired a considerable amount of richness and diversity over the last three decades or so. The chapters in this volume fully reflect this. We have classified these chapters into two broad groups: (1) those dealing with the ethical aspects of the theory of social choice and (2) those concerned with the positive theory of social choice. This division is to be treated as only a rough one. The demarcating line between normative and positive social choice theory is not always very clear. Positive analysis can often have profound normative significance (as in the case of the Gibbard–Satterthwaite manipulability theorem). Also, some chapters (e.g. those by Chichilnisky and Heal included in the first part of this volume) deal with the question of strategic misrevelation of preferences which we have classified as positive analysis, as well as with the problem of finding an ethically acceptable group decision rule.

The chapters in the first part of this volume, in their turn, are divided into two further subgroups — those concerned with the Arrow-type aggregation problem or aspects of it, and those concerned with more specific questions relating to optimality, justice, and welfare (again the distinction is only a rough one).

Following the tradition of economic theory, Arrow (1963) assumed individual weak preferences to be ordering (i.e. binary relations satisfying reflexivity, connectedness, and transitivity). While this assumption has proved to be a simple and powerful tool in a wide range of areas in economics, the empirical justification for it is by no means clear (in fact, a considerable amount of negative evidence has been turned up by psychologists and others). Barthélémy's contribution in Chapter 1 seeks to relax this assumption underlying Arrow's impossibility theorem. The main change that Barthélémy introduces into Arrow's framework is the assumption that the individual, as well as the social, weak preference relations are reflexive and connected with the corresponding strict preference relations being transitive. (Actually, Barthélémy uses a somewhat different, though logically equivalent, formulation: he starts with the strict preference relation and assumes it to be a partial order.) The negative impact of Arrow's theorem remains virtually unaltered in this modified framework too.

In Chapter 2 Barbera introduces the notion of "pivotal voters". Under a given social welfare function, a voter i is said to be pivotal at a specific preference profile, if, given the other individual's preference orderings in that profile, there exists some switch in i's ordering which can change the social ordering. Using this notion Barbera provides an alternative proof of Arrow's theorem.

As in Barthélémy's chapter, the motivation of Heiner and Pattanaik (Chapter 3) is also to widen Arrow's framework by adopting more general formulations of individual (and also social) preferences. Assuming that each individual has a "lottery" over possible preference orderings rather than one deterministic preference ordering, Heiner and Pattanaik examine the structure of power under aggregation rules which arrive at a lottery over possible social preference orderings given the individual lotteries. The results parallel earlier results of Barbera and Sonnenschein who considered random orderings for the society based on deterministic individual orderings.

In Chapter 4, McManus takes up the condition of positive association originating in Arrow (1963) and considers several variants of it. The interrelationship of these different versions of the basic "monotonicity" property is discussed. In the process several ambiguities are cleared up and the role of these properties in the context of familiar impossibility theorems is clarified.

In Chapter 5, Monjardet concentrates on the mathematical concept of ultrafilters and its use in social choice theory. In the process he extends an earlier impossibility result due to Blau (1979), and Blair and Pollack (1979), and provides a compact proof for the generalized theorem.

In Chapter 6, Chichilnisky gives a lucid survey of recent results and insights provided by the topological approach to social choice and game theory — an approach to which she herself has contributed much. As Chichilnisky points out, application of topological tools has often clarified the structure of already existing theorems and has yielded new results. Since the topological approach is somewhat new, and technically unfamiliar, in social choice theory, we expect Chichilnisky's survey to be widely useful.

Heal's chapter (Chapter 7) focuses on the condition that individual preferences form a "contractible" space and the significance of this condition for several important concerns of social choice theory (e.g. the existence of ethically desirable

rules for preference aggregation and the existence of straightforward group decision rules). The notion of contractibility first analysed by Chichilnisky, and
used in several recent papers of Heal and Chichilnisky, can be intuitively viewed
as coming within the general tradition of restricted preference conditions in social
choice theory, initiated by Black.

Suzumura's chapter (Chapter 8), as its title suggests, takes up the problem of
reconciling conflicting views of individuals about justice in social choice. He
starts with the basic distinction between an individual's subjective preferences
and his ethical preferences. The ethical preferences are derived from the individual's extended utility function (see Sen, 1970a) through a function which reflects the individual's moral sense of justice. Suzumura considers different types
of aggregation rules which use the ethical as well as the subjective preferences of
individuals in arriving at social choice. Two specific examples of the decision
rules considered by Suzumura are: (1) the choice rule given by the transitive
closure of the majority preferences relation defined in terms of subjective preferences but restricted to the Pareto optimal alternatives, Pareto optimality being
specified in terms of ethical preferences, and (2) the converse case where again
one considers the transitive closure of the majority preference relation, this time
defined in terms of ethical preferences but restricted to the alternatives which
are Pareto optimal in terms of subjective preferences.

Ng (Chapter 9) addresses himself to some of the basic conceptual issues in
welfare economics. Distinguishing between an individual's preferences and his
welfare, he considers whether individuals' welfares or their preferences should
constitute the basis of social choice. He argues for a utilitarian social welfare function, and for the maximization of total utility rather than average utility in the
case of a society of variable size.

Hammond's contribution (Chapter 10) deals with Pareto optimality under
uncertainty. The concept of Pareto efficiency defined relative to a consumer's
ex-ante expected utilities has, according to the author, a limited ethical appeal.
An alternative approach is based on individuals' utilities ex-post or, more inter-
estingly, on an ex-post welfare function. The contrast between ex-ante and ex-
post under uncertainty is similar to the problem of inconsistency of dynamic
choice. Hammond uses a reduced form of the decision problem: maximization
is made once and for all. (This does not mean that the optimal choice does not
depend on the tree structure of the problem, but that the objective does not.)
This question is formally described and its implications are derived.

In Chapter 11, dynamic consistency is discussed again. Plans made in one period without regard to the fact that tastes will change in the future are said to be
naive or myopic. Otherwise a plan is sophisticated. Grout compares naive and sophisticated plans in using the concepts of Pareto optimality and social welfare

functions. The main conclusion is that using sophisticated consistent planning in place of naive inconsistent planning does not guarantee welfare improvement.

In Part II, which deals with the positive aspects of social choice, several chapters discuss the problem of strategic misrevelation of preferences by individuals. The first chapter here (Chapter 12) by Bandyopadhyay and Deb is concerned with this problem. In a recent paper McIntyre and Pattanaik (1981) showed that a very broad class of democratic group decision functions are manipulable if one adopts the sure thing rule. However, their result does not hold when the domain of the functions are restricted to n-tuples (profiles) of strict individual orderings. By slightly strengthening some of their assumptions, Bandyopadhyay and Deb obtain again the manipulability results with strict orderings.

Dutta's contribution (Chapter 13) extends a former analysis of Dutta and Pattanaik (1978) and Peleg (1978) on consistent voting systems. (The concept of consistency is related to the concept of implementability.) It is shown that under some decision rules which endow individuals with a veto power, the sincere preference profile is an equilibrium. Maskin's result (1979) on implementability is also extended to the case of a strong equilibrium incorporating the possibility of counter-threats formation.

Chapter 14 by Peleg investigates the relationship between simple games and social choice correspondences. First, three simple games are associated with every social choice correspondence. Several examples are considered and an interesting concept of tightness is defined. Sufficient conditions for this concept are derived. The author also deals with the inverse problem of representing simple games by social choice correspondences. Sufficient conditions for the existence of tight and "nice" representations are given. Finally, this representation theory is related to the core solution concept.

In electoral competition models, when the policy space is one-dimensional and individual preferences are slightly restricted, a local core may exist for a large class of voting games. On the other hand, in two or more dimensions a core would be empty for most simple games. Schofield (Chapter 15) considers a smooth locally Euclidean topological manifold of dimension w. He shows that, given a simple game, if w is no greater than some integer calculated from Nakamura's number of the game referred to above, then local cycles cannot exist. A specific treatment of q-majority games (quota-games) is given. These results extend Greenberg's analysis to general voting games.

Chapter 16, by Coughlin and Nitzan, explores the electoral competition model with multi-dimensions policy space when (a) there are two candidates, (b) the choice must be taken among local options (i.e. within a small neighbourhood of the status quo), and (c) voting behaviour is random. The authors derive a necessary and sufficient condition for two directions from a given status quo to be an equilibrium strategy for the candidates. They prove the existence of a status quo with a stationary electoral equilibrium and find a characterization of status quo's having a local electoral equilibrium.

In Chapter 17, Gardner uses a voting device in a fixed-price-equilibrium model. He assumes that the agents currently trading in the market vote, at the close of trading, on next period's price. He shows that in Böhm-Bawerk's horse market, the price dynamics obtained from majority rule lead to Walrasian equilibrium in at most two periods. But Walrasian equilibrium is not always stable relative to these dynamics. However, in a large economy modelled according to Böhm-Bawerk's, the same two-period convergence is observed.

References

Abrams, R. (1980) *Foundations of Political Analysis* (Columbia University Press, New York).

Arrow, K.J. (1963) *Social Choice and Individual Values*, 2nd edn. (Wiley, New York).

Arrow, K.J. (1977) "Extended Sympathy and the Possibility of Social Choice", *American Economic Review*, 67.

Barbera, S. (1977) "Manipulation of Social Decicion Functions", *Journal of Economic Theory*, 15, 266–278.

Black, D. (1948) "On the Rationale of Group Decision Making", *The Journal of Political Economy*, 56, 23–34.

Black, D. (1958) *The Theory of Committees and Elections* (Cambridge University Press, Cambridge).

Blackorby, C. and D. Donaldson (1977) "Utility vs. Equity: Some Plausible Quasi-orderings", *Journal of Public Economics*, 7, 365–381.

Blackorby, C. and D. Donaldson (1979) "Interpersonal Comparability of Origin- or Scale-Independent Utilities: Admissible Social Evaluation Functionals", Discussion Paper No. 79-04 (Department of Economics, University of British Columbia).

Blair, D.H. and R.A. Pollack (1979) "Collective Rationality and Dictatorship: The Scope of the Arrow Theorem", *Journal of Economic Theory*, 21, 186–194.

Blair, D.H., G. Bordes, J.S. Kelly and K. Suzumura (1976) "Impossibility Theorems without Collective Rationality", *Journal of Economic Theory*, 13, 361–379.

Blau, J.H. (1975) "Liberal Values and Independence", *Review of Economic Studies*, 42, 413–420.

Blau. J.H. (1979) "Semiorders and Collective Choice", *Journal of Economic Theory*, 21, 195–206.

Blau, J.H. and R. Deb (1977) "Social Decision Functions and the Veto", *Econometrica*, 45, 871–879.

Bloomfield, S. (1971) *An Axiomatic Formulation of Constitutional Games*, Technical Report No. 71-18 (Operations Research House, Stanford University).

Borda, J.-Ch. de (1781) "Mémoire sur les élections au scrutin", *Mémoires de l'Académie Royale des Sciences*, 657–665.

Condorcet, Marquis de (1785) "Essai sur l'Application de l'Analyse à la Probabilité des Decisions Rendues à la Pluralité des Voix", in: A. Condorcet, O'Connor and M.F. Arago, eds., *Oeuvres de Condorcet* (Paris, 1847–1849).

Craven, J. (1971) "Majority Voting and Social Choice", *The Review of Economic Studies*, 38, 265–267.

Danielsson, S. (1974) "The Group Preference Problem as a Problem of Distributive Justice", Filosofiska Institutionen, Uppsala Universitet.

d'Aspremont, C. and L. Gevers (1977) "Equity and Informational Basis of Collective Choice", *Review of Economic Studies*, 46, 199–210.

Deschamps, R. and L. Gevers (1978) "Leximin and Utilitarian Rules: A Joint Characterization", *Journal of Economic Theory*, 17, 143–163.

Downs, A. (1957) *An Economic Theory of Democracy* (Harper and Row, New York).

Dutta, B. and P.K. Pattanaik (1978) "On Nicely Consistent Voting Systems", *Econometrica*, 46, 163–170.

Farquharson, R. (1969) *Theory of Voting* (Yale University Press, New Haven, Conn.).

Ferejohn, J. and D.M. Grether (1974) "On a Class of Rational Social Decision Procedures", *Journal of Economic Theory*, 8, 471–482.

Fine, K. (1972) "Some Necessary and Sufficient Conditions for Representative Decision on Two Alternatives", *Econometrica*, 40, 1083–1090.

Fine, B. and K. Fine (1974) "Social Choice and Individual Ranking", *Review of Economic Studies*, 41, 303–322, 459–475.

Fishburn, P.C. (1973) *The Theory of Social Choice* (Princeton University Press, Princeton).

Gaertner, W. and L. Kruger (1979) "From Hand-Cuffed Paretianism to Self Consistent Libertarianism: A New Possibility Theorem", mimeograph.

Gaertner, W. and M. Salles (1981) "Procédures d'Agrégation avec Domaines Restreints et Théorèmes d'Existence", in: P. Batteau, E. Jacquet-Lagrèze and B. Monjardet, eds., *Analyse et Agrégation des Préférences* (Economica, Paris).

Gardenfors, P. (1973) "Positional Voting Functions", *Theory and Decision*, 4, 1–24.

Gardenfors, P. (1976) "Manipulation of Social Choice Functions", *Journal of Economic Theory*, 13, 217–228.

Gibbard, A. (1973) "Manipulation of Voting Schemes, A General Result", *Econometrica*, 41, 587–601.

Gibbard, A. (1974) "A Pareto-Consistent Libertarian Claim", *Journal of Economic Theory*, 7, 338–410.

Gibbard, A. (1977) "Manipulation of Schemes that Mix Voting with Chance", *Econometrica*, 45, 665–681.

Gibbard, A. (1978) "Social Decision, Strategic Behaviour, and Best Outcomes", in: H.W. Gottinger and W. Leinfellner, eds., *Decision Theory and Social Ethics* (D. Reidel Publishing Co, Dordrecht, Holland).

Graaff, J. de V (1957) *Theoretical Welfare Economics* (Cambridge University Press).

Greenberg, J. (1979) "Consistent Majority Rules over Compact Sets of Alternatives", *Econometrica*, 47, 627–636.

Hammond, P. (1976) "Equity, Arrow's Conditions and Rawls' Difference Principle", *Econometrica*, 44, 793–804.

Hammond, P. (1979) "Liberalism, Independent Rights and the Pareto Principle", Department of Economics, University of Essex.

Harsanyi, J.C. (1953) "Cardinal Utility in Welfare Economics and the Theory of Risk-Taking", *Journal of Political Economy*, 61, 434–435.

Harsanyi, J.C. (1955) "Cardinal Welfare, Individualistic Ethics, and Interpersonal Comparisons of Utility", *Journal of Political Economy*, 63, 309–321.

Harsanyi, J.C. (1977) *Rational Behavior and Bargaining Equilibrium in Games and Social Situations* (Cambridge University Press).

Kelly, J. (1976) "Rights-Exercising and a Pareto Consistent Libertarian Claim", *Journal of Economic Theory*, 13, 138–153.

Kelly, J.S. (1978) *Arrow Impossibility Theorems* (Academic Press, New York).

Kramer, G.H. (1973) "On a Class of Equilibrium Conditions for Majority Rule", *Econometrica*, 41, 285–298.

Luce, R.D. and H. Raiffa (1957) *Games and Decisions* (Wiley, New York).

Mas-Colell, A. and H. Sonnenschein (1972) "General Possibility Theorems for Group Deci-
    sions", *The Review of Economic Studies*, 39, 185–192.
Maskin, E. (1978a) "Nash Equilibrium and Welfare Optimality", *Mathematics of Operations
    Research*, forthcoming.
Maskin, E. (1978b) "A Theorem on Utilitarianism", *Review of Economic Studies*, 45, 93–96.
Maskin, E. (1979) "Implementation and Strong Nash Equilibrium", in: J. Laffont, ed.,
    Aggregation and Revelation of Preferences (North-Holland, Amsterdam).
May, K.O. (1952) "A Set of Independent, Necessary and Sufficient Conditions for Simple
    Majority Decision", *Econometrica*, 20, 680–684.
May, K.O. (1953) "A Note on Complete Independence of the Conditions for Simple Majority
    Decision", *Econometrica*, 21, 172–173.
McIntyre, I. and P.K. Pattanaik (1981) "The Sure-Thing Rule and Strategic Voting under
    Minimally Binary Group Decision Functions", *Journal of Economic Theory*, 25, 338–352.
Moulin, H. (1981) *The Strategy of Group Choice* (Laboratoire D'Économétrie, École
    Polytechnique).
Murakami, Y. (1968) *Logic and Social Choice* (Routledge and Kegan Paul, London).
Nakamura, K. (1979) "The Vetoers in a Simple Game with Ordinal Preferences", *Interna-
    tional Journal of Game Theory*, 8, 55–61.
Ng, Y.-K. (1975) "Bentham or Bergson? Finite Sensibility, Utility Functions and Social Wel-
    fare Functions", *Review of Economic Studies*, 42, 545–569.
Pattanaik, P.K. (1971) *Voting and Collective Choice* (Cambridge University Press).
Pattanaik, P.K. (1978) *Strategy and Group Choice* (North-Holland Publishing Company,
    Amsterdam).
Peleg, B. (1978) "Consistent Voting Systems", *Econometrica*, 46, 153–161.
Peleg, B. (1980) "Game Theoretic Analysis of Voting in Committees", mimeographed.
Pigou, A.C. (1932) *The Economics of Welfare* (Macmillan, London).
Plott, C.R. (1967) "Equilibrium and Majority Rule", *The American Economic Review*, 57,
    787–806.
Rashed, R. (1974) *Condorcet: Mathématique et Société* (Harmann, Paris).
Rawls, J. (1971) *A Theory of Justice* (Clarendon Press, Oxford).
Riker, W.H. and P.C. Ordeshook (1973) *An Introduction to Positive Political Theory* (Pre-
    ntice-Hall, Englewood Cliffs).
Roberts, K.W.S. (1980a) "Interpersonal Comparability and Social Choice Theory", *Review
    of Economic Studies*, 47, 421–439.
Roberts, K.W.S. (1980b) "Possibility Theorems with Interpersonally Comparable Welfare
    Levels", *Review of Economic Studies*, 47, 409–420.
Samuelson, P. (1967) "Arrow's Mathematical Politics", in: S. Hook, ed., *Human Values and
    Economic Policy* (New York University Press, New York).
Satterthwaite, M.A. (1975) "Strategy-proofness and Arrow's Conditions: Existence and Cor-
    respondence Theorems for Voting Procedures and Social Welfare Functions", *Journal of
    Economic Theory*, 10, 187–217.
Schofield, N. (1981) *Social Choice and Democracy*, forthcoming.
Sen, A.K. (1968) "Quasi-Transitivity, Rational Choice and Collective Decisions", *The Re-
    view of Economic Studies*, 36, 381–393.
Sen, A.K. (1970a) *Collective Choice and Social Welfare* (Holden-Day, San Francisco).
Sen, A.K. (1970b) "The Impossibility of a Paretian Liberal", *Journal of Political Economy*,
    72, 152–157.
Sen, A.K. (1974) "Informational Bases of Alternative Welfare Approaches: Aggregation and
    Income Distribution", *Journal of Public Economics*, 3, 387–403.
Sen, A.K. (1976a) "Welfare Inequalities and Rawlsian Axiomatics", *Theory and Decision*, 7,
    243–262.
Sen, A.K. (1976b) "Liberty, Unanimity and Rights", *Economica*, 43, 217–245.
Sen, A.K. (1977) "Social Choice Theory: A Re-examination", *Econometrica*, 45, 53–89.

Sen, A.K. (1979a) Social Choice Theory, mimeo, forthcoming in: K.J. Arrow and M.D. Intriligator, eds., *Handbook of Mathematical Economics*, vol. III (North-Holland Publishing Company, Amsterdam).

Sen, A.K. (1979b) "Personal Utilities and Public Judgments: or What's Wrong with Welfare Economics?", *Economic Journal*.

Sen, A.K. (1982) "Social Choice Theory", in: K.J. Arrow and M.D Intriligator, eds., *Handbook of Mathematical Economics*, vol. III (North-Holland Publishing Company, Amsterdam).

Shubik, M. (1981) "Game Theory Models and Methods in Political Economy", in: K.J. Arrow and M.D. Intriligator, eds., *Handbook of Mathematical Economics*, vol. I (North-Holland Publishing Company, Amsterdam).

Smith, J.H. (1973) "Aggregation of Preferences with Variable Electorate", *Econometrica*, 41, 1027–1041.

Wilson, R. (1972) "The Game-Theoretic Structure of Arrow's General Possibility Theorem", *Journal of Economic Theory*, 5, 14–20.

Young, H.P. (1974) "An Axiomatization of Borda's Rule", *Journal of Economic Theory*, 9, 43–52.

PART IA

THE ETHICAL ASPECTS OF SOCIAL CHOICE:
THE AGGREGATION PROBLEM

CHAPTER 1

Arrow's theorem: Unusual domains and extended co-domains

J.-P. BARTHELEMY
Ecole Nationale Supérieure des Télécommunications

1. Introduction

Arrow's theorem asserts that if a social welfare function satisfies the unrestricted domain condition, the independence of irrelevant alternatives, and the weak Pareto principle, then it is a dictatorship. Since Arrow's earliest work (1962), which uses weak orders as both individual and social preferences (strict preference and indifference are both transitive), the axiomatic approach of social welfare has been developing in three directions.

(1) Restricting the domain. Some profiles of weak orders may be forbidden as profiles of individual preferences. Since the work of Black (1958) this is surely the more classical and the more explored approach (for the state of the art on these problems, see Gaertner and Salles, 1981).

(2) Enlarging the co-domain. Some other kind of relations (in the co-domain) are useful in the economic, psychological, or sociological areas. Such a point of view seems to go back to Murakami (1968) and Sen (1969), and has been illustrated by Mas-Colell and Sonnenschein (1972), Guha (1972), Blair and Pollak (1979), and Blau (1979). For all those authors individual preferences need to be weak orders.

(3) Finding other significant axiomatics. These studies seem to be only at their beginning. We mention only an axiomatic approach to the Borda'rule (as a choice function) by Young (1974) and an axiomatic approach of median linear orders by Young and Levenglick (1978).

Social Choice and Welfare, edited by P.K. Pattanaik and M. Salles
© North-Holland Publishing Company, 1983

This chapter is devoted to a fourth direction:

(4) Changing the domain and (eventually) enlarging the co-domain. The reason for this new direction is that taking weak orders as individual preferences is indeed a very special feature, practically as well as technically. From a practical point of view, the use of weak orders appears as a heritage of utility theories. Psychologists and other social scientists very well know that other kinds of binary relations, like semi-orders and interval orders (the indifference is not a transitive relation), constitute much more realistic models for individual preferences. Similarly, other ordinal aggregations are of interest in areas other than social choice: for example, the aggregation of tree posets which occurs in mathematical taxonomy.

From a technical point of view, the structure of a weak order is a very strong — and perhaps a very strange — one; some remarks and examples become invalid when transitivity of the incomparability is no longer required. Many classical aggregations (defined on weak orders) cannot be extended to partial orders.

In this chapter Arrow's theorem is established in the case of enlarged co-domains and when some order configurations are allowed in the domain. These configurations are compatible with most models for preferences, except the weak orders! Therefore, the classical Arrow theorem will not be a consequence of this one (and conversely!).

We asserted that direction (4) is a new one. Indeed, as is well known, nothing is new! This chapter, devoted to Arrow's theorem for partial orders, comes after a paper by Mirkin (1975) about the aggregation of equivalence relations and a paper by Monjardet (1978) about the aggregation of tournaments. Notice also in the book by Mirkin (1979) the very general conditions on the domain (but compensated by very strong conditions on the functions).

2. Notation

A binary relation on a set X is a subset of the cartesian product of $X \times X$. Hence, we use set theoretic notations for binary relations: $P \subseteq Q, P \cap Q, P \cup Q$, and $(x, y) \in P$ (instead of xPy). However, if P is a partial order we shall sometimes write: $x < y \ (P)$ instead of $(x, y) \in P$, and $x \parallel y \ (P)$ instead of $(x, y) \notin P$ and $(y, x) \notin P$.

Binary relations occurring in this chapter are considered as models for *strict preferences* and they are assumed to be asymmetric. Hence, throughout this text "relation" and "asymmetric relation" will be synonymous.

The reader is assumed to be familiar with some elementary vocabulary about partial orders. All information about this vocabulary can be found in Fishburn's *Mathematics of Decision Theory* (1972).

We shall denote by $\mathcal{O}$, the set of partial orders on X; $\mathcal{W}$, the set of weak orders on X; and $\mathcal{L}$, the set of linear orders on X.

If $\mathcal{D}$ and $\mathcal{M}$ are two sets of relations on X, and if k is an integer, we say that $\mathcal{D}$ is *k-stable* in $\mathcal{M}$ when the intersection of any family of k elements of $\mathcal{D}$ is in $\mathcal{M}$. For example, $\mathcal{D}$ is 1-stable in $\mathcal{M}$ means $\mathcal{D} \subseteq \mathcal{M}$. If K is the set of integers k such that $\mathcal{D}$ is k-stable in $\mathcal{M}$, we say that $\mathcal{D}$ is *K-stable* in $\mathcal{M}$.

Lastly, $|A|$ will denote the cardinality of the set A.

3. From individual preferences to social preferences

Let X be a finite set, $|X| = n, n \geqslant 3$, whose elements are called *alternatives*. We consider two sets of binary relations on X:

$\mathcal{D}$: the set of *individual preferences* (on the set of "data");
$\mathcal{M}$: the set of *social preferences* (or the set of "models").

We shall assume that the choice of any alternative against another one is a priori possible: for each ordered pair (x, y) of distinct alternatives there exists, at least, a relation P in $\mathcal{D}$ such that $(x, y) \in P$ ($\mathcal{D}$ *separates* X).

Let $V = \{1, ..., v\}$ be a finite set, $|V| = v$, whose elements are called *voters* (or "individuals"). A *profile* of individual preferences is a v-tuple $\pi = (P_1, ..., P_v)$ of relations in $\mathcal{D}$, P_i being the preference of the voter i. The set $\mathcal{P} = \mathcal{D}^v$ is the set of all profiles.

We are concerned with functions F from $\mathcal{P}$ to $\mathcal{M}$ assigning to each profile π a social preference $F(\pi)$. Notice that, considering F, we assume the "unrestricted domain condition" to be satisfied. Among the properties such a function may satisfy we recall the more classical ones.

Independence, or *binariness* (condition I). For any pair x, y of alternatives and every profile π, consider the restriction $F_{xy}(\pi)$ of $F(\pi)$ to $\{x, y\} \times \{x, y\}$. Let $\pi = (P_1, ..., P_v)$ and $\pi' = (P'_1, ..., P'_v)$ be two profiles. If the voters choosing y against x and the voters choosing x against y are the same for π and for π', then the choice between x and y is the same by $F(\pi)$ and by $F(\pi')$. Technically:

$$\{i/(x, y) \in P_i\} = \{i/(x, y) \in P'_i\},$$

and

$$\{i/(y, x) \in P_i\} = \{i/(y, x) \in P'_i\},$$

implies

$$F_{xy}(\pi) = F_{xy}(\pi').$$

(Weak) Pareto principle, or *unanimity* (condition P). For each pair x, y of alternatives, if y is chosen against x by each voter, then y is the winner against x in the social preference. Formally:

$$\bigcap_{i=1}^{v} P_i \subseteq F(\pi), \quad \text{for each profile } \pi = (P_1, \ldots, P_v).$$

This condition can be greatly weakened:

Very weak Pareto principle (condition P′). For each profile $\pi = (P_1, \ldots, P_v)$ such that $P_i = P$ for $1 \leqslant i \leqslant v, P \subseteq F(\pi)$. Obviously, P implies P′.

Autonomy, or citizen's sovereignty (condition A). For each ordered pair of distinct alternatives (x, y), there exists a profile π such that $(x, y) \in F(\pi)$. Notice that P′ implies A (since $\mathscr{D}$ separates X).

Anonymity, or *symmetry* (condition S). For every profile π and for each permutation σ of $V, F(\pi_\sigma) = F(\pi)$, with $\pi_\sigma = (P_{\sigma(1)}, \ldots, P_{\sigma(v)})$.

We now describe three strengthenings of the notion of independence. Following the terminology of Ferejohn and Fishburn (1979), we call them decisiveness, neutrality, and monotony.

Decisiveness (condition D). For each ordered pair (x, y) of alternatives the social choice of y against x depends only upon the individual choices of y against x (there is no intervention of the individual choices of x against y). Technically:

$$\{i / (x, y) \in P_i\} = \{i / (x, y) \in P_i'\}$$

implies

$$(x, y) \in F(\pi), \quad \text{if and only if} \quad (x, y) \in F(\pi').$$

Monotony (condition M). In condition I, equalities are replaced by inclusions:

$$\{i / (x, y) \in P_i\} \subseteq \{i / (x, y) \in P_i'\},$$

and

$$\{i / (y, x) \in P_i\} \supseteq \{i / (y, x) \in P_i'\},$$

implies

$$(x, y) \in F(\pi) \quad \text{implies} \quad (x, y) \in F(\pi').$$

Neutrality (condition N). This condition is obtained from I by replacing, in the profile π', the alternatives x, y by two other alternatives u, v such that $(y, x) \neq (u, v)$:

$$\{i/(x, y) \in P_i\} = \{i/(u, v) \in P_i'\},$$

and

$$\{i/(y, x) \in P_i\} = \{i/(v, u) \in P_i'\},$$

implies

$$(x, y) \in F(\pi), \quad \text{if and only if} \quad (u, v) \in F(\pi')$$

By a standard argument, we know that N is equivalent to the two following conditions:

(1) $\quad \{i/(x, y) \in P_i\} = \{i/(x, v) \in P_i'\},$

and

$$\{i/(y, x) \in P_i\} = \{i/(v, x) \in P_i'\},$$

implies

$$(x, y) \in F(\pi), \quad \text{if and only if} \quad (x, v) \in F(\pi').$$

(2) $\quad \{i/(x, y) \in P_i\} = \{i/(u, y) \in P_i'\},$

and

$$\{i/(y, x) \in P_i\} = \{i/(y, u) \in P_i'\},$$

implies

$$(x, y) \in F(\pi), \quad \text{if and only if} \quad (u, y) \in F(\pi').$$

4. Dictators and oligarchies

When there exists a voter j such that, for every profile $\pi = (P_1, ..., P_v), P_j \subseteq F(\pi)$, we say that j is a *dictator* and F a *dictatorship*.

A set W of voters is an *oligarchy* when, for every profile π,

$$\bigcap_{i \in W} P_i \subseteq F(\pi)$$

and

$$(x, y) \in \bigcup_{i \in W} P_i \quad \text{implies} \quad (y, x) \notin F(\pi)$$

(each member of the oligarchy is a vector). In this case we say that F is *oligarchic*.

Strengthening those notions we get the absolute dictators and absolute oligarchies: j is an *absolute dictator* (and F an *absolute dictatorship*) when $F(\pi) = P_j$, for each profile π; W is an *absolute oligarchy* (and F is *absolutely oligarchic*) when $\bigcap_{i \in W} P_i = F(\pi)$.

Recall the *fundamental theorem of social choice*:

Theorem 1. Assume that $\mathscr{D} = \mathscr{W}$ and let F be a function from $\mathscr{P}$ to $\mathscr{M}$ satisfying conditions I and P.
  (i) (Arrow) if $\mathscr{M} = \mathscr{W}$, F is a dictatorship.
  (ii) (Mas-Colell, Sonnenschein) if $\mathscr{M} = \mathscr{O}$, F is oligarchic.

A recent result by Blau (1979) and Blair and Pollack (1979) asserts that when $\mathscr{M}$ is the set of semi-orders on X, then F is still a dictatorship.

Unfortunately, this theorem does not entirely characterize the function F (what becomes the social choice when the dictator is indifferent?). However, in the general case ($\mathscr{D} = \mathscr{W}$ is not assumed):

Lemma. Assume that $\mathscr{D}$ separates X. For any function F from $\mathscr{P}$ to $\mathscr{M}$ the two following statements are equivalent:
  (i) F is a dictatorship and satisfies the condition D.
  (ii) F is an absolute dictatorship.

Proof. Assume that F fulfils (i) but not (ii). Then there exists a profile $\pi = (P_1, ..., P_v)$ and a pair x, y of alternatives such that $(x, y) \notin P_j$ and $(x, y) \in F(\pi)$, j being the dictator. Consider the new profile $\pi' = (P_1', ..., P_v')$, with $P_i = P_i'$ if $i \neq j$, P_j' being such that $(y, x) \in P_j'$. By condition D: $(x, y) \in F(\pi)$ implies $(x, y) \in F(\pi')$. This is impossible since $(y, x) \in P_j$ and j is a dictator. ∎

The following notation will be useful in the statement of our theorem. If the absolute· oligarchy W has the cardinality w we say that F is w-(absolutely) oligarchic. In this case $\mathscr{D}$ will be necessary w-stable in $\mathscr{M}$. Notice that an (absolute) dictatorship is a 1-(absolutely) oligarchic function.

5. Hypothesis on individual preferences

We now assume $\mathscr{D} \subseteq \mathscr{O}$ ($\mathscr{D}$ is a set of partial orders). $\mathscr{D}$ will be called a *regular set of partial orders* if every configuration on three alternatives (except the trivial one) is in $\mathscr{D}$: for every ordered three distinct alternatives (x, y, u) there exists P_1, P_2, P_3, P_4 in $\mathscr{D}$ such that:

$x < y\ (P_1), \quad x \parallel u\ (P_1), \quad y \parallel u\ (P_1);$

$x < y\ (P_2), \quad x < u\ (P_2), \quad u < y\ (P_2);$

$x \parallel y\ (P_3), \quad u < x\ (P_3), \quad u < y\ (P_3);$

$x \parallel y\ (P_4), \quad x < u\ (P_4), \quad y < u\ (P_4).$

If $\mathscr{D}$ is regular, $\mathscr{D}$ separates X.

The following sets of partial orders are regular sets: semi-orders; interval orders; orders of dimension 2; semi-lattices ($n \geqslant 5$); tree posets ($n \geqslant 5$); lattices ($n \geqslant 6$); distributive, modular, etc. lattices ($n \geqslant 6$); Boolean lattices ($n \geqslant 8$); graded orders; partial orders, etc.

6. Arrow's theorem

Theorem 2. Suppose that $\mathscr{D} \subseteq \mathscr{M} \subseteq \mathscr{O}$ and that $\mathscr{D}$ is regular. For any function F from $\mathscr{P}$ to $\mathscr{M}$, the following statements are equivalent:

(i) F satisfies I and P′.
(ii) F satisfies I and P.
(iii) F satisfies N and P.
(iv) F satisfies M and A.
(v) F satisfies D and P.
(vi) $\mathscr{D}$ being K-stable in $\mathscr{M}$, F is w-absolutely oligarchic with $w \in K$.

Notice that if $\mathscr{D}$ is just $\{1\}$-stable in $\mathscr{M}$, (vi) means that F is an absolute dictatorship. If $K \neq \{1\}$, since $\mathscr{D} \subseteq \mathscr{M}$ (i.e. $1 \in K$) (vi) does not exclude the dictatorial case.

Before giving the proof of this theorem, we point out some consequences. First, we remark that in the case where $\mathscr{L}$ is contained in $\mathscr{D}$, (vi) leads to a discussion about the dimension of partial orders in $\mathscr{D}$ (the dimension of a partial order P is the minimum number of linear orders whose P is the intersection).

Notice also that we obtain a characterization of the Pareto rule.

Corollary. Suppose that $\mathscr{D} \subseteq \mathscr{M} \subseteq \mathscr{O}$ and that $\mathscr{D}$ is regular. Then:

(1) If $\mathscr{D}$ is not v-stable in $\mathscr{M}$ there is no function from $\mathscr{P}$ to $\mathscr{M}$ satisfying I, P, and S.

(2) If $\mathscr{D}$ is v-stable in $\mathscr{M}$ (e.g. if $\mathscr{M} = \mathscr{O}$), the only function F from $\mathscr{P}$ to $\mathscr{M}$ satisfying I, P′, and S is the Pareto rule: $F(\pi) = \bigcap_{i=1}^{v} P_i$.

Finally, notice that an analogous oligarchic result has been obtained by Mirkin (1975) (namely, (iv) equivalent to (vi)) in the case of equivalence relations.

7. Proof of the theorem

(i) implies (ii). Just imagine that F satisfies I and P'. Let π be a profile such that $(x, y) \in P_i$ for $1 \leqslant i \leqslant v$. Consider the profile $\pi' = (P'_1, ..., P'_v)$ with $P'_1 = P_1$ for every voter i. By condition P', $P_1 \subseteq F(\pi')$: $(x, y) \in F(\pi')$. By condition I, $(x, y) \in F(\pi)$. F satisfies the condition P.

(ii) implies (iii). We shall restrict ourself to the first part of the condition N (the proof of the second part being just the same). Suppose that F satisfies I and P. Consider three alternatives, v, x, and y, such that, π, π' being two profiles:

$$\{i/(x, y) \in P_i\} = \{i/(x, v) \in P'_i\},$$

$$\{i/(y, x) \in P_i\} = \{i/(v, x) \in P'_i\},$$

it is sufficient, in order to establish N, to suppose that $\pi = \pi'$ (then apply condition I). Let $L, \overline{L}$, and $\overline{\overline{L}}$ be the sets:

$$L = \{i/(x, y) \in P_i\},$$

$$\overline{L} = \{i/(y, x) \in P_i\},$$

$$\overline{\overline{L}} = V - (L \cup \overline{L}).$$

$\mathscr{D}$ being regular, we can consider a new profile π' such that

$$x < y < v \quad (P'_i), \qquad \text{if } i \in L,$$

$$y < v < x \quad (P'_i), \qquad \text{if } i \in \overline{L},$$

$$y < v, \ v \parallel x, \ v \parallel y \quad (P'_i), \qquad \text{if } i \in \overline{\overline{L}}.$$

By condition P: $y < v \ (F(\pi'))$.

Suppose $x < y \ (F(\pi))$ then, by condition I, $x < y \ (F(\pi'))$, and by transitivity, $x < v \ (F(\pi'))$. Applying again condition I, we get $x < v \ (F(\pi))$.

(iii) implies (iv). Consider two profiles, $\pi = (P_1, ..., P_v)$ and $\pi' = (P'_1, ..., P'_v)$, and two alternatives, x, y, such that $L \subset L'$ and $\overline{L} \subset \overline{L}'$, with $L = \{i/(x, y) \in P_i\}$, $L' = \{i/(x, y) \in P'_i\}$, $\overline{L} = \{i/(y, x) \in P_i\}$, and $\overline{L}' = \{i/(y, x) \in P'_i\}$. We write also: $\overline{\overline{L}} = V - (L \cup \overline{L})$ and $\overline{\overline{L}}' = V - (L' \cup \overline{L}')$.

Assume that $(x, y) \in F(\pi)$. Since P implies A it will be sufficient to assume that F satisfies N and P and to prove that it satisfies M.

$\mathscr{D}$ being regular, we can consider a new profile $\pi'' = (P_1'', ..., P_v'')$ such that, u being an alternative distinct from x and y:

$$x < u < y \quad (P_i''), \qquad \text{if } i \in L;$$

$$x < u, \ x < y, \ u \parallel y \quad (P_i''), \quad \text{if } i \in L' = L;$$

$$x < u, \ x \parallel y, \ u \parallel y \quad (P_i''), \quad \text{if } i \in \bar{\bar{L}}' - \bar{L} = \bar{\bar{L}} - L';$$

$$x < u, \ x \parallel y, \ y < u \quad (P_i''), \quad \text{if } i \in \bar{L} - \bar{L}';$$

$$y < x < u \quad (P_i''), \qquad \text{if } i \in \bar{L}'.$$

We notice that:

$$\{i/(x, y) \in P_i''\} = L', \qquad \{i/(y, x) \in P_i''\} = \bar{L}',$$

$$\{i/(u, y) \in P_i''\} = L, \qquad \{i/(y, u) \in P_i''\} = \bar{L}.$$

Hence by condition N: $(u, y) \in F(\pi'')$; by condition P: $(x, u) \in F(\pi'')$; and by transitivity in $\mathscr{M}$: $(x, y) \in F(\pi'')$. Applying I (implied by N) we obtain: $(x, y) \in F(\pi')$.

(iv) implies (v). Consider a profile π and a pair x, y of alternatives such that $(x, y) \in F(\pi)$. We shall use, as previously (with the same definitions), the sets $L, \bar{L}$, and $\bar{\bar{L}}$. Assume that F satisfies M and A, then clearly, F satisfies I and P (to get P use a straightforward argument), and hence P and N. Consider an alternative u distinct from x and y. Let $\pi'' = (P_i'', ..., P_v'')$ be a profile such that:

$$x < u < y \quad (P_i''), \qquad \text{if } i \in L;$$

$$y < x, \ y \parallel u, \ x \parallel u \quad (P_i''), \quad \text{if } i \in \bar{\bar{L}};$$

$$y < u < x \quad (P_i''), \qquad \text{if } i \in \bar{L}.$$

Notice that:

$$L = \{i/(x, u) \in P_i''\} = \{i/(u, y) \in P_i''\},$$

$$\bar{L} = \{i/(u, x) \in P_i''\} = \{i/(y, u) \in P_i''\}.$$

Then applying N: $(x, u) \in F(\pi'')$ (since $(x, y) \in F(\pi)$), and $(u, y) \in F(\pi'')$. Hence, by transitivity, $(x, y) \in F(\pi'')$.

Now by condition M, if π' is a profile such that $\{i/(x,y) \in P_i'\} = L$, we will get, since $\{i/(y,x) \in P_i''\} = V - L \supseteq \{i/(y,x) \in P_i'\}, (x,y) \in F(\pi')$. F satisfies condition D.

(v) implies (vi). Assume that F satisfies D and P. We shall use the "decisive set" technique. Consider two distinct alternatives $x, y \in X$. Let W be a set of voters such that, for every profile π:

$$(x,y) \in F(\pi), \quad \text{when } (x,y) \in \bigcap_{i \in W} P_i,$$

$$(y,x) \in F(\pi), \quad \text{when } (y,x) \in \bigcap_{i \in W} P_i.$$

Then:

(1) $\quad \bigcap_{i \in W} P_i \subseteq F(\pi)$ (see the proof below) for every profile π.

Let Δ be the set of subsets W of V satisfying statement (1). Δ is not empty: $V \in \Delta$, by condition P. Let M be a minimal element of Δ (ordered by the inclusion). Then, for any voter $j \in M$ and for every profile π:

(2) $\quad F(\pi) \subseteq P_j, \quad \text{if } |M| > 1.$

Two cases can occur:

(a) $|M| = 1$, i.e. $M = \{j\}$, and $P_j \subseteq F(\pi)$: j is a dictator. Applying the lemma of section 4, j will be an absolute dictator.

(b) $|M| > 1$, statement (2) holds and $F(\pi) = \bigcap_{i \in M} P_i$. In this case, necessarily $\mathscr{D}$ is $|M|$-stable in $\mathscr{M}$.

Proof of statement (1). Let $\pi = (P_1, ..., P_v)$ be a profile such that $(x,y) \in P_i$ if $i \in W$. Consider two alternatives, u, v, with $u \neq y, v \neq x$, and $u \neq v$ (if $n = 3$, $u = x$) such that $(u, v) \in P_i$ when $i \in W$. Let $\widetilde{W}$ be the set of voters i such that $(u,v) \in P_i$: $W \subseteq \widetilde{W}$. Consider a new profile π' such that:

$$u < x < y < v \ (P_i), \quad \text{if } i \in \widetilde{W},$$

$$y < v < u < x \ (P_i), \quad \text{if } i \notin \widetilde{W}.$$

By condition P: $(u, x) \in F(\pi')$ and $(y, v) \in F(\pi')$. By definition of W: $(x,y) \in F(\pi')$. Hence, by transitivity, $(u, v) \in F(\pi')$. Now, from condition D: $(u, v) \in F(\pi)$ and statement (1) is proved.

Proof of statement (2). Assume $|M| > 1$. We consider a voter $j \in M$ and a profile π such that $(x, y) \in F(\pi)$ and $(x, y) \notin P_j$. Let L be the set $\{i/(x, y) \in P_i\}: j \notin L$. Let u be an alternative distinct from x and y and let π' be a profile such that:

$$u < x < y \ (P_i'), \quad \text{if } i \in L \cap M;$$

$$y < u < x \ (P_j'),$$

$$x < y < u \ (P_i'), \quad \text{if } i \in L \cap (V - M);$$

$$y < x < u \ (P_i'), \quad \text{if } i \in (V - L) \cap (V - M);$$

$$u < y < x \ (P_i'), \quad \text{if } i \in (V - L) \cap (M - \{j\}).$$

We notice that $\{i/(x, y) \in P_i'\} = L$, $\{i/(u, x) \in P_i'\} = M$, and $\{i/(u, y) \in P_i'\} = M - \{j\}$. By definition of M: $(u, x) \in F(\pi')$. By condition D: $(x, y) \in F(\pi')$. Hence, $(u, y) \in F(\pi')$, by transitivity. Since D implies I and I + P implies M, if π'' is any profile such that $M - \{j\} \subseteq \{i/(u, y) \in P_i''\}$, we get, by condition M: $(u, y) \in F(\pi'')$. Applying statement (1): $M - \{j\} \in \Delta$, M is not minimal.

(vi) implies (i). This is obvious. ∎

8. Remarks about weak orders

The regularity of $\mathcal{D}$ has been intensively used throughout the proof of the theorem. Hence, it cannot apply to weak orders. However, (i) equivalent to (ii) is true for any sets $(\mathcal{D}, \mathcal{M})$ of binary relations.

It is well known that if $\mathcal{D} = \mathcal{W}$, (i) implies (vi) is false. We give here two examples (as an illustration, not from an exhaustive point of view) in order to establish that other steps are also false.

Example 1. $\mathcal{D} = \mathcal{W}$ and $\mathcal{M} = \mathcal{O}$. a, b are two fixed alternatives and $F(\pi)$ is such that:

(1) $(a, b) \in F(\pi)$ if and only if $(a, b) \in \cap_{i=1}^v P_i$ or $a < b \ (P_1)$ and $a \parallel b \ (P_i)$ if $i \neq 1$;

(2) if $(x, y) \neq (a, b)$, $(x, y) \in F(\pi)$ if and only if $(x, y) \in \cap_{i=1}^v P_i$. F satisfies I, and P, but does not satisfy M, N, and D.

Example 2. $\mathcal{D} = \mathcal{W}$, $\mathcal{M} = \mathcal{O}$. $F(\pi)$ is defined by $(x, y) \in F(\pi)$ if and only if $(x, y) \in \cap_{i=1}^v P_i$ or $x < y \ (P_1)$ and $x \parallel y \ (P_i)$ for $i \neq 1$. F satisfies P, I, and N, does not satisfy D and M.

However, we remark that in the proof of the statement (v) implies (vi), we have only used:

- D implies M.
- Any four and three alternatives can be linearly ordered by a relation in $\mathcal{D}$.

When this second assertion is verified we say that $\mathcal{D}$ is *quasi-regular*. Regular sets are quasi-regular sets; moreover, weak orders and linear orders are quasi-regular sets. Hence, *suppose that $\mathcal{D} \subseteq \mathcal{M} \subseteq \mathcal{O}$ and that $\mathcal{D}$ is quasi-regular. A function F from $\mathcal{P}$ to $\mathcal{M}$ satisfies D, M and P' if and only if F is w-absolutely oligarchic and $\mathcal{D}$ w-stable in $\mathcal{M}$*. Notice that this result has been established by Mirkin (1979) (quasi-regular sets being the ordinal version of Mirkin's "universal" sets).

References

Arrow, K.P. (1962) *Social Choice and Individual Values*, 2nd edn. (Wiley, New York).
Black, D. (1958) *The Theory of Committees and Elections* (Cambridge University Press, London).
Blair, D.H. and R.A. Pollack (1979) "Collective Rationality and Dictatorship: The Scope of the Arrow Theorem", *Journal of Economic Theory*, 21, 186–194.
Blau, J.H. (1979) "Semiorders and Collective Choice", *Journal of Economic Theory*, 21, 195–206.
Ferejohn, J.A. and P.C. Fishburn (1979) "Representations of Binary Decision Rules by Generalized Decisiveness Structures", *Journal of Economic Theory*, 21, 28–45.
Fishburn, P.C. (1972) *Mathematics of Decision Theory* (Mouton, The Hague).
Gaertner, W. and M. Salles (1981) "Procédures d'Agrégation avec Domaines Restreints et Théorèmes d'Existence", in: P. Batteau, E. Jacquet-Lagrèze and B. Monjardet, eds., *Analyse et Agrégation des Préférences* (Economica, Paris).
Guha, A.S. (1972) "Neutrality, Monotonicity and the Right to Vote", *Econometrica*, 40, 821–826.
Mas-Colell, A. and H. Sonnenschein (1972) "General Possibility Theorems for Group Decisions", *The Review of Economic Studies*, 39, 185–192.
Mirkin, B.G. (1975) "On the Problem of Reconciling Partitions", in: *Quantitative Sociology. International Perspectives on Mathematical and Statistical Modeling* (Academic Press, New York).
Mirkin, B.G. (1979) in: P.C. Fishburn, ed., *Group Choice* (Winston, Washington).
Monjardet, B. (1978b) "Axiomatiques et Propriétés des Quasi-ordres", *Math. Sci. Hum.*, 63, 51–82.
Monjardet, B. (1978a) "An Axiomatic Theory of Tournament Aggregation", *Math. Open. Res.*, 3, 4, 334–351.
Murakami, Y. (1968) *Logic and Social Choice* (Dover, New York).
Sen, A. (1969) "Quasi-Transitivity, Rational Choice and Collective Decisions", *Review of Economic Studies*, 36, 381–389.
Young, H.P. (1974) "An Axiomatization of Borda's Rule", *Journal of Economic Theory*, 9, 43–52.
Young, H.P. and A. Levenglick (1978) "A Consistent Extension of Condorcet's Election Principle", *SIAM Journal of Applied Mathematics*, 35, 285–300.

CHAPTER 2

Pivotal voters: A simple proof of Arrow's theorem

SALVADOR BARBERA*
Universidad de Bilbao

This chapter presents a new proof of Arrow's "General Possibility Theorem". Since there is no need to elaborate on the importance and the widespread impact of the theorem, we limit our comments here to an outline of the main features of the present approach to its proof.

Arrow's theorem deals with social welfare functions, i.e. rules which assign one "social" preference ordering of the alternatives facing society to each n-tuple (profile) of logically possible "individual" preference orderings of the same alternatives. One way to describe a social welfare function is by appropriately specifying a rich enough structure of coalitions of individuals which are "decisive", in the sense that unanimity of strong preferences within the group regarding a given pair of alternatives is sufficient to determine society's preference vis-à-vis those alternatives under the given social welfare function. Most proofs of Arrow's theorem consist in analyzing the structure of the family of decisive coalitions associated with a Paretian social welfare function independent of irrelevant alternatives, and show that these families must contain one decisive coalition consisting of one individual only — a dictator.

Our approach does not focus so much on the "social" image of given profiles, but on the way "social" preferences change in response to changes in the preferences of individuals. One individual is *pivotal* for a pair of alternatives at a preference profile if he could change the social ordering of these alternatives by just changing his preferences. Once we know what the "social" ordering will be for

* I am grateful to a referee for his help in improving the exposition.

some given profile (and this is what the Paretian requirement does for us), describing a social welfare function is describing who can change the outcome of the function, when, and by what actions — it is a matter of distributing among individuals the ability to act as pivots. Our proof of Arrow's theorem consists in showing that, under Paretian and independent of irrelevant alternatives social welfare functions, pivotality must be essentially concentrated in the hands of a single individual — the dictator. The essential role of the independence condition, even in the absence of any Paretian requirement, is emphasized by a lemma.

It is hoped that this alternative way of looking at a classical problem might be complementary to others in reaching a better understanding of how to design mechanisms for collective decision-making. In particular, the idea of pivotality has proved basic in the literature on the strategy-proof allocation of public goods, and it might prove a useful bridge between this parallel flow of work and that of social choice theory.

Individuals

Let $I = \{1, 2, ..., n\}$, an initial segment of the integers. Elements of I are called the *individuals*.

Alternatives

Let A be a set (finite or infinite). Elements of A are denoted by $x, y, z, ...$, and are called the *alternatives*.

Preference relations

Let $\mathscr{R}$ be the set of complete, transitive, reflexive binary relations on A. Elements of $\mathscr{R}$ are denoted by $R, R', R_i, R_j, ...$, and are called *preference orderings*. Given $R \in \mathscr{R}$, the *strict preference relation P associated with R* is defined so that $(\forall x, y \in A) [xPy \longleftrightarrow (xRy \text{ and } \sim yRx)]$.

Let $\overline{\mathscr{R}} \subset \mathscr{R}$ be the set of preference orderings which are antisymmetric. Elements of $\overline{\mathscr{R}}$ are called *strong preference orderings*. They stand for preferences where no alternative is indifferent to any other. We say that $x, y \in A$ *are contiguous in* $R \in \overline{\mathscr{R}}$ iff $(\forall z \notin <x, y>) [zRx \longleftrightarrow zRy]$.

Preference profiles

Let $\mathscr{R}^n$ stand for the *n*-fold Cartesian product of $\mathscr{R}$. Elements of $\mathscr{R}^n$ are denoted by $R, R', ...$, and are called *preference profiles*. The set of *strong preference profiles* $\overline{\mathscr{R}}^n$ is defined likewise.

When there is no ambiguity, R_i and P_i stand for the *i*th element of R and for its associated strict relation (respectively), R_j' and P_j' for the *j*th element of R' and its strict relation, and so on.

Given $R \in \mathscr{R}^n$ and $R' \in \mathscr{R}, R/_i R'$ denotes the profile R', where $R'_i = R'$ and $(\forall j \neq i) R_j = R'_j$.

Social welfare functions

A social welfare function (SWF) is a function $w: \mathscr{R}^n \longleftrightarrow \mathscr{R}$.[1] Whenever there is no ambiguity, we denote $w(R)$ by R, $w(R')$ by R', etc. Similarly, $P, P', \dots$, will then denote the strict preference orderings associated with $w(R), w(R'), \dots$. A SWF w is *Paretian* iff $(\forall R \in \mathscr{R}^n)(\forall x, y \in A)[(\forall i \in I) x P_i y \rightarrow x P y]$. A SWF w is *independent of irrelevant alternatives* (IIA) iff $(\forall R, R' \in \mathscr{R}^n)(\forall x, y \in A)[(\forall i \in I)(x R_i y \longleftrightarrow x R'_i y)$ and $(y R_i x \longleftrightarrow y R'_i x) \rightarrow (x R y \longleftrightarrow x R' y)]$.[2]

A SWF w is *dictatorial* iff $\exists d \in I$ such that $(\forall x, y \in A)(\forall R \in \mathscr{R}^n)[x P_d y \rightarrow x P y]$. Otherwise, w is *nondictatorial*.

Arrow's theorem. Let $A > 2$. There exists no social welfare function which is Paretian, independent of irrelevant alternatives, and nondictatorial.

Pivotal individuals

Individual $i \in I$ is *pivotal* at profile $R \in \mathscr{R}^n$ under a social welfare function w iff $\exists R' \in \mathscr{R}$ such that $w(R/_i R') \neq w(R)$. For $x, y \in A$, individual $i \in I$ is *xy-pivotal* at $R \in \mathscr{R}^n$ under SWF w iff $\exists R' \in \mathscr{R}$ such that $\sim [x \, w(R) \, y \longleftrightarrow x \, w(R/_i R') \, y]$. For $x, y \in A$, individual $i \in I$ is *positively xy-pivotal* at $R \in \mathscr{R}^n$ under SWF w iff it is xy-pivotal and, for all $R' \in \mathscr{R}$ such that $x P'_i y$, $\sim [y \, w(R/_i R') \, x]$.

It is clear from the definitions that whenever i is xy-pivotal it is also yx-pivotal. The same symmetric implication is not necessarily true for positive pivotality. Also, note that when w is IIA, if i is xy-pivotal (resp. positively xy-pivotal) at R, it is also xy-pivotal (resp. positively xy-pivotal) at any R' such that $(\forall j \neq i, j \in I)$ $[x R_i y \longleftrightarrow x R'_i y]$.

A lemma on IIA social welfare functions. Under an IIA social welfare function, there can be no strong preference profile at which two individuals are pivotal for two different nondisjoint pairs of alternatives.

---

[1] Note that Arrow's condition of universal domain, whereby an image in $\mathscr{R}$ has to be attributed to each preference profile, is included in our definition of a SWF.

[2] The condition above is sometimes called binarity. It is *equivalent*, when applied to social welfare functions, to Arrow's original condition of independence of irrelevant alternatives.

Proof. Let w be an IIA social welfare function, and suppose there were such a strong preference profile, individuals, and alternatives. Then, without loss of generality,[3] $\exists R \in \overline{\mathcal{R}}, R_i', R_j'' \in \overline{\mathcal{R}}, i, j \in I$ and $x, y, z \in A$ such that [where $R' = w(R/_iR_i'), R'' = w(R/_jR_j'')$]:

(a) $xRyRz$, $yP'x$, and $zP''y$;

(b) x and y (resp. y and z) are contiguous in R_i and R_i' (resp. in R_j and R_j''); and

(c) $sR_it \longleftrightarrow sR_i't$ (resp. $sR_jt \longleftrightarrow sR_j''t$) for all pairs of alternatives $\langle s, t \rangle \neq \langle x, y \rangle$ (resp. $\langle s, t \rangle \neq \langle y, z \rangle$).

But then, i and j's pivotality would imply that, where $\hat{R} = w [(R/_jR_j'')/_iR_i']$, $z\hat{P}y$, $y\hat{P}x$ and yet $x\hat{R}z$ – a contradiction to the transitivity of $\hat{R}$.   ∎

A proof of Arrow's theorem

We start from any *given* Paretian and IIA social welfare function w, and prove that some individual $d \in I$ will be positively pivotal under w for any ordered pair of alternatives at every possible profile – i.e. a dictator.

We first restrict our attention to strong preference profiles, and for all distinct $x, y \in A$, define $I_{xy} = \{i \in I \mid$ for some $R \in \overline{\mathcal{R}}^n$, i is positively xy-pivotal at $R\}$.

(1) By the Pareto rule, $I_{xy} \neq \varnothing$ for all distinct $x, y \in A$. That is, *for every ordered pair of alternatives x, y there will be at least one strong preference profile at which some individual is positively xy-pivotal.*

(2) For any $x, y, z, w \in A$ ($x \neq y, z \neq w$), and for all $i, j \in I$, if $i \in I_{xy}$ and $j \in I_{zw}$, then $i = j$. That is, *for all strong profiles where some individual d is positively pivotal, this individual must be one and the same.*

To prove this, suppose not; i.e. $\exists x, y, z, w \in A$ ($x \neq y, z \neq w$) and $i, j \in I$, such that $i \neq j, i \in I_{xy}, j \in I_{zw}$.

(a) If the pairs (x, y) and (z, w) have exactly one element in common, we can construct one profile where i and j are pivotal, in violation of the lemma.

(b) Suppose $x = w$ and $y = z$. Then, for any $v \in A$ ($v \neq x, v \neq y$), there is a $k \in I_{yv}$ such that either $i \neq k$ or $j \neq k$. This brings us back to situation (a).

(c) If (x, y) and (z, w) have no element in common, there must be a $k \in I_{yz}$ such that either $i \neq k$ or $j \neq k$. This, again, leads to situation (a).

(3) Thus, there exists $d \in I$ such that $I_{xy} = d$ for all distinct $x, y \in A$. This individual d, is positively pivotal for all pairs of alternatives at all strong profiles. To prove it, suppose not – i.e. that for some $R \in \mathcal{R}^n$ and some $x, y \in A$, d is not positively xy-pivotal at R. Since, by (1) there are strong profiles where d is posi-

---

[3] Use is made here of the facts that w is IIA and that we start from a *strong* preference profile. The latter guarantees that none of the pivots is indifferent between the alternatives upon which he can act. The Lemma does not hold true on the larger set of all possible profiles. A counterexample to such a (false) extension is provided by a sequential dictatorship.

tively xy-pivotal, there must exist two strong profiles which only differ in the preferences of one individual $h \neq d$, and such that d is positively xy-pivotal in one of these profiles while not in the other. But then, there must be a strong profile where $h \neq d$ is xy-pivotal, and thus one where h is xy-pivotal and d is yz-pivotal. This contradicts the lemma.

(4) *Individual d is positively pivotal for all pairs of alternatives at all profiles,* i.e. *a dictator*. To prove it, suppose not. Then, there would exist a profile $\hat{R} \in \mathscr{R}^n$ and alternatives $x, y \in A$, such that $x\hat{P}_d y$ and yet $y\hat{R}x$ (where $\hat{R} = w(\hat{R})$). Consider a strong profile $R \in \bar{\mathscr{R}}^n$ such that $xP_d zP_d y$, for some arbitrary, fixed alternative $z \notin \langle x, y \rangle$, and such that x and y are contiguous at all preferences other than d's at the profile R. According to (3), zPy. Now, define a new profile R' in such a way that $(\forall i \in I)\ (xR_i'y \longleftrightarrow x\hat{R}_i y)$, and for all $\langle v, w \rangle \neq \langle x, y \rangle$, $(\forall i)$ $(vR_i'w \longleftrightarrow vR_i w)$. Independence of irrelevant alternatives would require that $yR'x$, $xP'z$, and $zP'y$ – in contradiction with R's transitivity.

CHAPTER 3

The structure of general probabilistic group decision rules

R.A. HEINER*
Brigham Young University

and

P.K. PATTANAIK
University of Birmingham

1. Introduction

The purpose of this chapter is to complete a line of enquiry initiated by Barberá and Sonnenschein (1978) and subsequently pursued by McLennan (1980).[1] These writers have sought to widen the well-known framework of Arrow (1963) in which the group decision procedure yields a deterministic social weak preference relation for every profile of determinate individual orderings by introducing group decision procedures which admit lotteries over social weak preference relations in their ranges. The basic motivation for this was to explore the possibility of escaping the trivial power structure yielded by the deterministic Arrow-type framework (a possibility suggested by examples such as random dictatorship). Also, an additional motivation for admitting non-trivial lotteries over social weak

* Our greatest debt is to M. Salles for numerous, and extremely valuable suggestions. We are also grateful to C. Blackorby, R. Deb, B. Dutta, P. Hammond, J. Mirrlees, Y.K. Ng, A. Rubinstein, and A.K. Sen for their very helpful comments.
 [1] See also Bandyopadhyay, Deb and Pattanaik (1982) and Barberá and Valenciano (1980).

Social Choice and Welfare, edited by P.K. Pattanaik and M. Salles
© *North-Holland Publishing Company, 1983*

preference relations arose from the fact that the probabilistic framework can often accommodate considerations of fairness better than the deterministic framework. However, the case for introducing probabilistic social preferences becomes much stronger if, as we argue below, there are reasons to believe that either the individual preferences or information about them is probabilistic in nature. For example, if everyone prefers x to y with probability 0.5, and also y to x with probability 0.5, then it seems unreasonable to demand that society must rank x and y in a deterministic fashion.

In this chapter we consider the structure of a more general type of decision procedures than those considered by Barberá and Sonnenschein and McLennan. Not only the ranges of the decision procedures consist of lotteries over social weak preference relations, but also their domains permit profiles of non-trivial lotteries (one lottery for each individual over possible preference orderings). Thus, the probabilistic features enter into our analysis not only with respect to social preferences but with respect to individual preferences as well. There are several contexts in which a probabilistic approach to individual preferences is of interest. For example, Sen (1977) in discussing the informational basis of alternative types of preference aggregation problems, rightly points out that social welfare judgements are often based on information about individual preferences, which may not have been acquired by direct enquiry. Often decision-makers in a democratic set-up may not have direct information about individual preferences (over the relevant alternatives) as expressed by the individuals themselves. In such circumstances the decision-makers may base the decisions on what they think the individual preferences may be, on the basis of various bits of indirect evidence. The information about individual preferences in such cases may be less firm than information collected through direct enquiry,[2] and may take a probabilistic form. Note that in this case there may not be anything non-deterministic about the "true" individual preferences so far as the individuals themselves are concerned. The probabilistic features arise because of the decision-maker's imperfect information about these preferences.

However, sometimes the individual himself may not be sure about his own true preferences; alternatively, if the group choice made now affects the individual after a significant lapse of time, then the effect on the individual's welfare may depend on the individual's preferences in the future and he may not be sure about his future preferences. Though in general social choice theory has not been much concerned with the notion of probabilistic preferences for individuals,[3]

---

[2]   We are ignoring here the problem of strategic manipulation of preferences when one tries to collect information about preferences through direct enquiry.

[3]   For some important exceptions see Intriligator (1973) and Fishburn and Gehrlein (1977).

the concept has been commonly used in psychological experiments relating to individual choice behaviour (see Tversky, Coombs and Dawnes 1970; see also Coombs, 1958; Luce and Suppes, 1965; Myers and Atkinson, 1964; and Rumelhart and Greeno, 1971).

Note that while in the first case that we mentioned above probabilistic considerations arise because of the decision-maker's imperfect knowledge of the individual preferences on which the decision-maker wants to base the group decisions, in the second case they arise because of the individual's uncertainty about his own preferences. However, in both cases it seems desirable to extend the analytical framework so that the decision procedure can take into account probabilistic information about individual preferences.

The introduction of probabilistic individual preferences makes the model significantly more realistic for the reasons outlined above. In addition, it also suggests some interesting possibilities from the technical point of view. Consider the case where the stochastic element is inherent in the individual preferences (rather than arising from the policy-maker's imperfect knowledge of individual preferences). This is the case which psychologists have sought to analyse by developing a stochastic meaning of preferences under which the strength of strict preference for x over y is supposed to increase as the probability of observing x chosen over y approaches 1. If this is accepted then the probabilistic individual preferences (interpreted in terms of the individual's choice behaviour) can be regarded as implicitly containing information about the intensity of individual preferences. The question then arises as to whether the use of such additional though implicit cardinal information helps one to go beyond the negative results of the Arrow type. It is also interesting to note the *formal* similarity between randomized individual preferences and the notions of mixed strategies, so successfully used in game theory,[4] a similarity which raises one's hope of possibly reducing the impact of Arrow's negative theorem in this wider framework.

The main purpose of this chapter is to explore the structural properties of group decision procedures which permit in their domains profiles of non-degenerate individual lotteries (or probability distributions) over possible preference orderings in addition to permitting in their ranges non-degenerate probability distributions over possible social preferences. We show that a sub-additive power structure closely related to Arrow's original theorem prevails even in our expanded framework. In the process we generalize the earlier results of Barberá and Sonnenschein (1978) and McLennan (1980), in which full additivity of the power structure is implied with six or more options.

---

[4] The similarity referred to here is only a formal one since our motivation for introducing probabilistic individual preferences is not related to the question of strategy in group decision-making.

This introduction is followed by five sections. In section 2 we introduce our basic notation and definitions. In section 3 we prove some general results. Section 4 discusses the implications of imposing the property of stochastic transitivity on individual or social preferences. We conclude in section 5. In the appendix we discuss an alternative but closely related formulation in terms of probabilistic social choice as distinguished from probabilistic social preferences.

2. Notation and definitions

Let Y ($\infty > |Y| \geqslant 3$) be the set of alternatives and N ($\infty > |N| \geqslant 2$) be the set of individuals constituting the society. Let A be the set of all possible orderings over Y. The elements of A are indicated by R, R', etc. For all $x, y \in Y$, xPy iff [xRy and $\sim yRx$]. Similarly, we have P' corresponding to R'.

We shall use the notion of lotteries on different sets such as A and Y. etc. In general, a *lottery* over any given set X is a function $p: X \to [0,1]$ such that $\Sigma_{x \in X} p(x) = 1$. The set of all possible lotteries over A will be indicated by $\mathscr{A}$. Let $\mathscr{A}_0 = \{p \in \mathscr{A} \mid$ for all $R \in A$, either $p(R) = 1$ or $p(R) = 0\}$. For all $r \in \mathscr{A}$ and for all $x, y \in Y$, $r(xRy) = \Sigma_{R \in A'} r(R)$, where $A' = \{R \in A \mid xRy\}$. In general, $r(...)$ stands for $\Sigma_{R \in A'} r(R)$, where A' is the set of all $R \in A$ for which the statement ... holds.

We now introduce the basic notion of a GSWF.

Definition 1. A *general social welfare function* (GSWF) is a function $f: \tilde{\mathscr{A}}^n \to \mathscr{A}$, where $\varnothing \neq \tilde{\mathscr{A}} \subseteq \mathscr{A}$.

The elements in the domain $\tilde{\mathscr{A}}^n$ of a GSWF f will be indicated by $q = (q^1, ..., q^n)$, where for all $i \in N$, $q^i \in \tilde{\mathscr{A}}$ (q^i is to be interpreted as the ith individual's lottery over possible preference orderings). We write $p = f(q)$, $\hat{p} = f(\hat{q})$, etc. $p, \hat{p}$, etc. have the obvious interpretation as lotteries over social weak preference relations, corresponding to $q, \hat{q}$, etc. The domain and the range of f are indicated by D_f and E_f, respectively. It may be noted that (i) the social welfare function of Arrow (1963), and (ii) the probabilistic decision rules discussed by Barberá and Sonnenschein (1978) and McLennan (1980) are special cases where we have respectively (i) a GSWF f with $D_f = \mathscr{A}_0^n$ and $E_f = \mathscr{A}_0$, and (ii) a GSWF f with $D_f = \mathscr{A}_0^n$ and $E_f = \mathscr{A}$.

For all ordered pairs of distinct alternatives x and y, let $G_f(x,y) = \{g \in [0,1]^n \mid$ there exists $q \in D_f$ such that for all $i \in N$, $q^i(xPy) = g_i\}$.

We now define certain properties of a GSWF.

Definition 2. Let f be a GSWF with domain $\tilde{A}^n$, f satisfies the property of:

(2.1)   unrestricted domain (UD) iff $\tilde{\mathscr{A}} = \mathscr{A}$;

(2.2)   regular domain (RD) iff $\tilde{\mathscr{A}}$ satisfies the following condition: for all r, $r' \in \mathscr{A}$, if r, $r' \in \tilde{\mathscr{A}}$, then $\tilde{\mathscr{A}}$ also contains all $r'' \in \mathscr{A}$ such that for all $R'' \in A$ ($[r''(R'') = r(R) + r'(R')$ for some R, $R' \in A]$, or $[r''(R'') = |(r(R) - r'(R'))|$ for some R, $R' \in A]$, or $[r''(R'') = r(R)$ for some $r \in A]$, or $[r''(R'') = r'(R')$ for some $R' \in A]$);

(2.3)   *Independence of irrelevant alternatives* (IIA) iff for all $x, y \in Y$ and for all $\hat{q}$, $q \in \tilde{A}^n$ such that $[q^i(xPy) = \hat{q}^i(xPy)$ and $q^i(yPx) = \hat{q}^i(yPx)]$ for all $i \in N$, we have $[p(xPy) = \hat{p}(xPy)$ and $p(yPx) = \hat{p}(yPx)]$;

(2.4)   Pareto criterion (PC) iff for all $x, y \in Y$ and for all $q \in \tilde{A}^n$ such that for all $i \in N$, $q^i(xPy) = 1$, we have $p(xPy) = 1$;

(2.5)   PC* iff for all $t \in [0,1]$, and for all $x, y \in Y$, and for all $q \in \tilde{\mathscr{A}}^n$ such that $q^i(xPy) \geqslant t$ for all i, we have $p(xPy) \geqslant t$.

UD, IIA, and PC are the natural probabilistic counterparts of corresponding conditions in the original framework of Arrow (1963). RD and PC* need some explanation. Essentially what RD means is that if probability distributions q^i and $\tilde{q}^i$ over A are permissible for an individual i, then so is any other probability distribution $\hat{q}^i$ over A, where each coordinate of $\hat{q}^i$ is either identical to some coordinate of q^i or $\tilde{q}^i$, or is equal to the sum or difference of a coordinate of q^i and a coordinate of $\tilde{q}^i$ (note that q^i and $\tilde{q}^i$ may be identical). PC* is somewhat stronger than PC. If everybody prefers x to y with probability greater than or equal to t, then PC* requires that the probability of society preferring x to y must be at least as great as t. Though stronger than PC, PC* has a considerable amount of appeal.

We note the following obvious result.

Lemma 1. If a GSWF satisfies UD or has $\mathscr{A}_0^n$ for its domain, then it must satisfy RD but the converse is not necessarily true.

3.   The structure of GSWFs

In this section we explore the structural properties of GSWFs. First we prove some preliminary lemmas.

Lemma 2. Let f be a GSWF. Let $q \in D_f$ and let $p = f(q)$. For all $x, y, z \in Y$:

(2.1) $[p(xPy) + p(yPz) \geqslant p(xPz)]$ and $[p(xRy) + p(yRz) \geqslant p(xRz)]$;

(2.2) $[p(xPz) \geqslant p(xPy) + p(yRz) - 1]$ and $[p(xPz) \geqslant p(xRy) + p(yPz) - 1]$.

Proof.

(2.1) If R is an ordering, then $[(zRy \text{ and } yRx) \to zRx]$ and hence $[xPz \to (xPy \text{ or } yPz)]$. Therefore, given that f is a GSWF, it follows that $\boldsymbol{p}(xPz \to [xPy \text{ or } yPz]) = 1$. Hence, $\boldsymbol{p}(xPy \text{ or } yPz) \geqslant \boldsymbol{p}(xPz)$. Therefore, $\boldsymbol{p}(xPy) + \boldsymbol{p}(yPz) \geqslant \boldsymbol{p}(xPy \text{ or } yPz) \geqslant \boldsymbol{p}(xPz)$. The other part of lemma 2.1 can be proved similarly.

(2.2) If R is an ordering, then $(xPy \text{ and } yRz)$ implies xPz. Therefore, given that f is a GSWF $\boldsymbol{p}(xPz) \geqslant \boldsymbol{p}(xPy \text{ and } yRz) = \boldsymbol{p}(xPy) + \boldsymbol{p}(yRz) - [\boldsymbol{p}(xPy \text{ and } \sim yRz) + \boldsymbol{p}(yRz \text{ and } \sim xPy) + \boldsymbol{p}(xPy \text{ and } yRz)] \geqslant \boldsymbol{p}(xPy) + \boldsymbol{p}(yRz) - 1$. Similarly, it can be proved that $\boldsymbol{p}(xPz) \geqslant \boldsymbol{p}(xRy) + \boldsymbol{p}(yPz) - 1$. ∎

Lemma 3. Let f be a GSWF if f satisfies RD, then for all $x, y, z, w \in Y$ such that $x \neq y$ and $z \neq w$, we have $G_f(x, y) = G_f(z, w)$; and if f satisfies UD, then $G_f(x, y) = [0,1]^n$ for all distinct $x, y \in Y$.

The proof of this lemma is trivial and is omitted.

Throughout this section we consider GSWFs satisfying RD. Therefore, by lemma 3 we write simply G_f to indicate $G_f(x, y)$, $G_f(z, w)$, etc. (Where the GSWF f is unambiguous, we omit the subscript f and write G only.)

Let the GSWF f satisfy RD and IIA. Then for all $a \in G$ and for all distinct x, $y \in Y$, we define $V(a; x, y)$ and $W(a; x, y)$ to be $\boldsymbol{p}(xPy)$ and $\boldsymbol{p}(xRy)$, respectively, where $\boldsymbol{p} = f(q)$ for some $q \in D_f$ such that for all $i \in N, a_i = \boldsymbol{q}^i(xPy)$ and $(1 - a_i) = \boldsymbol{q}^i(yPx)$. Thus, $V(a; x, y)$ is the probability of x being socially better than y when the probabilities of the individuals strictly preferring x to y are given by $a = (a_1, ..., a_n)$ and the probabilities of the individual strictly preferring y to x are given by $(1 - a_1, ..., 1 - a_n)$. $W(a; x, y)$ is interpreted similarly for weak rather than strict social preferences. Looked at from a slightly different angle, V (resp. W) can be interpreted as reflecting the degree of strict (resp. weak) veto power of different coalitions over different ordered pairs of alternatives. To see this, consider any coalition L and any $a \in G$ such that for all $i \in L, a_i = \alpha > 0.5$ and for all $j \in (N - L), a_j = \beta < 0.5$. Then $V(a; x, y)$ stands for the degree of strict veto power which L exercises for x against y, when the degree of support of every number of L for x is given by α and the degree of support of every member of $(N - L)$ for y is given by $(1 - \beta)$. (In this example we have stipulated that $\alpha > 0.5$ and $\beta < 0.5$ so that we can intuitively speak of L as supporting x and $(N - L)$ as supporting y; however, one could take any $\alpha, \beta \in [0,1]$.) The following lemma shows that a basic neutrality property holds with respect to W and V.

Lemma 4. Let the GSWF f satisfy RD, PC, and IIA. Then for all $a \in G$ and for all $x, y, x', y' \in Y$ such that $x \neq y$ and $x' \neq y'$, (1) $V(a; x, y) = V(a; x', y')$, and (2) $W(a; x, y) = W(a; x' y')$.

Proof.

(1) Let z be an alternative distinct from x and y. We first show that $V(a; x, y) = V(a; x, z)$.

Let $D_f = \mathcal{A}^n$. Consider $q \in \mathcal{A}^n$ such that for all $i \in N$, q^i (xPy and yPz and xPz) $= a_i$ and q^i(yPz and zPx and yPx) $= 1 - a_i$. (Note that since $a \in G$, by RD we can find such $q \in \mathcal{A}^n$.) By PC, $p(yPz) = 1$. $V(a; x, y) = p(xPy)$. Let $p(xPy) = \alpha$. Then by lemma 2.2, $V(a; x, z) = p(xPz) \geqslant \alpha$.

We now show that $p(xPz)$ cannot be greater than α. Suppose $p(xPz) > \alpha$. Then construct $\hat{q} \in \mathcal{A}^n$ such that for all $i \in N$, $\hat{q}^i$(xPz and zPy and xPy) $= a_i$ and $\hat{q}^i$(zPy and yPx and zPx) $= 1 - a_i$. (As before, this is possible given RD and given that $a \in G$.) By PC, $\hat{p}(zPy) = 1$ and by IIA, $\hat{p}(xPz) = p(xPz) > \alpha$. Then by lemma 2.2 we have $\hat{p}(xPy) > \alpha$. However, by IIA, $p(xPy) = \hat{p}(xPy)$. Therefore $[p(xPy) = \alpha$ and $\hat{p}(xPy) > \alpha]$ leads to a contradiction. Hence, $\sim [p(xPz) > \alpha]$.

Since $p(xPz) \geqslant \alpha$ and $\sim [p(xPz) > \alpha]$, we have $V(a; x, z) = p(xPz) = \alpha$.

Similarly, it can be shown that $V(a; x, y) = V(a; z, y)$.

Since $V(a; x, y) = V(a; x, z) = V(a; z, y)$ for all z distinct from x and y, the well-known Arrow (1963, pp. 99–100) technique of interchanging alternatives can now be used to complete the proof.

(2) The proof of the second part of the lemma is similar to the proof of the first part. ■

In view of lemma 4 we can drop x, y, etc. from $W(a; x, y)$, $V(a; x, y)$, etc. and simply write $W(a)$, $V(a)$, and so on.

Theorem 1. Let the GSWF f satisfy RD, IIA, and PC.

(1.1) For all $a \in G$ [if $a_i = 0$ for all $i \in N$, then $a \in G$ and $V(a) = 0$] and [if $a_i = 1$ for all $i \in N$, then $a \in G$ and $V(a) = 1$].

(1.2) For all $a, a' \in G$, if $a \geqslant a'$ (i.e. for all $i \in N$, $a_i \geqslant a'_i$), then $V(a) \geqslant V(a')$.

(1.3) Consider any $a, a', a'' \in G$ such that for all $i \in N$ (if $a_i + a'_i \leqslant 1$, then $a''_i = a_i + a'_i$) and (if $a_i + a'_i > 1$, then $a''_i = 1$). Then $V(a) + V(a') \geqslant V(a'')$.

(1.4) For all $a \in G$, $W(a) = V(a)$.

(1.5) Suppose $|Y| \geqslant 6$. Then for all $a, a', a'' \in G$ such that for all $i \in N$, $a_i + a'_i \leqslant 1$ and $a''_i = (a_i + a'_i)$, we must have $[V(a) + V(a') = V(a'')]$.

Proof.

(1.1) The proof of (1.1) follows immediately from RD and PC.

(1.2) Consider three distinct alternatives, x, y, and z. Construct $q \in D_f$ such that for all $i \in N$, q^i(xPy and yPz and xPz) $= a'_i$; q^i(yPz and yPx and xPz) $= a_i - a'_i$; and q^i(yPz and yPx and zPx) $= 1 - a_i$. (Given RD and given the fact that $a, a' \in G$ and $a \geqslant a'$ it is possible to construct such $q \in D_f$.) Then $V(a') = p(xPy)$

and $p(yPz) = 1$. Then by lemma 2.2 we have $p(xPz) \geqslant p(xPy)$. Since $p(xPz) = V(a)$ and $p(xPy) = V(a')$, we have $V(a) \geqslant V(a')$.

(1.3) Consider three distinct alternatives, x, y, and z. Construct $q \in D_f$ such that for all $i \in N$:

if $(a_i + a_i' \leqslant 1)$, then $[q^i(xPz \text{ and } zPy \text{ and } xPy) = a_i$ and $q^i(yPx \text{ and } xPz \text{ and } yPz) = a_i'$ and $q^i(zPy \text{ and } yPx \text{ and } zPx) = 1 - a_i - a_i']$;

and

if $(a_i + a_i' > 1)$, then $[q^i(yPx \text{ and } xPz \text{ and } yPz) = 1 - a_i$ and $q^i(xPy \text{ and } yPz$ and $xPz) = a_i + a_i' - 1 = a_i - (1 - a_i')$ and $q^i(xPy \text{ and } xPz \text{ and } zPy) = 1 - a_i']$

It can easily be checked that RD and the fact that a and a' belong to G, together ensure the existence of such $q \in D_f$.

For all $i \in N$, $q^i(xPy) = a_i$; $q^i(yPx) = 1 - a_i$; $q^i(yPz) = a_i'$; $q^i(zPy) = 1 - a_i'$; $q^i(xPz) = a_i''$; and $q^i(zPx) = 1 - a_i''$. Hence, $V(a) = p(xPy)$; $V(a') = p(yPz)$; and $V(a'') = p(xPz)$. Therefore applying lemma 2.1 we have $V(a) + V(a') \geqslant V(a'')$.

(1.4) Let $a \in G$. Let $a' = (1 - a_i, ..., 1 - a_n)$. By RD, $a' \in G$. By definitions of W and V, $W(a) + V(a') = 1$. Construct $q \in \mathscr{T}^n$ such that for all $i \in N$, $q^i(xPy$ and zPy and $xPz) = a_i$ and $q^i(yPx \text{ and } yPz \text{ and } xPz) = a_i'$. Clearly, $[V(a) = p(xPy)$ and $V(a') = p(yPz)$ and $p(xPz) = 1]$. Then by lemma 2.1, $V(a) + V(a') \geqslant 1$. However, $V(a) + V(a') \leqslant W(a) + V(a') = 1$. Hence, $V(a) + V(a') = W(a) + V(a') = 1$. Hence, $V(a) = W(a)$.

(1.5) Theorem 1.3 shows that $V(a) + V(a') \geqslant V(a'')$. Therefore, we have only to show that $[V(a) + V(a') > V(a'')]$ leads to a contradiction given that for all $i \in N$, $a_i + a_1' \leqslant 1$ and that $|Y| \geqslant 6$.

Suppose $V(a) + V(a') > V(a'')$. Consider six distinct alternatives $x_1, ..., x_6 \in Y$. Construct $q \in D_f$ such that for all $i \in N$, $q^i(x_1 Px_3$ and $x_3 Px_2$ and $x_2 Px_5$ and $x_5 Px_6$ and $x_6 Px_4) = a_i$; $q^i(x_1 Px_5$ and $x_5 Px_6$ and $x_6 Px_3$ and $x_3 Px_2$ and $x_2 Px_4) = a_i'$; and $q^i(x_5 Px_3$ and $x_3 Px_4$ and $x_4 Px_1$ and $x_1 Px_6$ and $x_6 Px_2) = 1 - a_i'' = 1 - (a_i + a_i')$. (Note that such construction would not be possible if we had $a_i + a_i' > 1$ for some i. Also, note that under the given specifications, $q^i(x_1 Px_2$ and $x_3 Px_2$ and $x_3 Px_4$ and $x_5 Px_4$ and $x_5 Px_6$ and $x_1 Px_6) = 1$ for all $i \in N$.) Let $p = f(q)$.

Let J be the set of ordered pairs $\{(1,2), (3,2), (3,4), (5,4), (5,6), (1,6), (2,5), (6,3), (4,1)\}$. For all $(i, j) \in J$ and for all $r \in \mathscr{A}$, let $r_{ij} = r(x_i Px_j)$. For all $r \in \mathscr{A}$, let $\theta(r) = \Sigma_{(i,j) \in J} r_{ij}$.

Note that by the construction of q and by theorem 1.1, $p_{12} = p_{32} = p_{34} = p_{54} = p_{56} = p_{16} = 1$. Also, by the construction of q we have $p_{25} = V(a)$; $p_{63} = V(a')$; and $p_{41} = V(1 - a_1'', ..., 1 - a_n'')$. Therefore,

$$\theta(p) = 6 + V(a) + V(a') + V(1 - a_1'', ..., 1 - a_n'')$$

$$\geqslant 6 + V(a) + V(a') + V(1, 1, ..., 1) - V(a''),$$

by theorem 1.3,

$$\geqslant 7 + V(a) + V(a') - V(a''), \quad \text{by theorem 1.1,}$$

$$> 7, \quad \text{since } V(a) + V(a') > V(a'').$$

For all $R \in A$, let r^R stand for the lottery in $\mathscr{A}$ such that $r^R(R) = 1$. (This means that for all $(i, j) \in J, r_{ij}^R = 1$ if $x_i P x_j$, and $r_{ij}^R = 0$ otherwise.) Then

$$\theta(p) = \sum_{(i,j)\in J} p_{ij} = \sum_{(i,j)\in J} \left[\sum_{R\in A} r_{ij}^R \cdot p(R) \right]$$

$$= \sum_{R\in A} p(R) \left[\sum_{(i,j)\in J} r_{ij}^R \right] = \sum_{R\in A} p(R) \cdot \theta(r^R).$$

Thus, $\theta(p)$ is a convex combination of $\{\theta(r^R) \mid R \in A\}$. Since $\theta(p) > 7$, there must exist $R^* \in A$ such that $\theta(r^{R^*}) > 7$ which implies that at least eight of the elements of $\{r_{ij}^{R^*} \mid (i, j) \in J\}$ must be equal to 1. Consider fig. 3.1 in which an ar-

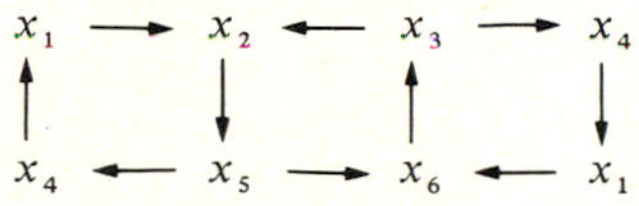

$$
\begin{array}{cccc}
x_1 \longrightarrow & x_2 \longleftarrow & x_3 \longrightarrow & x_4 \\
\uparrow & \downarrow & \uparrow & \downarrow \\
x_4 \longleftarrow & x_5 \longrightarrow & x_6 \longleftarrow & x_1
\end{array}
$$

Figure 3.1

row from any x_i to any x_j would indicate that $r_{ij}^{R^*} = 1$ (i.e. $x_i P^* x_j$) and which has been drawn for the hypothetical case where each of the nine elements of $\{r_{ij}^{R^*} \mid (i, j) \in J\}$ is equal to 1. For this *hypothetical* case, it is clear that R^* will involve at least three P^*-cycles ($x_3 P^* x_4 P^* x_1 P^* x_6 P^* x_3$ and $x_3 P^* x_2 P^* x_5 P^* x_6 P^* x_3$ and $x_1 P^* x_2 P^* x_5 P^* x_4 P^* x_1$). Note that although fig. 3.1 is drawn for the hypothetical case where each element of $\{r_{ij}^{R^*} \mid (i, j) \in J\}$ is equal to 1, all that we actually know is that at least eight of these elements must be equal to 1. However, with the help of the diagram the reader can easily check that if *any* eight elements of $\{r_{ij}^{R^*} \mid (i, j) \in J\}$ are separately equal to 1, then at least one P^*-cycle must be present in R^*, which is a contradiction. This completes the proof. ∎

The following corollary of theorem 1 is of interest.

Corollary of theorem 1. Let f be a GSWF satisfying UD, IIA, and PC. Then there exists a unique non-empty subset L^* of N such that for all $a \in [0,1]^n$, if $a_i = 1$ for all $i \in L^*$, then $V(a) = 1$, and if $a_i > 0$ for some $i \in L^*$, then $V(a) > 0$.

Proof. For every non-empty subset L of N, let $b[L]$ stand for $a \in [0,1]^n$ such that for all $i \in L$, $a_i = 1$ and for all $i \in (N - L)$, $a_i = 0$. To economize notation we write $b[1,2]$, $b[3]$, etc. instead of $b[\{1,2\}]$, $b[\{3\}]$, etc.

By theorem 1.2, $V(b[N]) = 1$. Hence, given theorem 1.3 it is clear that for some $k \in N$, $V(b[k]) > 0$. Now consider any $a \in [0,1]^n$ such that $a_k > 0$. Since $V(b[k]) > 0$, by theorem 1.3 it follows that $V(b[k]/2^t) > 0$, where t is a positive integer. By letting t be sufficiently large so that $a_k > 1/2^t$, and by applying theorem 1.2, it follows that $V(a) > 0$.

Let $L^* = \{i \in N \mid$ for all $a \in [0,1]^n$, if $a_i > 0$, then $V(a) > 0\}$. By what we have said in the proceeding paragraph, $L^* \neq \varnothing$. To complete the proof we have to show that for all $a \in [0,1]^n$ if $a_i = 1$ for all $i \in L^*$, then $V(a) = 1$. Suppose $V(a) < 1$. Let $a' = (1 - a_i, \ldots, 1 - a_n)$. Since $V(a) + W(a') = 1$, given $V(a) < 1$, it follows that $W(a') > 0$. Hence, by theorems 1.2 and 1.4, $V(b[N - L^*]) > 0$. Now, by repeatedly applying theorem 1.3 as in the previous paragraph, it can be shown that there exists $J \in (N - L^*)$ such that for all $a \in [0,1]^n$, if $a_j > 0$, then $V(a) > 0$. However, this contradicts the definition of L^*. Hence, for all $a \in [0,1]^n$, if $a_i = 1$ for all $i \in L^*$, then $V(a) = 1$.

Suppose there exists $\hat{L}$ ($\varnothing \neq \hat{L} \subseteq N$) such that $\hat{L} \neq L^*$; and for all $a \in [0,1]^n$, if $a_i = 1$ for all $i \in \hat{L}$, then $V(a) = 1$ and if $a_i > 0$ for some $i \in \hat{L}$, then $V(a) > 0$. Then either $L^* - \hat{L} \neq \varnothing$ or $\hat{L} - L^* \neq \varnothing$. Without loss of generality assume $L^* - \hat{L} \neq \varnothing$ and that $k \in (L^* - \hat{L})$. Consider $a \in [0,1]^n$ such that for all $i \neq k$, $a_i = 1$ and $a_k = 0$. Since $k \in L^*$, by the definition of L^* and by theorem 1.4, $W(a) = V(a) < 1$. Since for all $i \in \hat{L}$, $a_i = 1$, $V(a) = 1$. This is a contradiction. Hence, L^* is the unique non-empty subset of N fulfilling the two properties under consideration. This completes the proof. ∎

The results of this section show that some of the basic features of the model of Arrow (1963) remain intact even when we extend the framework so as to permit lotteries over individual as well as social preferences. One such feature is the symmetry of coalitional power as between different pairs of alternatives when individuals' indifferences are ruled out (we refer to this as quasi-neutrality in the context of the Arrow framework). Our lemma 4 shows that the probabilistic counterpart of quasi-neutrality holds for GSWFs satisfying IIA and PC. Of course, this, as in the Arrow model, severely reduces the richness of possible structures for GSWFs by making it impossible (when individual indifferences have zero probability) to take into account any information about the nature of the social alternatives as such, apart from the individual preferences, in social decision-making.[5]

---

[5]   See Sen (1979).

A conspicuous feature of Arrow's model is the undesirable power structure which takes the form of a dictatorship. Theorem 1, however, does not imply any such concentration of power. Theorem 1 does imply the existence of an individual such that whenever he attaches positive probability to any ordering in which an alternative, say, x, is preferred to another alternative, say, y, no matter how small this positive probability may be and no matter what the probability distributions of other individuals may be, society cannot attach zero probability to x being at least as good as y. However, it is worth noting that under GSWFs, such power need not necessarily be unequally distributed as it is the case in Arrow's analysis.

One aspect of theorem 1.5 may be worth noting here. Consider the restriction $(a_i + a_i'' \leqslant 1$ for all $i \in N)$ figuring in theorem 1.5. The question arises whether, by analogy with theorem 1.3, it is possible to relax this restriction to [for all $i \in N$ (if $a_i + a_i' < 1$, then $a_i' = a_i + a_i'$) and (if $a_i + a_i' > 1$, then $a_i'' = 1$)]. That this cannot be done without affecting the validity of the result can be seen from the following counter-example. Consider the GSWF f such that: (1) $D_f = \mathscr{A}_0^n$ and $E_f = \mathscr{A}_0$; and (2) for all $q \in \mathscr{A}_0^n, p(\hat{R}) = 1$, where $\hat{R} \in A$ is such that for all $x, y \in Y$, $x\hat{R}y$ iff $\sim$[for some $k \in N$, $q_k (yPx) = 1$; and for all $i \in N$, if $i < k$, then $q_i(xIy)$ = 1]. It is clear that f is a GSWF which satisfies RD, IIA, and PC (in fact, f is nothing but lexicographic dictatorship of a deterministic type). However, taking a, a', and a'' such that for all $i \in N$, $a_i = a_i' = a_i'' = 1$, it is clear that $V(a) + V(a')$ $= 2 > V(a'') = 1$.

We conclude this section by considering some special classes of GSWFs and relating our theorem 1 to several earlier results in the literature. One can think of at least three special classes of GSWFs: (1) $f: \mathscr{A}_0^n \to \mathscr{A}_0$ (considered by Arrow, 1963); (2) $f: \mathscr{A}_0^n \to \mathscr{A}$ (considered by Barberá and Sonnenschein, 1978, and McLennan, 1980); and (3) $f: \mathscr{A}^n \to \mathscr{A}_0$.

The reader can easily check that the corollary of our theorem 1 implies the impossibility result of Arrow (1963). Similarly, the central results of Barberá and Sonnenschein (1978) is a special case of our theorems 1.1 through 1.3 and McLennan's (1980) theorem is a special case of our theorem 1.5. Our theorem 1 is also applicable to case 3 listed above (where $D_f = \mathscr{A}^n$ and $E_f = \mathscr{A}_0$). However, as shown by the following theorem, our theorem 1 covers case 3 above only in a vacuous fashion.

Theorem 2. There does not exist any GSWF with domain $\mathscr{A}^n$ and range $\mathscr{A}_0$ which satisfies IIA and PC.

We omit the proof here, since theorem 2 follows directly from our theorem 4 in the next section. Theorem 2 shows (not unexpectedly) that attempts to aggregate probabilistic individual preferences into a deterministic social ordering creates even greater problems than the problem faced by Arrow in aggregating determinate individual orderings into a determinate social ordering.

4. Stochastic transitivity

Psychologists have often assumed (or predicted) various types of "stochastic transitivity" for probabilistic individual preferences.[6] In this section we investigate the implications of imposing a version of stochastic transitivity on individual and social preferences.

A lottery $r \in \mathcal{A}$ satisfies *stochastic transitivity* (ST) iff for all $x, y, z \in Y$ $[r(xRy) \geqslant 0.5$ and $r(yRz) \geqslant 0.5]$ implies $[r(xRz) \geqslant 0.5]$.[7] ST can be interpreted in a descriptive sense as a property which probabilistic individual preferences are supposed to satisfy in real life. There is some evidence in support of ST interpreted in this fashion, although the case is by no means conclusive.[8] An alternative interpretation of ST can be in normative terms: one can view it as a condition which one would expect to be satisfied by "rational" probabilistic preferences. When interpreted in this way, the property can be imposed on social preferences as well as on individual preferences.

Let $\mathcal{B} = \{r \in \mathcal{A} \mid r$ satisfies stochastic transitivity$\}$. In the context of a GSWF f one can think of at least three combinations of domain and range restrictions involving ST: (i) $D_f = \mathcal{B}^n$ and $E_f = \mathcal{B}$; (ii) $D_f = \mathcal{A}^n$ and $E_f = \mathcal{B}$; and (iii) $D_f = \mathcal{B}^n$ and $E_f = \mathcal{A}$.

Our theorem 3 shows that given IIA and PC*, case (i) leads to a high concentration of strict veto power in the hands of some individuals (as we have noted above, such concentration of strict veto power could not be deduced from the assumptions figuring in theorem 1).

We proceed to theorem 3 through the following lemmas.

Lemma 5. Let f be a GSWF such that $D_f = \mathcal{B}^n$. Then for all distinct $x, y \in Y$, $G_f(x, y) = [0,1]^n$.

[6]   See Davidson and Marschak (1959), Edwards (1961), Tversky, Coombs and Dawnes (1970), and Restle and Greeno (1970).

[7]   This is slightly stronger than weak stochastic transitivity (as defined by Tversky, Coombs and Dawnes, 1970) which, in terms of our notation, requires that for all $x, y, z \in Y$, $([p(xPy) \geqslant 0.5$ and $p(yPz) \geqslant 0.5] \to [p(xPz) \geqslant 0.5])$.

[8]   See Coombs (1958), Davidson and Marschak (1959), and Edwards (1961) among others.

The proof of lemma 5 is obvious and is omitted.

In view of lemma 5, whenever $D_f = \mathscr{B}^n$ we shall write simply G_f (or G if there is no ambiguity about f).

Lemma 6. Let f be a GSWF satisfying IIA and PC*. Let $D_f = \mathscr{B}^n$ and $E_f = \mathscr{B}$. Then for all $x, y, x', y' \in Y$ ($x \neq y$ and $y \neq y'$), for all $i \in N$, and for all $a, a' \in [0,1]^n = G$ such that ($a'_i = a_i > 0.5$ and $a_j = 0$ for all $j \neq i$), we have $V(a'; x', y') \geqslant V(a; x, y)$.

Proof. Let $z \in (Y - \{x, y\})$. Construct $q \in \mathscr{A}^n$ such that: (1) $[q'(xPy$ and yPz and $xPz) = a'_i = a_i$ and $q^i(yPz$ and zPx and $yPx) = 1 - a'_i = 1 - a_i]$; (2) for all $j \neq i$, $[q^j(yPx$ and xPz and $yPz) = a'_j$ and $q^j(yPz$ and zPx and $yPx) = 1 - a'_j]$; and (3) for all $k \in N, q^k$ satisfies ST.

Given that $a'_i = a_i > 0.5$, clearly it is possible to construct such q, and it is clear that $q \in \mathscr{B}^n = D_f$. (Note that if a_i were equal to 0.5, (1) would have been incompatible with (3).)

Using lemma 2.2 and PC*, $V(a'; x, z) = p(x, z) \geqslant p(x, y) + p(y, z) - 1 = p(x, y) = V(a; x, y)$. Similarly, it can be shown that $V(a'; z, y) \geqslant V(a; x, y)$. The proof of the lemma can now be completed by following the well-known technique of Arrow (1963, pp. 99–100). ■

Theorem 3. Let f be a GSWF satisfying IIA and PC*. Let $D_f = \mathscr{B}^n$ and $E_f = \mathscr{B}$. Then there exists $i \in N$ such that for all $a \in [0,1]^n = G$, if $a_i > 0.5$, then for all distinct $x, y \in Y, V(a; x, y) > 0.5$.

Proof. The proof follows the familiar pattern of Arrow's (1963) proof. Consider any real number t such that $1 > t > 0.5$. By PC*, there exists a coalition L such that for some distinct $w, w' \in Y, V(a; w, w') > 0.5$, where $a_k = t$ for all $k \in L$ and $a_j = 0$ for all $j \in (N - L)$. Let L^* be the smallest such coalition. Then $L^* \neq \varnothing$ (by PC*), and for some distinct $x, y \in Y, V(a; x, y) > 0.5$, where $a_k = t$ for all $k \in L$ and $a_j = 0$ for all $j \in (N - L)$. Let $z \in (Y - \{x, y\})$. Let $i \in L^*$. Let $q \in \mathscr{A}^n$ be such that: (1) $[q^i(xPy$ and yPz and $xPz) = t$ and $q^i(yPx$ and yPz and $zPx) = 1 - t]$; (2) [for all $j \in (N - L^*), q^j(yPz$ and zPx and $yPx) = 1]$; (3) [for all $j \in (L^* - \{i\}), q^j(zPx$ and xPy and $zPy) = t$ and $q^j(zPx$ and yPx and $yPz) = 1 - t]$; and (4) [for all $j \in N, q^j$ satisfies ST].

It can easily be checked that given $t > 0.5$, such q exists and it is clear that $q \in \mathscr{B}^n$. By the specification of $L^*, p(xPy) > 0.5$ and $p(zPy) \leqslant 0.5$. Hence, $p(xPy) > 0.5$ and $p(yRz) \geqslant 0.5$. Suppose $\sim[p(xPz) > 0.5]$. Then $p(zRx) \geqslant 0.5$. Given $p(yRz) \geqslant 0.5, [p(zRx) \geqslant 0.5]$ implies $[p(yRx) \geqslant 0.5]$ which contradicts $p(xPy) > 0.5$. This contradiction shows that $p(xPz) > 0.5$. Then by lemma 6, it follows that for all $\hat{a} \in [0,1]^n$ if $\hat{a}_i = t$, then for all distinct $x', y' \in Y$, $V(\hat{a}; x', y') \geqslant V(a; x, z) = p(xPz) > 0.5$.

What we have so far provided is that for all $t \in [0.5,1]$ there exists an individual $i(t)$ such that for all $a \in [0,1]^n$, if $a_{i(t)} = t$, then for all distinct $x, y \in Y$, $V(a; x, y) > 0.5$. Let $t, t' \in [0.5,1]$ and let $t \neq t'$. Then we show that $i(t) = i(t')$. Suppose $i(t) \neq i(t')$. Construct $a \in [0,1]^n$ such that $a_{i(t)} > 0.5$ and $a_{i(t')} < 0.5$. Then for all distinct $x, y \in Y$, we have $V(a; x, y) > 0.5$ and $V(a; y, x) > 0.5$ which is a contradiction. Hence, $i(t) = i(t')$. Thus, there exists a unique individual $i \in N$ such that for all $a \in [0,1]^n$ if $a_i > 0.5$, then for all distinct $x, y \in Y$, $V(a; x, y) > 0.5$. ∎

We now consider case (ii) where $D_f = \mathscr{A}^n$ and $E_f = \mathscr{B}$.

Theorem 4. There does not exist any GSWF f which satisfies IIA and PC and which has $\mathscr{A}^n$ for its domain and $\mathscr{B}$ for its range.

Proof. Let f be a GSWF satisfying IIA and PC. Let $D_f = \mathscr{A}^n$ and $E_f = \mathscr{B}$. Let $Y = \{x_1, ..., x_m\}$ and let $\hat{R}$ and $\tilde{R}$ be two orderings over Y such that $x_1 \hat{P} x_2 \hat{P} x_3 \hat{P} x_4 \hat{P} ... \hat{P} x_m$ and $x_3 \tilde{P} x_1 \tilde{P} x_2 \tilde{P} x_4 \tilde{P} ... \tilde{P} x_m$. Construct $q \in \mathscr{A}^n$ such that for all $i \in N$, $q_i(\hat{R}) = q_i(\tilde{R}) = 0.5$. Then by lemma 4, $p(x_3 P x_2) = p(x_2 P x_3) = p(x_3 P x_1) = p(x_1 P x_3) = \alpha (0 \leqslant \alpha \leqslant 1)$; and $p(x_1 P x_2) = 1$. If $\alpha \geqslant 0.5$, then $p(x_2 P x_3) = p(x_3 P x_1) \geqslant 0.5$, and given $p(x_1 P x_2) = 1$ this contradicts stochastic transitivity of p. If $\alpha < 5$, then $p(x_1 P x_3) = p(x_3 P x_2) < 0.5$. Then $p(x_2 R x_3) = p(x_3 R x_1) \geqslant 0.5$, and given $p(x_1 P x_2) = 1$ this again violates stochastic transitivity of p. ∎

The non-existence result embodied in theorem 4 is not surprising since the degree of rationality postulated for the social preference lotteries happens to be stronger than that postulated for individual lotteries. Since $\mathscr{A}_0 \subseteq \mathscr{B}$, theorem 2 follows as a corollary of theorem 4.

Of the three cases listed at the beginning of this section we are left with case (iii), where $D_f = \mathscr{B}^n$ and $E_f = \mathscr{A}$. We conjecture that the counterpart of theorem 1 can be proved for the case. However, so far we have not been able to prove (or disprove) this conjecture and therefore we leave it as an open problem.

5. Concluding remarks

In this chapter we have proved general results which show that some of the basic features of Arrow's (1963) deterministic model remain intact even when we consider a much broader type of decision-making mechanism which permits non-trivial lotteries over both individual preferences and social preferences. The impossibility theorem of Arrow (1963) as well as the central theorems of Barberá and Sonnenschein (1978) and McLennan (1980) emerge as special cases within our general framework.

We have concentrated on the generalized probabilistic version of Arrow's social welfare function where transitivity of the social weak preference relation constitutes the relevant condition of collective rationality. Consequently, weaker collective rationality conditions such as quasi-transitivity of the social weak preference relation or acyclicity of the social strict preference relation have not been analysed. However, Bandyopadhyay, Deb and Pattanaik (1982) and Barberá and Valenciano (1980) have considered such weaker collective rationality conditions in the Barberá–Sonnenschein type framework which permits probabilistic preferences for society but not for individuals. We leave it to the interested reader to check that it is possible to derive results parallel to those of Bandyopadhyay, Deb and Pattanaik, and Barberá and Valenciano, when both individual and social preferences are assumed to be probabilistic in nature.

Appendix

In the main body of this chapter we have posed our problem in terms of probabilistic *social preferences*. The purpose of this appendix is to develop an alternative framework in terms of probabilistic social choice.

Let Z be the set of all possible non-empty subsets of Y. A *choice function* over Z is a function $h: Z \to Z$, such that for all $Y' \in Z, h(Y') \subseteq Y'$ (we call $h(Y')$ the choice set for Y'). Let H be the set of all possible choice functions over Z. Let $\mathscr{L}, \mathscr{Y}$, and $\mathscr{H}$ be the set of all possible lotteries over Z, Y, and H, respectively.

Consider the following definitions. *A type I probabilistic social choice rule* (PSCR(I)) is a function $F: \mathscr{A}^n \times Z \to \mathscr{Y}$ such that for all $(q, Y') \in \mathscr{A}^n \times Z$, and for all $x \in Y, ([u(x) > 0] \to [x \in Y']$, where $u = F(q; X')$. *A type II probabilistic social choice rule* (PSCR(II)) is a function $F: \mathscr{A}^n \times Z \to \mathscr{L}$ such that for all $(q, Y') \in \mathscr{A}^n \times Z$ and for all $Y'' \in \mathscr{L}$ $([u(Y'') > 0] \to [Y'' \subseteq Y'])$, where $u = F(q, Y')$. *A type III probabilistic social choice rule* (PSCR(III)) is a function $F: \mathscr{A}^n \to \mathscr{H}$.

Intuitively speaking, given a profile of individual lotteries over preference orderings and given a feasible set of alternatives, a PSCR(I) specifies a lottery over this feasible set of alternatives, while a PSCR(II) specifies a lottery over the set of possible choice sets from this feasible set of alternatives. Clearly, a PSCR(I) can be thought of as a special case of a PSCR(II) where the choice sets are constrained to be singletons. Also, a PSCR(II) constitutes the exact counterpart of the notion of a deterministic social choice rule which for every profile of individual orderings and for every feasible set of alternatives, specifies a non-empty subset (not necessarily a singleton) of the feasible set of alternatives as the choice set. In view of this we concentrate below on PSCR(II).

It is well known that in the deterministic framework if social choice satisfies certain consistency conditions then they become rationalizable in terms of a binary social weak preference relation. Thus, in the presence of these consistency conditions a model formulated in terms of social choices in the non-probabilistic framework can be readily translated in terms of social weak preference relations. In the probabilistic framework also, one may like to impose such consistency conditions on the final choice of society, which emerge after the random mechanism adopted to implement the lottery has worked itself out. For example, consider a PSCR(II) F. Suppose we are given $q \in \mathscr{A}^n$, x, $y \in Y$ and Y', $Y'' \in \mathscr{L}$ such that $x, y \in (Y' \cap Y'')$. Let $u' = F(q, Y')$ and $u'' = F(q, Y'')$. Presumably in each of these two cases society would use a random mechanism so as to decide the final choice set. Then one may want to impose the probabilistic counterpart of the weak axiom of revealed preference (WARP) on the final choice sets which ultimately emerge after the random mechanism has been gone through. Thus, one may want to ensure zero probability for the event that in the first case the society finally "chooses" x (i.e. x belongs to the choice set which ultimately emerges in the first case) while in the second case society finally chooses y but rejects x (i.e. y but not x belongs to the choice set which ultimately emerges in the second case). In other words, one may want to require that for all $x, y \in (Y' \cap Y'')$, the joint probability of x figuring in the ultimately emerging choice set in the first case, and y, but not x, figuring in the choice set which finally results in the second case, should be zero. However, it is not possible to articulate this intuitive requirement in the framework of a PSCR(II) since the notion of a PSCR(II) does not contain any information about such joint probabilities. If we want to impose intuitive requirements of the type discussed above, then information about such joint probabilities has to be explicitly introduced into the structure. This is where the notion of a PSCR(III) becomes relevant.

Let F be a PSCR(III). Given $q \in \mathscr{A}^n$, F first specifies a lottery u over $\mathscr{H}$. Then a random mechanism is actuated to give effect to this lottery. The random mechanism leads to the final selection of a choice function and this choice function then determines the choice set for any feasible set of alternatives that may come up for decision. It is clear that under this type of procedure the sum of probabilities attached by the lottery u to all choice functions h such that $[x \in h(Y')$ and $y \in h(Y'')$ and $x \notin h(Y'')]$, gives the joint probability of x being in the final choice set for Y' and y (but not x) being in the final choice set of Y''. For all $u \in \mathscr{H}$, let $u[...]$ stand for $\Sigma_{h \in \hat{H}}$, $u(h)$, where $\hat{H}$ is the set of all $h \in H$ such that the statement $[...]$ is true of h. Now consider the following property that may be postulated for the PSCR(III) F.

WARP*. For all $q \in \mathscr{A}^n$, for all $x, y \in Y$, and for all Y', $Y'' \in Z$ if $x, y \in (Y' \cap Y'')$, then $\boldsymbol{u}\,[x \in h\,(Y')$ and $y \in h\,(Y'')$ and $x \notin h\,(Y'')] = 0$, where $u = F(q)$.

WARP* is the direct probabilistic counterpart of the Arrow (1959) version of the weak axiom of revealed preference. The reader can easily check the truth of the following proposition.

Proposition. Let F be a PSCR(III) satisfying WARP*. Then there exists a unique PSWF f with domain $\mathscr{A}^n$ and satisfying the following property: for all $q \in \mathscr{A}^n$ and for all $h \in H$, if $u\,(h) > 0$ (where $u = F(q)$), then there exists exactly one $R \in A$ such that $p\,(R) = u\,(h)$ (where $p = f(q)$) and for all $Y' \in Z$ the set of R-greatest elements in Y' coincides with $h\,(Y')$. Conversely, let f be a PSWF with domain $\mathscr{A}^n$. Then there exists a unique PSCR(III) F satisfying WARP* in addition to the following property: for all $q \in A^n$ and for all $R \in A$, if $p\,(R) > 0$ (where $p = f(q)$), then there exists exactly one $h \in H$ such that $u\,(h) = p\,(R)$ (where $u = F(q)$) and for all $Y' \in Z, h(Y')$ coincides with the set of R-greatest elements in Y'.

Thus, as in the deterministic models, a probabilistic social choice framework can be seen to be "equivalent" to a probabilistic social preference framework provided one imposes certain consistency conditions on the final social choice sets which emerge as the result of the random mechanisms adopted to implement the social lotteries.

References

Arrow, K.J. (1959) "Rational Choice Functions and Orderings", *Economica*.

Arrow, K.J. (1963) *Social Choice and Individual Values*, 2nd edn. (Wiley, New York).

Bandyopadhyay, T., R. Deb and P.K. Pattanaik (1982) "The Structure of Coalitional Power under Probabilistic Group Decision Rules", *Journal of Economic Theory*.

Barberá, S. and H. Sonnenschein (1978) "Mixture Social Welfare Functions", *Journal of Economic Theory*.

Barberá, S. and F. Valenciano (1980) "Collective Probabilistic Judgements" mimeograph.

Coombs, C.H. (1958) "On the Use of Inconsistency of Preferences in Psychological Measurement", *Journal of Experimental Psychology*.

Davidson, I. and J. Marschak (1959) "Experimental Tests of a Stochastic Decision Theory", in: C.W. Churchman and P. Ratoosh, eds., *Measurement: Definitions and Theories* (Wiley, New York).

Edwards, W. (1964) "Behavioural Decision Theory", *Annual Review of Psychology*; reprinted in: W. Edwards and A. Tversky, *Decision Making* (Penguin Books Ltd., Harmondsworth, 1967).

Fishburn, P.C. and W.V. Gehrlein (1977) "Towards a Theory of Elections with Probabilistic Preferences", *Econometrica*.

Gibbard, A. (1969) "Intransitive Social Indifference and Arrow's Dilemma", mimeograph.

Guha, A. (1972) "Neutrality, Monotonicity and the Right of Veto", *Econometrica*.

Intriligator, M.D. (1973) "A Probabilistic Model of Social Choice", *Review of Economic Studies*.

Luce, R.D. (1959) *Individual Choice Behaviour* (Wiley, New York).

Luce, R.D. and P. Suppes (1965) "Preferences, Utility and Subjective Probability", in: R.D. Luce, R.R. Bush and E. Galanter, eds., *Handbook of Mathematical Psychology*, Vol. III (Wiley, New York).

McLennan, A. (1980) "Randomized Preference Aggregation: Additivity of Power and Strategy-Proofness", *Journal of Economic Theory*.

Myers, J.L. and R.C. Atkinson (1964) "Choices Behaviour and Reward Structure", *Journal of Mathematical Psychology*.

Restle, J. and J.G. Greeno (1970) *Introduction to Mathematical Psychology* (Addison-Wesley Publishing Co., Reading, Mass).

Rumelhart, D.L. and J.G. Greeno (1971) "Similarity Between Stimuli: An Experimental Test of the Luce and Restle Choice Models", *Journal of Mathematical Psychology*.

Sen, A.K. (1977) "Social Choice Theory: A Re-examination", *Econometrica*.

Sen, A.K. (1979) "Personal Utilities and Public Judgements: Or What's Wrong with Welfare Economics?", *Economic Journal*.

Tversky, A.C., C. Coombs and R. Dawnes (1970) *Mathematical Psychology: An Elementary Introduction* (Prentice-Hall, New Jersey).

CHAPTER 4

Positive association and its relatives

MAURICE McMANUS*
The University of New South Wales

1. Introduction

Positive association is one of the properties introduced by Arrow (1963) in his famous model of social choice. Several extensions of the original idea have been proposed since then for particular reasons. This chapter attempts to purify the various concepts and examines the fundamental interrelationships among them in a setting more general than the usual one. There is considerable significance for the classic impossibility results.

2. The context

Assume that a society consists of a fixed set of individuals N, and is faced by a given set of alternative social states A. The individuals and society have certain sets of potential (weak) preference binary relations over A, the $\mathscr{P}_i$, $i \in N$, and $\mathscr{P}_S$. The usual symbol R is used generically for such relations, with subscripts as for $\mathscr{P}$. Negation is denoted by $\sim$, and it is convenient to write, for example, $x \sim R y$ rather than the logically preferable but more cumbersome $\sim(xRy)$. For all x, y in A, the associated strict preference relation P is defined by xPy whenever xRy and $y \sim Rx$, and indifference I by xIy whenever xRy and yRx. An individual's R relation need not be complete, so it is useful to supplement it by defining a relation

* This study stems from a disputed point made in an earlier paper supported by an SSRC Personal Research Grant in 1975/6. The author is grateful to Professor Salles for useful comments and references, but bears full responsibility for the final product.

of non-comparability J by xJy if and only if (iff) $x{\sim}Ry$ and $y{\sim}Rx$. The relation of non-preference (either way) K then means indifference or non-comparability. For simplicity, however, society's relations are assumed to be complete. For any $x \in A$, let $A_x = A - \{x\}$. Given an $x \in A$ and an R for society, use is sometimes made of $Rx = \{y \in A_x : yRx\}$, $xR = \{y \in A_x : xRy\}$, and the analogous sets Px, xP, and Ix (or xI). A preference profile is a family of preference relations, one per individual, so that the set of potential profiles $\mathscr{D}$ is a subset of $X_{i \in N} \mathscr{P}_i$. Superscripts on relations or sets denote profiles, e.g. for a given $p \in \mathscr{D}$, write R_i^p, $i \in N$, R_S^p, Rx^p, $x \in A$. Given a preference profile, the society is assumed to form a unique social preference relation. This defines a social choice function (SCF):

$$\text{SCF}: \mathscr{D} \to \mathscr{P}_S, \tag{1}$$

which is broader than most functions encountered in social choice theory because no special types of preference relations are specified except when needed for particular results.

Postulating such a function already involves certain social value judgements, and various further judgements have been proposed which limit the class of function deemed to be reasonable. Those of particular interest here are variations on the theme that increased preference by individuals should be reflected in increased social preference. Such monotonicity in a given preference profile is tantamount to the Paretian idea. This enters in a somewhat incidental manner below, but the main concern is with inter-profile monotonicity. The definitions in the literature offer variations in each of the required basic ingredients, namely the kind of profile changes considered, which associated social preferences are constrained, and what kind of constraint is proposed. The number of sensible combinations of these is so large that a chronological approach is subordinated to a taxonomic and analytic one, though a respect for tradition results in a somewhat unfelicitous nomenclature.

3. The founder and immediate family

The starting point must be the original concept of positive association (PA), due to Arrow (1963, pp. 25–26). An increase in preference for x relative to y in going from R to R' will mean that either yPx and $y{\sim}P'x$ or else xKy and $xP'y$. Thus, J is treated in the same way as I. This is done in order to show that no additional difficulty is involved, since transitivity questions do not arise. If this generalization is not to the reader's taste, then the parts involving J can simply be ignored, or else individuals' R relations can be assumed to be complete. Now define the relation U from A to $\mathscr{D} \times \mathscr{D}$ by $xU(s, t)$ iff the only difference between the profiles s and t is that at least one individual increases preference for x over at least one other alternative in the shift from s to t. Then positive association means that

$$\forall x \in A,\ \forall s, t \in \mathscr{D}\!: xU(s, t) \Rightarrow xP^s \subseteq xP^t. \tag{2}$$

Together with his other assumptions, this is sufficient for Arrow's purposes, but the underlying philosophy of monotonicity suggests that more than just (2) is involved. For example, it would surely be difficult to advocate that monotonicity be applied to social strict preference but not to social indifference. The earliest recognition of this is by May (1952) whose condition is examined in section 8. For the moment, it is apparent that a condition which is no less reasonable than positive association is

$$\forall x \in A,\ \forall s, t \in \mathscr{D}\!: xU(s, t) \Rightarrow xI^s \subseteq xR^t, \tag{3a}$$

and some might even argue for the stronger

$$\forall x \in A,\ \forall s, t \in \mathscr{D}\!: xU(s, t) \Rightarrow xI^s \subseteq xP^t. \tag{3b}$$

Murakami (1968, p. 55) calls the combination of (2) and (3a) monotonicity, but this term is used in a more general sense here, so the cue is taken from May instead. Call (3a) non-negative responsiveness to (social) indifference (NRI), (3b) positive responsiveness to indifference (PRI), (2) and (3a) non-negative responsiveness (NR), and (2) and (3b) positive responsiveness (PR). Thus:

(a)   NR = PA ∧ NRI,

(b)   PR = PA ∧ PRI.
$$\tag{4}$$

Moreover, it is clear that the general idea of monotonicity applies to decreases as well as to increases in preference. The same names for the various properties can be used, with the downward and upward versions distinguished as such or by the respective subscripts d and u when required. It is only sensible to say that a decrease in preference for y relative to x means the same as an increase in preference for x relative to y. Now let D denote the counterpart to U, that is, the relation showing that the only change in preferences is that some fixed social state moves downward in at least one individual's preferences. Then PA_d, NRI_d, and PRI_d are respectively defined by

$$\forall x \in A,\ \forall s, t \in \mathscr{D}\!: xD(t, s) \Rightarrow Px^t \subseteq Px^s, \tag{5}$$

(a) $xD(t, s) \Rightarrow Ix^t \subseteq Rx^s$,

(b) $xD(t, s) \Rightarrow Ix^t \subseteq Px^s$,   (6)

and these are used in (4) to give NR_d and PR_d. The switching of the labels s and t compared with those in (2) and (3) is logically innocuous but will soon be seen to be convenient.

4. Genealogy

Dependencies among the conditions are to be expected since they are rooted in the same philosophy, but there are fewer that one could wish for. In particular, PA_u and PA_d are independent. This is illustrated in table 4.1, assuming that

Table 4.1   Transitive preferences

Profile	Individual 1	Society
s	$yPzPx$	$xIyPz$
t	$xPyPz$	$yPxPz$

$A = \{x, y, z\}$ and that in s and t the preferences of individuals other than individual 1 are mixed but the same in s as they are in t. It is seen that $xU(s, t)$ with s, t satisfying PA_u, while $xD(t, s)$ with PA_d violated. Clearly, this example could be an extract from an SCF satisfying PA_u. Reversing all these preferences yields an example with PA_d satisfied and PA_u violated. Notice that x moving up over z and y means the same as z moving down over x and then y moving down over x. This sort of link between U and D, however, does not lead to a link between PA_u and PA_d, because the social preferences involved are quite different.

Apart from PRI in a given direction being stronger than NRI in the same direction, the main connections are summarized in

Theorem 1.

(a) $PA_u \Rightarrow NRI_d$;   (b) $PA_d \Rightarrow NRI_u$,   (7)

(a) $NR_u \Longleftrightarrow NR_d$;   (b) $PR_u \Longleftrightarrow PR_d$.   (8)

Much turns on the obvious equivalence

$$\forall x \in A, \ \forall s, t \in \mathcal{D}: xU(s, t) \Longleftrightarrow xD(t, s).$$ (9)

First, to prove (7a) assume that PA_u holds, and consider any $x, y \in A$ and $s, t \in \mathcal{D}$. If $xD(t, s)$ then $xU(s, t)$ from (9), and so $xI_S^t y \Rightarrow x{\sim}P_S^t y \Rightarrow x{\sim}P_S^s y \Longleftrightarrow yR_S^s x$, which shows that NRI_d holds.

Next, three different ways of proving (7b) are briefly sketched: directly, or as applications of a principle of duality, or by a simple transformation. For the first, simply repeat the proof of (7a) but interchange u and d, U and D, and xPy and yPx throughout. It is convenient but not logically necessary to interchange the s and t labels too. Each step in the arguments can be seen to be valid, and the conclusion is (7b).

The duality method elevates the above idea to the status of a general principle. The simplest formulation is that if the above interchanges are made in any logically valid argument involving the eight properties, then the result is another valid argument. The proof of duality consists of three parts. First, it is easily checked from the definitions that the upward and downward versions of each of PA, NRI, PRI, NR, and PR are duals. Secondly, any implication intrinsic to relations has the duality property. For example, the dual of $x{\sim}P_S^s y \Longleftrightarrow yR_S^s x$ is $y{\sim}P_S^t x \Longleftrightarrow xR_S^t y$, which is equally true. Finally, the two sides of (9) are dual to each other and provide the crucial link between upward and downward shifts of preference. Together, these three lots of duality give the full conclusion. As a first application, (7b) is true since (7a) is.

The transformation method is a variant of duality, and provides further insight into the logical structure of the results. For any relation R, its inverse R^{-1} is defined by

$$xR^{-1} y \Longleftrightarrow yRx, \quad x, y \in A. \tag{10}$$

If an SCF is re-written in terms of its R^{-1} relations, then it has the appearance of another SCF, namely that one with precisely opposite preferences throughout. Now an upward shift of x in a relation means exactly the same thing as a downward shift of it in the associated inverse. Similarly, a Px set transforms to an xP^{-1} set, and conversely. Thus, if PA_u is defined in terms of the individuals' and society's inverse relations, then it looks the same as does PA_d in its ordinary clothes, and conversely. The same idea applies to NRI. This shows, in particular, that (7b) as defined is the same as (7a) using the R^{-1} form. Consequently, given that (7a) is a true theorem about the class of SCFs, so is (7b).

The proof of the theorem can be conducted in set-theoretic terms instead for those who prefer this, as illustrated now in proving (8). For any $B \subseteq A_x$, denote its complement in A_x by $C(B)$. Suppose that NR_u holds. This certainly implies that $xR^s \subseteq xR^t$ whenever $xU(s, t)$. It follows from (9) that, whenever $xD(t, s)$, $Px^t = C(xR^t) \subseteq C(xR^s) = Px^s$, i.e. PA_d holds. Moreover, NRI_d from (4a) and (7a). Hence, NR_d holds, which proves half of (8a). Any of the three methods for tackling the duals yields the converse. Finally, (8b) follows immediately from (7) and the complementation result that $xR^s \subseteq xP^t$ iff $Rx^t \subseteq Px^s$ for any $x \in A$ and $s, t \in \mathcal{D}$.

This simple theorem prompts the following remarks. The two PA conditions should be regarded as the most basic properties, since (7) shows that each implies NRI for the other direction. Consequently, PA_u and PA_d together are sufficient for all these four conditions to hold. So are PA and NRI in the same single direction, as shown by (8a), but in opposite directions these two yield no more, as is clear from (7). Moreover, neither one-way nor two-way NRI (resp. PRI) leads further. For example, let $xU(s, t)$ and suppose that transitive social preferences include $yPxIwPz$ in s and $zPyIxPw$ in t. This satisfies PRI – and hence NRI – in both directions and yet violates both PA_u and PA_d. Finally, since the two versions of NR – and of PR – are equivalent, they need no longer be distinguished and their subscripts can be omitted.

5. A weaker stream

Murakami (1968, pp. 55–56) also defines a condition he calls strong monotonicity, which can best be discussed by defining analogues of the properties described in section 3.

First, for any $x \in A$ and $s, t \in \mathcal{D}$, define $U_x^{st} \subseteq A_x$ by $y \in U_x^{st}$ iff $xU(s, t)$ and some individual's preference between x and y changes in the shift from s to t. Now use these new sets to define weak versions of positive association, non-negative, and positive, responsiveness to indifference for upward changes (WPA_u, $WNRI_u$, and $WPRI_u$) by, respectively,

$$\forall x \in A, \forall s, t \in \mathcal{D}: U_x^{st} \cap xP^s \subseteq xP^t, \tag{11}$$

$$\text{(a)} \quad U_x^{st} \cap Ix^s \subseteq xR^t; \quad \text{(b)} \quad U_x^{st} \cap Ix^s \subseteq xP^t. \tag{12}$$

Of course, if $x \sim U(s, t)$ then $U_x^{st} = \varnothing$ and so (11) and (12) hold trivially. Also, define the D_x^{st} in the same way as the U_x^{st} with D substituted for U. Obviously,

$$\forall x \in A, \forall s, t \in \mathcal{D}: U_x^{st} = D_x^{ts}. \tag{13}$$

The analogues to (11) and (12) for downward shifts of preference (WPA_d, $WNRI_d$, and $WPRI_d$) are:

$$\forall x \in A, \forall s, t \in \mathcal{D}: D_x^{ts} \cap Px^t \subseteq Px^s, \tag{14}$$

(a) $D_x^{ts} \cap Ix^t \subseteq Rx^s$; (b) $D_x^{ts} \cap Ix^t \subseteq Px^s$. (15)

Finally, it almost goes without saying that properties called weak non-negative, and positive, responsiveness in each direction (WNR_u, WPR_u, WNR_d, and WPA_d) can be defined by analogues of (4).

The definitions of these properties are so similar to those of the previous ones that it is not surprising that similar relations among them hold. In fact, there is complete analogy. The examples in section 4 show that WPA_u and WPA_d are independent, and theorem 1 has its parallel in:

Theorem 2.

(a) $\text{WPA}_u \Rightarrow \text{WNRI}_d$; (b) $\text{WPA}_d \Rightarrow \text{WNRI}_u$, (16)

(a) $\text{WNR}_u \Longleftrightarrow \text{WNR}_d$; (b) $\text{WPR}_u \Longleftrightarrow \text{WPR}_d$. (17)

To prove (16a), assume WPA_u and consider any $x \in A$ and $s, t \in \mathscr{D}$. Then, using (13), $D_x^{ts} \cap Ix^t \subseteq U_x^{st} \cap C(xP^t) \subseteq U_x^{st} \cap C(xP^s) = D_x^{ts} \cap Rx^s$. The other parts of the theorem can be proved by similar adaptations of the proofs of the corresponding parts of theorem 1, and are left to the reader.

According to (17b), WPR_u is sufficient for two-way WPR, whereas Murakami calls for the latter, asserting (1968, p. 36) that the one-way property is not enough in the absence of his "self-duality".

6. An alternative view

Blau (1957) looks at monotonicity in yet another way. It is best appraised in terms which parallel those in sections 3 and 5. The same names are used again, except for the distinguishing adjective "alternative" (A).

First define a relation U^* from $A \times A$ to $\mathscr{D} \times \mathscr{D}$ to mean that $(x, y)U^*(s, t)$ iff at least one individual increases his preference for x relative to y in the move from s to t, and no one changes this pair-preference in any other way, nothing being specified about what happens to other pair-preferences. Alternative types of positive association (APA), non-negative (resp. positive) responsiveness to indifference (ANRI) (resp. APRI) can now be defined respectively by

$$\forall x, y \in A, \ \forall s, t \in \mathscr{D}: (x, y)U^*(s, t) \Rightarrow (xP_S^s y \Rightarrow xP_S^t y), \tag{18}$$

(a) $(x, y)U^*(s, t) \Rightarrow (xI_S^s y \Rightarrow xR_S^t y)$,

(b) $(x, y)U^*(s, t) \Rightarrow (xI_S^s y \Rightarrow xP_S^t y)$.   (19)

In order to facilitate discussion of downward shifts of relative preference, substitute "decreases his preference" for "increases his preference" in the definition of U^* to get the corresponding relation D^*. The place of (9) is taken by the more extensive

$$\forall x, y \in A, \ \forall s, t \in \mathscr{D}: (x, y)U^*(s, t) \Longleftrightarrow (y, x)D^*(s, t) \Longleftrightarrow (y, x)U^*(t, s).$$
                                                                                        (20)

Substitution of the first equivalence in (20) into (18) and (19) makes them read

$$\forall x, y \in A, \ \forall s, t \in \mathscr{D}: (y, x)D^*(s, t) \Rightarrow (xP_S^s y \Rightarrow xP_S^t y), \tag{21}$$

(a) $(y, x)D^*(s, t) \Rightarrow (xI_S^s y \Rightarrow xR_S^t y)$,

(b) $(y, x)D^*(s, t) \Rightarrow (xI_S^s y \Rightarrow xP_S^t y)$.   (22)

which are clearly proper definitions of the downward versions of APA, ANRI, and APRI, respectively. Thus, in marked contrast to PA and NRI or PRI as defined in section 3, and also to the weaker versions of section 5, there is no distinction between the upward and downward versions of the new alternatives.

As a result of this, something stronger than the mere analogue of theorems 1 and 2 holds; specifically, APA implies ANRI regardless of directions. It suffices to prove any one of the four equivalent expressions. For example, suppose that (18) is satisfied. If $(x, y)U^*(s, t)$ then $(y, x)U^*(t, s)$ by (20) and so, interchanging x and y and also s and t in (18), $xI_S^s y \Rightarrow y{\sim}P_S^s x \Rightarrow y{\sim}P_S^t x \Rightarrow xR_S^t y$. This proves that (18) implies (19a). Even APRI, however, does not imply APA.

Now reinterpret (4) in terms of the alternative concepts to define alternative non-negative (resp. positive) responsiveness ANR (resp. APR). Again, of course, the upward and downward descriptions are equivalent. Moreover, ANR is actually logically redundant since the ANRI part is already implied by APA and therefore adds no further restriction to it. Occam, however, is not the sole arbiter. For instance, ANR states that if someone's preference between a pair of social states changes and no one's changes in the other direction, then neither can the social preference between them change in the opposite direction. This conveys far more information than, say, just the bald statement of APA, and yet the two are logically equivalent.

The above relationships can be summarized as

Theorem 3. There is no distinction between upward and downward versions of APA, ANRI, APRI, ANR, and APR; APA implies ANRI and hence is equivalent to ANR.

7. Interconnections

Having looked at three broad types of monotonicity separately, the next task is to compare and contrast them.

The second sort differ from the first only by not placing any restrictions on the social preferences between x and y in s and t when $xU(s, t)$ or $xD(t, s)$ but individual's preferences between x and y are unchanged. Each condition defined in section 5 is therefore weaker than its counterpart in section 3. Moreover, for any $x \in A$ and $s, t \in \mathscr{D}$, $xU(s, t)$ implies that $(x, y)U^*(s, t)$ for $y \in U_x^{st}$, and equivalently, $xD(t, s)$ implies that $(x, y)D^*(t, s)$ for $y \in D_x^{ts}$. A comparison of the definitions now shows that each section 5 condition is also weaker than the corresponding condition in section 6. The reasons for the qualification "weak" are now apparent, and are summarized formally in the elementary but fundamental

Theorem 4. For each of the generic terms, positive association, non-negative (resp. positive) responsiveness, the type called weak is weaker than the other two types, given the same direction of shift, upwards or downwards.

The other fundamental point that needs to be established is that the original and alternative types are genuine alternatives in that neither implies the other. The original types places no restriction on the social preferences between x and y in the shift from s to t when $(x, y)U^*(s, t)$ but neither $xU(s, t)$ nor $yD(s, t)$, and the alternative type is quiet about what happens to the social preference between x and z when $xU(s, t)$ — equivalently, $xD(t, s)$ — and $z \in C(U_x^{st})$. For instance, the example in table 4.1 above satisfies PA_u but not APA since $(y, x)U^*(t, s)$, $yP_S^t x$ but $y \sim P_S^s x$. Conversely, it is easily checked that the preferences in table 4.2 (assuming that those of individuals other than the first are mixed but the

Table 4.2 Transitive preferences

Profile	Individual 1	Society
s	$yPxPz$	$xPzPy$
t	$xPyPz$	$zPxPy$

same in s as in t) satisfy APR — and therefore WPR by theorem 4 — but neither PA_u nor PA_d.

Independence of irrelevant alternatives is now brought into the picture for the first time. Also introduced by Arrow (1963, p. 27), it is used in the form of binariness (B)

$$\forall x, y \in A, \ \forall s, t \in \mathscr{D}: (xR_i^s y \Longleftrightarrow xR_i^t y, i \in N)$$

$$\Rightarrow (xR_S^s y \Longleftrightarrow xR_S^t y). \tag{23}$$

It can be counted as a distant relative of the alternative branch of the family monotonicity in that it requires a social pair preference not to change if the individuals' preferences between that pair do not change.

Secondly, recall that the domain of (1) is deliberately not specified closely in order to define properties very generally. So as not to specialize any more than is necessary, let an appropriate domain (AD) simply mean that any profiles needed for the purpose at hand are included. In order to obviate any difficulties, assume the same domain whenever one result involving AD is combined with another.

These assumptions bind the monotonicity properties together much more firmly, founded in

Theorem 5.   For $i = u, d$:

(a) $APA_i \wedge B \Rightarrow NR$;   (b) $WPA_i \wedge B \Rightarrow PA_i$,

(c) $WPA_i \wedge AD \wedge B \Rightarrow ANR$;
$$\tag{24}$$

(a) $WNRI_i \wedge B \Rightarrow NRI_i$;   (b) $WNRI_i \wedge AD \wedge B \Rightarrow ANRI_i$,
$$\tag{25}$$

(c) $WPRI_i \wedge AD \wedge B \Rightarrow APRI_i$;

$$WPR_i \wedge AD \wedge B \Rightarrow APR. \tag{26}$$

To prove (24a), assume APA_u (resp. APA_d) and B. Then theorem 3 yields ANR. Now consider any $x \in A$ and $s, t \in \mathscr{D}$ for which $xU(s, t)$, and any $y \in xP^s$. If $y \in U_x^{st}$, then $(x, y)U^*(s, t)$ and so $xP_S^t y$ by ANR. If $y \in C(U_x^{st})$, then the individuals' preferences between x and y are unchanged, and so B shows that again $xP_S^t y$. In either case, PA_u is satisfied. A parallel argument proves NRI_u, substituting Ix^s for xP^s, R_S^t for the first P_S^t, and I_S^t for the second. The consequent NR follows from (4a) and (8a). Alternatively, prove PA_d by duality and use (7) and (4a).

Next, assume WPA_u and B, and consider any $x, y \in A$ and $s, t \in \mathscr{D}$ for which $xU(s, t)$ and $y \in xP^s$. If, also, $y \in U^{st}_x$, then $y \in xP^t$ by WPA_u. If $y \notin U^{st}_x$, then the individuals' preferences between x and y are the same in t as in s and so $y \in xP^t$ by B. This proves (24b) for $i = u$, and the case $i = d$ is dual to it.

This time assume WPA_u, AD, and B, and consider arbitrary $x, y \in A$ and $s, t \in \mathscr{D}$. Suppose that $(x, y)U^*(s, t)$. By AD, the shift from s to t could be made in two stages, one to profile r in which only the position of x is moved to produce the preferences between it and y in t, and then moving the remaining alternatives around as required. Thus, $xU(s, r)$ and $y \in U^{sr}_x$. By WPA_u, $xP^s_S y$ implies $xP^r_S y$, and this implies $xP^t_S y$ by B. Hence, $xP^s_S y \Rightarrow xP^t_S y$, which proves APA, i.e. ANR. Duality shows that WPA_d can be substituted for WPA_u and produce the same result. This proves (24c).

After making the obvious substitutions, (25a) can be proved in similar fashion to (24b), and (25b, c) to (24c). Finally, (26) follows from (4b), (8b), (24c), and (25c).

Substitutions from previous results, especially theorem 4, yield several weak corollaries. For instance, the weak properties in (24c), (25b, c) and (26) can be replaced by the corresponding properties of the original type, WNRI_i in (25a) by ANRI_i, and the consequents in (24a and c) by WNP_i. A particularly vivid proposition is obtained by starting with (24c), then substituting it into (24a), and also applying theorem 4 to both ends. The conclusion is that, in the presence of AD and B, any one of the three types of positive association, even one-way, is sufficient for all three types of non-negative responsiveness both ways.

The special case of only two alternatives is important in tracing the development of the literature on monotonicity. Its properties are very strict because of its triviality.

Theorem 6: Given a set A^* of only two alternatives:

(a) $\quad \mathrm{WPA}_u \Longleftrightarrow \mathrm{WPA}_d \Longleftrightarrow \mathrm{PA}_u \Longleftrightarrow \mathrm{PA}_d \Longleftrightarrow \mathrm{WNR} \Longleftrightarrow \mathrm{NR} \Longleftrightarrow \mathrm{ANR},$

(b) $\quad \mathrm{WNRI}_u \Longleftrightarrow \mathrm{WNRI}_d \Longleftrightarrow \mathrm{NRI}_u \Longleftrightarrow \mathrm{NRI}_d \Longleftrightarrow \mathrm{ANRI},$

(c) $\quad \mathrm{WPRI}_u \Longleftrightarrow \mathrm{WPRI}_d \Longleftrightarrow \mathrm{PRI}_u \Longleftrightarrow \mathrm{PRI}_d \Longleftrightarrow \mathrm{APRI},$

(d) $\quad \mathrm{WPR} \Longleftrightarrow \mathrm{PR} \Longleftrightarrow \mathrm{APR}.$

$$(27)$$

The proof turns upon the obvious equivalences

$$\forall x, y \in A^*, x \neq y, \forall s, t \in \mathscr{D}:$$
$$xU(s, t) \Longleftrightarrow yD(s, t) \Longleftrightarrow (x, y)U^*(s, t).$$

$$(28)$$

The definition of each of the five distinguishable varieties of positive association can be re-cast so as to start with the appropriate term from (28) as it stands and finish with the statement "implies that if $xP_s^s y$ then $xP_s^t y$". For example, PA_d means that

$$\forall x, y \in A^*, x \neq y, \forall s, t \in \mathcal{D}: yD(s, t) \Rightarrow (xP_S^s y \Rightarrow xP_S^t y). \tag{29}$$

All five are therefore equivalent, and the remaining implications in (27a) are simply applications of (4a) and theorems 1, 2, and 3. The rest of the theorem can be proved in analogous fashion.

8. Comparisons with the usual definitions

Only now can the usual definitions of the alternative stream be properly appraised. By assuming B and dropping transitivity, May (1952) boils the social choice question down to one of only two alternatives, and defines his positive responsiveness in this context as APR_u. Blau (1957, p. 305) defines his condition 2′ (monotonicity) just like APA_u, but adds in B parenthetically. The definition of non-negative responsiveness by Sen (1970), p. 74) makes it identical to ANR_u, though it is put forward as being in the same spirit as May's condition which he (1970, pp. 69, 71) properly describes as: "For CCRs that satisfy the independence of irrelevant alternatives ...".

It is clearly better to keep B out of the definitions of the other conditions, since otherwise the monotonicity aspects cannot properly be isolated and yet B can still stand on its own. Theorem 3 shows that the definitions of the alternative stream are complete and satisfying without the gratuitous appendage. Moreover, theorem 5 shows precisely how B links the three different streams of monotonicity. Blau (1957, pp. 307, 309, 311) and Sen (1970, pp. 69, 77) mention both B and the relevant monotonicity condition together in various propositions, which is an indication that they do not intend B to be included in the other. Yet Blau (1957, pp. 305, 309) maintains that his condition is stronger than Arrow's. This is confirmed by (24a) if B is an integral part of his condition, but otherwise table 4.2 is a counter-demonstration. His omission of B in the equivalence assertion immediately following on p. 305 is presumably unintentional, as indicated by the corrected proposition on p. 311. May (1952, p. 682) points out that his condition is stronger than Arrow's, and theorem 6 confirms this, though his assumption of B must be remembered if the proposition is to be carried over to the general case. Finally, the analogous claim by Sen (1970, p. 69) is more confusing. It is clear from his footnote 24 that he is referring to the report of Blau's condition by Arrow (1963, pp. 96–97), which is faithful even down to the parenthetical B and the assertion of comparative strength. Now theorem 3 shows that ANR is only equivalent to APA_u by itself, and this makes it actually weaker than the Blau–Arrow condition if the latter includes B. If B is part of both Sen's and Blau's conditions, then again they are only equivalent.

Murakami (1968) develops his general case from the two-alternative one. In the latter, his strong monotonicity property is proposed as a two-way extension of May's condition. In the general case, May's condition, like Blau's, is firmly rooted in the relation called here U^*, whereas Murakami's is explicitly based on the relation U. It could be that this divergence stems from the equivalence of U and U^* in the two-alternative case, in the sense of (28). The difference in general cases can be substantial for, as (26) in theorem 5 indicates, it takes quite a lot more to bring WPR up to the strength of APR.

9. Some uses of the properties

The previous sections explain what the monotonicity properties are, and how they relate to each other, but not much about how they can be used. A full examination cannot be undertaken here, but this section takes a new look at the classic debate on impossibility as a prime example.

First, familiar additional terms required are recalled. Non-imposition or citizens' sovereignty (CS) means that

$$\forall x, y \in A, \exists p \in \mathcal{D}: xP_S^p y; \tag{30}$$

the weak Pareto superiority principle (WP) means that

$$\forall x, y \subset A, \forall p \subset \mathcal{D}: xP_i^p y, \quad i \subset N, \Rightarrow xP_S^p y; \tag{31}$$

and non-dictatorship means that

$$\forall i \in N, \exists x, y \in A, \exists p \in \mathcal{D}: xP_i^p y \wedge x \sim P_S^p y. \tag{32}$$

The next theorem is a useful extension of well-known results. The symbol 0 (for "original") refers to the monotonicity concepts defined in section 3.

Theorem 7.

(a) $AD \wedge WP \Rightarrow CS,$

(b) $AD \wedge XPA_i \wedge B \wedge CS \Rightarrow WP,$ $X = 0, W,$ $i = u, d,$ (33)

(c) $APA \wedge B \wedge CS \Rightarrow WP.$

The proof of (a) is obvious. Blau (1957, p. 307) accepts the argument by Arrow (1963, pp. 52–54) as a proof of (b) for PA_u in the standard preference context, provided that Arrow's domain assumption is adequately strengthened. Arrow (1963, p. 97) accordingly truncates his result to (c) on the ground that his "Consequence 1...is identical with condition $2'$ [Blau's]", though the former reads weaker. Proofs in the more general context are no different. It is seen from theorem 5 that all four implications in (b) are equivalent and that (c) is stronger.

Assume now that there is a finite number of individuals, more than two social states, and that individuals' and society's preference relations are complete, reflexive, and transitive. Blau (1957) produces a counter-example to the famous original impossibility claim by Arrow (1963, p. 51) and proceeds to prove

Theorem 8.   AD, APA, B, WP, and ND are mutually incompatible.

It follows from theorem 7 that CS can be substituted for WP in theorem 8 to produce

Theorem 9.   For $X = 0, A, W,$ and $i = u, d,$ AD, XPA_i, B, CS, and ND cannot hold simultaneously.

That for PA_u is due to Blau (1957, p. 311), and is his correction to Arrow's original assertion, making it appropriate to call it the Arrow-Blau theorem. Arrow's proof for APA is described below. It is clear from theorems 5 and 7 that theorem 8 and the five parts of theorem 9 (recall that APA_u and APA_d are the same) are all equivalent to each other. If any pride of place among these equivalents is to be given, it must go to those involving WPA_u and WPA_d, since these conditions are the weakest varieties. The other three parts of theorem 9 are on a par with each other as useful alternatives, whereas Blau's contention that his new form of monotonicity is stronger than Arrow's might give the misleading impression that the APA part of theorem 9 is less important that the PA_u one.

Arrow (1963, pp. 97–100) neatly strengthens Blau's theorem to

Theorem 10.   AD, B, WP, and ND are simultaneously impossible.

He combines this with (33c) to yield the APA part of theorem 9, and leaves the Arrow–Blau theorem to be inferred from a corollary to (24c). Thus, having eliminated APA from Blau's theorem, Arrow re-introduces it via (33c). This is quite unnecessary if the final objective is the Arrow–Blau theorem. More generally, each part of theorem 9 can be obtained by combining the corresponding part of theorem 7 with theorem 10. Arrow really has no need of Blau's alternative type of positive association at all!

This point is so interesting that it is worth making sure of it. Arrow's proof of the PA_u part of (33b) not only requires amendment but is very long and involved. The following proof is short, simple, direct, is in the more general context, and applies to the other three parts of (33b) as well. Start with any $x, y \in A$ and $t \in \mathcal{D}$ for which $xP_i^t y$, $i \in N$. By CS there is an $s \in \mathcal{D}$ for which $xP_S^s y$. If $xP_i^s y$ for all i in N, then $xP_S^s y$ follows from B. In the contrary case, AD allows of a profile r for which $xU(s, r)$ (resp. $yD(s, r)$) and $xP_i^r y$ for all $i \in N$. Then PA_u or even WPA_u (resp. PA_d or WPA_d) implies $xP_S^r y$, and thence $xP_S^t y$ by B. There is no mention of APA anywhere.

Murakami (1968, pp. 89–90) repeats some old assertions that PA_u and CS together imply WP, despite the counter-example by Blau (1957, p. 305). A step-by-step comparison with the above proof of (33b) soon shows where the claim fails.

In order to isolate the comparative effects of the various monotonicity properties, all the above comparisons are based on the assumption of a common domain. It should be kept in mind, however, that the domain requirements of the various theorems differ. Keeping to the spirit of the originators for simplicity, the assumption by Blau (1957, p. 309) that all triples be free is sufficient for AD in the results concerning APA and also for theorem 10, whereas results concerning the ordinary or weak properties generally require more profiles. This further emphasizes the power of Arrow's theorem and makes the APA version of theorem 9 stronger than the other parts. Arrow (1963, p. 97) recognizes that his unrestricted domain is an unnecessarily strong assumption.

10. Concluding remarks

The family monotonicity is large, closely knit, and rich. It is natural that its members should play a large role in the theory of social choice. This study looks at the family in greater detail than usual, and leads to generalization of some old propositions, the generation of some new propositions, the clarification and removal of certain ambiguities, the correction of some minor errors, and a more efficient way of proving a classic result. One could also re-appraise other studies involving monotonicity, e.g. Mas-Colell and Sonnenschein (1972), Blair, Bordes, Kelly and Suzumura (1976), Blau and Deb (1977), and Bordes and Salles (1978). It might also be worth making a similar investigation into monotonicity properties in other theories, such as game theory.

The family monotonicity can be expanded further. For instance, as with the Pareto principle, conditions weaker than those given here can be postulated by not requiring those social responses unless a larger minimum number of individuals — perhaps all individuals — change preferences as described. The most interesting extension, however, is to allow incomplete preference relations for society as well as for individuals. Most of the results still hold up, but the proofs are considerably more involved.

This chapter looks only at the logical aspects of monotonicity. The properties are, however, expressions of certain value judgements and must ultimately be judged as such. Contini (1966) shows that positive association is irrelevant in an "economic" context, and McManus (1981) analyses this issue in depth. It is shown by McManus (1982b) that sufficient Paretianism and certain weak topological assumptions bar alternative positive association, in line with the result about binariness by McManus (1982a). Furthermore, it is argued that all the present monotonicity conditions are unreasonable, the analysis pointing to an acceptable substitute.

References

Arrow, Kenneth J. (1963) *Social Choice and Individual Values*, 2nd edn. (Yale University Press, New Haven and London).

Blair, Douglas H., Georges Bordes, Jerry S. Kelly and Kotaro Suzumura (1976) "Impossibility Theorems without Collective Rationality", *Journal of Economic Theory*, 13, 361–379.

Blau, Julian H. (1957) "The Existence of Social Welfare Functions", *Econometrica*, 25, 302–313.

Blau, Julian H. and Rajat Deb (1977) "Social Decision Functions and the Veto", *Econometrica*, 45, 871–879.

Bordes, Georges and Maurice Salles (1978) "Sur l'Impossibilité des Fonctions de Décision Collective: Un Commentaire et un Résultat", *Revue d'Économie Politique*, 88, 442–448.

Contini, Bruno (1966) "A Note on Arrow's Postulates for a Social Welfare Function", *Journal of Political Economy*, 74, 278–280.

Mas-Colell, Andreu and Hugo Sonnenschein (1972) "General Possibility Theorems for Group Decisions", *Review of Economic Studies*, 39, 185–192.

May, Kenneth O. (1952) "A Set of Independent Necessary and Sufficient Conditions for Simple Majority Decision", *Econometrica*, 20, 680–684.

McManus, M. (1981) *Impossibility Theorems with Positive Association Vacuous*, The University of New South Wales Discussion Paper, 60, 1–22.

McManus, M. (1982a) "Some Properties of Topological Social Choice Functions", *Review of Economic Studies*, 49, 447–460.

McManus, M. (1982b) "Inter-Profile Monotonicity for Economists", University of New South Wales Discussion Paper, 1–18.
Murakami, Y. (1968) *Logic and Social Choice* (Routledge and Kegan Paul, London; Dover Publications, New York).
Sen, Armartya K. (1970) *Collective Choice and Social Welfare* (Holden-Day, San Francisco).

CHAPTER 5

On the use of ultrafilters in social choice theory

BERNARD MONJARDET*

Université Paris V et Centre de Mathématique Sociale

1. Notations and preliminaries

Let A be a set whose elements will be called alternatives. We denote by P an asymmetric (binary) relation on A. We write xIy iff neither xPy nor yPx; we write xRy iff yPx is false. Thus, I is a symmetric relation and R is a complete (connected) relation.

The usual product (composition) of two arbitrary (binary) relations S and T on A is denoted by ST ($xSTy$ iff there exists a z in A such that xSz and zTy). S^p denotes the product of relation S with itself p times.

A relation S is *transitive* iff $S^2 \subseteq S$. A *partial order* is an asymmetric and transitive relation. A partial order P is a *weak order* iff $I^2 \subseteq I$ (or $PI \subseteq P$, or $IP \subseteq P$). We shall let $\mathscr{P}$ be the set of all weak orders on A.

Let s and t be two arbitrary integers. An asymmetric relation P on A is $s \sim t$ *transitive* iff $P^s I P^t \subseteq P$. We denote by $\mathscr{P}_{st}$ the set of all $s \sim t$ transitive asymmetric relations on A. Note that P in $\mathscr{P}_{st}$ implies $P^{s+t} \subseteq P$; we shall say that P is $s + t$ transitive. Thus, the sets $\mathscr{P}_{20} (= \mathscr{P}_{02})$ and $\mathscr{P}_{11}$ are two sets of partial orders on A. The partial orders in $\mathscr{P}_{11}$ (resp. $\mathscr{P}_{20}$) are called *interval orders* (resp. *semitransitive orders*). A partial order is a *semiorder* iff it is an interval order and a semitransitive order. For further information on these asymmetric relations see Blau (1979), Blair and Pollak (1979), Fishburn (1970), Mirkin (1979), Monjardet (1978b), and Roberts (1979).

* The author wishes to thank J.H. Blau and an anonymous referee for helpful comments on the first draft.

Let N a set whose elements shall be called individuals; we suppose $|N| > 1$ (thus N can be infinite). Throughout this chapter each i in N has a preference relation P_i on A which is assumed to be a weak order. I_i and R_i are the indifference and weak preference relations associated with P_i. A profile Π of individual preferences is a mapping from N into the set $\mathscr{P}$ of weak orders on A: $\Pi(i) = P_i \cdot \mathscr{P}^N$ denotes the set of all profiles.

We study collective choice rules defined as mappings F with domain $\mathscr{P}^N$ and with range $\mathscr{P}_{st}$ for some s and t. We shall say that such a mapping is a $(\mathscr{P}^N, \mathscr{P}_{st})$ aggregation function. Throughout this chapter the image of a profile Π under the mapping F is denoted by P; P is the collective preference, I and R are the (collective) indifference and weak preference associated with P. Also, $F(\Pi') = P'$.

We recall, for convenience, some classical definitions for functions F: F is *binary* (independent) iff for every set $\{x, y\}$ of alternatives and for every pair Π, Π' of profiles, the equality of Π and Π' on $\{x, y\}$ implies the equality of $F(\Pi)$ and $F(\Pi')$ on $\{x, y\}$.

F is *unanimous* (weak Pareto condition) iff for all x, y in A and for every profile Π in $\mathscr{P}^N$, xP_iy for all i, implies xPy. F is *dictatorial* iff there is an individual i in N such that, for all x, y in A and for every profile Π in $\mathscr{P}^N$, xP_iy implies xPy.

A set of individuals D is *almost decisive* for x against y iff xP_iy for every i in D and yP_jx for every j not in D, imply xPy. A set of individuals D is *decisive* for x against y iff xP_iy for every i in D implies xPy. A set of individuals D is *globally decisive* iff D is decisive for x against y for all x, y in A. We denote by $\mathscr{D}_F$ (or simply by $\mathscr{D}$) the set of globally decisive sets associated with the function F.

Throughout this chapter a family $\mathscr{F}$ on N is a set of subsets of N. We shall now define six properties which are satisfied by certain families:

(1) $[V \in \mathscr{F}, W \supseteq V] \Rightarrow [W \in \mathscr{F}]$,

(2) $[V \in \mathscr{F}, W \in \mathscr{F}] \Rightarrow [V \cap W \in \mathscr{F}]$,

(3) $[V \in \mathscr{F}] \Rightarrow [\overline{V} \notin \mathscr{F}]$ (where $\overline{V} = N{-}V$),

(4) $[\overline{V} \notin \mathscr{F}] \Rightarrow [V \in \mathscr{F}]$,

(5) $\varnothing \notin \mathscr{F}$,

(6) $[V \in \mathscr{F}, W \in \mathscr{F}, U \in \mathscr{F}, V \neq W \neq U] \Rightarrow [V \cap W \cap U \neq \varnothing]$.

We recall two classical definitions. A family $\mathscr{F}$ on N is a *filter* iff $\mathscr{F}$ satisfies conditions (1), (2), and (5). A filter $\mathscr{F}$ on N is an *ultrafilter* iff $\mathscr{F}$ is not contained in another filter. It is well known that a family $\mathscr{F}$ is an ultrafilter iff $\mathscr{F}$ satisfies conditions (1), (2), (3), (4), and (5); also, if N is finite, an ultrafilter is the family of all subsets of N containing an element i_0 in N.

Lemma 1. Let N be a set with $|N| \geqslant 3$. A family $\mathcal{F}$ on N is an ultrafilter iff $\mathcal{F}$ satisfies conditions (4) and (6).

The proof is purely combinatorial (see Monjardet, 1978a).

Remarks

(1) If $|N| = 2$ and $\mathcal{F}$ satisfies (4) and (6), $\mathcal{F}$ is an ultrafilter or a maximal ideal (for example, $\mathcal{F} = \{\varnothing, \{1\}\}$).

(2) Condition (6) was first introduced by Guilbaud (1952) in a proof of the Arrow theorem (under neutrality and linear orderings assumptions). In fact, Guilbaud proved lemma 1, with $\mathcal{F}$ satisfying conditions (1), (3), (4), and (6).

(3) Making use of the simple game vocabulary, we say that a simple game is a family of subsets of N satisfying condition (5) (Monotonicity condition (1) is not assumed.) For such a simple game $\mathcal{F}$, the Nakamura number (Nakamura, 1975; Peleg, 1978) is the minimum number of subsets in $\mathcal{F}$ such that their intersection is empty; if $\mathcal{F}$ is weak ($\cap \mathcal{F} \neq \varnothing$) we shall write $v(\mathcal{F}) = \infty$. Lemma 1 is equivalent to saying that a strong simple game (conditions (4) and (5)) is an ultrafilter iff $v(\mathcal{F}) \neq 3$. An immediate corollary is that if N is finite and $\mathcal{F}$ is a strong simple game the three following conditions are equivalent: $\mathcal{F}$ is essential (i.e. $\cap \mathcal{F} = \varnothing$); $\mathcal{F}$ is not a filter; $v(\mathcal{F}) = 3$. See Ishikawa and Nakamura (1979) for some particular cases of these results (proposition 3.2 and corollary 7.1).

2. A theorem

Theorem. Let A have at least $s + t + 2$ members with $s + t \geqslant 2$ and F be a binary and unanimous ($\mathcal{P}^N, \mathcal{P}_{st}$) aggregation function; then, the family $\mathcal{P}$ of globally decisive sets associated with F is an ultrafilter.

Corollary (Blair and Pollak, 1979; Blau, 1979). If N is finite and $|A| \geqslant s + t + 2 \geqslant 4$, a binary and unanimous ($\mathcal{P}^N, \mathcal{P}_{st}$) aggregation function is dictatorial.

We now prove the theorem. First, we recall a straightforward generalization of a classical lemma in social choice theory (Arrow, 1963; Murakami, 1968; Sen, 1970).

Lemma 2 (Blair and Pollak, 1979). Let A have at least $s + t + 1$ members with $s + t \geqslant 2$ and D be an almost decisive set for some ordered pair of alternatives under a binary and unanimous ($\mathcal{P}^N, \mathcal{P}_{st}$) aggregation function: then D is a globally decisive set.

Note that the proof of this lemma uses only the P^{s+t} transitivity of members of $\mathscr{P}_{st}$.

Let $\mathscr{D}$ be the family of globally decisive sets associated with the function F. In order to prove the theorem, it is sufficient to prove that $\mathscr{D}$ satisfies conditions (4) and (6) (see lemma 1).

$\mathscr{D}$ satisfies condition (4): Let D be not contained in $\mathscr{D}$. Consider a profile for which $x_1 P_i x_2 \ldots P_i x_{s+1} P_i x_{s+2} P_i \ldots P_i x_{s+t+2}$, for every i in D; $x_{s+2} P_i \ldots x_{s+t+2}$. $P_i x_1 P_i \ldots P_i x_{s+1}$, for every i in $\bar{D}$. By the weak Pareto condition, we have $x_1 P x_2 \ldots P x_{s+1}$ and $x_{s+2} P \ldots P x_{s+t+2}$. By definition of D and lemma 2, we have $x_{s+2} R x_{s+1}$. If $x_{s+1} I x_{s+2}$, then, P in $\mathscr{P}_{st}$ implies $x_1 P x_{s+t+2}$; hence, D is almost decisive for x_1 against x_{s+t+2}, and by lemma 2, D is in $\mathscr{D}$, a contradiction. Hence, we have $x_{s+2} P x_{s+1}$, and $\bar{D}$ is in $\mathscr{D}$.

N.B. This proof is the same as that in Blau (1979, p. 201).

$\mathscr{D}$ satisfies condition (6): Suppose that we have three different globally decisive sets, B, C, and D, such that $B \cap C \cap D = \varnothing$. Then, we can construct a profile for which $x_1 P_i \ldots P_i x_{s+t}$, for every i in B; $x_{s+t} P_i x_{s+t+1}$ for every i in C; $x_{s+t+1} P_i x_1$ for every i in D. Hence, we have socially $x_1 P \ldots x_{s+t} P x_{s+t+1} P x_1$, a contradiction with P in $\mathscr{P}_{st}$ (P is $s+t$ transitive).

3. Comments

For $s+t=1$, $\mathscr{P}_{st} = \mathscr{P}_{10} = \mathscr{P}_{01}$ contains the set $\mathscr{P}$ of all weak orders on A. The above proof remains valid for $\mathscr{P}$ and gives quickly the Hanssonn (1972, 1976) and Kirman–Sondermann (1972) theorem.

If N is an infinite set, it is well known that there exist ultrafilters containing no finite subsets (the so-called free or non-principal ultrafilters). Consequently, the Arrow or Blau–Blair–Pollak theorems for the finite case and their proofs cannot be directly extended. Hence, the use of ultrafilters is indispensable in the infinite case. Obviously, the interest for the results obtained depends on the interest for this case and can be challenged. See Fishburn (1970), Kirman–Sondermann (1972), Hanssonn (1976), Schmitz (1977), and Armstrong (1980) for related investigations.

If N is a finite set, the ultrafilter machinery gives an alternative proof to the Arrow or Blau–Blair–Pollak theorems and lemma 1 allows us to obtain a short proof. Working out a Guilbaud idea (see section 2, remark 2), we sketched such a proof of Arrow's theorem in Monjardet (1967, pp. 179–180) and we wrote it explicitly in Monjardet (1978a) (this proof is also valid for $|N| = 2$; see remark 1, section 2).

A profitable use of ultrafilters in social choice theory is not restricted to the above theorems. For example, we can use them to obtain the Gibbard—Satterthwaite theorem in the infinite (or finite case). The notion of a decisive set is replaced by the notion of a preventing set, and it is shown that the family of such preventing sets is an ultrafilter (Batteau, Blin and Monjardet, 1981; see also Pazner and Wesley, 1977, and Ishikawa and Nakamura, 1979). Hence, the known connection between Arrow's theorem and the Gibbard—Satterthwaite theorem is enlightened.

Finally, we notice an open problem. Blair and Pollak (1979) claim "that there is a sense in which their results imply that any rationality requirement stronger than quasi-transitivity implies dictatorship". This is true, but only in the sense that the stronger rationality requirement for the collective preference P is that P is not only transitive but also $s \sim t$ transitive. Thus, the dictatorial result is only obtained for semi-transitive orders, interval orders, and semi-orders (see Blau, 1979, for the earlier work on this late case). But the question of knowing if one obtains dictatorship or oligarchy is not solved for other sets of particular partial orders (for example, for partial orders of dimension $\leqslant k$; Barbut and Monjardet, 1971). Related results to this problem were obtained by Barthélémy (1982), but only when the set of individual preferences satisfies "regularity" conditions.

References

Armstrong, T.E. (1980) "Arrow's Theorem with Restricted Coalition Algebras", *Journal of Mathematical Economics*, 7, 55–75.

Arrow, K.J. (1951 and 1963), *Social Choice and Individual Values* (Wiley, New York).

Barbut, M. and Monjardet B. (1971) *Ordre et Classification, Algèbre et Combinatoire*, t.2 (Hachette, Paris).

Barthélémy, J.P. (1982) "Arrow's Theorem: Unusual Domains and Extended Co-domains", Chapter 1, this volume.

Batteau, P., J.M. Blin and B. Monjardet (1981) "Stability of Aggregation Procedures, Ultrafilters and Simple Games", *Econometrica*, 49, 527–534.

Blair, P.H. and R.A. Pollak (1979) "Collective Rationality and Dictatorship: The Scope of the Arrow Theorem", *Journal of Economic Theory*, 21, 186–194.

Blau, J.H. (1979) "Semiorders and Collective Choice", *Journal of Economic Theory*, 21, 195–206.

Fishburn, P.C. (1970) "Arrow's Impossibility Theorem: Concise Proof and Infinite Voters", *Journal of Economic Theory*, 2, 103–106.

Fishburn, P.C. (1978) "Intransitive Indifference in Preference Theory: A Survey", *Operations Research*, 18, 207–228.

Guilbaud, G.Th. (1952) "Les Théories de l'Intérêt Général et le Problème Logique de l'Agrégation", *Economie Appliquée*, 5, 501–584. English translation in P.F. Lazarsfeld and N.W. Henry, eds., *Readings in Mathematical Social Sciences* (Science Research Association, Inc., Chicago, 1965), pp. 262–307.

Hanssonn, B. (1972 and 1976) "The Existence of Group Preferences Functions (Working paper, Department of Philosophy, Lund) and *Public Choice*, 28, 89–98.

Ishikawa, S. and K. Nakamura (1979) "The Strategy-Proof Social Choice Functions", *Journal of Mathematical Economics*, 6, 283–295.

Kirman, A.P. and D. Sondermann (1972) "Arrow's Theorem, Many Agents and Invisible Dictators", *Journal of Economic Theory*, 5, 266–277.

Mirkin, B.G. (1979) in: P.C. Fishburn, ed., *Group Choice* (Winston and Sons, Washington).

Monjardet, B. (1967) "Remarques sur une Classe de Procédures de Votes et les Théorèmes de Possibilité", in: *La Décision* (Colloque du CNRS, Aix-en-Provence), pp. 117–184.

Monjardet, B. (1978a) "Une autre Preuve du Théorème d'Arrow", *R.A.I.R.O. Recherche Opérationnelle*, 12, 291–296.

Monjardet, B. (1978b) "Axiomatique et Propriétés des Quasi-ordres", *Mathématiques et Sciences Humaines*, 63, 51–82.

Monjardet, B. and E. Jacquet-Lagreze (1978) "Modélisations des Préférences et Quasi-ordres", *Mathématiques et Sciences Humaines*, 62, 5–10.

Murakami, Y. (1968) *Logic and Social Choice* (Dover, New York).

Nakamura, K. (1975) "The Core of Simple Games with Ordinal Preferences", *International Journal of Game Theory*, 4, 95–104.

Pazner, A. and E. Wesley (1977) "Stability of Social Choice in Infinitely Large Societies", *Journal of Economic Theory*, 14, 252–262.

Peleg, B. (1978) "Representation of Simple Games by Social Choice Functions", *International Journal of Game Theory*, 7, 81–94.

Roberts, F.S. (1979) *Measurement Theory* (Addison-Wesley, Reading, Massachussetts).

Schmitz, N. (1977) "A Further Note on Arrow's Impossibility Theorem", *Journal of Mathematical Economics*, 4, 189–196.

Sen, A.K. (1970) *Collective Choice and Sociale Welfare* (Holden-Day, San Francisco).

CHAPTER 6

Social choice and game theory: Recent results with a topological approach

G. CHICHILNISKY*
University of Essex and Columbia University

1. Introduction

This chapter presents a summary of recent results obtained in game and social choice theories, and highlights the application and the development of tools in algebraic topology. The purpose is expository: no attempt is made to provide complete proofs, for which references are given, nor to review the previous work in this area, which covers a significant subset of the economic literature.

The aim is to provide an oriented guide to recent results, through economic examples with geometric interpretations, and to indicate possibly fruitful avenues of research.

The use of topological tools has a long tradition in economic analysis, which gocs back to the work of Von Neumann on balanced economic growth of 1937 and 1945. He proved a generalization of Brouwer's fixed point theorem that was the basis of Kakutani's theorem. In game theory and in general equilibrium market analysis, fixed point methods are the topological methods most frequently utilized to show existence of solutions. As a matter of fact, fixed point theorems are the largest part of applications of topology to economics as a whole. Instead of topological methods, social choice theory has traditionally been formulated in a

* This research was supported partly by NFS Grant SES 791 4050. I thank G. Heal, C. Henry, J.M. Lasry, and M. Vergne for comments and suggestions. A French version of this chapter appears in E. Malinvaud, ed., *Cahiers du Seminaire d'économetrie* (CNRS, Paris, 1982).

Social Choice and Welfare, edited by P.K. Pattanaik and M. Salles
© *North-Holland Publishing Company, 1983*

combinatorial fashion, following the first formal works of Arrow (1951) and Black (1948) in this area.

However, we shall now show that many problems of game and social choice theories, when properly formulated, exhibit an intrinsic topological structure that may be fruitfully examined with algebraic topology tools that go beyond fixed point theorems, such as homotopy and cohomology theories. This allows us to tap a wealth of existing topological techniques, as well as to develop new ones, to resolve problems in social choice and game theories.

This chapter studies certain social choice paradoxes and their resolution, the relation of a fixed point theorem with the social choice paradox, the equivalence of the Pareto condition and the existence of a dictator, majority rules, aggregation in large economies, and the aggregation of Von Neumann—Morgenstern utilities for choices under uncertainty.

Within game theory, we summarize results on the manipulation of games, the existence of Nash equilibrium of certain non-convex games and the fairness of these games, and the existence and characterization of strategy-proof games, a problem that appears in the literature on economies with public goods.

2. Social choice

Social choice theory is concerned with providing a rationale for collective decisions when individuals have diverse opinions. Voting is an obvious way in which societies aggregate individual preferences into collective preferences. It has been known for a long time that majority voting may be in contradiction with certain basic criteria of rationality of preferences, such as the transitivity of the social choice; this phenomenon is usually called the "Condorcet" effect; Condorcet first formalized it in 1785 in a book on the theory of elections. The general theory of elections became a fertile field of research following the work of Black in 1948 and Arrow in 1951. Arrow stated formally a set of apparently reasonable criteria required for the aggregation of individual preferences, and proved that they are inconsistent.

One way of formalizing the problem is as follows: a voting procedure typically takes into account only the relative value that the individuals assign to different choices (i.e. ordinal preferences), rather than the intensity with which they prefer one choice to another (e.g. preferences derived from utilities). This is one source of the social choice paradox, because, as we shall see, spaces of ordinal preference are rather different from spaces of utility functions. Utility functions are real-valued functions and as such can be aggregated or summed. Spaces of utility functions are *linear*, and, in particular, topologically trivial or contractible.[1] Instead, spaces of ordinal utilities are not linear, they cannot be deformed into linear spaces, and furthermore they are *not* topologically trivial. This will be seen to be the source of the social choice paradox because contractible spaces, and only them, admit appropriate aggregation rules (see theorem 10).

We now need some definitions.

The social choice problems studied here are similar to procedures of selection of a vector of public goods, and therefore lend themselves naturally to representation in Euclidean space. Let X be a *space of alternatives* or *choices*, contained in the positive orthant of Euclidean space R^n, i.e. R^{n+}. Assume X is a cube in R^{n+}. One can also consider more general cases; however, since the results are topological, they will be automatically valid for continuous deformations of all objects under consideration.

We use here the notation of Chichilnisky (1980d) throughout, and the reader is referred to it. A preference p is a C^1 vector field over the space of alternatives, which is locally integrable, see Debreu (1972). This means that to each alternative x one attaches a vector $p(x) \in R^n$ (in a continuously differentiable fashion) which indicates a gradient or the direction of the largest increase of utility, i.e. the normal to an indifference surface of an utility. Since we are considering here *ordinal* preferences, it is the direction rather than the length of the vectors that matters. Therefore, we normalize the vectors at each point to be of length 1, i.e. $\|p(x)\| = 1 \; \forall x$ in X (see fig. 6.1). P represents the space of preferences over X.

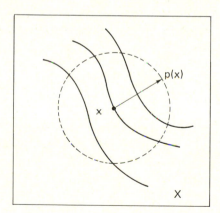

Figure 6.1. A preference over R^2: $p(x)$ is the gradient vector at a choice x.

---

[1] A topological space X is *topologically trivial* or *contractible* when it admits a continuous deformation through itself into one of its points. It is therefore topologically equivalent to a point. Formally, X is contractible if there exists a continuous map $f: X \times [0,1] \to X$ such that $f(x, 0) = x \; \forall x$ in X, and $f(x, 1) = x_0$, all x in X, some x_0 in X.

With k individuals, a *social choice rule* ϕ is thus a map that associates a collective preference to each k-tuple of individual preferences, i.e.

$$\phi: P^k \to P.$$

P^k is called the *space of profiles* of individual preferences. The continuity of ϕ is defined according to the usual topology for vector fields, implying that proximity of preferences in P is equivalent to the proximity of their indifference surfaces. *Anonymity* is defined by the condition $\phi(p_1, ..., p_k) = \phi(p_{n_1}, ..., p_{n_k})$, where n is any permutation of the set of integers $\{1, ..., k\}$. *Respect of unanimity* means that, whenever all the individuals have identical preference (for all possible choices), then the outcome has the same preference as well, i.e.

$$\phi = (p, ..., p) = p, \quad \forall p \text{ in } P.$$

ϕ is *Pareto* if the outcome $\phi(p_1, ..., p_k)$ prefers choice x to y whenever all preferences in the profile $(p_1, ..., p_k)$ prefer x to y. Note that respect of unanimity is a much weaker condition than Pareto, since it is only binding when all individuals have identical preferences for all choices. ϕ is *dictatorial* if $\phi(p_1, ..., p_k) \equiv p_d$ for some $d \in \{1, ..., k\}$, for all profiles $(p_1, ..., p_k)$ in P^k. Note that anonymity is a stronger condition than non-dictatorship.

In order to simplify the presentation, we now consider a particular case: preferences are linear, i.e. they are gradient fields of linear utilities and there are two voters. By an appropriate choice of origin, as explained in Chichilnisky

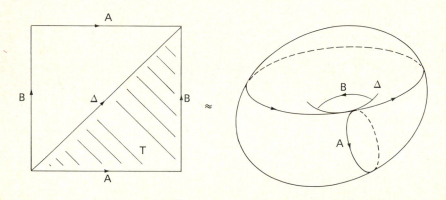

Figure 6.2. The space of profiles of linear preferences on R^2, with two voters.

(1979b), in this particular case the space of preferences $P = S^1$, the one-dimensional circle in R^2. The space of profiles of two voters is thus

$$P \times P = S^1 \times S^1,$$

called also the two-dimensional torus (see fig. 6.2).

In what follows D will represent the unit disk, $D = \{(x, y: x^2 + y^2 \leqslant 1)\}$, and ∂D its boundary. The circle $P \times P = S^1 \times S^1$ is equivalent to a square in which the points on opposite sides have been identified, as in the right-hand side of fig. 6.2. A is the set $\{(p, p_0), p \in S^1\}$, and $B = \{(p_0, p), p \in S^1\}$. The boundary of the triangle T is the union of the diagonal $\Delta = \{(p_1, p_2): p_1 = p_2\}$ with A and B, i.e. $\partial T = \Delta \cup A \cup B$. This can also be represented by three circles joined at one common point, as in fig. 6.3.

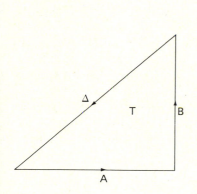 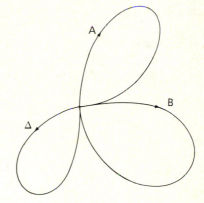

Figure 6.3

We need a definition from algebraic topology. The *degree* of a continuous map $f: S^1 \to S^1$, denoted deg (f), can be described as the number of times $f(S^1)$ "covers" S^1 with the same orientation. For instance, if f is the identity map on S^1, then deg $(f) = 1$; if $f(p) = 2p$ (p in radians), then deg $(f) = 2$; if $f(S^1)$ does not cover S^1 then deg $(f) = 0$. If a function f changes orientation (e.g. $f(x) = -x$), then deg (f) is negative. See Spanier (1966) for a complete definition of "degree".

2.1. Social choice paradoxes and fixed points theorems

The following theorem is valid for all preferences in P (not necessarily linear), any finite number of voters, and any finite dimensional space of choices; the proof of the general case is in Chichilnisky (1980d):

Theorem 1. There is no continuous, anonymous social choice rule

$$\phi: P^2 \to P$$

that respects unanimity.

In the particular case considered here, a simple geometrical proof can be given. Let Δ be the diagonal. Then Δ is equivalent to the circle S^1, and we can define the degree of ϕ on Δ, $\phi/\Delta: \Delta \to S^1$. If ϕ respects unanimity, then $\phi(p,p) = p \,\forall p$, and thus

$$\deg(\phi/\Delta) = 1. \tag{1}$$

We can also define the degree of the restriction of ϕ on A and B, since both these sets are equivalent to circles. Anonymity of ϕ implies

$$\deg(\phi/A) = \deg(\phi/B). \tag{2}$$

Since the circle Δ can be continuously deformed within $S^1 \times S^1$ into the union $A \cup B$ (see fig. 6.3) it follows that

$$\deg(\phi/\Delta) = \deg\phi/(A \cup B). \tag{3}$$

On the other hand, the degree of ϕ on $A \cup B$ is the sum of the degree of ϕ on A and on B:

$$\deg\phi/(A \cup B) = \deg(\phi/A) + \deg(\phi/B). \tag{4}$$

From (1)–(4) we obtain a contradiction because these equations imply that 1 is an even number. Thus, no continuous rule respecting unanimity can be anonymous.

Remark. The above result can be extended to preferences that admit satiation; see, for example, Chichilnisky (1982a). It should be pointed out that the linear preference whose gradient is zero (which is not considered here as a possible social outcome) is not merely a preference admitting satiation, but rather the preference which is indifferent among all possible choices. Clearly, such a social choice outcome would leave the social choice problem unresolved.

We now discuss briefly the connection between the paradox and fixed point theorems. The following result is proven in Chichilnisky (1979b).

Theorem 2. The existence of a continuous anonymous social rule respecting unanimity (as in theorem 1) is equivalent to the existence of a continuous function from the disk D into itself, without any fixed point.

The idea underlying this result is simple. One proves that the paradox of theorem 1 is equivalent to that of extending a continuous function g defined on the boundary of the disk ∂D, $g: \partial D \to \partial D$, into another function f from all of the disk D into ∂D, $f: D \to \partial D$. f is called an *extension* of g because it coincides with g in their common domain, i.e. the following diagram commutes:

$$\begin{array}{ccc} D & & \\ \uparrow & \searrow f & \\ \text{inclusion} & & \\ \partial D & \xrightarrow{ g } & \partial D \end{array} \qquad (5)$$

The equivalence between the paradox and the extension problem of (5) can be explained as follows. If T is the triangle in $S^1 \times S^1$ indicated in fig. 6.3, its interior $\mathring{T}$ is equivalent to the interior of disk $\mathring{D}$, and the frontier ∂D corresponds to $\Delta \cup A \cup B$. Note that on the set T, the conditions on the rule ϕ are only restrictions of the behaviour of ϕ on Δ, on A and on B: anonymity requires that $\phi/A \equiv \phi/B$, and unanimity is $\phi/\Delta = \text{id } \Delta$.

One sees immediately that a continuous anonymous map respecting unanimity *always exists* on ∂T; for example:

$$g/\Delta (p,p) = p, \quad \forall p \in S^1,$$

$$g/A \equiv p_0 \quad \text{and} \quad g/B \equiv p_0,$$

where $\Delta \cap A \cap B = (p_0, p_0)$. Therefore the paradox could be solved if such a function $g: \partial T \to S^1$ can be extended to another $f: T \to S^1$. Since $\partial T \cong \partial D$ and $S^1 \cong \partial D$, the problem is equivalent to the extension of $g: \partial D \to \partial D$ into $f: D \to \partial D$, as in diagram of (5). But such an extension exists if and only if deg $(g/\partial D)$

= 0. Since this latter statement is equivalent to Brouwer's fixed point theorem, see Chichilnisky (1979b), this explains the connection between a fixed point theorem and the paradox.

2.2.   *Topological equivalence of the Pareto condition and the existence of a dictator*

Theorems 1 and 2 show that the paradox appears because the seemingly natural properties of anonymity and respect of unanimity are in contradiction with each other. These properties are obviously related, but are different, from two axioms that are the basis of Arrow's theorem: *non-dictatorship and the Pareto condition*. However, the two sets of conditions (Arrow's and ours) are *not comparable*, because Pareto is stronger than respect of unanimity, while on the other hand anonymity is stronger than non-dictatorship. In addition, Arrow imposes another, somewhat controversial, axiom: the independence from irrelevant alternatives, while here continuity is required. A natural question is whether, despite the differences, Arrow's paradox has also a topological basis.

We now show that the Pareto condition is in fact topologically equivalent to the existence of a dictator, and thus establish the topological basis of Arrow's theorem. This also establishes that the controversial "independence" axiom is not needed intrinsically for his paradox, and can be understood as a device to reduce the problem to the study of a finite number of choices (indeed, three choices as in the Condorcet paradox).

A comment about the domain of preferences may be useful here. While Arrow's paradox appears to be valid in principle with monotone preferences (while our theorem requires that gradients may vary in all directions) in fact this is not so. This is because the axiom of independence in Arrow's work reduces effectively the problem to preferences over three choices only. Over these three choices, say a, b, and c, in order to obtain his paradox, Arrow must allow for "Condorcet triples", i.e. three preferences ranking these choices as (a, b, c), (c, a, b), and (b, c, a), respectively. Obviously, no reasonable definition of monotonicity can be given that makes such Condorcet triples into a set of monotone preferences. Therefore, Arrow's theorem requires lack of monotonicity as well.

In what follows the results are a special case of the results in Chichilnisky (1982b) that prove the topological equivalence of the Pareto condition and the existence of a dictator, for any (finite) dimension of the choice space and any number of voters, using algebraic topology tools.

The following is a proof for a special case, which admits a geometric interpretation. A rule ϕ is said to be *topologically equivalent* to another $\widetilde{\phi}$ when there exists a continuous deformation of ϕ into $\tilde{\phi}$, i.e. a continuous function

$$\Pi: (P \times P) \times [0, 1] \to P,$$

such that

$$\Pi(p_1, p_2, 0) = \phi(p_1, p_2), \quad \forall p_1, p_2 \quad \text{in} \quad PxP,$$
$$\Pi(p_1, p_2, 1) = \tilde{\phi}(p_1, p_2), \quad \forall p_1, p_2 \quad \text{in} \quad PxP.$$

We now examine geometrically the Pareto condition. If p_1 and p_2 are two preferences in P, the set of choices that *both* p_1 and p_2 prefer to x is the "dual cone"

$$E = \{q: (q \cdot p_1) \geqslant 0 \quad \text{and} \quad (q \cdot p_2) \geqslant 0\}.$$

The Pareto condition requires that $\phi(p_1, p_2)$ prefers also all such choices to x, i.e.

$$\phi(p_1, p_2) \in \{q: (q, r) \geqslant 0, \forall r \in E\}.$$

This can only happen if $\phi(p_1, p_2)$ is in the "dual" of the "dual cone" E, i.e. the cone generated by (p_1, p_2) denoted $C(p_1, p_2)$ (see fig. 6.4).

We can also show that if ϕ is Pareto, then deg (ϕ/A) and deg (ϕ/B) must be positive and at most 1. This is because as p varies over S^1, the outcome $\phi(p_0, p)$ must be in the cone $C(p_0, p)$. In particular, $\phi(p_0, p)$ cannot cover all of S^1 unless p has covered it. The proof of the next theorem will also show that a Pareto rule ϕ cannot have degree one simultaneously on A *and* on B. This is because a

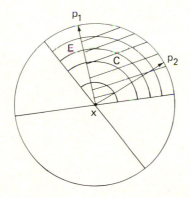

Figure 6.4. The set shaded in circular lines is the dual cone E corresponding to (p_1, p_2). The double shaded set is the cone generated by (p_1, p_2), $C(p_1, p_2)$.

Pareto rule is shown in the next theorem to be topologically equivalent to a dictatorial rule, and the degree of a map only depends on its topological equivalence class. Thus, since the degree of a dictatorial (i.e. a projection) map $\Pi: S^1 \times S^1 \to S^1$ is 1 on one of the sets A or B, and 0 on the other, the same must be true of a Pareto rule.

Theorem 3. If $\phi: P \times P \to P$ is Pareto, ϕ is topologically equivalent to a dictatorial rule.

Proof. Let p_1 and $-p_1$ be two diametrically opposed vectors in S^1. The Pareto condition and the continuity of ϕ together imply that either $\phi(p_1, -p_1) = p_1$, or else $\phi(p_1, -p_1) = -p_1$. Without loss of generality, assume $\phi = (p_1, -p_1) = p_1$. By continuity, we then have $\phi(p_2, -p_2) = p_2$ for all p_2 in S^1. Moreover, $\phi(p_1, q)$ must be different from $-p_1$ for all q in S^1 with $q \neq -p_1$, since $\phi(p_1, q)$ must belong to the cone $C(p_1, q)$. Thus, for all $p_1 \in S^1$, $\phi(p_1, q) \neq -p_1, \forall q$ in S^1. Let $\pi: P \times P \times [0,1] \to P$ be defined by

$$\pi(p_1, p_2, t) = \frac{t(p_1) + (1-t)\,\phi(p_1, p_2)}{\| t(p_1) + (1-t)\,\phi(p_1, p_2) \|} \ .$$

In view of the above remarks, the denominator of this expression never vanishes, and therefore π is a continuous map. In addition:

$$\pi(p_1, p_2, 0) = \phi(p_1, p_2)$$

and

$$\pi(p_1, p_2, 1) = p_1,$$

so that π defines a continuous deformation of ϕ into a dictatorial rule with the first voter as a dictator in this case. This proves theorem 3.

The result just proven is a special case of a general theorem proven in Chichilnisky (1982b), where it is shown that any Pareto rule, for any number $k \geq 2$ of voters and any dimension $n \geq 2$ of the space of choices, corresponds to a projection, i.e. a dictatorial rule. For $n > 2$ an extra condition of non-negative association is required.

Figure 6.5 gives an example of a social choice rule defined for two agents, with linear preferences and two-dimensional choices, $\phi: S^1 \times S^1 \to S^1$. The curve drawn in the left-hand figure is the set $\{\phi^{-1}(\bar{p})\}$, the inverse image under ϕ of an outcome $\bar{p}$ in S^1. Under the assumption of smoothness and regularity, $\{\phi^{-1}$

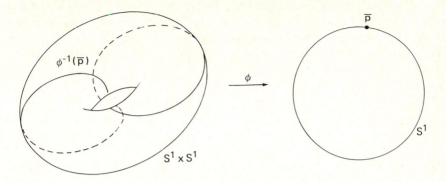

Figure 6.5

$(\overline{p})\}$ is a one-dimensional manifold, by the global version of the implicit function theorem. Note that each point $\overline{p}$ in S^1 is attained exactly twice (with the same orientation) as a value of the map ϕ restricted to either set A or B. Therefore degree $\phi/A = 2$, and thus ϕ cannot be Pareto in view of the above; of course, ϕ cannot be deformed into a dictatorial rule either.

2.3. *Decisive majority rules*

A social choice rule is said to satisfy a *decisive majority condition* if in certain particular cases the outcome chosen coincides with that of the majority, namely in those cases when the voters can be divided into two groups, within each graph voters have identical preferences, and across groups they have opposite preferences. Formally, ϕ is a decisive majority rule if for all profile $(p_1, p_2, ..., p_k)$ such that $p_i = p$ or $p_i = -p, \forall i = 1, ..., k$, then

$$\phi = (p_1, p_2, ..., p_n) = p$$

if the number of voters with preference p exceed those with preference $-p$.

A majority rule clearly satisfies a *decisive majority condition*, but the converse is obviously not true. This is because the decisive majority condition is only binding in the particular case in which the voters can be divided into two totally internally homogeneous groups for *all possible choices*, and the two groups are completely opposed to each other, also for all possible choices. Therefore, a decisive majority condition is much weaker than a majority condition.

In our next result we explore the structural stability of decisive majority rules. The overall continuity of a rule ϕ can be interpreted as structural stability, because it requires that a small variation (or observational error) of the data of the problem (individual preferences) does not produce drastic changes in the outcome. Since preferences are functions from the choice space with values of R^n (vector fields), continuity of ϕ corresponds to the notion of structural stability of maps on function spaces used frequently in mathematical physics and biology; with an appropriate topology, it corresponds also to the notion of Liapunov stability used frequently in economics. The following theorem is proved in Chichilnisky (1981):

Theorem 4. Any rule satisfying the decisive majority condition is structurally unstable.

The following is an immediate corollary:

Corollary 5. Majority rules are structurally unstable.

2.4. Intensity of preference and Von Neumann–Morgenstern utilities

The preferences considered until now have been ordinal, and the intensity of preferences was not recorded. Such preferences rank choices in a given order, but do not measure the difference in the intensity of preferences between, for example, choices a and b, and between c and another choice d. a may be preferred to b and c to d, but one may want to consider whether a is preferred to b *more* than c is preferred to d.

This is precisely formalized in the notion of *cardinal preferences*. Cardinal preferences are given by utility representations which are invariant under, and only under, linear positive transformations. By comparison, the invariance required of ordinal preferences is far greater, involving all monotonic transformation (not just linear ones). In the case of choice under uncertainty it is shown in Chichilnisky (1980b) that with this definition, cardinal preferences coincide with Von Neumann–Morgenstern utilities. The result obtained for the aggregation of cardinal preferences are thus applied directly to the aggregation of Von Neumann –Morgenstern utilities.

In contrast to all the previous results, we now consider discrete sets of choices, either finite or numerable. In the finite case the choice space is therefore $X = \{x_1, ..., x_n\}$, and we have shown in Chichilnisky (1980b) that the set of (nonzero) cardinal preferences can be represented by

$$R = \{(p_1, ..., p_n) \in R^{n+} : 0 \leqslant p_i \leqslant 1 \,\, \forall i; p_j = 0 \text{ and } p_k = 1 \text{ for } some \,\, j, k\}.$$

Each p_i describes the utility value of choice x_i. In addition, we also consider the null preference, which is indifferent among all choices, represented by the vector

$$\{0\} = (0, ..., 0).$$

The space of *all cardinal preferences* is therefore

$$Q = R \cup \{0\}.$$

This space has two connected components R and $\{0\}$. A similar definition can be given for the case where there are infinite (countably many) choices. In this case the space of cardinal preferences is a subspace of Banach space of infinite sequences (Chichilnisky, 1980b).

In what follows we consider rules for aggregation of cardinal preferences: with k voters, they are functions of the form

$$\phi: Q^k \rightarrow Q.$$

The social preference which is indifferent among all choices, i.e. $\{0\}$, is a permissible outcome.

Theorem 6. If the space X of choices is finite, then there exists no continuous aggregation rule for cardinal preferences $\phi: Q^k \rightarrow Q$ that respects unanimity and anonymity. This result is also valid for the aggregation of Von Neumann–Morgenstern utility functions.

This result is proved in Chichilnisky (1980b) through the study of the topological structure of spaces of cardinal preferences and spaces of Von Neumann–Morgenstern utilities. In particular, the following lemma is obtained.

Lemma 7. With a finite set of alternatives, the space of Von Neumann–Morgenstern utilities is not contractible.

It turns out that the topology of the spaces of cardinal preferences changes drastically with infinitely many alternatives. In this case the spaces of cardinal preferences become topologically trivial or contractible, and we have the following:

Theorem 8. With an infinite (countable) number of alternatives, there exists a continuous anonymous aggregation rule for cardinal preferences $\phi: Q^k \to Q$ respecting unanimity, and it is a deformation of a Bergson–Samuelson welfare function. However, this function is the limit of dictatorial rules on finite subsets of choices. The same result applies to the aggregation of Von Neumann–Morgenstern utilities with countably many alternatives. (See Chichilnisky, 1980b.)

The above results show the difference between spaces of cardinal and ordinal preferences. For ordinal preferences, we obtained non-existence results when the choice space X is infinite, such as the cube in Euclidean space of the previous sections. With cardinal preferences, and Von Neumann–Morgenstern utilities, we obtain instead *non-existence* results with *finitely* many choices, and *existence* results with *infinitely* many choices. One reason for this difference is that spaces of ordinal preferences are finite dimensional even when the choices are infinitely many; by contrast, cardinal preferences and Von Neumann–Morgenstern utilities define infinite dimensional spaces whenever the set of choices is infinite. The following subsection will explore another characteristic of infinity, namely the case of large economies or economies with infinite populations. Recall that all the results until now have referred to finitely many voters only. The following results study finite dimensional choice spaces but infinitely large populations.

2.5. *Social choice in large economies*

As seen above, infinite dimensionality produces significant differences in the results. The reason is that the topology of infinite dimensional spaces is rather different from that of Euclidean spaces. A particular characteristic that affects our results is that while in Euclidean spaces the circle S^1 and in general any (hollow) sphere is *not contractible* or topologically trivial, in infinite dimensional Banach spaces show hollow spheres *are* contractible (see, for example, Kuiper, 1971).

Theorem 8. Let $P^\infty = X_{i=1}^\infty P$ be the space of profiles of a countable number of agents and P the space of ordinal preferences defined on n-dimensional Euclidean choice space. Then the rule $\phi(p_1, ..., p_k, ...) = \lim_{k \to \infty} p_k$ is continuous, Pareto, and non-dictatorial (see Chichilnisky and Heal, 1979b).

A note on the concept of limit: if the sequence of vectors $\{p_i(x)\}$ has a standard limit in Euclidean space for all choices x, then the outcome of the rule coincides with this limit. Otherwise, the limit is defined by means of a free ultrafilter of the integers $\{1, 2, ..., k, ...\}$. (See definition in Chichilnisky and Heal,

1979b.) It can be seen that the rule ϕ is well defined, and continuous with respect to the standard product topology of P^∞. It is worth noting that the literature in this area succeeded previously in proving the existence of Pareto, non-dictatorial rules (see, for example, Brown, 1974), but not the existence of such continuous rules. An example is provided in fig. 6.6. In this figure, $p(x) = \lim_i p_i(x)$ is by definition the image ϕ of the sequence of vectors $\{p_1(x), p_2(x), ..., p_n(x), ...\}$,

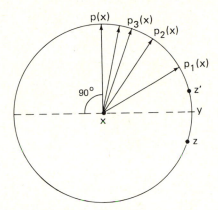

Figure 6.6

as in theorem 8 above. In contrast, in Brown (1974) the "winning coalitions" that decide the outcome are the subsets of a free ultrafilter F of the integers N. If F is the free ultrafilter over N consisting of the complements of finite subsets of N, then the collective preference according to Brown (1974) prefers y *strictly* to x while $\lim_i p_i(x)$ (our definition) is indifferent between y and x. Note that the rules of Brown (1974) are in effect discontinuous, because they prefer x strictly to any point z in the circle to the right of y, while they prefer strictly any point z' to the left of y in the circle, and y, to x.

2.6. Necessary and sufficient conditions for a resolution of the social choice paradox

The results discussed above show that without restrictions on preferences it is impossible to eliminate the aggregation paradox. A traditional approach has been to study *conditions* to eliminate the paradox, these being given as restrictions on the domain of individual preferences. The first such conditions were given by Black (1948) who introduced the notion of "single peakedness", meaning that one can order the (finite) set of choices in a line in such a way that each agent has a unique alternative who he or she prefers best (called peak), and that to the right and to the left of this alternative choices become progressively less desirable as they are further away from the peak. This remains the only sufficient condition which is generally accepted and utilized to solve the paradox (see also Sen, 1970).

In another paper Chichilnisky and Heal (1979a) found that there exists a domain restriction which is *both necessary and sufficient* to eliminate the paradox of theorem 1, and this is that the space of preferences be *contractible or topologically trivial*. This condition is equivalent to "topological" unanimity of preferences since, as we saw, a preference space is contractible if it can be continuously deformed through itself into one of its points. The relationships between this condition and Black's single peakedness are studied in Chichilnisky (1980c). In another chapter in this volume (Chapter 7, to which the reader is referred) contractibility is discussed in some detail.

It should be noted that the following result on the existence of an aggregation rule $\phi: R^k \to R$, is for *any domain R*, and R need not be a sphere of preferences of the sort discussed here. For instance, R could be a set of agendas, or of agendas and preferences over these agendas, without any requirement of the consistency of an individual's preference over different agendas. Alternatively, R could be any space of parameters describing individual characteristics; if these are preferences, one can also include the total indifference (as in theorems 6 and 7) as well as incomplete preferences on a Euclidean choice space.

Theorem 10. Let R be a manifold representing individual characteristics. Then a continuous rule $\phi: R^k \to R$ that respects anonymity and unanimity exists if and only if R is contractible.

For a proof see Chichilnisky and Heal (1979a). It is of interest to note that if such a rule exists, then it is topologically equivalent to a Bergsonian welfare function:

Theorem 11. If the dimension of R exceeds 5, and the boundary ∂R is simply connected,[2] then any continuous rule $\phi: R^k \to R$ which is anonymous and respects unanimity is topologically equivalent to the rule

$$\phi(p_1, ..., p_k) = \frac{1}{k} \sum_{i=1}^{k} p_k.$$

This result follows from theorem 10. This is because if such a ϕ exists, then R

---

[2]   I.e. the first homotopy group $\pi_1(\partial R)$ is zero; see Spanier (1966) for a description of homotopy groups.

must be contractible, and when R is contractible any map $\phi: R^k \to R$ will be a deformation of a convex addition rule, because by the proof of the Poincaré conjecture (under the conditions) R is deformable into a convex set.

Finally we mention the following:

Theorem 12. A continuous deformation of the (restricted) space of preferences R satisfies the "single peakedness" condition if and only if R is contractible, i.e. if and only if a continuous anonymous rule $\phi: R^k \to R$ respecting unanimity exists.

For a proof, see Chichilnisky (1980c).

3. Game theory

The basic mathematical structure of game theory is rather similar to that of social choice theory. A *game* consists of two objects: a *map* that associates an outcome to each k-tuple of individual strategies, denoted

$$g: S^k \to A,$$

where S is the *space of messages or strategies* and A the *space of outcomes*; and of a k-tuple of *individual preferences* over outcomes.[3] The basic properties of such a game form g are the subject of game theory, much the same way that the study of the aggregation maps $\phi: P^k \to P$ are those of social theory. In both cases one is concerned with maps from a product space to another space.

An initial difference between these two fields arises from the fact that the players of the game are aware of the game form g, and therefore choose their messages in S strategically. In social choice theory, instead, the properties of the map ϕ are the concern of the planner only (individuals are assumed simply to announce their preferences) and the relevant properties of a social choice rule ϕ are those of justice. In game theory, instead, the properties of a game form g are of direct interest to the players, and they choose their strategies in order to maximize the value of the outcome, according to their own preferences.

A direct link between the two problems arises with the issue of manipulability of social choice rules. In this case the agents are assumed to know the aggregation rule ϕ, and to choose strategically the preference they announce to the planner in order to influence the outcome in their favour. For instance, with an ade-

---

[3] The function g is called a *game form*.

quate definition of distance between preferences, the goal of the manipulation of messages would be to obtain a collective preference as close as possible to one's own. This section studies such problems. A large body of literature exists in this area and is not reviewed here. For references see, for example, Chichilnisky (1982c) and Chichilnisky and Heal (1982), and the original work of Vickrey (1960), Gibbard (1973) and Satterthwaite (1975).

An obvious technical difference between social choice and game theories is that the space of outcomes A can be rather different from the space of messages. Since an aggregation rule is a map $\phi: P^k \rightarrow P$, while a game form is $g: S^k \rightarrow A$, where in general $A \neq S$, the two problems have a somewhat different structure. This difference does not appear to be a fundamental one, because the properties of a map defined on the k-product of a space with itself with values in the same space, are related to the property of the product space into other spaces that are significantly simpler, such as outcome spaces generally are.

A second difference appears because of the equilibrium concepts of game theory. This displaces the topology structure of the problem, towards the geometry or differential topology, since notions of equilibrium are generally based on maximization.

Manipulation of games

As will be seen in what follows, the manipulation of a social choice rule, or more generally of a game, is in many cases a topological problem, while the existence and properties of an equilibrium are better studied instead by geometric or differentiable means. Under certain conditions, however, the topological analysis will serve also to establish the existence and properties of the equilibrium of a game. In particular, the following theorem will show that certain games have a Nash equilibrium only if they are "unfair" in the sense that they can be manipulated by one player more than by others and this is a topological property. Thus "more cooperative" solutions than Nash equilibrium are needed in order to secure the equity of games.

Within the games studied below, the players' strategies consist of announcing a preference, and the outcomes are aggregate preferences. The player wishes, ideally, to attain an outcome as close as possible to his or her true preference, so that preference over outcomes are given by distance functions.

If one considers more general outcome spaces, the results can be extended by noting, for instance, that a social choice in R^n may be obtained from the maximization of social preferences on R^n. Therefore, one can construct games h where outcomes are arbitrary vectors in R^n deriving them from the games g constructed here by the rule

$$h = M \circ g,$$

or

$$h = P^k \overset{g}{\to} P \overset{M}{\to} A,$$

where M denotes the maximization operator.

The following result is proven in Chichilnisky (1979a) utilizing homotopy theory:

Theorem 13. If $g: P^k \to P$ is a continuous game respecting unanimity, then it is either dictatorial, or else there exists a player that can obtain any outcome he or she desires by announcing a false preference. In addition, if g is Pareto such a manipulative player is unique.

Formally, we say that a player (say the first) is a *strong manipulator* if $\forall p_1^* \in P$, and all $p_2 \in P$, $\exists p_1 = p_1(p_2)$ such that

$$\phi(p_1, p_2) = p_1^*.$$

Theorem 13 establishes therefore the existence of a strong manipulator for continuous games which respect unanimity.

Proof of theorem 13 in a special case. Consider now, as before, the special case where there are two players with linear preferences, so that

$$g: S^1 \times S^1 \to S^1.$$

As seen in theorem 1, if g respects unanimity,

$$\deg(g/\Delta) = 1.$$

Since $\deg(g/(A \cup B) = \deg(g/\Delta) = 1$, and $\deg g/(A \cup B) = \deg g/A + \deg g/B$, it follows that either $\deg(g/A) \neq 0$, or $\deg(g/B) \neq 0$. Assume, without loss of generality, that $\deg(g/A) \neq 0$. Then the first player is a strong manipulator, because the image of A under g, $g/A(A)$, must cover S^1, otherwise $\deg(g/A)$ would be zero. This means that when the second player states p_0, there exists some $p_1 = p_1(p_0)$ such that

$$g(p_1, p_0) = p_1^*,$$

for *any* p_1^* in S^1. Since it can be seen that deg $(g/A) \neq 0$ implies that deg (g/A') $\neq 0$ for any set $A' = \{(p, q): q = q_0, p \in S^1\}$, then the first part of the theorem is proven. To prove the second part, note that when g is Pareto, as seen above, then

$$0 \leqslant \deg (g/A) \leqslant 1$$

and

$$0 \leqslant \deg (g/B) \leqslant 1;$$

therefore deg (g/A) + deg (g/B) = 1 implies the existence of a *unique* manipulator. When g is not dictatorial, then the manipulator must lie.

One can now introduce the notion of equity in such a game. Assume $g: (S^1)^2 \to S^1$ is *equitable*, or *fair* when either both players can manipulate the game, or when neither of them can. An example of a game which has one strong manipulator is shown in fig. 6.7.

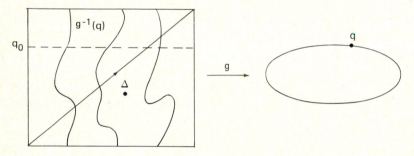

Figure 6.7. The curves in the left-hand diagram indicate three different hypersurfaces of the game $g: S^1 \times S^1 \to S^1$. Since by unanimity deg $g/\Delta = 1$, then for any q in S^1, $\phi^{-1}(q) \cap \Delta = q$. Note that for all q and any q_0, there is a p such that $g(p, q_0) = q$.

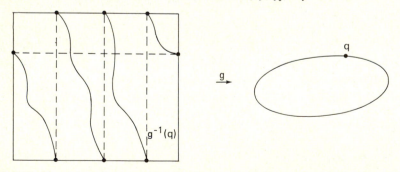

Figure 6.8. The union of the curves in the left-hand diagram represents *one* hypersurface of the game. This game has two manipulators: for any q_0 there is a p_1 such that $g(p_1, p_0)$ = q, and a p_2 such that $g(q_0, p_2) = q$.

The game in fig. 6.7 is clearly *not* dictatorial. An example of a game with two manipulators is shown in fig. 6.8.

Clearly, a game with two strong manipulators cannot have a Nash equilibrium when the two players have different "true" preferences, since each player can attain the most desirable outcome by an appropriate choice of strategy once the other player's announcement is known. The following theorem establishes the relationship between existence of Nash equilibria and fairness of games.

Theorem 14. A continuous game g that satisfies unanimity has a Nash equilibrium only if it is unfair.

This is established by an application of theorem 13. The game is fair when there are no manipulators, or when both players can manipulate the game. The first case is eliminated by theorem 13. In the second case there is no Nash equilibrium. Unfairness is therefore necessary for the existence of a Nash equilibrium.

We conclude this section with recent results on the existence and characterization of non-manipulable games. Clearly, if one wishes to preserve respect of unanimity, in order to prevent manipulability one must restrict the domain of individual preferences. This is the same procedure that was followed in the first part of this paper to find solutions to the social choice paradox.

The following results will therefore study games with arbitrary strategy and outcome spaces; these need not be preference spaces.

The spaces considered here are smooth manifolds X, of dimension at least 5, and with simply connected boundaries (i.e. the first homotopy group $\Pi_1(\partial X) = 0$). A *straightforward game* is one in which the announcement of an agent's true characteristic is a *dominant strategy* for each player. We consider here games which are onto, i.e. the image of $g: X^k \to X$ covers X.

Theorem 15. A continuous straightforward game $g: X^k \to X$ respecting anonymity exists if and only if X is contractible.

For a proof see Chichilnisky (1982c). This last theorem shows the close link between the conditions needed to solve the social choice paradox (theorem 10) and those needed for the existence of straightforward games: the necessary and sufficient condition in both cases is *contractibility*, or topological triviality. Aggregation problems and manipulable games exist in those cases where the relevant spaces (of preferences, or strategies and outcomes, respectively) are topologically complex.

Consider now the case where *choices* are vectors in R^n, *messages* are single peaked preferences, of the form shown in fig. 6.9, given by the distance function

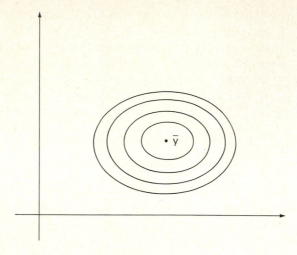

Figure 6.9. A single peaked preference on R^2 : the curves indicate the indifference surfaces.

$$d\,(x,\overline{y}) = \sum_{i=1}^{k} a_i\,(x_i - \overline{y}_i)^2, \quad a_i > 0, \quad \forall i = 1, ..., n,$$

where $\overline{y}$ denotes the "bliss" point. *Outcomes* are vectors in R^n as well. The space of messages in denoted M, and the space of outcomes A.

A function $g: (R^n)^k \rightarrow R^n$ is said to be *locally simple* if it is continuous and separable, i.e.

$$g\,(r_1^1, ..., r_n^1, r_1^2, ..., r_n^2, ..., r_1^k, ..., r_n^k)$$
$$= g_1\,(r_1^1, ..., r_n^1), g_2\,(r_1^2, ..., r_n^2), ..., g_k\,(r_1^k, ..., r_n^k),$$

and for almost all $(x_1, ..., x_k) \in (R^n)^k$, g is either constant, or dictatorial (i.e. a projection) on *some* neighbourhood of $(x_1, ..., x_k)$ in $(R^n)^k$.

The following is a characterization of all straightforward games in this context.

Theorem 16. $g: M^k \rightarrow A$ is a straightforward game if and only if the function g is locally simple. For a proof see Chichilnisky and Heal (1982).

Remark. Note that theorem 15 implies, in particular, that whenever g is straightforward, then g is continuous.

For such straightforward games continuity is therefore a *result* rather than a condition.

A final result gives conditions for a game to be Nash implementable, i.e. for the truthful revelation of characteristics, when each player plays a Nash equilibrium strategy. Since straightforward games require a more stringent equilibrium concept, i.e. that truthful revelation is a *dominant* strategy. It may appear that one could obtain larger classes of Nash implementable than straightforward games; the following result shows that, at least for separable games, this is not the case:

Theorem 17. A separable regular game $g: M^k \to A$ is Nash implementable only if g is locally simple. For a proof see Chichilnisky and Heal (1981).

Remark. The regularity condition requires that g be smooth, and a transversality condition which is generally satisfied. See Chichilnisky and Heal (1981).

References

Arrow, K.J. (1951) *Social Choice and Individual Values* (Yale University Press).
Black, D. (1948) "On the Rationale of Group Decision Making", *Journal of Political Economy*.
Brown, D. (1974) "Aggregation of Preferences", *Quarterly Journal of Economics*.
Chichilnisky, G. (1976) "Manifolds of Preferences and Equilibria", Project for Efficiency of Decision Making in Economic Systems, Harvard University.
Chichilnisky, G. (1978) "Spaces of Economic Agents", *Journal of Economic Theory*.
Chichilnisky, G. (1979a) "A General Result on Strong Manipulability", The Economic Workshop, Columbia University.
Chichilnisky, G. (1979b) "On Fixed Points and Social Choice Paradoxes", *Economic Letters*.
Chichilnisky, G. (1980a) "Continuous Representation of Preferences", *Review of Economic Studies*.
Chichilnisky, G. (1980b) "Intensity of Preferences and von Neuman Morgenstern Utilities", Working Paper, University of Essex.
Chichilnisky, G. (1980c) "Single Peakedness and the Contractibility of Preference Spaces", Working Paper, University of Essex.
Chichilnisky, G. (1980d) "Social Choice and the Topology of Spaces of Preferences", *Advances in Mathematics*.
Chichilnisky, G. (1981) "The Structural Instability of Decisive Majority Rules", *Journal of Mathematical Economics*.
Chichilnisky, G. (1982a) "Social Aggregation Rules and Continuity", *Quarterly Journal of Economics*.
Chichilnisky, G. (1982b) "The Topological Equivalence of the Pareto Condition and the Existence of a Dictator", *Journal of Mathematical Economics*.
Chichilnisky, G. (1982c) "Incentive Compatible Games: A Characterization of Strategy and Outcome Spaces", Working Paper No. 139, Columbia University.
Chichilnisky, G. and G. Heal (1979a) "Necessary and Sufficient Conditions for a Resolution of the Social Choice Paradox", *Journal of Economic Theory*, in press.

Chichilnisky, G. and G. Heal (1979b) "Social Choice with Infinite Population: Construction of a Rule and Impossibility Results", The Economic Workshop, Columbia University.

Chichilnisky, G. and G. Heal (1980) "Patterns of Power: Bargaining and Implementation in two person games", Discussion Paper, University of Essex.

Chichilnisky, G. and G. Heal (1981) "Incentive Compatibility and Local Simplicity", Working Paper, University of Essex.

Chichilnisky, G. and G. Heal (1982) "A Necessary and Sufficient Condition for Straight Forward Games", Working Paper No. 138, Columbia University.

Debreu, G. (1972) "Regular Economies", *Econometrica*.

Gibbard, A. (1973) "Manipulation of Voting Schemes: A General Result", *Econometrica*.

Kuiper, N.H. (1971) *Variétés Hilbertiennes. Aspects Géométriques*, Séminaire de mathématiques Supérieures (la Pressé de l'Université de Montréal).

Satterthwaite, M.A. (1975) "Strategy-Proofness and Arrow's Conditions: Existence and Correspondence Theorems for Voting Procedures and Social Welfare Functions", *Journal of Economic Theory*.

Sen, A.K. (1970) *Collective Choice and Social Welfare* (Holden-Day, San Francisco).

Spanier, E. (1966) *Algebraic Topology* (McGraw-Hill, New York).

Vickrey, W. (1960) "Utility, Strategy and Social Decision Rules", *Quarterly Journal of Economics*.

CHAPTER 7

Contractibility and public decision-making

GEOFFREY HEAL*
University of Essex

1. Introduction

In the area of social choice theory, restrictions on the domain of preferences are
a device that has long been used to assure the existence of solutions to certain
problems. In particular, there has been an extensive discussion of domain restrictions sufficient to ensure that majority voting is a "well-behaved" social choice
rule, and a rather less extensive discussion of conditions which permit the existence of straightforward (i.e. non-manipulable) social choice rules. In the former
category come single peakedness (Black, 1948), value restrictedness (Pattanaik
and Sen, 1969) and many others; conditions discussed in connection with straightforwardness include again single peakedness (Moulin, 1980) and also rich domain
(Dasgupta, Hammond and Maskin, 1979).

More recently, the condition that preferences form a contractible space has
been introduced. It was first analysed in Chichilnisky (1976), and its implications
for the existence of social choice rules were explored in Chichilnisky and Heal
(1979a). It was shown there to be a necessary and sufficient condition for the
existence of continuous social choice rules which are anonymous and respect
unanimity. Chichilnisky and Heal (1981) and Chichilnisky (1981) explore the
implications of contractibility for incentive compatibility. In the former it is
shown that if the space of preferences is unrestricted, and in particular non-contractible, then amongst continuous social choice rules only those that are constant or dictatorial can be implemented by either Nash or strong equilibria. It is

* The framework adopted in this review was introduced by Graciela Chichilnisky, to
whom I am grateful for very helpful comments.

also shown that in this case, if a continuous rule satisfies a degree condition, then at least one agent must be a "strategic dictator", i.e. must have the power, through suitable misrepresentation of preferences, to ensure that any outcome he or she chooses is selected by the social choice rule. Such an agent therefore has an incentive to misrepresent preferences. In Chichilnisky (1981), restricted domains of preferences are considered, and it is shown that contractibility of the preference space is a necessary and sufficient condition for the existence of straightforward (or non-manipulable or strategy-proof) rules.

It is clear from this that contractibility is an important condition in social choice theory, being necessary and sufficient both for the existence of acceptable social choice rules, and for the existence of interesting straightforward or strategy-proof rules. It is also a new and unfamiliar one. It is therefore the purpose of this chapter to examine its meaning and implications, and to review the role that it plays. We shall note that, although new to social choice theory, it is not new to mathematical economics: it was used by Debreu (1953) in a basic existence theorem, and by Kuhn (1954) in establishing results in game theory. More recently it has been discussed by Heal (1981) in the context of non-convex programming and the welfare economics of non-convex economies. One of the reasons why contractibility is of importance in resource allocation theory is that under certain mild assumptions contractible spaces have the fixed-point property: contractibility may therefore replace convexity in some existence arguments (Debreu, 1953; Chichilnisky and Heal, 1979a). The relationship between, and indeed equivalence of, fixed-point problems and social choice paradoxes was noted in Chichilnisky (1979). Another reason for its interest is that through morse-theoretic arguments (Milnor, 1963a), contractibility conditions can be used to determine the optimality of critical points of constrained maximisation problems. It is certainly not without interest that the same condition arises naturally and in an important way in both social choice theory and resource allocation theory, particularly in view of the traditional divorce between their methodologies.

2.   Basic definitions and concepts

We begin this section with a definition of contractibility, and we then explore the relationship between this and other concepts more commonly used in economics, such as convexity. Finally, we introduce some concepts which will be needed in the following section, which deals with the applications of contractibility to social choice theory.

Let X be a topological space and let I be the unit interval of the real line. Then:

Definition. X is said to be *contractible* if there exists a point $x_0 \in X$ and a continuous function $F: X \times I \to X$ such that $F(x, 0) = x$ for all $x \in X$ and $F(x, 1) = x_0$ for all $x \in X$.

In this definition we can think of F as defining a parameterised family of maps from X into itself. Denote a typical member of this family by f_t for $t \in [0,1]$. Then f_t is defined by

$$f_t: X \to X, \quad f_t(x) = F(x, t).$$

Clearly, f_0 is the identity map on X, i.e. the map that for all $x \in X$ sends x into itself, as $F(x, 0) = x$ for all x. Similarly, f_1 is the constant map that sends all $x \in X$ into a constant point $x_0 \in X$, as $F(x, 1) = x_0$ for all x. The parameterised family is jointly continuous in $x \in X$ and in the parameter $t \in [0, 1]$. This means that the identity map $F(x, 0) \equiv f_0(x)$ can be continuously deformed into (technically, is homotopic to) the constant map $F(x, 1) \equiv f_1(x)$.

The next step is to explore the geometrical implications of this definition, and to set out the relationship between contractibility and convexity. We first remind the reader of the meaning of the term *homeomorphic*. Two topological spaces A and B are said to be homeomorphic if there exists a function $h: A \to B$ which is continuous, one to one, onto B, and has a continuous inverse. Such a function is said to be a *homeomorphism*. Roughly speaking, two spaces are homeomorphic if one can be continuously deformed into the other.

Next, we introduce an assumption that will remain effective for the rest of the chapter, namely that all the spaces that we are dealing with are CW complexes. We do not give a formal definition of such a space here (one can be found in Maunder, 1970, p. 273). Intuitively, this can be described as a space which can be constructed inductively by joining to a 1-cell a 2-cell in a suitably regular manner, then attaching a 3-cell, and so on up the dimensions. Here an n-cell is simply $\{x \in R^n : d(x, 0) \leqslant 1\}$, where d is a metric on R^n. A CW complex can be shown to be a very general type of space: any polyhedron, or any space homeomorphic to a polyhedron, is a CW complex. Most if not all spaces likely to arise naturally in economics are CW complexes, and the usual examples of spaces which are not CW complexes are rather pathological. One example of such a space is the subspace of R^1 consisting of the points 0 and $1/n$, for all integers $n \geqslant 1$ (Maunder, 1970, p. 277). Another more complex one is the double comb space (Maunder, p. 301) defined as the subspace of R^2 consisting of straight line segments joining the point $(0,1)$ to the points $(0,0)$ and $(1/n, 0)$ for all positive integers n, and the straight line segments joining $(0,-1)$ to the points $(0,0)$ and $(-1/n, 0)$. This is shown in fig. 7.1.

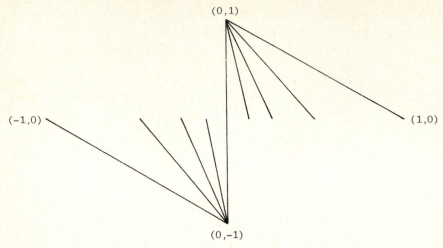

Figure 7.1. The double comb space which is not a CW complex.

We can now note that any convex space is contractible. To prove this, take a convex space X and a point $x_0 \in X$. By convexity, $\{t\,x + (1 - t)\,x_0\} \in X$ for any $t \in [0,1]$. We then set

$$F(x, t) = t\,x + (1 - t)\,x_0,$$

which is a map of $X \times [0,1] \to X$, with $F(x, 1) = x$ and $F(x, 0) = x_0$ as required. A relaxation of convexity sometimes used is that of being star-shaped (Arrow and Hahn, 1971). X is star-shaped if there exists $x_0 \in X$ such that $\{t\,x + (1-t)x_0\} \in X$ for all $t \in [0,1]$ and any $x \in X$. Thus, there is a point in a star-shaped set to which every other point can be joined by a straight line segment contained in the set. Clearly, the proof given above also suffices to show that any star-shaped space is contractible. More generally, any space X homeomorphic by a homeomorphism h to a convex set C can be shown to be contractible. Choose any $x_0 \in X$ and set

$$F(x, t) = h^{-1}\,\{t\,h(x) + (1 - t)\,h(x_0)\},$$

which sends $X \times [0,1] \to X$ with $F(x, 0) = x$ and $F(x, 1) = x_0$. This amounts to sending points in X into points in C by h, contracting them in C, and then sending the result back to X by h^{-1} and using it as the result of a contraction in X. It should be emphasised that although any space homeomorphic to a convex space is contractible, the converse is not true. Fig. 7.2 shows a contractible space which

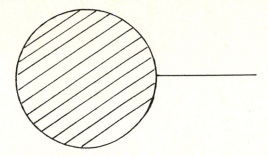

Figure 7.2.   A contractible space which is not homeomorphic to a convex space.

is not homeomorphic to a convex one. This example is the unit disk in R^2 with a line segment joined to its boundary.

Figure 7.2 is star-shaped and so contractible: it cannot however be put into one-to-one bicontinuous correspondence with a convex set. Although it is not true that any contractible space is homeomorphic to a convex one, it is true that a space which is contractible and satisfies certain regularity conditions is homeomorphic to a convex space. In particular, any contractible manifold of dimension at least five, and with a simply connected boundary, can be shown to be homeomorphic to a convex set. The concept of a manifold is discussed in Milnor (1963b), and the property of being simply connected (having the first homotopy group zero) in Maunder (1970). A proof of this result uses the generalised Poincaré conjecture, and is given in Chichilnisky (1981).

Another aspect of the relationship between these two concepts is that any contractible space is a retract of a convex space. The property of being a retract is defined as follows. Consider two topological spaces A and B, $A \subset B$. Then A is a *retract* of B if there exists a continuous function $f: B \to A$ such that $f(a) = a$ for all $a \in A$. In this case, f is said to be a *retraction*. Intuitively, B can be "pushed in" to give A. Thus, one can prove that given any contractible space A, there exists a convex space B, with $A \subset B$ such that A is a retract of B.

Now that the relationship between contractibility and convexity has been clarified, the reader will have no difficulty in obtaining examples of contractible spaces. What kinds of spaces are not contractible? A simple example is the circle in R^2, or any figure homeomorphic to it, such as the boundary of a square or triangle. A torus is also non-contractible: these figures are all illustrated in fig. 7.3. As these examples imply, the property of being non-contractible is preserved by a homeomorphism. This is because if A and B are homeomorphic, with B contractible and f_t the appropriate family of parameterised maps from B to B, then if

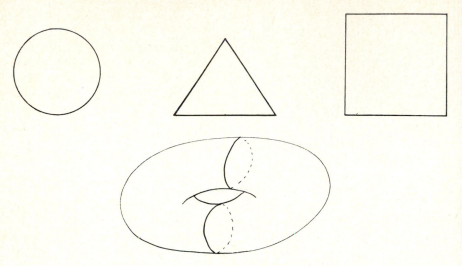

Figure 7.3.   Some non-contractible spaces.

h is the homeomorphism $h: A \to B$, we can define a suitable family of parameterised maps $q_t: A \to A$ by $q_t(a) = h^{-1}(f_t(h(a)))$ for any $a \in A$. Hence, A non-contractible and B contractible produces a contradiction. This puts us in a position, given one non-contractible space, to generate many more.

What is the formal criterion for recognising a non-contractible space? Intuitively, this is that it has a hole of some kind in it. Clearly, the examples in fig. 7.3 are all of this type, and because of this none can be deformed continuously through itself into one of its points. Equally clearly, all of the examples we have seen of contractible spaces have no holes in. Unfortunately the presence or absence of holes cannot be taken as the test of contractibility or non-contractibility, since there are spaces which have no holes and yet are non-contractible. The double comb space of fig. 7.1 is such an example. (Formally, one can show that contractibility implies all homotopy groups zero, which implies all homology groups zero, which implies that there are no holes of any dimension in the space. However, the reverse set of implications is true only if the first homotopy group of the space is zero or abelian. A space with all homology groups zero is said to be acyclic, and contractibility is thus equivalent to acyclicity if and only if the first homotopy group is zero or abelian.) From this we can conclude that the presence of holes certainly makes a space non-contractible, and their absence usually but not always makes it contractible.

One final but rather important point to note in connection with contractibility and its properties is the relationship between contractibility and aggregation (see Chichilnisky, 1976). This can be approached via the relationship between contractibility and convexity, and in particular via the fact that any contractible space is a retract of a convex one. By aggregation in a space X, one might reasonably mean taking a k-tuple of points $(x_1, ..., x_k)$ each of which is in X and assigning to them another point y in X which is their aggregate, and which is felt in some sense to be representative of them. An aggregation rule f is therefore a map from the k-fold product of X with itself, into $X: f: (X)^k \to X$. In general one will wish to impose supposedly desirable properties on f, although for the moment we shall suppose only that it is continuous. Note now that if X is convex, it certainly admits continuous aggregation rules. For example:

$$f(x) = \frac{1}{k} \sum_{i=1}^{k} x_i,$$

which is just convex addition, is a continuous map from $(X)^k$ to X. Aggregation in this sense is therefore possible in convex spaces, and the fact that a contractible space is a retract of a convex space enables us to make the same assertion for contractible spaces. To see this, consider $Y \subset X$, X convex, Y contractible, and $r: X \to Y$ a retraction. Then we can define the rule $g: (Y)^k \to Y$ by:

$$g(y_1, ..., y_k) = r(f(y_1, ..., y_k)).$$

Here the function f sends the k-tuple $(y_1, ..., y_k)$ into a point in X, and r then brings this back to Y. Hence, one can also aggregate continuously in contractible spaces. Note that in this discussion the example of a convex addition rule was not chosen at random: viewed as a map $f(x_1, ... x_k) = x$ this rule has the properties that:

(i) $f(x, ..., x) = x$, i.e. if all the arguments of f are the same, then the outcome is this common point, and

(ii) $f(x_1, ..., x_k) = f(x_{\pi_1}, ..., x_{\pi_k})$ where $(\pi_1, ..., \pi_k)$ is any permutation of the indices 1 to k.

As we shall see below, these two conditions are important in a social choice framework where they correspond to respect of unanimity and to anonymity, respectively.

Now that contractibility has been defined and its properties explored, we introduce the framework within which the social choice problem will be studied.

Let Y be the *choice space*, such as a unit cube in R^n, denoted I^n, or the positive orthant of R^n, R^{n+}. Since our framework is topological, it suffices to consider a space which is homeomorphic to I^n.

A preference p on Y is a family of smooth indifference surfaces: formally, it is defined by giving for each choice y in Y a preferred direction or, equivalently,

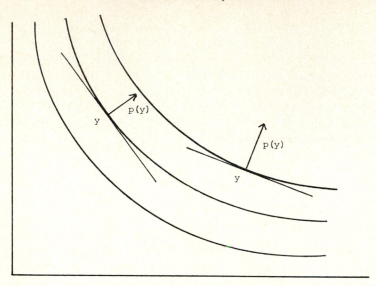

Figure 7.4

the normal to the indifference surface at y, a vector denoted $p(y)$. As is usual in social choice theory, preferences are ordinal and intensities of preferences are not considered. We therefore normalise the vector fields that give our preferences to be of unit length, i.e. $\| p(y) \| = 1$ for all y^1. A preference is thus a map $y \to p(y)$ from choices y into the tangent space of Y, $T(Y)$, such that for each choice y, $p(y)$ is the normal to the indifference surface at y. Fig. 7.4 illustrates this idea. With each point in the choice space, in this case R_+^2, we associate a vector normalised to be of unit length, which defines the slope of the indifference curve at that point. A preference is therefore a map from R^2 to R^2 which associates with each point in R^2 a vector which defines the slope of the indifference surface at that point.

We topologise the spaces Y and $T(Y)$ as usual, and we assume that the preferences are defined by continuously differentiable locally integrable vector fields, i.e. that $p(y)$ is locally the gradient of a real-valued utility function on Y. The space P of all such locally integrable preferences is characterised within the space

---

[1] The fact that the vector field can be normalised to be of unit length implies that it is no where zero in the interior of the choice space. A general discussion of social choice problems with vanishing gradients within the present framework is contained in Chichilnisky (1982).

of all vector fields on Y, $V(Y)$, by the Frobenius integrability conditions.[2] $V(Y)$ is given the C^1 topology.[3] The Frobenius conditions and the normalization assumption $\| p(y) \| = 1$ are both closed conditions, so that the space P endowed with the topology inherited from $V(Y)$ is a complete space since it is a closed subspace of the space of vector fields $V(Y)$.

We assume that there are k voters indexed by $i = 1, ..., k$. A *profile* of k voters' preferences is given by a sequence $\{p_i\} = (p_1, p_2, ..., p_k)$. We denote the space of profiles by L; this is in general a subset of the product of the space P with itself k times. We denote this product space XP_i; P_i denotes the space of preferences of the ith voter and thus $P_i = P$ for all i, so that $XP_i = XP$.

A *social aggregation rule* or *social choice rule* is a map from profiles to social preferences in P. Therefore

$$\phi: L \subset XP \to P.$$

A social choice rule ϕ is said to be *anonymous* if for any permutation $\{m_1, ..., m_k\}$ of the set of integers $\{1, ..., k\}$,

$$\phi(p_1, p_2, ..., p_k) = \phi(p_{m_1}, ..., p_{m_k}).$$

The outcome of the social choice rule thus depends only on the set of preferences of the individuals, and not on who holds which preference. This is an equal treatment condition: it implies that there is no one individual whose preference determines the social choice, so that in particular the rule is non-dictatorial. The social choice rule is said to *respect unanimity* if

$$\phi(p, p, ..., p) = p, \quad \text{for all } p \in p,$$

i.e. if all individuals have identical preferences over all choices. Then the social choice rule yields that preference as an outcome. This is clearly a very natural requirement. It was shown in Chichilnisky (1980a) that with unrestricted domains of preferences there is no social choice rule ϕ,

$$\phi: XP \to P,$$

---

[2]   The Frobenius integrability conditions are usually given by a set of partial differential equations. They are necessary (but not sufficient) for a vector field to be the gradient of a real-valued function. For a discussion of these conditions see, for instance, Debreu (1972).

[3]   We give V the C^1 topology in order to obtain a nice topological structure on V; any topology on V that is restricted to linear preferences and coincides with the convergence of vectors in R^n, will also give our result.

which is simultaneously continuous, anonymous, and respects unanimity.

The space *XP* has the natural product topology inherited from that of the space *P*, and continuity of the social choice rule ϕ is defined with respect to this topology on *XP*. Continuity of the rule ϕ and of the preferences implies that the social preference at a point $y \in Y$ is continuous in profiles and choices. Although we do not require the axiom of independence of irrelevant alternatives, these continuity properties will ensure that a social choice rule satisfies a related *global independence condition* (see Chichilnisky and Heal, 1979c).

A topological space *X* is connected when it does not contain two subsets *A* and *B* such that both *A* and *B* are open and closed in $X, A \cap B = \phi$, and $X = A \cup B$. $X \supset Y$ is called a connected component of *X* if *Y* is connected, and there is no connected subset $\mathscr{S}$ of *X* such that $Y \neq\!\!\!\!{}^{c}\; Z$.

3. Examples of preferences spaces

It is now possible to flesh out the earlier discussion by giving examples of particular preferences spaces, and of the conditions on individual preferences which make these spaces contractible.

Example 1. We consider first the case of linear, ordinal, non-satiated preferences on R^n, for *n* finite. Such a preference has indifference surfaces given by a family of parallel hyperplanes. A family of parallel hyperplanes is fully determined once the normal to one of its members is known, and since preferences are ordinal all preferences represented by the same normal will be identified. We can therefore take all normals to be of unit length, and represent every linear, ordinal non-satiated preference on R^n by a vector in R^n of unit length, the normal to its indifference surfaces. Fig. 7.5 illustrates this for $n = 2$. If we permit preferences to increase in all possible directions, then every unit vector in R^n represents a possible preference, and the space of preferences can be identified with the set of all unit vectors in R^n, which is of course the $(n-1)$-dimensional unit sphere S^{n-1} in R^n. If, however, we were to restrict our attention to preferences that do not decrease in any variable, then these preferences could have as normals only nonnegative vectors, so that the preference space in this case would be the intersection of S^{n-1} with the positive cone of R^n. Fig. 7.6 again illustrates for $n = 2$.

In this case it is easy to check when the preference space is contractible. We have already seen that the circle S^1 in R^2 is not contractible, and by similar arguments the sphere S^{n-1} in R^n is non-contractible for any finite *n*. Hence, with linear, ordinal, and non-satiated preferences, the space *P* of preferences obtained by allowing all possible directions of increase is non-contractible. We refer to this as the unrestricted domain.

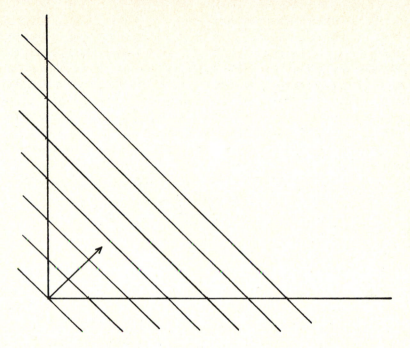

Figure 7.5. An ordinal, linear, non-satiated preference on R^2 is identified by its normal vector *P*.

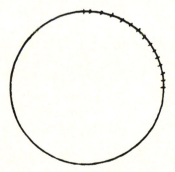

Figure 7.6. With all possible directions of increase, the preference space is the circle S^1. With monotone preferences, it is the hatched subset of S^1.

Figure 7.6 makes it clear that, at least for R^2, if we restrict our attention to the space of monotone increasing preferences, then this is contractible. This is generally true: the intersection of S^{n-1} with R_+^n, the positive cone of R^n, is contractible. The easiest way to prove this is to note that $S^{n-1} \cap R_+^n$ is homeomorphic to the unit simplex Q in R^n, i.e. $\{x \in R^n : \Sigma_i x_i = 1, x_i \geqslant 0, i = 1, ..., n\}$. The homeomorphism can be constructed by considering the ray from the origin to each point s in $S^{n-1} \cap R_+^n$, and then associating the point $s \in S^{n-1} \cap R_+^n$ with the point x in the simplex lying on the same ray. It is routine to show that this map is one-to-one, onto, continuous, and has a continuous inverse. Note now that Q is convex: this establishes by the results of the last section that $S^{n-1} \cap R_+^n$ is contractible. Hence, the space of preferences which are monotone increasing, ordinal, and linear is a contractible space.

In fact one can find much larger contractible spaces of linear preferences. Let C be an arbitrarily small cone with a non-empty interior in R^n. Consider now the space P^c of linear preferences given by all points in S^{n-1} except these also in C, i.e.

$$P^c = S^{n-1} - (S^{n-1} \cap C).$$

Figure 7.7 illustrates this case for R^2, and it is clear from this that, at least for R^2, the space P^c is contractible, since it is homeomorphic to a connected interval of R^1. In fact P^c is contractible for any finite n. This can be proven along the following lines. Choose a point $x \in S^{n-1} \cap C$. Let y be the other point in S^{n-1}

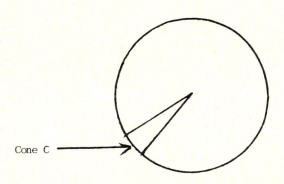

Cone C

Figure 7.7. $P^c = S^{n-1} - (S^{n-1} \cap C)$.

where the ray through x and the origin meets S^{n-1}. Let H be the hyperplane which supports S^{n-1} at y. We establish a homeomorphism between $S^{n-1} - (S^{n-1} \cap C)$ and H as follows. For any point $s \in (S^{n-1} \cap C)$, consider the straight line $\langle x, s \rangle$ through x and s. Let $f(s)$ be the point at which this line intersects H. Then $f: S^{n-1} - (S^{n-1} \cap C) \to H$, with $f(s)$ defined as above, can be shown to be a homeomorphism. Since H is convex, this establishes the point. Note that this construction could not be applied to the whole of S^{n-1}, because there would be no way of determining the image of x: the rule would not be well-defined in this case. For the case of R^2, this construction is shown in fig. 7.8.

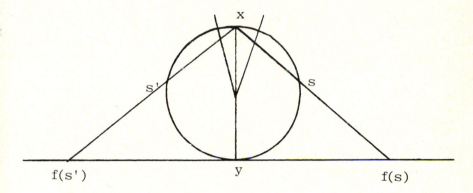

Figure 7.8. A homeomorphism f between $S^1 - (S^1 \cap C)$ and H.

Within the space of linear preferences, the contractible space P^c is extremely general. The cone C can be arbitrarily small, as long as its interior is non-empty. There is thus a direction from which all normals are bounded away. In economic terms, there is one preference from which all others are bounded away: there is one direction in which nobody wants to move. Sen (1970, p. 169) discusses a domain restriction condition entitled "limited agreement"; although it was used quite differently by Sen, it seems that limited agreement, perhaps very limited agreement, is exactly what one has in a space P^c.

Example 2. Next we consider general smooth preferences, as defined in the previous section. In this case, for each point y in the choice space Y, the preference defines a unit vector $p(y)$ which is the normal to the tangent to the indifference surface at y. Unlike the linear case, this normal will typically vary from point to point in Y. However, at any fixed choice $y \in Y$ we have exactly the same structure as in example 1, because a preference p can locally be approximated by a linear preference, the indifference surface of which is the tangent plane to the indifference surface of p at y.

If P is the overall space of preferences we are studying, we let P_y denote its evaluation at the point y, i.e. the space of all normals that elements of P can give rise to at y, or, equivalently, the space of all approximating linear preferences at y. Clearly, if P is not restricted in any way, then P_y is S^{n-1}, by the arguments of the previous example. Hence, the evaluation of P at y, P_y, is non-contractible at any y, and from this it can be shown that P itself is not contractible. The argument in this case is a little complicated, but uses the fact that the contractibility of P would imply that of P_y for every y.

It emerges, then, that the space of smooth preferences is not contractible. What restrictions on it will make it so? One economically appealing sufficient restriction is a generalisation of that considered in the previous example. Let C be a cone with a non-empty interior in R^n. Define a subspace $\tilde{P}$ of the space P of smooth preferences as follows:

$$\tilde{P} = \{p \in P: p(y) \notin C \; \forall y \in Y\}.$$

This is just the set of smooth preferences whose normals never lie in the cone C, i.e. which never increase in a direction in C. As with P^c of example 1, it is a space of preferences such that all individuals agree that there is some particular direction that is unattractive. In particular, the space of all smooth non-decreasing preferences is contained in $\tilde{P}$, and is contractible: the same is true of the space of all smooth, convex, and monotone preferences, a space frequently considered in general equilibrium theory.

The restriction implied by the definition of $\tilde{P}$ is very mild, and clearly many quite general preference spaces are contractible. In fact, weaker restrictions are sufficient to ensure contractibility. For example, the cone C of excluded directions need not be constant. Consider the space

$$\tilde{\tilde{P}} = \{p \in P: p(y) \notin C_y \; \forall y \in Y\},$$

where C_y is now a cone of excluded directions at y which varies with y, and does so in a suitably continuous manner. Then this space may still be shown to be contractible.

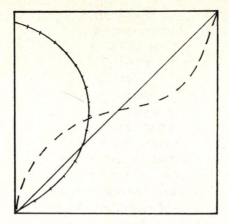

Figure 7.9. Three candidates for D, indicated by ———, ++++, and ———.

Example 3. We have seen two rather similar examples of contractible preference spaces: both were constructed by limiting the set of gradients allowable at any point. The next example is constructed quite differently. Recall that the choice space is I^n, the unit cube in R^n. Let D be a one-dimensional submanifold with a boundary of I^n, the boundaries of D being contained in those of I^n, and D containing the origin. (Such a submanifold is said to be a *neat* submanifold.) D could, for example, be the diagonal ray $\{x \in R^n : x_1 = x_2 = ... = x_n\}$ in I^n, or any continuous deformation of it, or any other path in I^n starting at the origin and meeting the boundary of I^n once more at some point other than the origin. Fig. 7.9 shows possible candidates for D when $n = 2$. For any given D, we shall denote by P^D the family of all C^1 locally integrable preferences which are strictly increasing along D. Fig. 7.10 shows, for a given D in R^2, two preferences which increase along D. Preference spaces P^D were introduced and studied by Chichilnisky (1976), and she shows there that such spaces are homeomorphic to convex spaces, and so in particular are contractible.

The above examples make it clear that from an economic viewpoint contractibility is a very weak condition to impose on the space of preferences, much weaker than most other domain restrictions studied. It is, however, recognisably of the same type as these: all of the sufficient conditions for contractibility discussed above involve in some way limiting the range of permitted variation in individual preferences. This is of course exactly the impact of such conditions as single peakedness or value restrictedness, and indeed it is shown in Chichilnisky (1980b) that contractibility is a generalisation of these earlier domain restrictions.

Figure 7.10.   Two preferences increasing along *D*.

4. Properties of contractible preference spaces

The property of contractibility has now been defined and analysed in some detail. What remains is to study its implications. In this section we therefore summarise the results in which contractibility of the preference space plays an important role. All of these results are stated in detail with proofs elsewhere, so that no more than a review is attempted here.

The first result concerns the classic problem of social choice theory — the existence of "acceptable" social choice rules. This result, proven in Chichilnisky and Heal (1979a), shows that contractibility of the preference space is necessary and sufficient for the existence of social choice rules which are continuous and anonymous, and which respect unanimity. The proof of sufficiency is given here, since it builds upon a point noted in section 2, namely the existence of certain types of aggregation rule on convex or on contractible spaces. This point was first noted in Chichilnisky (1976).

Theorem 1.   If the space of preference profiles is the *k*-fold Cartesian product of the space of preferences, so that all logically possible combinations of preferences are admitted, then a necessary and sufficient condition for the existence of a social choice rule which is continuous, anonymous, and respects unanimity for all $k > 2$ is that the space of preferences P be contractible.

Proof. Let P be a contractible space. Suppose first that P is also convex. By definition, in a convex space averaging is always possible. It follows immediately that a continuous anonymous rule ϕ respecting unanimity exists; for instance, the example considered in section 2, namely

$$\phi(p_1, ..., p_k) = \frac{1}{k} \Sigma p_i,$$

where Σ denoted the vector sum in the space of C^1 vector fields $V(Y)$ induced by summing vectors at each point. The social preference is just the mean of the individual preferences. In fact, even if P is not convex a similar construction can still be used. Note first that since P is a contractible CW complex, it is therefore a retract of a convex set C.

Let r be a retraction from $V(Y)$ onto P. It follows that the composite map

$$\phi(p_1, ..., p_k) = r \phi \left(\frac{1}{k} \Sigma p_i \right)$$

defines a continuous anonymous rule that respects unanimity. Therefore to construct the social preference we perform an averaging operation on the convex space of which P is a retract, and then compose this with the retraction on P. This completes the proof of sufficiency. The proof of necessity is in Chichilnisky and Heal (1979a).

The next result provides a characterisation of the social choice rules that can be defined on a contractible space. It says that all rules which are continuous, anonymous, and respect unanimity are essentially of the type indicated in the proof of theorem 1. More precisely, such rules are all equivalent to the construction in the sufficiency proof in the following sense.

Let $f, g: X \to Y$ be continuous maps of a topological space X into a topological space Y. We say that f is *equivalent to* g if there exists a continuous map $F: X \times [0,1] \to Y$ such that

$$F(x,0) = f(x) \ \forall x \in X,$$
$$F(x,1) = g(x) \ \forall x \in X.$$

This is obviously reminiscent of the definition of contractibility, and says in essence that two maps are equivalent if they can be linked by a parameterised family of maps $F(x, t)$ which are jointly continuous in x and the parameter t.

Theorem 2. Let the preference space P be contractible. Then any continuous anonymous social choice rule that respects unanimity is equivalent to a rule f constructed as follows. Take a convex space C of which P is a retract, with r the retraction, $r: C \to P$. Then define a convex averaging rule on C, and let f be the composition of this with r.

The proof of this is also in Chichilnisky and Heal (1979a).

The next theorems relate to the strategic properties of social choice rules. To study these we use a slightly different framework from that above. We now suppose that a preference can be represented as an element of a finite-dimensional space R^q: preferences are functions (e.g. polynomials) which can be fully defined by q parameters. The space of preferences is therefore a subset P of the space R^q. Example 1 of the previous section has this characteristic. There we saw that the space of linear preferences on R^n is identical with S^{n-1}, a subset of R^n. A social choice rule is then a continuous map from $(P)^k$ to R^q. The outcome, a social preference, is an element of $P \subset R^q$. If p_i^* is individual i's true preference, then it is assumed that agent i behaves strategically so as to obtain an outcome as near as possible to p_i^*. We are therefore concerned with games, where the game form is the social choice rule f, the strategy spaces are P, the space of possible preferences, and individual i's objective is to minimise the distance between the outcome and p_i^*.

We say that a social choice rule f is *straightforward* (or strategy-proof or non-manipulable) if for each agent i, p_i^* is a dominant strategy, i.e. if for each i:

$$d[f(P_i^*, P_{-i}), P_i^*] \leqslant d[f(P_i, P_{-i}), P_i^*], \forall P_i,$$

where $d(x, y)$ is the Euclidean distance between points x and y, and p_{-i} is the vector of strategies of all agents other than i. We say that a rule is *non-trivially straightforward* if it is straightforward and neither dictatorial nor constant. The point of this is that dictatorial and constant rules are clearly straightforward, and in discussing the existence of straightforward rules one may wish to eliminate these cases. Proofs of theorems 3 and 4 can be found in Chichilnisky (1981).

Theorem 3. Let $f: P^k \to P$ be continuous, anonymous, and non-trivially straightforward. Then P is contractible.

Contractibility of the preference space is thus a necessary condition for the existence of anonymous straightforward rules. In outline, the proof of this result is as follows. One first proves that if f is anonymous and straightforward, then it must also respect unanimity. This implies that f is continuous, anonymous, and respects unanimity. Theorem 1 then implies that P must be contractible, for otherwise such an f would not exist.

Theorem 4. Let $P \subset R^q$ be a contractible manifold with a simply connected boundary. Then there exists a continuous $f: P^k \to P$, and preferences over outcomes in P such that f is non-trivially straightforward.

The assumption here that P is contractible manifold with simply connected boundary implies, as remarked in section 2, that P is homeomorphic to a convex set. In particular, P can be taken as homeomorphic to the unit hypercube. The proof of theorem 4 works by deforming P into the cube, constructing a suitable f and suitable preferences over outcomes in this case, and then pulling these back to P via the homeomorphism.

References

Arrow, Kenneth and Frank H. Hahn (1971) *General Competitive Analysis* (Holden-Day).

Black, Duncan (1948) "On the Rationale of Group Decision-Making", *Journal of Political Economy*, 56.

Chichilnisky, Graciela (1976) "Manifolds of Preferences and Equilibria", Report No. 27, Project on Efficiency of Decision-making in Economic Systems, Harvard University.

Chichilnisky, Graciela (1979) "On Fixed Point Theorems and Social Choice Paradoxes", *Economics Letters*.

Chichilnisky, Graciela (1980a) "Social Choice and the Topology of Preference Spaces", *Advances in Mathematics*.

Chichilnisky, Graciela (1980b) "Contractibility and Single-peakedness", Essex Economics papers.

Chichilnisky, Graciela (1981) "Strategy and Outcome Spaces Admitting Straightforward Games", Discussion Paper.

Chichilnisky, Graciela (1982) "Social Aggregation Rules and Continuity", *Quarterly Journal of Economics*, February.

Chichilnisky, Graciela and Geoffrey Heal (1979a) "Neccessary and Sufficient Conditions for a Resolution of the Social Choice Paradox", *Journal of Economic Theory*, to appear.

Chichilnisky, Graciela and Geoffrey Heal (1979b) "The Welfare Economics of Competitive General Equilibrium with Variable Endowments", Columbia University Economics Discussion paper.

Chichilnisky, Graciela and Geoffrey Heal (1979c) "Social Choice with Infinite Populations", Columbia University Economics Discussion paper.

Chichilnisky, Graciela and Geoffrey Heal (1981) "Incentive Compatibility and Local Simplicity", Essex Discussion Paper.

Dasgupta, Partha, Peter Hammond and Eric Maskin (1979) "The Implementation of Social Choice Rules – General Results on Incentive Compatibility", *Review of Economic Studies*.

Debreu, Gerard (1953) "A Social Equilibrium Existence Theorem", *Proceedings of the National Academy of Sciences of the U.S.A.*

Debreu, Gerard (1972) "Smooth Preferences", *Econometrica*, 40 (4), 606-616.

Heal, Geoffrey (1981) "The Equivalence of Optima and Saddle-points for Non-convex Programmes", *Advances in Applied Mathematics*, to appear.

Kuhn, Harold (1954) "Contractibility and Convexity", *Transactions of the American Mathematical Society*.

Maunder, Richard (1970) *Algebraic Topology* (Cambridge University Press).

Milnor, John (1963a) *Morse Theory* (Princeton University Press).

Milnor, John (1963b) *Topology from a Differentiable Viewpoint* (University of Virginia Press).

Moulin, Hervé (1980) "Strategy-proofness and Straightforwardness", *Public Choice*.

Pattanaik, Prasanta and Amartya Sen (1969) "Necessary and Sufficient Conditions for Rational Choice Under Majority Decision", *Journal of Economic Theory*.

Sen, Amartya (1970) *Collective Choice and Social Welfare* (Holden-Day).

PART IB

THE ETHICAL ASPECTS OF SOCIAL CHOICE: JUSTICE, OPTIMALITY, AND WELFARE

CHAPTER 8

Resolving conflicting views of justice in social choice

KOTARO SUZUMURA*

Hitotsubashi University

0. Introduction

In order to introduce our problem intuitively and to motivate our approach in-
formally, let us start with a simple problem of dividing a cake among three individuals. Consider the following four alternative divisions:

$$x = (\tfrac{1}{2}, \tfrac{1}{2}, 0), \quad y = (\tfrac{1}{2}, 0, \tfrac{1}{2}), \quad z = (0, \tfrac{1}{2}, \tfrac{1}{2}), \quad w = (\tfrac{1}{3}, \tfrac{1}{3}, \tfrac{1}{3}),$$

where the component i of each vector denotes the proportion of the cake to be
given to individual i ($i = 1, 2, 3$). The subjective preferences over these divisions
by each and every individual, which represent each one's preference ranking of
the alternatives from one's personal point of view, are likely to be (R_1: $[x, y]$,
w, z), (R_2: $[x, z]$, w, y), and (R_3: $[y, z]$, w, x), where R_i denotes the preference
ordering over the set $S = \{x, y, z, w\}$ by individual i ($i = 1, 2, 3$).[1] Equipped only
with this intrapersonally ordinal and interpersonally non-comparable profile (R_1,
R_2, R_3), which alternative out of S should this society of three choose? This is
probably the simplest possible, yet non-trivial distributional problem and any sensible social choice rule should help us resolve this conflict situation.

* I am indebted to Professors Georges Bordes, Peter Coughlin, Bhaskar Dutta, Peter
Hammond, and Amartya Sen for their discussions with me on the topics related to this chap-
ter. Thanks are also due for helpful comments of the referees appointed by the editors.
Needless to say I am solely responsible for any remaining defects.

[1] Preference orderings are written horizontally with the more preferred state to the left
of the less preferred; the indifferent states, if any, being put together by square brackets.

Social Choice and Welfare, edited by P.K. Pattanaik and M. Salles
© *North-Holland Publishing Company, 1983*

Consider first what the simple majority decision rule — the SMD rule for short hereafter — recommends in this situation. We may easily verify that x and y, y and z, and z and x all tie with each other, while each element of $C(S) = \{x, y, z\}$ beats w by a two to one majority. There is no Condorcet winner in S, which beats all other alternatives in the SMD contest, so that there is no unambiguous choice recommended by the SMD rule. One way to proceed is to declare that each one of x, y, and z is equally eligible from S in the exclusion of w. This verdict is endorsed by the transitive closure extension of the SMD rule analysed by Bordes (1976) and others, which "does provide an interesting resolution of the social choice paradox with what appears to be a relatively slight weakening of the condition of rationality of social preference" (Arrow, 1977b, p. 620). Note that the Borda method of rank-order decision as well as the Copeland method, both of which extend the SMD rule to the non-binary choice situation, also declare that each element of $C(S)$, among the elements of which social indifferences are declared to prevail, is strictly better than w. Remember, however, that eventually a single alternative should be chosen from among alternatives in $C(S)$, and whatever tie-breaking mechanism we may use for this purpose, a fact remains that it is "best", according to these celebrated social choice rules, to sacrifice an unlucky individual for the benefit of the lucky majority coalition. It seems to us that a social choice rule which always empowers a majority in the resolution of distributional conflict exemplified above, *even though there is a perfectly egalitarian alternative which is available for implementation*, is most likely to be rejected in the primordial game of constitutional choice, in which individuals choose a rule of conflict resolution once and for all without knowing the actual realization of the social and personal contingencies.[2]

To make progress, let us suppose that information is now available about individuals' extended preferences of the form: It is better (or worse) for me to be in individual i's position in one social state than to be in individual j's position in another social state. People in fact seem to be prepared to make comparisons of this type and in the context of our specified example, it makes good sense to assume that the following extended preference *ordering* is commonly held by all individuals: $[(x, 1), (x, 2), (y, 1), (y, 3), (z, 2), (z, 3)], [(w, 1), (w, 2), (w, 3)],$ $[(x, 3), (y, 2), (z, 1)]$, where $(x, 1)$ signifies to be put in the position of individual 1 when the social state x prevails and so on. Note that the *subjective* preference or-

---

[2]   Suppose that the even-chance random mechanism is used to single out the final choice out of $C(S) = \{x, y, z\}$ and consider an individual whose von Neumann–Morgenstern utility function v exhibits risk aversion. The even-chance lottery with prizes x, y, and z gives him the expected utility of $(2/3) v (1/2) + (1/3) v (0)$, which is smaller than $v (1/3)$ generated by the certain choice of w. Therefore risk-averting individuals will not voluntarily agree to adopt such a conflict resolution rule in the primordial game of constitutional choice.

derings subsumed in this extended preference ordering are precisely those which were originally specified. Equipped with this wider informational basis of social choice, there are two possible approaches which suggest themselves in the context of distributional social choice problem.

(a) According to the extended preference, $(x, 1)$ is better than $(x, 3)$, $(y, 3)$ is better than $(y, 2)$, and $(z, 2)$ is better than $(z, 1)$. It then follows that individual 3 envies individual 1's position if the state x prevails, individual 2 envies individual 3's position if the state y prevails, while individual 1 envies individual 2's position if the state z prevails. If we say, following Foley (1967) and Varian (1974, 1975) that a social state is *equitable* if and only if no individual envies the position of another individual when the chosen state prevails, there is only one state in S which is equitable in this sense, i.e. w. Since w is Pareto-efficient in S as well, it is the unique *fair* state in S in the Foley–Varian sense. Why not choose w for this good reason?

(b) Consider the fate of the worst-off individual under respective social states. On inspection, it turns out that it is better to be in anyone's position under w than to be in the worst-off individual's position under x, y, or z. Let us say, following Rawls (1971) and Sen (1970), that a social state is more just than another state if the welfare level of the worst-off individual under the latter state is less than the corresponding level under the former state. Since we are interested in the choice of a constitutional conflict resolution rule behind the "veil of ignorance" (which in particular prevents us from knowing who is going to be the worst-off individual under the state to be realized), why do we not design our rule so that the resolution by the majority voting is applied only to those states which are justice-undominated? In our cake-division problem, there is only one justice-undominated state in S, namely w, so that it is *the* choice without any further ado.

In this chapter, we will explore the avenue suggested by this simple exercise of a cake-division problem. In so doing, an attempt will be made to see how the extended sympathy approach in social choice theory à la Suppes (1966), Arrow (1963, pp. 114–115, 1977b) and Sen (1970, ch. 9 and 9*) fares in the context of Arrovian impossibility theorems. It is also hoped that our analysis will shed some light on Harsanyi's (1955) concepts of *impersonality, ethical preferences*, and *subjective preferences* and the interconnection thereof, supplementing Pattanaik's (1968) seminal contribution.

1. Extended preferences, equity, and justice

1.1. Extended preferences which designate the welfare comparisons of the extended sympathy type may be operationally formulated by an extended utility function defined on the Cartesian product $X \times N$, where X denotes the set of all conceivable social states and $N = \{1, 2, ..., n\}$ stands for the set of all individuals. We assume that $2 \leqslant n < \infty$. Let E stand for the set of all real numbers and let $\mathscr{U}$ be the set of all extended utility functions, i.e. the set of all functions from $X \times N$ into E. When $u \in \mathscr{U}$, $x, y \in X$, and $i, j \in N$ are specified, the inequality $u(x, i) \geqslant u(y, j)$ is construed to mean that it is no worse (in the evaluator's judgement) to be an individual i in the social state x than to be an individual j in the social state y. We assume that every individual $i \in N$ has an extended utility function $u_i \in \mathscr{U}$ of his own, which represents i's intrapersonal and intersituational comparisons of welfare in the sense of Alchian (1953) and "[i]n effect, we are asking each agent to put himself in the position of each other agents to determine if that is a better or worse position than the one he is now in" (Varian, 1975, p. 240).

A list of extended utility functions, one function for each individual, will be called a *profile* and alternative profiles will be indexed by $\alpha \in \mathscr{A}$ like $\alpha = (u_1^\alpha, u_2^\alpha, ..., u_n^\alpha)$, where $\mathscr{A}$ denotes the set of all logically possible profiles.

$\mathscr{S}$ denotes the set of all non-empty *finite* subsets of X, each and every $S \in \mathscr{S}$ being construed to represent a set of available social states under the specified environmental conditions. A *choice function* on $\mathscr{S}$ is a function C which maps each and every $S \in \mathscr{S}$ into a non-empty subset $C(S)$ of S.

What we call a *collective choice rule* (CCR) is a method or rule of choosing, for each profile, a *social choice function* (SCF) on $\mathscr{S}$. Given a profile $\alpha = (u_1^\alpha, u_2^\alpha, ..., u_n^\alpha) \in \mathscr{A}$, a CCR Ψ amalgamates this into an SCF: $C^\alpha = \Psi(\alpha)$. When a set $S \in \mathscr{S}$ of available states is specified, $C^\alpha(S)$ represents the set of socially chosen states from S when the profile α prevails. Note that this concept of a CCR is nothing other than a formalization of what we intuitively understand by the conflict resolution rule.

1.2.   Take any profile $\alpha = (u_1^\alpha, u_2^\alpha, ..., u_n^\alpha) \in \mathscr{A}$ and let individual i's *subjective preference ordering* R_i^α be defined by

$$R_i^\alpha = \{(x, y) \in X \times X \mid u_i^\alpha(x, i) \geqslant u_i^\alpha(y, i)\} \tag{1}$$

for each and every $i \in N$, which expresses i's actual preferences on the basis of his personal interests. Clearly, R_i^α is an ordering on X, being connected and transitive.[3] The first desideratum which we want our CCR to satisfy is the Pareto una-

---

[3]   We refer to Arrow (1963, ch. II) and Sen (1970, ch. 1*) for the standard terminology on the properties of a binary relation.

nimity condition, which refers only to the profile of subjective preference orderings corresponding to a given profile.[4]

Condition P (Pareto principle). For every profile $\alpha = (u_1^\alpha, u_2^\alpha, ..., u_n^\alpha) \in \mathscr{A}$ and every $x, y \in X$, if $(x, y) \in \cap_{i \in N} P(R_i^\alpha)$, then $[x \in S \to y \notin C^\alpha(S)]$ for all $S \in \mathscr{S}$, where $C^\alpha = \Psi(\alpha)$.

Condition SP (Strong Pareto principle). For every profile $\alpha = (u_1^\alpha, u_2^\alpha, ..., u_n^\alpha) \in \mathscr{A}$ and every $x, y \in X$, if $(x, y) \in P(\cap_{i \in N} R_i^\alpha)$, then $[x \in S \to y \notin C^\alpha(S)]$ for all $S \in \mathscr{S}$, where $C^\alpha = \Psi(\alpha)$.

1.3. We are now ready to examine how the suggested resolutions of the cake-division problem fare in our generalized context of designing a satisfactory CCR. The first approach via the concept of equity as no-envy à la Foley (1967) and Varian (1974, 1975) has been explored already in Suzumura (1981a, 1981b), so that we will focus our attention on the second approach referring occasionally to the first approach only to the extent that may help highlight the second approach by contrast.

Recollect that our problem is to design a "just" CCR based on the profile of extended utility functions, which will be voluntarily agreed on by all individuals in the primordial game of constitutional choice. Our second approach provided one reasonable argument to this effect in the special context of the cake-division problem where a single extended preference ordering is commonly held by all individuals and the Rawls–Sen maximin principle of justice represents the moral principle shared by all. How can we generalize this?

Our generalization begins with the concept of a *principle of justice* which is a rule by which the extended utility function incorporating the extended sympathy type intersituational comparisons is boiled down to an ethical judgement over the set of social states. Let ω denote a principle of justice. For each extended utility function $u \in \mathscr{U}$, $\omega(u)$ denotes a binary relation on X such that $x \in X$ is judged by the evaluator whose moral sense of justice is represented by ω to be at least as just as $y \in X$ if and only if $(x, y) \in \omega(u)$. We require that $\omega(u)$ always satisfies a logical property of transitivity. If, in addition, $\omega(u)$ satisfies connectedness as well, we say that ω is a complete principle of justice. There is one more re-

---

[4] In what follows, $P(\cdot)$ denotes the *asymmetric part* of the binary relation in the parenthesis, so that

$$P(R) = \{(x, y) \in X \times X \mid (x, y) \in R \text{ and } (y, x) \notin R\}$$

for every binary relation R on X.

quirement on the admissible principle of justice, which arguably underlies *any* moral value judgements. As an auxiliary step, let Π_N stand for the set of all permutations on N and, for any extended utility function $u \in \mathcal{U}$, define a binary relation $\omega_S(u)$ by

$$\forall x, y \in X: (x,y) \in \omega_S(u) \longleftrightarrow \exists \pi \in \Pi_N: \begin{cases} \forall i \in N: u(x,i) \geqslant u(y,\pi(i)) \\ \text{and} \\ \exists j \in N: u(x,j) > u(y,\pi(j)). \end{cases} \tag{2}$$

Note that $(x, y) \in \omega_S(u)$ holds true if and only if we may start from the utility distribution under y to arrive at that under x following two steps: (1) interpersonal permutation of utility levels at y, and then (2) making Pareto-wise improvement. By making interpersonal permutation of utility levels ethically irrelevant, the ethical judgements incorporated in $\omega_S(u)$ crystallize the intuitive idea of *impartiality* in an operational way. In what follows we require that any admissible principle of justice ω satisfies the following condition.

Condition IM (Impartiality).   For every extended utility function $u \in \mathcal{U}$, $\omega_S(u)$ $\subset P(\omega(u))$ holds true.

Note in particular that ω_S in itself is a legitimate principle of justice, which is known as Suppes' (1966) grading principle of justice.[5] Let us emphasize that the condition IM is indeed a fairly weak and natural requirement of impartiality, which is satisfied by a number of well-known principles, e.g. Rawls (1971) and Sen (1970, p. 138) and the Benthamite principle of utilitarian justice.[6]

1.4.   Before going further, it is useful to have a brief look at the no-envy equity concept due to Foley (1967) and others in this context. Take any profile $\alpha = (u_1^\alpha, u_2^\alpha, ..., u_n^\alpha) \in \mathcal{A}$ and define, for each $i \in N$ and each $S \in \mathcal{S}$, a set

$$E_{qi}^\alpha(S) = \{x \in S \mid \forall j \in N: u_i^\alpha(x, i) \geqslant u_i^\alpha(x,j)\}. \tag{3}$$

If $x \in E_{qi}^\alpha(S)$, individual i feels no envy to anybody else, so that x is no-envy-equitable as far as individual i is concerned. A state x is Foley-equitable in S if and only if $x \in \cap_{i \in N} E_{qi}^\alpha(S)$. To examine the ethical relevance of this equity-as-no-envy concept, we define the no-less-equitable relation for individual i by

---

[5]   It is shown by Sen (1970, theorem 9*1) that $\omega_S(u)$ is a strict partial ordering on X, being asymmetric and transitive, for every extended utility function $u \in \mathcal{U}$.

[6]   See Arrow (1977a), d'Aspremont and Gevers (1977), Hammond (1976, 1979) and Sen (1970, p. 158, Footnote 4, and p. 159, Theorem 9*7, 1977).

$$R_{qi}^\alpha = \{(x,y) \in X \times X \mid \sim [y \in E_{qi}^\alpha(X) \text{ and } x \notin E_{qi}^\alpha(X)]\}, \tag{4}$$

where $\sim$ denotes logical negation. It is easy to verify that R_{qi}^α is an ordering on X. Note, however, that R_{qi}^α fails to satisfy the condition IM, thereby casting rather serious doubt on its ethical relevance.

Example 1 (Suzumura, 1982). Let there be two individuals, 1 and 2, and two social states, x and y. Let a profile $\alpha = (u_1^\alpha, u_2^\alpha)$ be such that

$$u_1^\alpha(x,2) > u_1^\alpha(x,1) > u_1^\alpha(y,1) \geqq u_1^\alpha(y,2).$$

Note that individual 1 feels that x is strictly better than y whoever he happens to be, so that it is intuitively appealing to say that x is a better state than y in individual 1's impartial judgement. Yet this is not endorsed by the "ethical" ordering R_{q1}^α, since $E_{q1}^\alpha(\{x,y\}) = \{y\}$ entails $(y,x) \in P(R_{q1}^\alpha)$. ∎

1.5. Returning to the main stream of our discourse, let us now assume that a list of the impartial principles of justice, one principle ω_i for each individual $i \in N$, is given, which summarizes the distribution of individuals' impartial moral sense of justice in the society.

Let a profile $\alpha = (u_1^\alpha, u_2^\alpha, ..., u_n^\alpha) \in \mathscr{A}$ be given. Then we obtain, for each and every individual $i \in N$, his "social" preferences over social states $\omega_i(u_i^\alpha)$, which corresponds to what Harsanyi (1955) calls his *ethical preferences* or his *social welfare function*. We also obtain his *subjective preferences* R_i^α, which are defined by (1). Corresponding to a profile α, we have thus generated a *subjective profile* $\sigma(\alpha) = (R_1^\alpha, R_2^\alpha, ..., R_n^\alpha)$ and an *ethical profile* $\omega(\alpha) = (\omega_1(u_1^\alpha), \omega_2(u_2^\alpha), ..., \omega_n(u_n^\alpha))$. Note that, in this framework,

cach individual is supposed to have a social welfare function of his own, expressing his own individual value — in the same way as each individual has a utility function of his own, expressing his own individual taste. ... Even if both an individual's social welfare function and his utility function in a sense express his own individual preferences, they must express preferences of different sorts: the former must express what this individual prefers (or, rather, would prefer) on the basis of impersonal social considerations alone, and the latter must express what he actually prefers, whether on the basis of his personal interests or on any other basis. The former may be called his "ethical" preferences, the latter his "subjective" preferences.[7]

[7] Harsanyi (1955, p. 315).

Both subjective and ethical preferences express authentic individual preferences and our problem is to design a CCR which aggregates this double heterogeneity as it were into a "just" social choice function.

2. Non-paternalism and the lexical combination of preferences

2.1. Unless otherwise circumscribed, it is desirable to have a CCR having the widest possible domain of applicability, the extreme form of this requirement being the following:

Condition U (Unrestricted domain). The domain of Ψ consists of all logically possible profiles.

A very simple impossibility theorem due essentially to Sen (1970, pp. 149–150) negates the possibility of having a CCR with such a wide domain, which also serves to motivate an axiom which requires the sympathetic acceptance of others' subjective preferences by each and every member of the society. Consider the following unanimity requirements on the ethical profile, which are the counterpart of the Pareto unanimity condition on the subjective profile.

Condition JU (Justice unanimity condition). For every profile $\alpha = (u_1^\alpha, u_2^\alpha, ..., u_n^\alpha) \in \mathcal{A}$ and every $x, y \in X$, if $(x, y) \in \cap_{i \in N} P(\omega_i(u_i^\alpha))$, then $[x \in S \rightarrow y \notin C^\alpha(S)]$ for all $S \in \mathcal{S}$, where $C^\alpha = \Psi(\alpha)$.

Condition SJU (Strong justice unanimity condition). For every profile $\alpha = (u_1^\alpha, u_2^\alpha, ..., u_n^\alpha) \in \mathcal{A}$ and every $x, y \in X$, if $(x, y) \in P(\cap_{i \in N} \omega_i(u_i^\alpha))$, then $[x \in S \rightarrow y \notin C^\alpha(S)]$ for all $S \in \mathcal{S}$, where $C^\alpha = \Psi(\alpha)$.

Theorem 1. There exists no CCR which satisfies U (Unrestricted domain), SP (Strong Pareto principle), and JU (Justice unanimity condition).[8]

Proof. Suppose that there exists an eligible CCR Ψ. Take any $x, y \in X$ such that $x \neq y$, and let a profile $\alpha = (u_1^\alpha, u_2^\alpha, ..., u_n^\alpha)$ be such that

$$u_1^\alpha(x, 2) > u_1^\alpha(y, 1) > u_1^\alpha(x, 1) > u_1^\alpha(y, 2),$$

$$u_2^\alpha(x, 1) > u_2^\alpha(y, 2) > u_2^\alpha(x, 2) > u_2^\alpha(y, 1),$$

---

[8] It is easy, if tedious, to weaken the condition SP into the condition P. See Kelly (1978, theorem 8-12).

$$\forall i \in N \backslash \{1, 2\}, \forall (z, k) \in \{x, y\} \times \{1, 2\}: u_i^\alpha(z, k) = u_2^\alpha(z, k),$$

$$\forall i \in N, \forall k \in N \backslash \{1, 2\}: u_i^\alpha(x, k) = u_i^\alpha(y, k).$$

We have

$$(y, x) \in P(R_1^\alpha) \cap P(R_2^\alpha) \cap \left[\bigcap_{k \in N \backslash \{1,2\}} I(R_k^\alpha) \right],$$

so that the condition SP entails that $\{y\} = C^\alpha(\{x, y\})$. On the other hand, we may easily see that $(x, y) \in \omega_S(u_i^\alpha)$ for all $i \in N$, so that we have $(x, y) \in \cap_{i \in N} P(\omega_i(u_i^\alpha))$ by impartiality. It then follows from the condition JU that $\{x\} = C^\alpha(\{x, y\})$, a contradiction. ∎

2.2. We need not look for long in order to track down the culprit of this simple impossibility theorem. Take any profile $\alpha = (u_1^\alpha, u_2^\alpha, ..., u_n^\alpha) \in \mathscr{A}$ and let a binary relation R_{ij}^α on X be defined for every $i, j \in N$ by

$$\forall x, y \in X: (x, y) \in R_{ij}^\alpha \longleftrightarrow u_i^\alpha(x, j) \geqslant u_i^\alpha(y, j). \tag{5}$$

Note that $(x, y) \in R_{ij}^\alpha$ means that individual i judges that it is no worse for individual j to be in x rather than in y, while $(x, y) \in R_j^\alpha$ means that j himself feels to be no worse in x than in y. It is clear then that $R_i^\alpha \equiv R_{ii}^\alpha$ for all $i \in N$. If we now examine the profile α which we used in establishing theorem 1, we may immediately recognize that $(y, x) \in P(R_1^\alpha)$, $(x, y) \in P(R_{21}^\alpha)$, $(y, x) \in P(R_2^\alpha)$, and $(x, y) \in P(R_{12}^\alpha)$. There is a clear pattern in this. Although individual 1 feels better to be in y rather than in x, individual 2 maintains that it is better for individual 1 to be in x rather than in y, and vice versa. No wonder we cannot find a CCR which accommodates such a mutually meddlesome preference pattern.[9] Once this general feature is recognized, it is easy to get rid of the source of trouble, which lies in the fact that each individual makes comparisons of individuals' positions in terms of his own tastes without making any effort to take into consideration the other's subjective preferences when he places himself in the position of others through the imaginary exchange of circumstances. Let us now introduce the following condition due to Sen (1970, p. 156), which stipulates straightforwardly that "each individual is required to have a nonpaternalistic view of other individuals' welfare (in the sense that the judgement of any individual

---

[9] It is indeed quite well recognized that "without sympathetic identification or some such assumption, the analysis may lead to some odd results" (Pattanaik, 1968, p. 157). See also Sen (1970, pp. 149-150).

regarding his own relative welfare positions in any two social states is being respected)" (Pazner, 1979, p. 163).

Condition UID (Unrestricted domain under identity axiom). The domain of Ψ consists of all profiles α such that $R_{ij}^\alpha = R_j^\alpha$ holds true for all $i, j \in N$.

Even though the admissible class of profiles is restricted so that the identity axiom is satisfied, the subjective and ethical preferences, respectively, have every reason to differ among individuals. Note also that an individual's subjective preferences, which represent his personal likes and dislikes, and his ethical preferences, which represent his value judgements incorporating his impartial sense of justice, may well differ from each other for the simple reason that we do not always prefer what we consider to be ethically just for the society. Therefore the restriction of the domain of a CCR to the extent of replacing the condition U by the condition UID still leaves us quite substantial problems of preference aggregation.

2.3. In addition to the already stated impartiality condition, we assume that each and every ω_i $(i \in N)$ satisfies the following:

Condition IE (Informational efficiency). If u^1, $u^2 \in \mathcal{U}$ and $S \in \mathcal{S}$ are such that $u^1(x, i) = u^2(x, i)$ for all $(x, i) \in S \times N$, then $\omega(u^1) \cap (S \times S) = \omega(u^2) \cap (S \times S)$.

This is essentially a requirement of informational efficiency of the principle of justice ω, since a principle satisfying it need only be fed interpositional welfare information about the opportunity set S in comparing relative justice among social states in S. Note that ω_B (the Benthamite principle of utilitarian justice), ω_R (the Rawlsian principle of leximin justice), and ω_S (the Suppes' grading principle of justice) all satisfy this informational efficiency requirement.

2.4. Let us now define several concrete CCRs whose domain is specified by

$$\mathcal{A}_{ID} = \{\alpha = (u_1^\alpha, u_2^\alpha, ..., u_n^\alpha) \mid \forall i, j \in N: R_{ij}^\alpha = R_j^\alpha\}. \tag{6}$$

Take any $\alpha \in \mathcal{A}_{ID}$ and let $\sigma(\alpha) = (R_1^\alpha, R_2^\alpha, ..., R_n^\alpha)$ and $\omega(\alpha) = (\omega_1(u_1^\alpha), \omega_2(u_2^\alpha), ..., \omega_n(u_n^\alpha))$ be, respectively, the corresponding subjective and ethical profiles. Let M_ϵ^α denote the simple majority relation with respect to the ethical profile $\omega(\alpha)$ corresponding to the profile α, namely $(x, y) \in M_\epsilon^\alpha$ if and only if

$$\#\{i \in N \mid (x, y) \in \omega_i(u_i^\alpha)\} \geqslant \#\{i \in N \mid (y, x) \in \omega_i(u_i^\alpha)\} \tag{7}$$

holds true, where # denotes the cardinality of a set thereinafter. Similarly, M_σ^α denotes the simple majority relation with respect to the subjective profile $\sigma(\alpha)$ corresponding to the profile α, namely $(x, y) \in M_\sigma^\alpha$ if and only if

$$\#\{i \in N \mid (x, y) \in R_i^\alpha\} \geqslant \#\{i \in N \mid (y, x) \in R_i^\alpha\} \tag{8}$$

holds true. Take any $S \in \mathscr{S}$ and let $C_\epsilon^\alpha(S)$ and $C_\sigma^\alpha(S)$ be defined, respectively, by

$$C_\epsilon^\alpha(S) = \{x \in S \mid \forall y \in S: (y, x) \notin P(\omega_N(\alpha))\} \tag{9}$$

and

$$C_\sigma^\alpha(S) = \{x \in S \mid \forall y \in S: (y, x) \notin P(R_N^\alpha)\}, \tag{10}$$

where $\omega_N(\alpha) = \cap_{i \in N} \omega_i(u_i^\alpha)$ and $R_N^\alpha = \cap_{i \in N} R_i^\alpha$. Note that $C_\sigma^\alpha(S)$ is nothing but the Pareto-optimal subset of S, given the profile α, and $C_\epsilon^\alpha(S)$ may be interpreted similarly. Note also that both $C_\epsilon^\alpha(S)$ and $C_\sigma^\alpha(S)$ are non-empty subsets of S for each $S \in \mathscr{S}$ and each $\alpha \in \mathscr{A}_{\mathrm{ID}}$, because $\omega_N(\alpha)$ and R_N^α are transitive by construction. It is easy to verify that

$$\forall S \in \mathscr{S}: C_\epsilon^\alpha(S) \subset C_\sigma^\alpha(S). \tag{11}$$

Suffice it to notice that we have $P(R_N^\alpha) \subset P(\omega_N(\alpha))$, which follows from the impartiality of each ω_i $(i \in N)$ and $P(R_N^\alpha) \subset \omega_S(u_i^\alpha)$ for all $i \in N$.

Let $M_\epsilon^\alpha(S) = M_\epsilon^\alpha \cap (S \times S)$ and $M_\sigma^\alpha(S) = M_\sigma^\alpha \cap (S \times S)$ denote the restriction of M_ϵ^α and M_σ^α on S, respectively, and let $T(M_\epsilon^\alpha(S))$ and $T(M_\sigma^\alpha(S))$ be the transitive closure of $M_\epsilon^\alpha(S)$ and $M_\sigma^\alpha(S)$, respectively.[10] With these definitions in hand, we may now define two functions $C_{\epsilon\tau}^\alpha$ and $C_{\sigma\tau}^\alpha$ on $\mathscr{S}$ by

$$\forall S \in \mathscr{S}: \begin{cases} C_{\epsilon\tau}^\alpha(S) = \{x \in S \mid \forall y \in S: (x, y) \in T(M_\epsilon^\alpha(S))\} \\ \text{and} \\ C_{\sigma\tau}^\alpha(S) = \{x \in S \mid \forall y \in S: (x, y) \in T(M_\sigma^\alpha(S))\}. \end{cases} \tag{12}$$

---

[10] The transitive closure of a binary relation R on X is the smallest transitive superset of R, the formal definition thereof being as follows. For any two binary relations, R^1 and R^2, let the composition thereof, $R^1 R^2$, be defined by $(x, y) \in R^1 R^2$ if and only if $(x, z) \in R^1$ and $(z, y) \in R^2$ for some $z \in X$. To define the transitive closure $T(R)$ of R, let a sequence $R(t)$, $t = 0, 1, 2, \ldots$, be defined by $R(0) = R$, $R(t) = RR(t - 1)$ for $t \geqslant 2$. Then $T(R) = \cup_{t=0}^{\infty} R(t)$.

In view of the transitivity of $T(M_\epsilon^\alpha(S))$ and $T(M_\sigma^\alpha(S))$ for each $S \in \mathscr{S}$ and each $\alpha \in \mathscr{A}_{\mathrm{ID}}$, both $C_{\epsilon\tau}^\alpha$ and $C_{\sigma\tau}^\alpha$ are well-defined choice functions on $\mathscr{S}$. $C_{\epsilon\tau}^\alpha$ and $C_{\sigma\tau}^\alpha$, in their turn, are instrumental in defining the following functions: $C_{\epsilon\epsilon}^\alpha, C_{\epsilon\sigma}^\alpha, C_{\sigma\epsilon}^\alpha$, and $C_{\sigma\sigma}^\alpha$ on $\mathscr{S}$ by $C_{\epsilon\epsilon}^\alpha(S) = C_{\epsilon\tau}^\alpha(C_\epsilon^\alpha(S))$, $C_{\epsilon\sigma}^\alpha(S) = C_{\epsilon\tau}^\alpha(C_\sigma^\alpha(S))$, $C_{\sigma\epsilon}^\alpha(S) = C_{\sigma\tau}^\alpha(C_\epsilon^\alpha(S))$, and $C_{\sigma\sigma}^\alpha(S) = C_{\sigma\tau}^\alpha(C_\sigma^\alpha(S))$ for all $S \in \mathscr{S}$. Clearly, $C_{\epsilon\epsilon}^\alpha, C_{\epsilon\sigma}^\alpha, C_{\sigma\epsilon}^\alpha$, and $C_{\sigma\sigma}^\alpha$ are all well-defined choice functions on $\mathscr{S}$, so that by associating each one of these choice functions with the profile $\alpha \in \mathscr{A}_{\mathrm{ID}}$ we have started from, we have completed our description of a series of CCRs, which are to be denoted by $\Psi_{\epsilon\epsilon}, \Psi_{\epsilon\sigma}, \Psi_{\sigma\epsilon}$, and $\Psi_{\sigma\sigma}$, respectively.

2.5. Complicated though our procedure in defining these CCRs may look, they represent in fact quite intuitive ideas. They use in common the transitive closure of the SMD rule restricted to the efficiency frontier. The use of the transitive closure is motivated by the need to circumvent the well-known majority voting cycle, whereas restricting it to the efficiency frontier is motivated by the need to avoid the choice of an inefficient state from the opportunity set. $\Psi_{\epsilon\epsilon}$ uses only the ethical profile in defining the SMD rule as well as in defining the efficiency frontier and $\Psi_{\sigma\sigma}$ uses only the subjective profile for both purposes, while $\Psi_{\epsilon\sigma}$ and $\Psi_{\sigma\epsilon}$ combine both subjective and ethical profiles hierarchically. $\Psi_{\epsilon\sigma}$ uses the subjective profile in defining the efficiency frontier $C_\sigma^\alpha(S)$, to which the transitive closure of the SMD rule with respect to the ethical profile is applied, while $\Psi_{\sigma\epsilon}$ reverses the order of application of the subjective and ethical profiles.[11]

2.6. As an auxiliary step in our analysis of these CCRs, we put forward a theorem which summarizes what we can generally assert about the choice sets generated by $\Psi_{\epsilon\epsilon}, \Psi_{\sigma\sigma}, \Psi_{\epsilon\sigma}$, and $\Psi_{\sigma\epsilon}$.

Theorem 2. For any $\alpha = (u_1^\alpha, u_2^\alpha, ..., u_n^\alpha) \in \mathscr{A}_{\mathrm{ID}}$, we have

(a) $\forall S \in \mathscr{S}: C_{\sigma\sigma}^\alpha(S) \subset C_{\sigma\tau}^\alpha(S) \cap C_\sigma^\alpha(S)$;

(b) $\forall S \in \mathscr{S}: C_{\epsilon\epsilon}^\alpha(S) \subset C_{\epsilon\tau}^\alpha(S) \cap C_\epsilon^\alpha(S)$;

(c) $\forall S \in \mathscr{S}: C_{\epsilon\sigma}^\alpha(S) \subset C_{\epsilon\tau}^\alpha(S) \cap C_\sigma^\alpha(S)$;

(d) $\forall S \in \mathscr{S}: C_{\sigma\epsilon}^\alpha(S) \subset C_{\sigma\sigma}^\alpha(S)$ if and only if $C_\epsilon^\alpha(S) \cap C_{\sigma\sigma}^\alpha(S) \neq \varnothing$; and

(e) $\forall S \in \mathscr{S}: C_{\epsilon\epsilon}^\alpha(S) \subset C_{\epsilon\sigma}^\alpha(S)$ if and only if $C_\epsilon^\alpha(S) \cap C_{\epsilon\sigma}^\alpha(S) \neq \varnothing$, where

$C_{\epsilon\epsilon}^\alpha = \Psi_{\epsilon\epsilon}(\alpha), C_{\sigma\sigma}^\alpha = \Psi_{\sigma\sigma}(\alpha), C_{\epsilon\sigma}^\alpha = \Psi_{\epsilon\sigma}(\alpha)$, and $C_{\sigma\epsilon}^\alpha = \Psi_{\sigma\epsilon}(\alpha)$.

[11] An extensive study of the properties of $\Psi_{\sigma\sigma}$, which is definable in the traditional – intrapersonally ordinal and interpersonally non-comparable – informational framework, was conducted by Bordes (1979).

Proof of theorem 2(a). Take any $S \in \mathscr{S}$, any $x \in C^{\alpha}_{\sigma\sigma}(S)$, and any $z \in S$. If $z \in C^{\alpha}_{\sigma}(S)$ is the case, we have $(x, z) \in T(M^{\alpha}_{\sigma}(C^{\alpha}_{\sigma}(S)))$. Since it is true that $T(M^{\alpha}_{\sigma}(C^{\alpha}_{\sigma}(S))) \subset T(M^{\alpha}_{\sigma}(S))$ for all $S \in \mathscr{S}$ we then obtain:

$$\forall z \in C^{\alpha}_{\sigma}(S): \; (x, z) \in T(M^{\alpha}_{\sigma}(S)). \tag{13}$$

If, on the other hand, $z \in S \setminus C^{\alpha}_{\sigma}(S)$ is the case, the definition of $C^{\alpha}_{\sigma}(S)$ entails that $(y^1, z) \in P(R^{\alpha}_N)$ for some $y^1 \in S$. This y^1, in its turn, either belongs to $C^{\alpha}_{\sigma}(S)$ or satisfies $(y^2, y^1) \in P(R^{\alpha}_N)$ for some $y^2 \in S$. Repeating this procedure and taking the transitivity of R^{α}_N and the finiteness of S into consideration, we obtain:

$$\forall z \in S \setminus C^{\alpha}_{\sigma}(S), \; \exists y_z \in C^{\alpha}_{\sigma}(S): \; (y_z, z) \in P(R^{\alpha}_N). \tag{14}$$

Since $x \in C^{\alpha}_{\sigma\sigma}(S)$ and $y_z \in C^{\alpha}_{\sigma}(S)$ it follows that

$$(x, y_z) \in T(M^{\alpha}_{\sigma}(C^{\alpha}_{\sigma}(S))) \subset T(M^{\alpha}_{\sigma}(S)). \tag{15}$$

Clearly we have $P(R^{\alpha}_N) \cap (S \times S) \subset T(M^{\alpha}_{\sigma}(S))$ for all $S \in \mathscr{S}$, so that (14) and (15) imply that

$$\forall z \in S \setminus C^{\alpha}_{\sigma}(S): \; (x, z) \in T(M^{\alpha}_{\sigma}(S)). \tag{16}$$

Coupled with (13), (16) implies that $(x, z) \in T(M^{\alpha}_{\sigma}(S))$ for all $z \in S$, namely $x \in C^{\alpha}_{\sigma\tau}(S)$. Taking $C^{\alpha}_{\sigma\sigma}(S) \subset C^{\alpha}_{\sigma}(S)$ into consideration, we arrive at (a) as desired. ∎

Proof of theorem 2(b). If we replace all occurrences of σ in the above proof of (a) by ϵ, we have a valid proof of (b) thanks to the full symmetry of the definition. ∎

Proof of theorem 2(c). Once again the method of proof for theorem 2(a) essentially applies. We have only to invoke en route the fact that

$$P(R^{\alpha}_N) \cap (S \times S) \subset P(\omega_N(\alpha)) \cap (S \times S) \subset M^{\alpha}_{\sigma}(S). \quad ∎$$

Proof of theorem 2(d). In view of $T(M^{\alpha}_{\sigma}(S^1)) \subset T(M^{\alpha}_{\sigma}(S^2))$, which is true if $S^1 \subset S^2$, we have

$$\forall S^1, S^2 \in \mathscr{S}: S^1 \subset S^2 \to G(S^1, T(M^{\alpha}_{\sigma}(S^1))) \subset G(S^1, T(M^{\alpha}_{\sigma}(S^2))).^{12} \tag{17}$$

Since $T(M^{\alpha}_{\sigma}(S))$ is an ordering on S for every $S \in \mathscr{S}$, $C^*(\cdot) = G(\cdot, T(M^{\alpha}_{\sigma}(S)))$ defines a full rational choice function on a family of all non-empty subsets of S.[13] It then follows from Arrow's (1959) theorem that

$$\forall S^1, S^2 \in \mathscr{S}: S^1 \subset S^2 \text{ and } S^1 \cap G(S^2, T(M_\sigma^\alpha(S^2))) \neq \varnothing$$
$$\to S^1 \cap G(S^2, T(M_\sigma^\alpha(S^2))) = G(S^1, T(M_\sigma^\alpha(S^2))). \tag{18}$$

In view of (17), (18) implies that

$$\forall S^1, S^2 \in \mathscr{S}: S^1 \subset S^2 \text{ and } S^1 \cap G(S^2, T(M_\sigma^\alpha(S^2))) \neq \varnothing$$
$$\to G(S^1, T(M_\sigma^\alpha(S^1))) \subset G(S^2, T(M_\sigma^\alpha(S^2))). \tag{19}$$

We now use (19) to prove theorem 2(d). If we let $S^1 = C_\epsilon^\alpha(S)$ and $S^2 = C_\sigma^\alpha(S)$, it follows from (19) that

$$\forall S \in \mathscr{S}: C_\epsilon^\alpha(S) \cap C_{\sigma\sigma}^\alpha(S) \neq \varnothing \to C_{\sigma\epsilon}^\alpha(S) \subset C_{\sigma\sigma}^\alpha(S), \tag{20}$$

where we made use of (11). To complete the proof of (d), assume that $C_{\sigma\epsilon}^\alpha(S) \subset C_{\sigma\sigma}^\alpha(S)$. Then we have

$$C_\epsilon^\alpha(S) \cap C_{\sigma\sigma}^\alpha(S) \supset C_\epsilon^\alpha(S) \cap C_{\sigma\epsilon}^\alpha(S) = C_{\sigma\epsilon}^\alpha(S),$$

which is non-empty by construction. The proof of (d) is thereby complete. ∎

[12]   For any binary relation R and any set S, we define

$$G(S, R) = \{x \in S \mid \forall y \in S: (x, y) \in R\}$$

and

$$M(S, R) = \{x \in S \mid \forall y \in S: (y, x) \notin P(R)\}.$$

[13]   We say that a choice function C on $\mathscr{S}$ is *rational* if and only if there exists a binary relation R on X such that $C(S) = G(S, R)$ for all $S \in \mathscr{S}$. The intended interpretation of R, to be called a *rationalization* of C, is a weak preference relation which underlies the choice behaviour C, $(x, y) \in R$ being construed to mean that x is at least as desirable as y. If, in particular, C has a rationalization which is an ordering on X, we say that C is *full-rational*. A basic theorem of Arrow (1959) asserts that C is full-rational if and only if the following axiom is satisfied.

Arrow's axiom (AA).
$$\forall S^1, S^2 \in \mathscr{S}: S^1 \subset S^2 \to [S^1 \cap C(S^2) = \varnothing \vee S^1 \cap C(S^2) = C(S^1)].$$

We stress that the equivalence between full rationality and Arrow's axiom hinges squarely on the assumption that $\mathscr{S}$ contains all pair sets and all triple sets contained in X. If this assumption does not apply, the story of rational choice becomes much more complicated.

Proof of theorem 2(e). By reasoning in exactly the same way we may establish a statement which is the same as (18) save for the replacement of σ by ϵ, which we call (18: ϵ). Take any $S \in \mathscr{S}$ and let $S^1 = C_\epsilon^\alpha(S)$ and $S^2 = C_\sigma^\alpha(S)$ be substituted into (18: ϵ) to obtain:

$$\forall S \in \mathscr{S}: \ C_\epsilon^\alpha(S) \cap C_{\epsilon\sigma}^\alpha(S) \neq \varnothing \to C_{\epsilon\epsilon}^\alpha(S) \subset C_{\epsilon\sigma}^\alpha(S). \tag{20: ϵ}$$

Just as we could reverse the arrow in (20), we may reverse the arrow in (20: ϵ) to obtain the assertion of (e). ∎

Although $\Psi_{\epsilon\sigma}$ and $\Psi_{\sigma\epsilon}$ are quite symmetrically defined by exchanging the role played by the ethical and subjective profiles, the counterpart of theorem 2(c), which is a property of $\Psi_{\epsilon\sigma}$, does not hold true for $\Psi_{\sigma\epsilon}$, namely a plausible conjecture

$$\forall S \in \mathscr{S}: C_{\sigma\epsilon}^\alpha(S) \subset C_{\sigma\tau}^\alpha(S) \cap C_\epsilon^\alpha(S) \tag{21}$$

is *not* true in general as the following example shows.

Example 2. Let $N = \{1, 2, 3\}$, $\omega_i = \omega_R$ (the Rawlsian leximin principle) for all $i \in N$, $X = \{x, y, z\}$ and $\alpha = (u_*^\alpha, u_*^\alpha, u_*^\alpha)$, where $u_*^\alpha(z, 1) > u_*^\alpha(y, 1) > u_*^\alpha(x, 1) > u_*^\alpha(z, 3) > u_*^\alpha(x, 3) > u_*^\alpha(y, 2) > u_*^\alpha(x, 2) > u_*^\alpha(z, 2) > u_*^\alpha(y, 3)$. It is clear that $(\omega_R(u_*^\alpha): x, z, y)$, $(R_1^\alpha: z, y, x)$, $(R_2^\alpha: y, x, z)$, and $(R_3^\alpha: z, x, y)$. We may easily verify that $C_\epsilon^\alpha(S) = \{x\}$, $C_{\sigma\epsilon}^\alpha(S) = \{x\}$, $C_{\sigma\tau}^\alpha(S) = \{z\}$, where $S = X$. Obviously (21) is not true in this case. ∎

2.7. Let us now examine $\Psi_{\epsilon\sigma}$ – Pareto-constrained ethical majoritarianism – and $\Psi_{\sigma\epsilon}$ – justice-constrained subjective majoritarianism – with respect to their choice-consistency properties. To prepare for this, let us enumerate a series of weakened versions of Arrow's axiom, each one of which represents an intuitively appealing choice-consistency requirement, and present a diagram which summarizes the logical relationships among these axioms, where an arrow indicates a logical implication which cannot be reversed in general and the axioms in parentheses are jointly equivalent to the axiom above them.

Chernoff's axiom (CA):[14]

---

[14] Chernoff (1954).

$$\forall S^1, S^2 \in \mathscr{S}: S^1 \subset S^2 \to [S^1 \cap C(S^2) = \varnothing \vee S^1 \cap C(S^2) \subset C(S^1)].$$

Dual-Chernoff axiom (DCA):[15]

$$\forall S^1, S^2 \in \mathscr{S}: S^1 \subset S^2 \to [S^1 \cap C(S^2) = \varnothing \vee S^1 \cap C(S^2) \supset C(S^1)].$$

Nash's axiom (NA):[16]

$$\forall S^1, S^2 \in \mathscr{S}: [S^1 \subset S^2 \text{ and } C(S^2) \subset S^1] \to C(S^1) = C(S^2).$$

Superset axiom (SUA):[17]

$$\forall S^1, S^2 \in \mathscr{S}: [S^1 \subset S^2 \text{ and } C(S^2) \subset C(S^1)] \to C(S^1) = C(S^2).$$

Stability axiom (ST):[18]

$$\forall S \in \mathscr{S}: C(C(S)) = C(S).$$

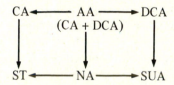

Note that the choice-consistency conditions referred to above are restrictions on the class of choice functions but, by extension, we may construe them to be restrictions on the class of CCRs. For example, we may say that a CCR Ψ is full-rational if $C^\alpha = \Psi(\alpha)$ is a full-rational choice function for all admissible profiles. We may then assert the following:

Theorem 3.

(a) $\Psi_{\epsilon\sigma}$ satisfies NA (Nash's choice-consistency axiom) on $\mathscr{A}_{\text{ID}}$; and

(b) $\Psi_{\sigma\epsilon}$ satisfies ST (Stability axiom of choice-consistency) on $\mathscr{A}_{\text{ID}}$.

---

[15] Bordes (1976).

[16] Nash (1950) introduced this choice-consistency condition for a single-valued choice function, while the general version thereof was discussed by Bordes (1979) under the name of *strong superset condition*. As a matter of fact, we may show that for a single-valued choice function Nash's axiom and Arrow's axiom are equivalent.

[17] Blair, Bordes, Kelly and Suzumura (1976).

[18] This condition is reportedly due to Robert Parks and is also discussed by Bordes (1979).

Proof of theorem 3(a). For each $\alpha \in \mathscr{A}_{ID}$ define a binary relation Q^{α} on X by:

$$Q^{\alpha} = \{(x, y) \mid (x, y) \in P(R_N^{\alpha}) \vee (y, x) \notin P(R_N^{\alpha})\}.$$

Q^{α} is reflexive and connected. We may also verify that $P(Q^{\alpha}) = P(R_N^{\alpha})$, which is transitive, and that

$$\forall S \in \mathscr{S}: G(S, Q^{\alpha}) = M(S, R_N^{\alpha}). \tag{22}$$

We now prove that

$$P(Q^{\alpha}) P(M_{\epsilon}^{\alpha}) \cup P(M_{\epsilon}^{\alpha}) P(Q^{\alpha}) \subset P(M_{\epsilon}^{\alpha}), \tag{23}$$

where, for example, $P(Q^{\alpha})P(M_{\epsilon}^{\alpha})$ is the composition of $P(Q^{\alpha})$ and $P(M_{\epsilon}^{\alpha})$. Let $x, y \in X$ be such that $(x, y) \in P(Q^{\alpha})P(M_{\epsilon}^{\alpha})$, so that $(x, z) \in P(Q^{\alpha}) = P(R_N^{\alpha})$ and $(z, y) \in P(M_{\epsilon}^{\alpha})$ for some $z \in X$. Since ω_i satisfies the condition IM for all $i \in N$, we have $P(R_N^{\alpha}) \subset \cap_{i \in N} P(\omega_i(u_i^{\alpha}))$. Since $\omega_i(u_i^{\alpha})$ is transitive for all $i \in N$, we obtain $(x, y) \in P(M_{\epsilon}^{\alpha})$, establishing $P(Q^{\alpha})P(M_{\epsilon}^{\alpha}) \subset P(M_{\epsilon}^{\alpha})$. We may similarly verify that $P(M_{\epsilon}^{\alpha})P(Q^{\alpha}) \subset P(M_{\epsilon}^{\alpha})$, completing the proof of (23). We may now invoke Bordes' lemma[19] for $R^1 \equiv M_{\epsilon}^{\alpha}$ and $R^2 \equiv Q^{\alpha}$ to conclude that

$$G[G(S, Q^{\alpha}), T(M_{\epsilon}^{\alpha}(G(S, Q^{\alpha})))] = G[M(S, R_N^{\alpha}), T(M_{\epsilon}^{\alpha}(M(S, R_N^{\alpha})))]$$
$$= G[C_{\sigma}^{\alpha}(S), T(M_{\epsilon}^{\alpha}(C_{\epsilon}^{\alpha}(S)))]$$
$$= C_{\epsilon\sigma}^{\alpha}(S)$$

satisfies Nash's choice-consistency axiom, where use is made of (22). Since $\alpha \in \mathscr{A}_{ID}$ and $S \in \mathscr{S}$ are arbitrary, this completes the proof. ∎

Proof of theorem 3(b). To begin with, let us show that

$$\forall S^1, S^2 \in \mathscr{S}: \ S^1 \subset C_{\epsilon}^{\alpha}(S^2) \to S^1 = C_{\epsilon}^{\alpha}(S^1) \tag{24}$$

---

[19] Bordes' (1979) lemma asserts the following. Suppose that two binary relations R^1 and R^2 on X satisfy

A(1): R^1 is connected and reflexive and $P(R^2)$ is transitive;
A(2): $P(R^2) \subset P(R^1)$; and
A(3): $P(R^1)P(R^2) \cup P(R^2)P(R^1) \subset P(R^1)$.

Then a choice function C on $\mathscr{S}$ defined by $C(S) = G[V_S, T(R^1(V_S))]$, where $V_S = G(S, R^2)$, satisfies Nash's axiom of choice-consistency.

for any $\alpha \in \mathscr{A}_{\mathrm{ID}}$. Since $C_\epsilon^\alpha(S^1) \subset S^1$ is always true, (24) can be false only if there exists an $x \in X$ such that $x \in S^1 \setminus C_\epsilon^\alpha(S^1)$, namely

$$\exists x \in S^1, \ \exists y \in S^1 : (y, x) \in P(\omega_N(\alpha))$$

even though we have $S^1 \subset C_\epsilon^\alpha(S^2)$. It then follows that

$$\exists (x, y) \in C_\epsilon^\alpha(S^2) \times S^2 : (y, x) \in P(\omega_N(\alpha)),$$

which is an apparent contradiction.

To show that $C_{\sigma\epsilon}^\alpha$ satisfies the choice-consistency condition ST, let $S \in \mathscr{S}$ be picked arbitrarily and define $S^0 \equiv C_{\sigma\epsilon}^\alpha(S)$. We then have

$$S^0 = C_{\sigma\tau}^\alpha(C_\epsilon^\alpha(S)) \subset C_\epsilon^\alpha(S), \tag{25}$$

so that (24) implies that $S^0 = C_\epsilon^\alpha(S^0)$, namely

$$C_\epsilon^\alpha(C_{\sigma\epsilon}^\alpha(S)) = C_{\sigma\epsilon}^\alpha(S). \tag{26}$$

If we put $S^1 \equiv C_\epsilon^\alpha(C_{\sigma\epsilon}^\alpha(S))$ and $S^2 \equiv C_\epsilon^\alpha(S)$, then we obtain

$$S^1 \subset S^2, \ C_{\sigma\tau}^\alpha(S^2) = C_{\sigma\epsilon}^\alpha(S) = S^1, \tag{27}$$

where we made use of (25) and (26). Since $C_{\sigma\tau}^\alpha$ satisfies Nash's axiom as was shown by Bordes (1976, 1979), we then obtain $C_{\sigma\tau}^\alpha(S^1) = C_{\sigma\tau}^\alpha(S^2)$. Since

$$C_{\sigma\tau}^\alpha(S^1) = C_{\sigma\tau}^\alpha(C_\epsilon^\alpha(C_{\sigma\epsilon}^\alpha(S))) = C_{\sigma\epsilon}^\alpha(C_{\sigma\epsilon}^\alpha(S))$$

and

$$C_{\sigma\tau}^\alpha(S^2) = C_{\sigma\tau}^\alpha(C_\epsilon^\alpha(S)) = C_{\sigma\epsilon}^\alpha(S),$$

are true, we are now home. ∎

Note that the choice-consistency axiom which $\Psi_{\sigma\epsilon}$ is asserted to satisfy is ST, which is strictly weaker than NA, which $\Psi_{\epsilon\sigma}$ is asserted to meet. We present an example showing that $\Psi_{\sigma\epsilon}$ indeed may fail to guarantee the satisfaction of NA. This is the second feature which separates $\Psi_{\epsilon\sigma}$ from $\Psi_{\sigma\epsilon}$ despite their symmetric definitions.

Example 3. Let $N = \{1, 2, 3\}$, $\omega_i = \omega_R$ for all $i \in N$, $X = \{x, y, z\}$ and consider the following profile $\alpha = (u_1^\alpha, u_2^\alpha, u_3^\alpha) \in \mathscr{A}_{ID}$:

$$u_1^\alpha(x, 3) = u_1^\alpha(y, 3) > u_1^\alpha(z, 3) > u_1^\alpha(x, 2) > u_1^\alpha(z, 2) > u_1^\alpha(y, 2) > u_1^\alpha(y, 1)$$
$$> u_1^\alpha(z, 1) > u_1^\alpha(x, 1),$$

$$u_2^\alpha(x, 3) = u_2^\alpha(y, 3) > u_2^\alpha(z, 3) > u_2^\alpha(y, 1) > u_2^\alpha(z, 1) > u_2^\alpha(x, 2) > u_2^\alpha(z, 2)$$
$$> u_2^\alpha(x, 1) > u_2^\alpha(y, 2),$$

$$u_3^\alpha(x, 3) = u_3^\alpha(y, 3) > u_3^\alpha(x, 2) > u_3^\alpha(z, 2) > u_3^\alpha(y, 1) > u_3^\alpha(z, 1) > u_3^\alpha(z, 3)$$
$$> u_3^\alpha(y, 2) > u_3^\alpha(x, 1).$$

We may easily verify that $(\omega_R(u_1^\alpha): y, z, x)$, $(\omega_R(u_2^\alpha): z, x, y)$, $(\omega_R(u_3^\alpha): z, y, x)$, $(R_1^\alpha: y, z, x)$, $(R_2^\alpha: x, z, y)$, $(R_3^\alpha: [x, y], z)$. Let $S^1 = \{x, y\}$ and $S^2 = X$. Since $(x, y), (y, x) \in M_\sigma^\alpha$, $(y, z) \in P(M_\sigma^\alpha)$, $(x, z) \in P(M_\sigma^\alpha)$ and $\cap_{i \in N} \omega_R(u_i^\alpha) = \Delta \cup \{(z, x)\}$, where Δ denotes the diagonal binary relation on X, we obtain $C_{\sigma\epsilon}^\alpha(S^1) = S^1 \supset \supset C_{\sigma\epsilon}^\alpha(S^2) = \{y\}$, even though $S^1 \subset S^2$, which is a clear violation of NA by $C_{\sigma\epsilon}^\alpha$. ∎

2.8. So much for the choice-consistency properties of $\Psi_{\sigma\epsilon}$ and $\Psi_{\epsilon\sigma}$. We now examine the performance of these CCRs with respect to some other social choice criteria.

(1) In the first place, $\Psi_{\sigma\epsilon}$ as well as $\Psi_{\epsilon\sigma}$ are Paretian in the sense that they satisfy the condition SP (strong Pareto principle).[20] Consider $\Psi_{\sigma\epsilon}$ first and let $\alpha \in \mathscr{A}_{ID}$, $S \in \mathscr{S}$, and $x, y \in X$ be such that $(x, y) \in P(R_N^\alpha)$, $x \in S$ and $y \in C_{\sigma\epsilon}^\alpha(S)$. But this is an immediate contradiction, since $(x, y) \in P(R_N^\alpha)$ and $x \in S$ imply $y \notin$

---

[20]   Suppose that we add the following quite natural requirement to the condition IM (impartiality):

$$[\exists \pi \in \Pi_N, \forall i \in N: u(x, i) = u(y, \pi(i))] \rightarrow (x, y) \in I(\omega(u)),$$

where $I(\cdot)$ denotes the *symmetric part* of the binary relation in the parenthesis, so that

$$I(R) = \{(x, y) \in X \times X \mid (x, y) \in R \text{ and } (y, x) \in R\}$$

for every binary relation R on X. We may then strengthen our verdict on the Paretian nature of $\Psi_{\sigma\epsilon}$ and $\Psi_{\epsilon\sigma}$ by proving that they satisfy the following condition as well.

Condition PI (Pareto indifference principle).   For every profile $\alpha = (u_1^\alpha, u_2^\alpha, ..., u_n^\alpha) \in \mathscr{A}$ and every $x, y \in X$, if $(x, y) \in \cap_{i \in N} I(R_i^\alpha)$, then $[x \in S$ and $y \in C^\alpha(S) \rightarrow x \in C^\alpha(S)]$ for every $S \in \mathscr{S}$.

$C_\sigma^\alpha(S)$, hence $y \notin C_\epsilon^\alpha(S)$ in view of (11), while $y \in C_{\sigma\epsilon}^\alpha(S) \subset C_\epsilon^\alpha(S)$. Only a few trivial changes are needed in the above proof to establish that $\Psi_{\epsilon\sigma}$ also satisfies the condition SP. ∎

(2) As a matter of fact, the case for $\Psi_{\sigma\epsilon}$ may be somewhat strengthened. The method of proof we used in (1) above essentially goes through to show that $\Psi_{\sigma\epsilon}$ satisfies the condition SJU (strong justice unanimity condition) on $\mathscr{A}_{\mathrm{ID}}$, which is stronger than SP. Note, however, that $\Psi_{\epsilon\sigma}$ does not admit similar generalization as the following counter-example shows.

Example 4. Let $N = \{1, 2\}$, $\omega_1 = \omega_2 = \omega_R$, $X = \{x, y, z, w\}$, and let a profile $\alpha = (u_1^\alpha, u_2^\alpha) \in \mathscr{A}_{\mathrm{ID}}$ be defined as follows:

$$u_1^\alpha(z, 2) > u_1^\alpha(w, 2) > u_1^\alpha(y, 2) > u_1^\alpha(x, 2) > u_1^\alpha(x, 1) > u_1^\alpha(w, 1) > u_1^\alpha(y, 1)$$
$$> u_1^\alpha(z, 1);$$

$$u_2^\alpha(z, 2) > u_2^\alpha(w, 2) > u_2^\alpha(y, 2) > u_2^\alpha(x, 1) > u_2^\alpha(w, 1) > u_2^\alpha(y, 1) > u_2^\alpha(z, 1)$$
$$> u_2^\alpha(x, 2).$$

It may be easily seen that $(\omega_R(u_1^\alpha): x, w, y, z)$, $(\omega_R(u_2^\alpha): w, y, z, x)$, $(R_1^\alpha: x, w, y, z)$, and $(R_2^\alpha: z, w, y, x)$. Let $S = \{x, y, z, w\}$. We may compute that $C_\sigma^\alpha(S) = C_{\epsilon\sigma}^\alpha(S) = \{x, w, z\}$, which means that $(y, z) \in P(\omega_N(\alpha))$, $z \in C_{\epsilon\sigma}^\alpha(S)$, and $y \notin C_{\epsilon\sigma}^\alpha(S)$, negating the validity of the condition SJU for $\Psi_{\epsilon\sigma}$. ∎

(3) Let us now turn to the informational requirements of $\Psi_{\sigma\epsilon}$ and $\Psi_{\epsilon\sigma}$. It is quite true that they require far more information than the intrapersonally ordinal and interpersonally non-comparable informational inputs needed, for example, by $\Psi_{\sigma\sigma}$, but there is a sense in which the informational requirements of $\Psi_{\sigma\epsilon}$ and $\Psi_{\epsilon\sigma}$ are *minimal*. Recollect that a CCR is needed so as to enable people to arrive at a social choice from each and every set $S \in \mathscr{S}$ reflecting a fair amalgamation of people's welfare judgements, so that it seems obvious that a CCR should be provided with information at least about the characteristics of each profile restricted on $S \times N$. An important fact is that these necessary informational imputs are all we need in order to arrive at the social choice via $\Psi_{\sigma\epsilon}$ and/or $\Psi_{\epsilon\sigma}$. Formally, both $\Psi_{\sigma\epsilon}$ and $\Psi_{\epsilon\sigma}$ satisfy the following requirement of informational modesty, which is a counterpart in our context of Arrow's (1963) *independence of irrelevant alternatives*.

Condition I (Independence). Suppose that two profiles $\alpha = (u_1^\alpha, u_2^\alpha, ..., u_n^\alpha)$, $\beta = (u_1^\beta, u_2^\beta, ..., u_n^\beta)$, and an $S \in \mathscr{S}$ are such that $u_i^\alpha(x, j) = u_i^\beta(x, j)$ for all $i \in N$ and all $(x, j) \in S \times N$. Then $C^\alpha(S) = C^\beta(S)$ holds true, where $C^\alpha = \Psi(\alpha)$ and $C^\beta = \Psi(\beta)$.

(4) The next property we examine is whether $\Psi_{\sigma\epsilon}$ and $\Psi_{\epsilon\sigma}$ treat individuals without prejudice or favouritism. In other words, do they treat similar individuals similarly? Care should be taken with the concept of similarity in our context, since an individual is characterized in our framework not only by his extended preferences but also by his principle of justice, so that the relevant concept of anonymity should read thus. If the profile of extended utility functions and the profile of the principles of justice are simultaneously and identically permuted among individuals, the social choice function should remain the same. To make this point explicit, let a CCR be parameterized as Ψ^ω when a profile $(\omega_1, \omega_2, ..., \omega_n)$ prevails. For any $\alpha \in \mathscr{A}$ and any $\pi \in \Pi_N$, let the permuted profile $\pi \circ \alpha$ be defined by

$$\pi \circ \alpha = (\pi \circ u^\alpha_{\pi(1)}, \ \pi \circ u^\alpha_{\pi(2)}, \ ..., \ \pi \circ u^\alpha_{\pi(n)}).$$

Note that, after applying the permutation $\pi \in \Pi_N$, individual i will have a principle of justice $\omega_{\pi(i)}$ and an extended utility function $u^{\pi \circ \alpha}_i = \pi \circ u^\alpha_{\pi(i)}$, so that $u^{\pi \circ \alpha}_i(x, j) = (\pi \circ u^\alpha_{\pi(i)})(x, j) = u^\alpha_{\pi(i)}(x, \pi(j))$ for all $(x, j) \in X \times N$. Therefore the total individual characteristics are interpersonally permuted by our procedure, as should naturally be the case. If we note that $C^\alpha_{\sigma\epsilon} = \Psi^\omega_{\sigma\epsilon}(\alpha)$ depends only on $\cap_{i \in N}$ $\omega_i(u^\alpha_i)$ and M^α_σ, while $C^\alpha_{\epsilon\sigma} = \Psi^\omega_{\epsilon\sigma}(\alpha)$ depends only on $\cap_{i \in N} R^\alpha_i$ and M^α_ϵ, it is clearly the case that $\Psi_{\sigma\epsilon}$ as well as $\Psi_{\epsilon\sigma}$ satisfies the following:

Condition A (Anonymity). For every $\alpha \in \mathscr{A}$ and every $\pi \in \Pi_N$, we have $C^{\pi \circ \alpha} = C^\alpha$, where $C^{\pi \circ \alpha} = \Psi^{\pi \circ \omega}(\pi \circ \alpha)$ and $C^\alpha = \Psi^\omega(\alpha)$.

2.9. Putting all the pieces together, we may summarize the overall performance of $\Psi_{\sigma\epsilon}$ and $\Psi_{\epsilon\sigma}$ as follows.

Theorem 4.

(a) $\Psi_{\epsilon\sigma}$ is a well-defined CCR which satisfies UID (unrestricted domain under identity axiom), SP (strong Pareto), I (independence), A (anonymity), and NA (Nash's axiom of choice-consistency).

(b) $\Psi_{\sigma\epsilon}$ is a well-defined CCR which satisfies UID, SJU (strong justice unanimity), I, A, and ST (stability axiom of choice-consistency).

3.　Discussion and remarks on the literature

Enough has been said so far about the formal properties of the Pareto-constrained ethical majoritarianism $\Psi_{\epsilon\sigma}$ and the justice-constrained subjective majoritarianism $\Psi_{\sigma\epsilon}$. We now move on to compare these CCRs with each other as well as with $\Psi_{\sigma\sigma}$ and $\Psi_{\epsilon\epsilon}$ with a view to clarifying these rules further by contrast. We will also make some remarks on the existing literature related to the subject of the present chapter.

(1)　The justice-constrained subjective majoritarianism $\Psi_{\sigma\epsilon}$ is founded on a very simple idea, suggested in the preliminary analysis of the cake-division problem, to the effect that the resolution by the SMD rule should be applied only to those states which are justice-undominated. Note, however, that $\Psi_{\epsilon\epsilon}$ satisfies all the formal properties enumerated in theorem 4(b) for $\Psi_{\sigma\epsilon}$ and goes one step further, namely $\Psi_{\epsilon\epsilon}$ satisfies a *stronger* Nash's choice-consistency axiom. Furthermore, in the context of the cake-division problem, not only $\Psi_{\sigma\epsilon}$ and $\Psi_{\epsilon\sigma}$ but also $\Psi_{\epsilon\epsilon}$ choose the egalitarian alternative w. An appeal of $\Psi_{\sigma\epsilon}$ and $\Psi_{\epsilon\sigma}$ over $\Psi_{\epsilon\epsilon}$ does seem to exist, however, in that the former combine ethical and subjective profiles lexically, while the latter makes use only of people's ethical preferences, which "express what can in only a qualified sense be called his 'preferences': they will, by definition, express what he prefers only in those possibly rare moments when he forces a special impartial and impersonal attitude upon himself".[21]

(2)　As Bordes (1979) has shown, $\Psi_{\sigma\sigma}$ scores fairly well in terms of the well-known social choice criteria and that it uses only the subjective profile. How many further niceties have we secured by additionally requiring the ethical profile? There are two points we would like to make here. First, $\Psi_{\sigma\epsilon}$ and $\Psi_{\epsilon\sigma}$ are "just" CCRs in the following sense. $\Psi_{\sigma\epsilon}$ is "just" in that it satisfies the justice unanimity condition, while $\Psi_{\epsilon\sigma}$ is "just" in that $C_{\epsilon\sigma}^{\alpha}(S) \subset C_{\epsilon\tau}^{\alpha}(S)$ for all $\alpha \in \mathscr{A}_{\mathrm{ID}}$ and all $S \in \mathscr{S}$, which follows from theorem 2(c). As a result, we have in the cake-division example that $C_{\sigma\sigma}(\{x, y, z, w\}) = \{x, y, z\}$ holds true, while we have $C_{\epsilon\sigma}(\{x, y, z, w\}) = C_{\sigma\epsilon}(\{x, y, z, w\}) = \{w\}$. Secondly, we should like to call attention to the relationship between the *selective power* of a rule and the *informational requirement* thereof. To make our point precise, let us consider an $\alpha \in \mathscr{A}_{\mathrm{ID}}$ and an $S \in \mathscr{S}$ such that $C_{\epsilon}^{\alpha}(S) \cap C_{\sigma\sigma}^{\alpha}(S) \neq \varnothing$. Thanks to theorem 2 we then have

$$C_{\sigma\epsilon}^{\alpha}(S) \subset C_{\epsilon}^{\alpha}(S) \cap C_{\sigma\sigma}^{\alpha}(S) \subset C_{\sigma\sigma}^{\alpha}(S) \subset C_{\sigma\tau}^{\alpha}(S) \cap C_{\sigma}^{\alpha}(S) \subset C_{\sigma\tau}^{\alpha}(S).$$

---

[21]　Harsanyi (1955, p. 315).

Note that $\Psi_{\sigma\tau}$, which is nothing other than the transitive closure extension of the SMD rule, uses only the SMD relation M_σ^α with respect to the subjective profile $\sigma(\alpha)$. As such, $\Psi_{\sigma\tau}$ is informationally less demanding at the cost of being less selective among $\Psi_{\sigma\epsilon}$, $\Psi_{\sigma\sigma}$, and $\Psi_{\sigma\tau}$. So low is the selective power of $\Psi_{\sigma\tau}$ that the choice set thereby generated may occasionally contain a Pareto-dominated state. This obvious defect of $\Psi_{\sigma\tau}$ may be rectified if we use $P(R_N^\alpha)$ along with M_σ^α and choose in accordance with the choice mechanism $\Psi_{\sigma\sigma}$ which, by definition, ensures that $C_{\sigma\sigma}^\alpha(S)$ is contained in the Pareto efficient set $C_\sigma^\alpha(S)$. Further strengthening of the informational requirement to the extent of having not only the subjective profile $\sigma(\alpha)$ but also the ethical profile $\omega(\alpha)$ enables us to choose in accordance with the choice mechanism $\Psi_{\sigma\epsilon}$. Not only is the choice by $\Psi_{\sigma\epsilon}$ "just", but also it is the most selective choice mechanism among $\Psi_{\sigma\epsilon}$, $\Psi_{\sigma\sigma}$, and $\Psi_{\sigma\tau}$.[22] What this argument in favour of $\Psi_{\sigma\epsilon}$ does *not* guarantee is that $\Psi_{\sigma\epsilon}$ is selective enough. Although the above argument seems to establish that $\Psi_{\sigma\epsilon}$ is the most selective among those nominated rules, $C_{\sigma\epsilon}^\alpha(S)$ may still be too inclusive.

(3)   In Suzumura (1981a, 1981b) we have examined the equity-as-no-envy concept in the extended sympathy social choice framework. We have shown in Suzumura (1981b) that there exists a "fair" CCR Ψ_{GS}, which we call the Goldman–Sussangkarn rule, with the following properties: (a) U (unrestricted domain), (b) CBEP (conditional binary exclusion Pareto), (c) I (independence), (d) A (anonymity), and (e) ST (stability axiom of choice consistency). Other than condition CBEP, all these performance criteria are already familiar to us. The condition CBEP is a variant of the Pareto principle and requires the following: if a profile $\alpha \in \mathscr{A}$ and $x, y \in X$ are such that $\cap_{i \in N} E_{qi}^\alpha(\{x, y\}) = \varnothing$ and $(x, y) \in \cap_{i \in N} P(R_i^\alpha)$, then $\{x\} = C^\alpha(\{x, y\})$ holds true, where $C^\alpha = \Psi(\alpha)$. We have also shown in Suzumura (1981a) that there exists no "fair" CCR having a property (b) if we want *either* to strengthen (e) into (e*) CA (Chernoff's axiom of choice consistency) *or* to replace (e) by (e**) SUA (superset axiom of choice consistency) even though we weaken (a) substantially into (a*) UID (unrestricted domain under identity axiom). Note that (c) and (d) have nothing to say in the context of these impossibility theorems.

(4)   The performance of $\Psi_{\sigma\epsilon}$ and $\Psi_{\epsilon\sigma}$ summarized in theorem 4 and the results on Ψ_{GS} reported in (3) immediately above are now to be evaluated in the con-

---

[22]   It is true that this argument is valid only when $C_\epsilon^\alpha(S) \cap C_{\sigma\sigma}^\alpha(S) \neq \varnothing$. If it so happens that $C_\epsilon^\alpha(S) \cap C_{\sigma\sigma}^\alpha(S) = \varnothing$, the case against $C_{\sigma\sigma}^\alpha(S)$ is that much strengthened, not weakened, since every alternative in $C_{\sigma\sigma}^\alpha(S)$ is then obviously justice-dominated. To assume that $C_\epsilon^\alpha(S) \cap C_{\sigma\sigma}^\alpha(S) \neq \varnothing$ is therefore to give $C_{\sigma\sigma}^\alpha(S)$ a fair chance in the contest with $C_{\sigma\epsilon}^\alpha$, in which $C_{\sigma\epsilon}^\alpha$ performs better.

text of Arrovian impossibility theorems. Recollect that Arrow's (1963) celebrated general possibility theorem asserts that *there exists no full-rational collective choice rule which satisfies unrestricted domain, Pareto principle, independence of irrelevant alternatives, and nondictatorship.* In Arrow's framework, use is made only of the intrapersonally ordinal and interpersonally non-comparable preference orderings in the process or rule of arriving at a social choice. There are many attempts in the literature which seek a way to circumvent Arrow's impossibility theorem by expanding the informational framework of social choice theory.[23] We have also examined this escape route in two ways. First, by lexically combining two profiles of individual preferences — the subjective preferences and the ethical preferences, both of which do represent an individual's authentic preferences — we have constructed two CCRs, $\Psi_{\sigma\epsilon}$ and $\Psi_{\epsilon\sigma}$, which show in effect that the lexical combination of the impartial sympathy and self-love generates a social choice mechanism which is always applicable, which works with the minimal informational inputs, which treats individuals without prejudice or favouritism, and which generates a "just" social choice function with some choice-consistency property. An essentially different second approach centred upon the equity-as-no-envy concept led us to a "fair" CCR, Ψ_{GS}, with very similar performance characteristics. What these CCRs commonly sacrifice is Arrow's collective full-rationality condition, which is replaced by a much weaker choice-consistency condition. They are also likely to yield rather unselective social choice functions in view of the common use of the transitive closure, so that they can hardly qualify as *the* resolution of Arrow's dilemma. Our modest hope is that our result might serve as an indication of the potentiality of the extended sympathy approach in social choice theory, thereby enticing further exploration thereof in the future.

References

Alchian, Armen S. (1953) "The Meaning of Utility Measurement", *American Economic Review*, 43, 26–50.

Arrow, Kenneth J. (1959) "Rational Choice Functions and Orderings", *Economica*, 26, 121–127.

Arrow, Kenneth J. (1963) *Social Choice and Individual Values*, 2nd edn. (John Wiley & Sons, New York).

Arrow, Kenneth J. (1977a) "Extended Sympathy and the Possibility of Social Choice", *American Economic Review*, 67, 217–225.

Arrow, Kenneth J. (1977b) "Current Development in the Theory of Social Choice", *Social Research*, 44, 607–622.

[23] See Arrow (1977a), d'Aspremont and Gevers (1977), Hammond (1976, 1979), Roberts (1980), and Sen (1977), among others.

Blair, Douglas H., Georges Bordes, Jerry S. Kelly and Kotaro Suzumura (1976) "Impossibility Theorems Without Collective Rationality", *Journal of Economic Theory*, 13, 361–379.

Bordes, Georges (1976) "Consistency, Rationality and Collective Choice", *Review of Economic Studies*, 43, 451–457.

Bordes, Georges (1979) "Some More Results on Consistency, Rationality and Collective Choice", in: Jean-Jacques Laffont, ed., *Aggregation and Revelation of Preferences* (North-Holland, Amsterdam), pp. 175–197.

Chernoff, Herman (1954) "Rational Selection of Decision Functions", *Econometrica*, 22, 422–443.

d'Aspremont, Claude and Louis Gevers (1977) "Equity and the Informational Basis of Collective Choice", *Review of Economic Studies*, 44, 199–209.

Fishburn, Peter C. (1973) *The Theory of Social Choice* (Princeton University Press, Princeton).

Foley, Duncan K. (1967) "Resource Allocation and the Public Sector", *Yale Economic Essays*, 7, 45–98.

Hammond, Peter J. (1976) "Equity, Arrow's Conditions and Rawls' Difference Principle", *Econometrica*, 44, 793–804.

Hammond, Peter J. (1979) "Equity in Two Person Situations: Some Consequences", *Econometrica*, 47, 1127–1135.

Harsanyi, John C. (1955) "Cardinal Welfare, Individualistic Ethics, and Interpersonal Comparisons of Utility", *Journal of Political Economy*, 63, 309–321.

Kelly, Jerry S. (1978) *Arrow Impossibility Theorems* (Academic Press, New York).

Nash, John F. (1950) "The Bargaining Problem", *Econometrica*, 18, 155–162.

Pattanaik, Prasanta K. (1968) "Risk, Impersonality, and the Social Welfare Function", *Journal of Political Economy*, 76, 1152–1169.

Pazner, Elisha A. (1976) "Recent Thinking on Economic Justice", *Journal of Peace Science*, 2, 143–153.

Pazner, Elisha A. (1979) "Equity, Nonfeasible Alternatives and Social Choice: A Reconsideration of the Concept of Social Welfare", in: Jean-Jacques Laffont, ed., *Aggregation and Revelation of Preferences* (North-Holland, Amsterdam), pp. 161–173.

Rawls, John (1971) *A Theory of Justice* (Harvard University Press, Cambridge).

Roberts, Kevin W.S. (1980) "Possibility Theorems with Interpersonally Comparable Welfare Levels", *Review of Economic Studies*, 47, 409–420.

Sen, Amartya K. (1970) *Collective Choice and Social Welfare* (Holden-Day, San Francisco).

Sen, Amartya K. (1977) "On Weights and Measures: Informational Constraints in Social Welfare Analysis", *Econometrica*, 45, 1539–1572.

Suppes, Patrik (1966) "Some Formal Models of Grading Principles", *Synthese*, 6, 284–306.

Suzumura, Kotaro (1981a) "On Pareto-efficiency and the No-envy Concept of Equity", *Journal of Economic Theory*, 25, 367–379.

Suzumura, Kotaro (1981b) "On the Possibility of 'Fair' Collective Choice Rule", *International Economic Review*, 22, 351–364.

Suzumura, Kotaro (1982) "Equity, Efficiency and Rights in Social Choice", *Mathematical Social Sciences*, 3, 131–155.

Varian, Hal R. (1974) "Equity, Envy and Efficiency", *Journal of Economic Theory*, 9, 63–91.

Varian, Hal R. (1975) "Distributive Justice, Welfare Economics, and the Theory of Fairness", *Philosophy and Public Affairs*, 4, 223–247.

CHAPTER 9

Some broader issues of social choice

YEW-KWANG NG
Monash University

(With contributions in an appendix from
John Harsanyi, University of California at Berkeley)

1. Introduction

Most chapters in this volume are highly technical and specialized, incorporating rigorous contributions. Partly to provide something different, I choose here to discuss some broader issues of social choice in a non-technical and even speculative way.

Three factors (concern for others, ignorance, irrationality) accounting for a divergence between the preference of an individual and his welfare are discussed and a distinction is made between a self-concerning and a self-minding individual (section 2). Individual welfares are more appropriate ingredients for social choice (section 3). Extending the weak majority preference criterion (a preferring majority should outweigh an indifferent minority) to cover a variable population size, the "correct" criterion for optimum population is the maximization of the sum instead of the mean of individual welfares. Similar extensions to non-human sentients are possible (section 5 and the appendix). This implies that existent human beings may have to sustain enormous sacrifice for the welfare of future generations and the welfare of other sentients. Attempts to bypass this by ignoring prospective persons are rejected as unable to provide a satisfactory solution to the Parfit paradox and the extinction paradox. Instead, prospective persons and non-human sentients should be treated on a par with existent human beings, at least on an ideal moralistic point of view. But our actual objective functions are largely based on our self-interests (section 6).

Social Choice and Welfare, edited by P.K. Pattanaik and M. Salles
© *North-Holland Publishing Company, 1983*

2. Preferences vs. welfare: a distinction

Social choice theorists typically ignore any divergences between the preferences of an individual and his welfare. Social welfare is then taken as a function of and usually only of individual preferences or welfares. The "only of" part is termed "welfarism" and vigorously attacked by Sen (1979). I have defended welfarism against Sen's criticism elsewhere (Ng, 1981). Here, I shall discuss factors accounting for a divergence between preference and welfare.

The welfare of an individual is defined as his (net) happiness. But the word "happy" may be used in a different sense than intended here. I use the word "happy" in its more subjective sense, referring to the subjective well-being of the individual. Sometimes "happy" is used in the similar sense as "preference". "I am happy taking a train" may mean "I prefer taking a train (to other means of travel)." It need not imply I positively enjoy the train ride; I may just hate driving more. I have to rule out this sense of the word "happy"; otherwise "preference" and "welfare" (as defined) are synonyms.

Three different factors may account for a divergence between the preference of an individual and his welfare. First, the preference of an individual may not only be affected by his own welfare but may also be affected by his consideration for the welfare of other individuals. Thus, it is possible for a person to prefer x to y and yet he himself be less happy in x than in y because he believes, for example, that other people are happier in x than in y. It is true that the belief that other people are happy may make oneself happy. But this may not be strong enough to outweigh the loss one has to suffer from changing from y to x. For example, a person may vote for party x, knowing that he himself will be better off with party y in government. The reason he votes for x is that he believes that the majority of the people will be much better of with x. This itself may make him feel better. However, this benefit may not be important enough to overbalance, in terms of his subjective happiness, his personal loss, say in income, under x. He may yet vote for x due to his moral concern for the majority. To give an even more dramatic example, consider an individual who expects to lead a very happy life. When his country is being invaded, he may volunteer for a mission which will bring him the certainty of death. The prospect of being a citizen of a conquered nation, especially with the guilty conscience of failing to volunteer for the mission, may not be too bright. But overall he may still expect to be fairly happy leading such a life. Yet he chooses death for the sake of his fellow countrymen. He is not maximizing his own welfare.[1]

---

[1] This source of divergence between welfare and preference due to a consideration for others is discussed in Ng (1969, p. 43) and Sen (1973).

Some people have difficulty in seeing the above distinction between preference and welfare, saying that whenever an individual prefers x to y, he must be,
or at least believe to be, happier in x than in y. This difficulty completely baffles
me. Clearly, a father (or mother) may sacrifice his (her) happiness for the welfare
of his (her) children. I cannot see why this cannot be extended to a friend or a
relative, and further to a countryman, any human being, and finally to any sentient creatures.

Assuming that the preference of an individual may be represented by a utility
function (on which see section 4), the difference between welfare and preference
discussed above may be illustrated below. The preference of a rational individual
with perfect knowledge (irrationality and ignorance will be discussed below) is in
general a function of the welfares of all individuals (where "individuals" may include non-human sentients):

$$U^i = U^i(W^1, W^2, ..., W^n).$$

In general, it is not true that individual i prefers x to y if and only if $W^i(x) >
W^i(y)$. This is so for the special (though it may be a very important) case of a
self-concerning individual with $U^i = U^i(W^i)$. His welfare may still assume the following general form:

$$W^i = W^i(X_1^1, ..., X_m^1, X_1^2, ..., X_m^2, ..., X_m^n; W^1 ..., W^{i-1}, W^{i+1}, ..., W^n)$$
$$\equiv W^i(X_{k=1,...,m}^{j=1,...,n}; W^{j \neq i}),$$

where X_k^j is the value of the kth variable (good, service, or activity) by the jth
individual, and $X_{k=1,...,m}^{j=1,...,n}$ is just a short-hand way of writing the $n \times m$ variables.

A self-concerning person may be distinguished from a "self-minding" one
with $W^i = W^i(X_{k=1,...,m}^{j=1,...,n})$ and $W^{j \neq i}$ do not affect W^i, and a "self-attending" one
with $W^i - W^i(X_{k=1,...,m}^i; W^{j \neq i})$ and $X_{k=1,...,m}^{j \neq i}$ do not affect W^i except through
their effects on W^j. The *preference* of a self-concerning person is not affected by
the welfare of others except in so far as his own welfare is affected. The *welfare*
of a self-minding person is not affected by the welfare of others. A self-concerning individual is more likely to exist than a self-minding one. (If my judgement is
right, over 90 percent are self-concerning except with respect to their immediate
family.) In fact, those who have difficulty seeing the distinction between a self-
concerning and a self-minding individual are likely to be self-concerning. A generous person who helps others a lot need not necessarily be non-self-concerning
since he may do so only because he himself feels happy doing so (i.e. he is non-
self-minding). Hence, operationally, it is very difficult to distinguish non-self-

concerning from non-self-minding. (But this distinction is not without policy significance; see below and also Ng, 1979, section 7.4.)

Secondly, preference may differ from welfare due to ignorance and imperfect foresight. While an individual may prefer x to y believing he will be better off in x than in y, it may turn out to be the other way around. This is the question of ex-ante versus ex-post. While the ex-ante concept is relevant for explaining behaviour, it is the ex-post one which is his actual welfare.

Thirdly, an individual may have irrational preferences. The preference of an individual is defined here to be irrational if he prefers x over y despite the fact that his welfare is higher in y than in x, neither due to a consideration of the welfare of other individuals (any sentient creature can be an individual here), nor to ignorance or imperfect foresight. The definition of irrationality here is such as to make the three factors discussed here exhaustive causes of divergence between preference and welfare.

There are at least two sources of irrational preference. First, an individual may stick rigidly to some habit, custom, "principles", or the like even if he knows that this is detrimental to his welfare and the welfare of others, even in the long run, taking account of all effects and repercussions. Customs, rules, moral principles, etc. have a rational basis since they may provide simple guides to behaviours which may be, at least on the whole, conducive to social welfare. It would be too cumbersome and time-consuming if an individual were to weigh the gain and loss in terms of social welfare or his own welfare each time he has to make a decision. Thus, he may stick to his routine, rules, principles, etc. without thinking about the gain and loss. If this results, occasionally, in decisions inconsistent with his welfare and the welfare of others, it may be regarded as a cost in pursuing generally good rules. If, say, there is a change in circumstances, the adherence to some rules may result in persistent net losses in welfare, taking everything into account. An individual may stick to these rules without knowing that they no longer are conducive to welfare. Then the divergence between preference and welfare can be traced to ignorance. If he knows this and yet sticks to the rules, he is irrational.

Many readers may disagree with the definition of irrationality adopted here. For example, suppose a man sticks rigidly to the principle of honesty and would not tell a lie even if that would save his happy life and contribute to the welfare of others, taking everything into account. According to our definition here, he is acting irrationally. For those who are willing to accept honesty as an ultimate good in itself, he may not be considered irrational. But let us consider such questions as: *Why* shouldn't a person tell a lie? Shouldn't one lie to an invading army which is cruel and dishonest? If we press hard enough with such questions, I believe most people would have gone ultimately to rely on social welfare as the final justification for any moral principle such as honesty. Personally, I take the (weighted or unweighted) aggregate welfare of all sentient creatures or a part thereof as the only rational ultimate end in itself (my basic value judgement, on which see Sen, 1967, and Ng, 1979, appendix 1A) and hence define irrationality accordingly. I know the controversial nature of this definition; fortunately, one does not have to agree on the definition of irrationality given here to agree with the arguments of this chapter.

The second source of irrational preference is the excessive fear of danger or pain and the excessive temptation of pleasure. For example, consider a person with an aching tooth which will cause nagging pain for a long time but can be treated by a dentist with just a once-and-for-all agony. With fear of the agony, the person may refuse to go to the dentist, thus subjecting himself to a greater amount of pain. His refusal to go to the dentist may be due to the ignorance of the greater amount of pain or to the ignorance of the fact that the agony of dental treatment is not really that bad. Then the cause of his preference that does not contribute to his welfare is classified under ignorance. But if he knows that very well but just cannot have the determination to undergo a once-and-for-all but present agony, he is being irrational. As another example, a drunkard may vote in favour of prohibiting Sunday drinking not for the sake of the public, road safety, or the like, but because he will then be forced to drink less. However, before the new law is effective, he may yet go out drinking on Sundays.

It may be objected that an individual himself is the sole judge of his own welfare and irrationality cannot therefore arise. But I think that some individuals will admit that some of their preferences are irrational. The first individual above may, after a few days, decide to face up to the dentist and agree that he should have done so days earlier. The drunkard may also agree that it is in his own interest to resist temptation.

However, the above source of irrational preference touches on the tricky question of the existence of free will. If an individual will be better off with x than with y but chooses y because x is not feasible, then obviously we would not call this irrational preference. Thus, a relevant question is whether x is within his feasible set. For example, one may argue that the individual in the first example above may have a psychological make-up that makes him *incapable* of deciding to go to the dentist before a few more days of pain help him to free himself of this incapability. Pursued to its logical conclusion, this line of argument will end up with the result that everything is predetermined and the feasible set open to any decision-maker consists only of one single point (or action). Little scope would be left for any theory of choice. To avoid this unpalatable result, we will not introduce too many constraints so as to leave an individual with some scope for exercising his preference.[2]

3.   Preference or welfare: which is the ingredient for social choice?

After distinguishing preference and welfare, let us ask: Which one should be the ingredient for social choice? Whether one is interested in preference or welfare depends partly on the problem at hand. Thus, a statesman is more interested in the welfare of the people while a politician is more interested in their preference. Preference is the relevant concept for the objective theories of production and distribution; welfare may be a more satisfactory criterion in assessing the performance of an economic, political, or social system. As an ultimate end, it seems that welfare is a more appropriate objective.

Where the divergence between preference and welfare is due to ignorance, the best way to deal with the problem may just be the provision of information. But what if the divergence persists? Or if it is very costly to provide the required information? And what if irrationality is also involved? Liberals may choose to ignore such divergences. This may be justified on the ground that, if we attempt to look after the welfare of people by overriding their preferences, this will lead to undesirable side-effects detrimental to the welfare of all in the long run. This just means that our objective is welfare but the best way to achieve welfare is to respect people's preferences even in the presence of divergences between preference and welfare. To a very large extent this is probably true. But what if preference and welfare do conflict even in the long run, taking all effects into account? I am prepared to go for welfare. It may also be noted that many actual instances of social decisions (e.g. prohibition of addictive drugs, compulsory wearing of seat-belts) cannot be adequately explained without invoking the divergence between preference and welfare due to ignorance and/or irrationality.

Consider now the divergence between preference and welfare due to a concern for the welfare of others. For simplicity, suppose our social welfare function is a utilitarian one of the sum of individual utilities or welfares. (The next section outlines an argument that this should be the case. Moreover, the use of a more general social welfare function does not change the problem of choosing between preference and welfares.) Take a simple case of a two-person society where person 1 is self-concerning with $U^1 = W^1$ and person 2 is perfectly non-self-concerning with $U^2 = W^1 + W^2$. Then the maximization of aggregate utilities gives us a social welfare function $W = U^1 + U^2 = 2W^1 + W^2$ and is quite different from the maximization of aggregate welfare $W = W^1 + W^2$. These two different social welfare functions have of course quite different implications for action. To illustrate,

---

[2]   This does not imply that the determinist view of the world is wrong. This is a matter of different types of problems; but I do not want to go into the depth of this philosophical problem.

consider two social alternatives x and y and assume utility and welfare measurability and comparability. The welfares of the two individuals under the two alternatives are as shown in table 9.1. Thus, the maximization of aggregate welfare

Table 9.1

	W^1	W^2	$W^1 + W^2$	$U^1 + U^2 = 2W^1 + W^2$
x	5	10	15	20
y	9	3	12	21

dictates that x should be chosen over y but the maximization of aggregate utility dictates the reverse. It might be argued that if person 2 takes account of the welfare of person 1 in his utility or preference function, he must himself be better off than is indicated by W^2. This argument misses my distinction between "self-concerning" and "self-minding" in section 2. Moreover, even if it is true that the welfare of person 2 is increased by that of person 1, this has already been taken into account in the values of W^2 in table 9.1. A non-self-concerning individual is one who has concern in his preference function for the welfare of others over and above the fact that his own welfare may be affected. I built a toy-house for my daughter which increases her welfare by 20 units. The fact that she feels happier by 20 units makes me feel happy by 5 units. But I suffer a decrease in welfare by 10 units in building the toy-house. Yet I preferred to build it, since I have concern over the welfare of my daughter over and above the fact that my own welfare is affected by her welfare.

In the above example where the divergence between preference and welfare is due to a concern for other individuals, it seems clear that the ingredient for social choice should be individual welfares instead of individual preferences. Using individual preferences as the ingredient in this case can be seen to involve some form of double-counting. In his private choice, it is not double-counting for person 2 to take account of person 1's welfare. But in the social choice, person 1's welfare already directly affects social choice and, to avoid double-counting, should not be allowed to have additional effect through its effect on person 2's utility function.

If the question is not non-self-concerning but non-self-minding, the double-counting argument should not in my view apply. If person 2 himself actually feels happier due to the increased happiness of person 1, the increases in happiness in both persons should be taken into account. In the case of non-self-concerning, the reason person 2 takes account of person 1's welfare is that he wants person 1's welfare to influence decision. In social choice that already allows for such an influence, no *additional* influence through person 1's preference should be permitted. In the case of non-self-minding, the reason why person 2 feels happier may be due to any reason but *not* because he wants person 1's welfare to influence decision. Hence, it is not double-counting to take account of both persons' increase in happiness. The following example further illustrates this point.

To abstract away secondary effects (incentives, etc.), consider an adult and a young child living on an isolated island with a given limited food supply. On their own each has the welfare function $W^i = \log F^i$, where F^i is the amount of food consumed by person i. (Differences in food requirement are abstracted away.) Ignore also the possible enjoyment of each due to the company of the other. The adult makes all decisions concerning the division of the given amount of food. If the consumption and welfare of the child enters neither the welfare function nor the preference function of the adult, the adult will appropriate all food for himself. Now let his welfare function to remain unchanged at $W^a = \log F^a$ but let him have a perfect concern for the child such that the welfare of the child W^c enters his preference function on a par with his own W^a. For simplicity, let $U^a = W^a + W^c = \log F^a + \log F^c$. (One could consider a more general function without changing the basic point.) He then chooses an equal division of food.

Now let the welfare of the child enter the *welfare* function of the adult. For example, the adult may *feel* bad if the child is suffering from hunger. For simplicity, let $W^a = \log F^a + W^c = \log F^a + \log F^c$. By assumption, the child is too young to have a similar welfare interdependency. Now something like a paradox arises. Should the adult maximize $U^a = W^a = \log F^a + \log F^c$ or $U^a = W^a + W^c = \log F^a + 2 \log F^c$? If he is self-concerning, he maximizes W^a. If he is perfectly non-self-concerning, as in the case of the previous paragraph, he maximizes $W^a + W^c$. The maximization of $W^a + W^c = \log F^a + 2 \log F^c$ dictates that the adult gives himself only one-third of the total food supply, half the amount given to the child. Does not this involve a double-counting of the significance of F^c? In a certain sense, yes. But this "double-counting" is done for a good reason. Since F^c positively affects both W^a and W^c, but F^a affects only W^a, the greater importance given to F^c can be justified, as is indeed required by the maximization of aggregate welfare.

One could construct examples where both persons are adults where the greater significance given to the self-minding person seems undesirable. But this can be explained by the long-run effects (incentives, etc.). The maximization of long-run aggregate welfare may not then involve giving more food to the self minding.

While welfare seems a more appropriate ultimate objective than preference, the pursuit of individual welfares may be best done by respecting individual preferences due to the argument of the liberals. Moreover, welfare is more subjective and preference more objective and easier to capture operationally. Hence, one may wish to use the preference of an individual as an indicator of his welfare unless there are specific important reasons to suggest a wide divergence between his preference and welfare. In what follows we will ignore such divergences and use preference (or utility) and welfare interchangeably.

4. An argument for a utilitarian social welfare function

Since we use preference or utility functions, let us ask: Is there a real-valued function U representing the preference of a person such that $U(x) > U(y)$ whenever he prefers x to y and $U(x) = U(y)$ whenever he is indifferent, and vice versa, where x and y are any two elements in the relevant set of alternatives X. It is convenient to define xRy as "x is regarded as at least as preferable as y". It is well known that if the relevant set of alternatives X is a countable set, then there exists a utility function U over X such that $U(x) \geqslant U(y) \Longleftrightarrow xRy$ if and only if the following two conditions are satisfied: (i) completeness; for all x, y in X, xRy and/or yRx; (ii) transitivity; for all x, y, z in X, xRy and yRz imply xRz.

If X includes a continuum of alternatives such as the set of all points in a Euclidean space, the set is uncountable. An additional continuity condition that preference does not jump still ensures the existence of a utility function.[3]

All these conditions, especially transitivity, sound very reasonable. It seems to be just a consequence of logical consistency. However, there is a reason suggesting that transitivity may be violated. This is due to the fact that human beings are not infinitely discriminative. For example, suppose an individual prefers two spoons of sugar (x) to one (y) in his coffee. If we increase the amount of sugar continuously from one spoon, we will reach a point y' (say 1.8 spoons) for which the individual cannot tell the difference between x and y'. There may exist another point y'' (say 1.6 spoons) for which he is indifferent to y' but he prefers x to y''. Hence, a perfectly rational individual may have intransitive indifference.[4] This intransitivity is well known in the literature of psychology on the concept of "just noticeable difference". The concept was touched on as far back as 1781 by Borda and in 1881 by Edgeworth. Edgeworth called it "minimum sensibile" and took it as axiomatic, or, in his words "a first principle incapable of proof", that the "minimum sensibile" or the just-perceivable increment of pleasure, of all

---

[3] The continuity condition is however not necessary for preference representation. The necessary and sufficient condition is given in Cantor's Theorem: There is a real-valued preference-representing function U on X if and only if P (the strict preference) on X is a weak order and there is a countable subset of X that is P-order dense in X (i.e. there exists a countable set $Y \subseteq X$ such that, whenever xPz and $x, z \epsilon X - Y$, there is a $y \epsilon Y$ such that $xPyPz$); see Fishburn (1972, p. 59).

[4] I have shown elsewhere (Ng, 1977) that we may even have "consistent" intransitivity of *preference* for choices involving multi-dimensions.

pleasures for all persons, are equatable (Edgeworth, 1881, pp. 7ff. 60 ff.). It has been shown (Ng, 1975) that this can be derived from more basic axioms.

With intransitivity of indifference, the (explicit) preference of an individual can no longer be represented by a utility function. However, it can be shown that his "underlying preference" (Ng, 1975, p. 549) may still be represented by a utility function. In terms of his explicit preference, the utility function can be scaled to have the following property:

$$yPx \Longleftrightarrow U(y) - U(x) > a,$$
$$xRy \Longleftrightarrow U(y) - U(x) \leqslant a,$$

where a is a constant, i.e. any number (say one) used to represent a utility difference of a marginal (or maximal) indifference.[5]

Using the above utility function (which is unique up to a positive afine transformation) for each individual, it has been shown elsewhere (Ng, 1975) that our social welfare function is just the unweighted sum of individual utilities (the Summation Theorem) if we accept the following value premise:[6]

Weak majority preference criterion (WMP). For any two alternatives, x and y, if no individual prefers y to x, and (i) if n, the number of individuals, is even, at least $n/2$ individuals prefer x to y; (ii) if n is odd, at least $(n-1)/2$ individuals prefer x to y and at least another individual's utility level has not decreased, then social welfare is higher in x than in y.

It can be seen that WMP is a very reasonable premise; it is roughly a combination of the majority rule and the (strong) Pareto principle. The rejection of WMP implies the rejection of both the Pareto principle and the majority rule.

The reason why WMP leads us to the utilitarian social welfare function may be briefly explained. The criterion WMP requires that utility differences sufficient to give rise to preferences of half of the population must be regarded as socially more significant than utility differences not sufficient to give rise to preferences (or dis-preferences) of the other half. Since any group of individuals comprising 50 percent of the population is an acceptable half, this effectively makes a just-perceivable increment of pleasure of any individual an interpersonally comparable unit of utility. Some people may find this unacceptable. But the rejection

---

[5] This is basically interval representation of explicit preferences explored earlier by other writers; see Fishburn (1970) for a survey.
[6] Some other assumptions involving purely technical details are also used.

of WMP means that we are not prepared to say "yes" even if half of the population say "yes" and the other half do not feel any difference. Then, it seems that we can say "yes" only if *all* individuals say "yes". This is not a palatable outcome. I have also provided a defence of WMP and the utilitarian principle in Ng (1975, especially sections 2 and 5).

5. Who are the individuals?

The social choice literature predominantly takes the set of individuals as given. With a given set of individuals, individual utility functions unique up to a positive afine transformation serve as a sufficient basis upon which social choice may be made.[7] With the number of individuals as a variable, one would like to work with utility functions unique up to a positive proportionate transformation (i.e. strict cardinal measurability, or ratio-scale measurability). From a utility function unique up to a positive afine transformation, what we need is the level of zero utility to get to ratio-scale measurability. This seems easy enough, at least conceptually.

> There can be little doubt that an individual, apart from his attitude of preference or indifference to a pair of alternatives, may also desire an alternative not in the sense of preferring it to some other alternative, or may have an aversion towards it not in the sense of contra-preferring it to some alternative. There seems to be [there certainly are] pleasant situations that are intrinsically desirable and painful situations that are intrinsically repugnant. It does not seem unreasonable to postulate that welfare is +ve in the former case and −ve in the later (Armstrong, 1951, p. 269).

If we have in mind a utility function for the whole lifespan of an individual, positive and negative utilities are still obvious in such remarks as: "If I had to lead such a miserable life, I'd wish not to have been born at all!"

When the number of individuals is given, the maximization of aggregate welfare (sum) is equivalent to the maximization of average welfare (mean). However,

---

[7] That purely ordinal utilities or individual *orderings* provide insufficient information basis for a reasonable social choice is established by Arrow's impossibility theorem for the multi-profile framework (i.e. where individual preferences may change) and established by the impossibility propositions of Kemp and Ng (1976) and Parks (1976) for the single-profile framework (i.e. a fixed set of individual preferences). See also Ng (1979, appendix 5A) which provides a proof of the incompatibility of individualism and ordinalism and Roberts (1980a, 1980b, 1980c).

if the number of individuals is a variable, such as in the problem of optimum population, sum and mean may have quite different results. More generally, consider the social welfare function $W = \Sigma(W^i)^{1-\alpha}/(1-\alpha)$, where α may be varied to accommodate different degrees of "egalitarianism". Faced with a variable population, one has to choose whether to maximize $\Sigma_{i=1}^n (W^i)^{1-\alpha}/(1-\alpha)$ or $\Sigma_{i=1}^n (W^i)^{1-\alpha}/(1-\alpha)n$ or somewhere in between. Utilitarians, who agree that $\alpha = 1$, are themselves quite divided on this issue of whether we should maximize the sum or the mean. A recent heated argument on this problem between Professor Harsanyi and myself is reproduced in the Appendix. Here, I shall just note that aggregate welfare is the appropriate objective if we accept the following extended WMP criterion to cover the case of a variable population.

Extended WMP. Social welfare is increased by bringing t (any positive integer) more individuals into existence if:

(i)   these t new individuals have positive utilities, i.e. enjoy their lives;

(ii)   none of the original s individuals prefers that the t new individual not to be born;

(iii)   if $s > t$, at least $(s - t)$ original individuals' utility levels have not decreased due to the birth of the t new individuals.

Using the above Extended WMP, one can then prove, in a similar way as the proof of the Summation Theorem in Ng (1975), that we should maximize aggregate welfare instead of average welfare.

Is our set of individuals confined to human beings? It is natural self-interest for the human race to be more concerned with its own welfare than that of other sentient creatures. Likewise for an individual and a nation. But on the level of ethics, I find it compelling to extend the set of individuals to cover all sentients. Again, one can see that this ought to be so if we accept the WMP criterion defined in the previous section, interpreting an individual to be any sentient creature.

A sentient is any creature which is capable of the feeling of well-being and/or suffering. All vertebrates are most probably included. It is less certain whether lower forms of animals are sentients. However, it cannot be ruled out that all animals and perhaps some plants are sentients. Nevertheless, personally I have not yet been persuaded by recent studies on the "secret lives" of plants (see, for example, Backster, 1968; Warr, 1969; Tompkins and Bird, 1974) that plants are sentients. Though it seems that plants react to outside stimuli, including human intention (or is it the change in humidity, etc. thus caused?), "reaction" as such does not constitute "feeling".

The inclusion of animals in our welfare function need not necessarily imply that we have to become vegetarians. But in all probability it does require the prohibition of or the imposition of special taxes on many forms of maltreatment of animals (including certain practices used in factory farming) and the encouragement of painless insecticides or at least "fast killers", etc. On a practical level, it seems to me that non-speciesists can more easily achieve the objective of reducing the suffering of animals without causing significant sacrifice on the part of mankind by agitating for these kinds of reform instead of undertaking the difficult task of persuading people to become vegetarians, at least as a first item on the agenda.

Even if we wish to confine ourselves to human beings, shall we include just our conscious selves or the subconscious as well? Psychology and parapsychology have revealed the possible enormous range of capabilities of the subconscious.[8] Do we have to take this into account? Suppose we have a machine that induces a person to have all sorts of ecstatic dreams without affecting his rest or health and without having any other good or bad side-effect on his conscious life. If he is awakened during the dream, he can recall his dream and confirm that it is joyful. But he cannot recall anything if awakened after the dream. If his welfare increased by having ecstatic dreams which he cannot recall? *His* welfare? Or the welfare of his subconscious? Should we encourage the invention of such a dream-making machine? If one were available, would you be willing to pay for its installation at your bedside?

When a colleague of mine said that he would not pay a single cent, I asked him the following question: "If you are constrained to use one machine but are free to choose between one inducing ecstatic dreams and another inducing horror dreams, would you be indifferent between the two?" He then answered that he preferred the ecstatic one and agreed that he should reconsider his answer to the first question.

Though I am prepared to keep an open mind, I am inclined to include the welfare of our subconscious or our welfare when we are in a subconscious state into our social welfare function. We cannot recall much of our past enjoyment and suffering experienced in our conscious state of mind. This does not render such experience worthless. One may argue that the welfare of our subconscious is really part of our own welfare. However, many individuals may not pay attention to this part of their welfare since they cannot remember its experience or even know of its existence. If it does exist, this may well be a cause of the divergence between preference and welfare which one may or may not wish to clas-

---

[8] Some psychologists object to the use of "subconsciousness" or "unconsciousness" as independent of consciousness and regard the subconscious as derived from the conscious, the unconscious is "forgotten consciousness" or "implicit non-sensory ideation"; see Klein (1977). The acceptance of this view does not invalidate the question raised here and in fact tends to favour the inclusion of the welfare of our "subconscious" into our objective function.

sify under "ignorance". If an individual were to take his subconscious welfare into account (if he knew of its existence), then the divergence is due to ignorance. If he did not, then this raises a more serious difficulty. Should we take the individual as the best judge of his own welfare including his subconscious welfare, or should society act to protect our subconscious welfare from our conscious prejudice or apathy?

6. Disturbing implications and a way out

The argument of the previous section has some disturbing implications even if we just take account of the size of (human) population and/or animal welfare. I shall consider these implications briefly and suggest a way of dealing with them.

Many people can be persuaded to oppose the maximization of welfare average or utility mean in the problem of optimum population. They will agree that a population of say 10 million persons each enjoying a utility of 1,000 units is preferable to one with 1 million persons each enjoying a utility of 1,001 units. Maximizing utility mean implies that one will refuse to trade-off any reduction, no matter how minute, in utility mean even if this would bring many happy lives to many more persons. But many people also regard the maximization of utility sum as having the reverse disturbing implication. Many people cannot accept the implication that a population of 10 million persons each with 1,000 utils (x) is inferior to one with 20,000 million each with one util (y). In my view, in such a comparison the 19,990 million prospective but non-existent persons under alternative x must be taken as having zero utils each. It is then easy to see that 10 million 1,000 utils plus 19,990 million zeros is inferior to 20,000 million ones. However, some people insist that a non-existent person should be ignored and not assigned a zero. This view is subject to the difficulty of the Parfit Paradox outlined below.[9]

Consider two alternative policies toward resources called (reasonable) Conservation and (rapid) Depletion that may be pursued by the present generation but that would have implications for people generations from now. The usual argument against Depletion is that it would drastically reduce the welfare of future generations with a relatively small gain to the present generations. But Parfit argues that there is no future person whose existence is independent of which policy is pursued. Conceptions at different times and even different marriages will be made, making different people being born under one policy than the other. Depletion would lower the quality of life in the far future, but the people who

---

[9]   Parfit (1982); see also the discussion of the paradox by Govier (1979).

would then be living would not have been born if instead we had adopted Conservation. Those who would be living would be another set of people. If these people's lives would be still worth living, Depletion would be better for them. Parfit concludes that Depletion would be worse for no one while it makes the present generation better off. Parfit is not advocating depletion of our resources. He presents his argument as a paradox but does not propose any solution.

In my view, Parfit's paradox can be solved easily if we regard a person who does not or would not exist under alternative x but would exist under y (whom I shall call a "prospective person") as having a zero utility under x, at least for the purpose of comparing the two alternatives x and y. Those prospective persons who would be living under Conservation can then be said to be worse off with Depletion. If we ignore prospective persons as many people do, we are not only subject to the Parfit paradox but also to the following "extinction paradox".

Suppose that a chemical has been invented which if released into the air will clean up the atmosphere and make us healthy, able to enjoy life better and not get any older. But it will also make us all sterile (but sexually still active, if not more so) and die painlessly after one hundred years. Suppose also that everyone regards the better health, etc. as more than compensating for the inability to have any more children. So all existing persons will be made better off and no new person will be born. Should the chemical be released? The answer is yes if we ignore prospective persons. I hope that this extinction paradox will persuade readers that prospective persons should not be ignored.

Many people will agree that the welfare of animals and prospective persons should be taken into account in our social choice. But few would go as far as putting their welfare on a par with our welfare. This "parity" does not imply that we should share our food equally with animals and let animals sleep on our beds. Because of biological and other differences, such a naive equality policy obviously does not maximize overall welfare. In addition, we have to take account of all sorts of indirect effects, including incentives. Nevertheless, even taking everything into account, man–animal parity may require man to sacrifice an enormous amount of his welfare if the welfare of animals can be increased by more. Most people (myself included) are not prepared to sustain such sacrifices. What justification can we provide to reject man–animal parity? I can think of a pure and simple one – self-interest. To those who object that this is hardly an acceptable *justification*, I have to agree. In fact, from an ideal moralistic point of view, I find parity for all sentients very compelling. But the acceptance of parity carries with it the disturbing implication of probable enormous sacrifice on the part of man. One way out of this is to make a distinction between the ideal moralistic and the actual objective functions. Most persons' and nations' objective functions are largely influenced by their own self-interests. Abstracting from the complications of ignorance and irrationality, a completely self-interested person is defined here as one who has neither positive concern nor positive "minding" about others' welfares. In other words, a completely self-interested person is both self-concerning and self-minding (as defined in section 2) except for possible negative concern and/or negative "minding" (e.g. envy). To the extent that a person's welfare is positively affected by others' welfares (e.g. sympathy) and/or to the extent that his preference is also positively affected by others' welfares directly, his utility function moves from the completely self-interested one towards the ideal moralistic one. Perhaps one may term non-self-concerning as non-self-interestedness in choice, and non-self-minding as non-self-interestedness in feeling.

From a global point of view, I cannot find any acceptable justification to reject parity for all sentients (where all effects have been taken into account). Mankind may nevertheless admit that it is self-interested just like a person or a nation is usually self-interested. But most persons are not completely self-interested and usually have some degree of non-self-interestedness in feeling, if not in choice. With the advancement of our civilization, perhaps mankind can move a little bit more towards non-self-interestedness with respect to other sentients.

Appendix: On maximizing utility sum vs. mean

(Correspondence during 1977 between Professor John C. Harsanyi of the University of California, Berkeley, and Dr. Yew-Kwang Ng of Monash University. The quotations below are exact quotations; no attempt has been made even to correct any grammatical mistakes.)

Ng (26 January):

I have just read your paper on Nonlinear social welfare functions[10] with great interest and find myself very much in agreement with it ...

There is only one comment I wish to make. You mention the arithmetic *mean* of utilities as the right SWF. This is OK with fixed number of individuals (or sentient creatures). With this as a variable, I think we should use the arithmetic *sum* of utilities. It is true that each lucky individual may prefer a higher mean to a higher sum, but what about the excluded individuals (prevented from birth by a restrictive policy maximising mean instead of sum)?

---

[10]   Harsanyi (1975).

Harsanyi (4 February):

I do feel that we should choose the arithmetic *mean*, rather than the *sum*, of individual utilities as our social welfare function. This is so because non-existing potential individuals have no moral claims on us, they have no "right" to exist. In contrast, our fellow humans already in existence do have the right not to have their standards of living depressed by our uncontrolled procreative activities. In short, I feel a world having a smaller but well-to-do population is morally preferable over a world having a larger but desperately poor population.

Ng (9 February):

I agree that a world having a smaller but well-to-do and happy population is preferable over a world having a larger but desperately poor population. But this is so only because the people in the later probably enjoy negative (or at best very low) utilities and hence smaller in terms of sums of utilities. To see that maximizing mean is not morally acceptable, consider the following hypothetical example. Suppose that we know with certainty that our world with one million (or one thousand, or ten) inhabitants in the future will maximize average utility = 100 units. And that the world can support a population of 4,000 million quite comfortably with average utility = 80 units. Suppose also that people do not care about the number of children they are having. Would you favour a policy that will reduce the world population to one million (or ten persons?) or one that maintains at 4,000 million? Whether it is the one million or the 4,000 million, they are all unborn now. No one has more "right" than another. In fact I am a little surprised that you bring in the abstract "right" argument. To be a good utilitarian, all rights are justified, in the final analysis, to utility (i.e. happiness minus pain, widely interpreted). Why doesn't a stone have "rights"? Because it is not sentient.

Ng (21 February):

It seems to me that, in my example of a future population of 4,000 million with average utility = 80 units versus a population of 10 million with average utility = 100 units, the superiority of the former can be shown to be so even by using your criterion of expected utility maximization under the veil of ignorance, properly interpreted. A person maximizing his expected utility will choose the second policy if he knows for sure that he will be one of the lucky 10 million. But under the veil of ignorance, how can one exclude the possibility that one may not be born at all. A fair comparison is the following: If the probability that one will be born as one of the 10 million is $x\%$, then the probability of being one of the 4,000 million is $400x\%$. It is then clear that a rational person maximizing expected utility will choose the first policy, assuming a non-person (unborn, hypothetical, non-existent being) to enjoy zero utility. (What else could it be?)

Harsanyi (15 March):

Mean utility and the veil of ignorance. I think it is a rather forced and unnatural interpretation of the "veil of ignorance" to assume that it would involve ignorance about one's own existence or non-existence. Surely, if I can make any decisions or moral value judgments at all, this will be a sure sign that I do exist. Of course, I can consider the possibility that I may *die* in the next moment, but I cannot reasonably consider the possibility that I may *not exist* or may never have been born.

All the same, I can make my point even if you insist on this strange interpretation of the "veil of ignorance". Suppose that under the "veil of ignorance" I would consider n different possible worlds, each having the same probability $1/n$ of coming into existence. Out of these n possible worlds, I would exist in the first k possible worlds, and would not exist in the remaining $(n - k)$ possible worlds. You seem to assume that in that situation the rational decision-making criterion for me would be to maximize the *unconditional* expectation of my utility function, i.e. to maximize the quantity

$$\epsilon(U) = \frac{1}{n} \sum_{i=1}^{n} U_i, \tag{1}$$

where U_i is the utility level I would enjoy in the ith possible world.

Yet, in actual fact, in that situation the only rational decision rule for me would be to maximize the *conditional* expectation of my utility function *on the condition that I would in fact exist.* This would amount to maximizing the quantity

$$\epsilon(U \mid \text{given my existence}) = \frac{1}{k} \sum_{i=1}^{k} U_i. \tag{2}$$

This is so because only existing people can have real utility levels since they are the only ones able to *enjoy* objects with a positive utility, *suffer* from objects with a negative utility, and *feel indifferent* to objects with zero utility. As for non-existing people, we may wish to assign purely theoretical *fictitious* utility levels to them (e.g., by setting $U = 0$ for them). But we must always keep in mind that these utility levels are purely fictitious since such people obviously cannot *experience* any utility level, whether high, or low, or in between.

I may rationally assign a high disutility to the possibility of *dying* (e.g., to having a high probability of dying in the near future, say, because of an incurable illness). But I cannot rationally assign any real utility or disutility (or even any real zero utility) to the possibility of *not being born* at all, because

(a) If I can assign any utility or disutility to anything then I must be alive and must have been born already;
and

(b) Assuming that I would not have been born, I could not derive any utility, disutility, or zero utility from this fact.

Accordingly, in moral decisions, the social welfare function to be maximized is the quantity defined under (2), rather than the quantity defined under (1). This means that our social welfare function must be the *mean utility* of all individuals now living or to be born in the future, rather than the *sum* of all individual utilities. This of course implies that a world of one million extremely happy people is preferable over a world of one hundred million somewhat less happy people. I fully endorse this implication. To my mind, the *quality* of life has absolute precedence over its *quantity*.

Ng (6 April):

I agree with you perfectly that the utility of a non-existent person is zero. But the point is that if a policy of maximizing utility sum is adopted, the probability that any "I" will in fact exist is increased. What you are assuming is that the "I" will certainly exist. (Probability = 100%.) It is then rational for him if he is purely self-interested to go along with the maximization of utility mean.

The maximization of utility mean does not just imply that a world of one million very happy people is preferable over a world of one hundred million somewhat less happy people. It also implies that a world of two (assuming that that is sufficient for reproduction, etc.) fairly happy people is preferable to a world of 4,000 million a little less but still quite happy people. If you can accept this moral implication without any uneasiness whether the two lucky persons happen to be the Ng's or the Harsanyi's or not, I must confess that your morality and mine must be miles apart.

I will give another example to persuade you. Compare the following three situations. A: 2 persons each with 100 utils; B: the same 2 persons each with 100 utils as in A plus another 8 persons each with 99 utils; C: ten persons each with 99.7 utils. Situation B has exactly the same 2 persons as in A each with exactly the same amount of utils. But in addition, there are another 8 quite happy people. These 8 people would, if given the choice, choose to be born than not. The two persons with 100 utils each do not mind whether the 8 persons exist or not. I can only conclude that B is preferable to A. On the other hand, B is indifferent to C whether according to utility mean or utility sum. I conclude therefore that C is preferable to A. Hence, the maximization of utility mean cannot be acceptable.

Harsanyi (20 April):

In my letter I have said that I want to maximize the *conditional expectation* of my utility function, *based on the condition* that I will exist. You now claim that this statement has the implication that I assign probability one to the assumption that I will exist. This is not the case at all: my statement does not have this implication. It seems to me that you misunderstand what probability theorists call the "conditional expectation" of a random variable: by using a conditional expectation, we do not assign any numerical probability to the condition, and certainly do not assign unity probability to it.

Ng (4 May):

I take it that you accept the moral implication of preferring a society of 2 individuals (not 2 million, just 2 persons) each with 100 utils to one of 4,000 million individuals each with 99.9 utils. ...

If you do not assume that the probability of the existence of the individual is 100%, then I think that a rational individual would not maximize the conditional expected utility *based on the condition that he will exist.* Rather, I think he would maximize the expected value of his conditional expected utility, i.e. his conditional expected utility times the probability that he will exist. At least I would. To assume that he will maximize the conditional expected utility is to assume that he will not care about the probability of his actual existence. Your "rational" individual would then prefer a conditional expected utility of 100 utils with only 0.1% probability of actual existence to another conditional expected utility of 99.9 utils with the certainty (i.e. 100% probability) of actual existence. I would not regard such a person as rational.

Harsanyi (23 May):

You want to compare two hypothetical societies: one (A), having only two members and having an average utility level of 100 units; and another, (B), having 4,000 million members and having an average utility level of 99.9 units. This raises two questions:

(i) Is it really possible that such a small society (like A) should have a utility level higher than a much larger society (like B)?

(ii) *If* this were possible, and were actually the case, would society A be preferable to society B?

I think the answer to question (i) is probably "*no*". A very small society would have to have a very low productivity level because it would have very little division of labor and could not use modern mass production methods. Therefore, it would have a very low economic standard of living. Its cultural and intellectual life would also be rather thin; and it would not offer enough opportunity to human companionship.

Of course, a very large society with an unduly high population density would be equally undesirable, because of the scarcity of basic raw materials and of agricultural land on this planet, because of the pollution problem, and because of the undesirable effects of sheer physical overcrowding as such. This is why many people are rightly worried about the possibility that world population may reach a high multiple of its present level in the near future.

Yet, even though I think it is unrealistic to assume that a very, very small society could have a higher utility level than a much larger (but not excessively large) society, we can ask question (ii) as a purely *hypothetical* question: *Would society A be preferable to society B if it did* have a slightly higher average utility level?

In my opinion, the answer must be clearly "*yes*". What does it mean to say that one society is preferable to another? It can only mean that a *rational* individual would *prefer* to be a member of the first society rather than of the second if he had a choice, assuming that he would not know which particular social position he would have in either society (but rather would think he would have the same chance of occupying *any* possible position in any given society)? In this sense, society A would be clearly *slightly preferable* to society B; a rational individual would *slightly prefer* to live in A rather than in B, simply because 100 is a slightly larger number than 99.9. How could he possibly have the opposite preference?

You might object that a morally sensitive individual should assign some weight to the interests of those not-as-yet-existing individuals who *would* exist if society B came into existence, but who would *never* exist if society A came into existence. But I think this would be an invalid argument. Surely, it would be irrational for us to feel sorry for those possible individuals who will never exist, since the latter will not experience any disutility at all as a result of their nonexistence — because nonexistent individuals cannot experience any disutility or utility at all. Unhappy existence is a hardship; but nonexistence is not.

In any case, in any possible world there will be only a *finite* number of existing individuals, but the number of possible individuals is presumably *infinite* (because there are infinitely many possible combinations of psychological characteristics). Thus, in *any* possible world, however large its population may be, and however long its history may be over time, only a negligibly small proportion of all possible individuals will exist. But I really cannot see why we should worry about this metaphysical fact.

I am glad that now you seem to appreciate that maximizing my *conditional* expected utility, based on the condition that I will actually exist, does *not* in any way mean assigning 100 per cent probability to my existence. It is regrettable that so much correspondence had to be devoted to dispelling this and other similar, technical misunderstandings. Now that this confusion is out of the way, we can at last consider the real problem, vix. whether a rational person will or will not maximize this *conditional* utility expectation.

In my view, a rational person will no doubt try to maximize this *conditional* utility expectation, rather that his *unconditional* utility expectation. The reason is this. If he is rational then he will surely realize that he *already exists*, and that he could not possibly worry about maximizing either utility expectation if he did not already exist. It is a general rule in decision theory that, if you know that a particular event E has in fact occurred, then you will never try to maximize your *unconditional* utility expectation but rather will try to maximize your *conditional* utility expectation, with event E as conditioning event. That is, you will not maximize $\epsilon(U)$ but rather will maximize $\epsilon(U \mid E)$.

Of course, in moral analysis, you may sometimes wish to *abstract* from the information you have about some event E. But there is one piece of information you cannot possibly abstract from, and this is information about your own existence. It is surely absurd to imagine that you want to maximize something even though you do not exist, or do not as yet exist. ...

In conclusion, it seems to me that the time has come to stop our correspondence on the remaining differences between us. I feel we have now reached the point of sharply decreasing returns. You will probably feel the same way. Perhaps one day we will meet personally in some part of the world, and will have an opportunity to discuss some of these problems personally.

References

Armstrong, W.E. (1951) "Utility and the Theory of Welfare", *Oxford Economic Papers*, 3.

Backster, C. (1968) "Evidence of a Primary Perception in Plant Life", *International Journal of Parapsychology*, 10.

Edgeworth, F.Y. (1881) *Mathematical Psychics* (Kegan Paul, London).

Fishburn, Peter C. (1970) "Intransitive Indifference in Preference Theory: A Survey", *Operations Research*, 18.

Fishburn, Peter C. (1972) *Mathematics of Decision Theory* (Mouton, The Hague).

Govier, Trudy (1979) "What Should We Do About Future People?", *American Philosophical Quarterly*, 16.

Harsanyi, John C. (1975) "Nonlinear Social Welfare Functions", *Theory and Decision*, 6.

Kemp, Murray C. and Yew-Kwang Ng (1976) "On the Existence of Social Welfare Functions, Social Orderings, and Social Decision Functions", *Economica*, 43.

Klein, D.B. (1977) *The Unconscious: Invention or Discovery? A Historico-critical Inquiry* (Goodyear, Santa Monica).

Ng, Yew-Kwang (1969) "A Study of the Inter-relationships Between Efficient Resource Allocation, Economic Growth, and Welfare and the Solution of these Problems in Market Socialism", Ph.D. thesis, University of Sydney.

Ng, Yew-Kwang (1975) "Bentham or Bergson? Finite Sensibility, Utility Function, and Social Welfare Functions", *Review of Economic Studies*, 42.

Ng, Yew-Kwang (1977) "Sub-semiorder: A Model of Multi-dimensional Choice with Preference Intransitivity", *Journal of Mathematical Psychology*.

Ng, Yew-Kwang (1979) *Welfare Economics: Introduction and Development of Basic Concepts* (Macmillan, London).

Ng, Yew-Kwang (1981) "Welfarism: A Defence Against Sen's Attack", *Economic Journal*, 91.

Parfit, Derek (1982) "Future Generations: Further Problems", *Philosophy and Public Affairs*, 11.

Parks, Robert P. (1976) "An Impossibility Theorem for Fixed Preferences: A Dictatorial Bergson-Samuelson Welfare Function", *Review of Economic Studies*, 43.

Prince, Walter F. (1927) *The Case of Patience Worth* (Boston Society for Psychic Research).

Roberts, Kevin W.S. (1980a) "Possibility Theorems with Interpersonally Comparable Welfare Levels", *Review of Economic Studies*, 47.

Roberts, Kevin W.S. (1980b) "Interpersonal Comparability and Social Choice Theory", *Review of Economic Studies*, 47.

Roberts, Kevin W.S. (1980c) "Social Choice Theory: The Single-profile and Multi-profile Approaches", *Review of Economic Studies*, 47.

Sen, Amartya K. (1967) "The Nature and Classes of Prescriptive Judgments", *Philosophical Quarterly*, 17.

Sen, Amartya K. (1973) "Behaviour and the Concept of Preference", *Economica*, 40.

Sen, Amartya K. (1979) "Personal Utilities and Public Judgments: Or What's Wrong with Welfare Economics?", *Economic Journal*, 89.

Tompkins, Peter and Christopher Bird (1974) *Secret Life of Plants* (Penguin, Harmondsworth).

Warr, de la G. (1969) "Do Plants Feel Emotion?" *Electso Technology*.

CHAPTER 10

Ex-post optimality as a dynamically consistent objective for collective choice under uncertainty

PETER HAMMOND*
Stanford University

1. Introduction: ex-ante and ex-post

Following the pioneering work of Arrow and Debreu on the economics of uncertainty, some kind of consensus appears to have emerged as to what welfare criterion should be used to assess the allocation of risk in an economy. Arrow and Debreu showed how the powerful device of contingent commodities (or securities) allows the economic theorist to treat allocations under uncertainty. In particular, the standard welfare propositions relating Pareto efficient allocations to competitive equilibria apply equally to economies with uncertainty and with contingent commodity markets. In such economies, Pareto efficiency is defined with respect to the preferences which govern consumers' market behaviour, as usual, with uncertainty, and under the Ramsey—Savage axioms which entail expected utility maximization by consumers, these preferences embody consumers' subjective

* This work was supported by National Science Foundation Grant SES-79-24831 at the IMSSS, Stanford University. My interest in the subject was aroused many years ago by my Ph.D. supervisors, Christopher Bliss and James Mirrlees; I have also benefited over the years from discussions with Jacques Drèze, Jack Mintz, Knud Munk, Agnar Sandmo, Amartya Sen, and Ross Starr; in deciding to write the chapter I was much encouraged by Kotaro Suzumura: my thanks to all of these.

An earlier version of parts of this chapter under the title "Some Uncomfortable Options in Welfare Economics Under Uncertainty" was presented to the IMSSS workshop, Summer 1980. My thanks to the workshop participants, especially Kenneth Arrow, Frank Hahn, Sergiu Hart, Mordecai Kurz, and Bob Wilson, for some perceptive comments which made me realize that I should consider explicitly a dynamic choice framework. They may still not agree with my position, however.

Social Choice and Welfare, edited by P.K. Pattanaik and M. Salles
© *North-Holland Publishing Company, 1983*

probabilities and their attitudes to risk. To put it more concisely, Pareto efficiency is then defined relative to consumers' ex-ante expected utilities.

Though this concept of ex-ante Pareto efficiency is the one which preserves the efficiency of competitive markets, its ethical appeal is perhaps more limited than economists have been willing to admit. The least controversial case is when some consumers have subjective probabilities based on poor information: then it becomes very hard to claim that a market allocation cannot be dominated in a proper welfare sense by another allocation which would emerge if consumers were fully informed.[1] And, though some extreme proponents of laissez faire might argue that, if consumers have chosen to be less than fully informed, this inefficiency is not really relevant, it is hard to know how consumers can always be expected to make optimal decisions on whether to buy information, for instance, until they know what the information is.[2] It is, moreover, ex-ante Pareto efficient to try to make consumers as optimistic as possible about the future, without regard to reality. And, insofar as welfare judgements of what is equitable are based on comparisons of utility levels, it is all too easy to give a pessimist disproportionate weight if one compares levels of ex-ante expected utility.[3]

An alternative approach to welfare economics under uncertainty is based on individuals' utilities ex-post. *Ex-post efficiency* means that it is impossible to make an individual i better off in some event E which has positive probability without making the same or another individual j worse off in the same or another event E' which has positive probability (see Hammond, 1981a; Harris, 1978; and Harris and Olewiler, 1979; compare Starr, 1973). This is a rather weak welfare criterion. Of rather more interest is ex-post (welfare) optimality based on an ex-post welfare function, constructed as follows. For each state of the world s, construct a measure of ex-post social welfare which depends on individuals' ex-post utilities in state s (and on interpersonal comparisons of those utilities). Then construct a social welfare function which is the expected value of this ex-post measure of social welfare, with appropriate probabilities. This is the ex-post approach to welfare economics, with social welfare the expected value of a social welfare function. By contrast, the ex-ante approach discussed previously makes

---

[1]   The question of whether more information improves the market allocation has recently received extensive discussion by, among others, Hirshleifer (1971), Marshall (1974), Ng (1975), and Hakansson, Kunkel, and Ohlson (1980). While it is true that extra information makes no difference in an economy of pure exchange with *additively separable* preferences, this is a very special case which has received undue emphasis in the literature. More generally, extra information improves a first-best allocation. For further discussion, see Hammond (1981b), where I advocate that a policy-maker maximize expected ex-post welfare based on the best information available to him.

[2]   A related problem is the difficulty a firm faces is knowing how much expenditure should be devoted to research and development. See, for example, Dasgupta and Heal (1979, pp. 425–427).

[3]   This elaborates a point I owe to a conversation many years ago with Christopher Bliss.

social welfare a function of individuals' ex-ante expected utilities.

The contrast between the ex-ante and ex-post approaches to welfare economics under uncertainty has already received extensive discussion by Diamond (1967a, 1967b), Drèze (1970), Starr (1973), Guesnerie and de Montbrial (1974), Mirrlees (1974), Harsanyi (1975), Harris (1978), Harris and Olewiler (1979), and Hammond (1981a). Though the contrast has been noted, however, there have been few if any suggestions for a satisfactory reconciliation of the two approaches.

One of the weaknesses of this literature has been its failure to realize that the contrast between ex-ante and ex-post under uncertainty is similar to the problem of inconsistency of dynamic choice, as discussed by Strotz (1956) and numerous successors. Here I propose to make full use of this analogy.

Now, in normative decision-making under uncertainty, we are accustomed to focusing attention on the eventual consequences in the various possible states of the world. The times at which crucial decisions are to be made and at which we are to learn of random events are of no relevance. In the language of game theory and decision theory, it is the normal or reduced form of the decision problem which matters, rather than the structure of the decision tree. It is simply a matter of maximizing once and for all a given preference ordering, defined on the space of contingent outcomes, subject to constraints which determine what contingent outcomes are feasible. This approach to decision-making I take to be basic. It is at variance with Koopmans' (1964) idea of preference for flexibility per se, with the implication that an agent prefers to defer crucial decisions even though they make no difference whatsoever to the final contingent outcome. It is also at variance with the view of Kreps and Porteus (1978) that an agent might prefer to have uncertainty resolved sooner rather than later because risk-aversion increases over time. Of course, delaying crucial decisions until there is more information, or resolving uncertainty earlier, are both changes that generally enable an agent to undertake better decisions leading to better eventual outcomes. But where this is not true — where the eventual consequences are completely unaltered — it seems to me that there is nothing to be gained by a rational agent delaying his choices or discovering the future earlier purely for the sake of it. Accordingly, I shall take no account of the Koopmans or of the Kreps and Porteus suggestions.[4] Notice that I am also ruling out the "timing effect" in collective choice problems, as considered by Myerson (1981), but I shall return to this below in subsection 6.5.

---

[4] Kreps and Porteus (1978) motivate their approach with an example of preference for earlier resolution of uncertainty in which a person's income for the next two years is determined by tossing a coin. As they point out, knowing one's income earlier facilitates the consumer budgeting problem. But it does so by relaxing informational constraints which bind either when some of the person's assets are imperfectly liquid, or when the expected utility function has the consistent Weller (1978) form $E[u(c(s), c(s + 1), ...)]$ without additive separability between time periods.

What has to be true, however, for this once and for all maximization to complete the solution to the decision problem is that the agent will not want to revise his contingent plan whenever he has the opportunity to do so later on. In other words, the possibility of making consistent dynamic choice must be guaranteed. The guarantee must be there, moreover, whatever may be the exact form of the decision tree. This is the property of metastatic consistency which was considered in Hammond (1977). There I showed how it had strong implications for choice with certainty. Here I shall use a similar argument to show that, with uncertainty, dynamic consistency of "consequentialist" welfare maximizing plans without regard to the structure of the decision tree requires use of an ex-post approach to welfare economics.

Let me emphasize that I am using the dynamically consistent consequentialist approach just in order to formulate an appropriate *objective* for economic policy under uncertainty. The eventual policy choice may well depend inevitably upon the precise structure of the decision tree. For example, if one faces constraints dictated by individual behaviour, and if individuals do not consistently maximize an appropriate personal objective function, their choices depend on the tree structure and so therefore does the feasible set of options available to the policy-maker. Thus, in the end, an optimal *choice* depends on the tree structure in this case; notice, however, that there is still no reason why the *objective* has to depend on the tree structure.

The rest of the chapter consists of a formal discussion of consistent consequentialist collective choice under uncertainty and of its implications. Section 2 prepares the ground by reviewing decision trees in an extension of the form considered by Weller (1978) which is appropriate for discussions of dynamic consistency. Then the notion of "individualistic consequentialism" is presented. Elsewhere (Hammond, 1982b) I show that dynamically consistent consequentialist choice by a single agent, for all possible probability distributions over the set of states of the world, entails maximizing the expected value of a von Neumann–Morgenstern utility function. Thus, I shall assume that society, acting like a single agent whose choices are dynamically consistent and consequentialist, should seek to maximize the expected value of a von Neumann–Morgenstern Bergson social welfare function.

Section 3 considers the dependence of such a von Neumann–Morgenstern Bergson social welfare function upon individuals' consequentialist utility functions. For each decision tree, there is a collection of dynamic social welfare functionals which depend on the individuals' consequentialist utility functions on the space of "dynamically relevant" consequences. These social welfare functionals determine social welfare in each state of the world as a function of the individualistic consequences. The postulate of "independence of dynamically irrelevant consequences" is adduced. In section 4 it is shown that this independence condition, together with dynamic consistency and consequentialism, imply independence of irrelevant alternatives. With two extra minor conditions this then leads to "expected ex-post utilitarianism", whereby the welfare criterion is the expected value of an ex-post welfare function which depends, in each state of the world, on the individual utilities in that state.

Having derived ex-post utilitarianism in this way, section 5 goes on to consider when it is consistent with the ex-ante criterion which is commonly used in making welfare judgements under uncertainty. Section 6 discusses some reservations over the ex-post approach. Section 7 then discusses a weakening of the postulate of "consequentialism", and considers ex-post welfare functions which depend upon ex-ante utilities as well as utilities ex-post. Section 8 puts forward some conclusions.

2. Collective dynamic choice under uncertainty

2.1. The decision tree

The model of dynamic choice to be used here is adapted from that of Weller (1978). The adaptation is to allow for a general sequence of events $\langle S(n)\rangle_{n \in N}$, where N is the set of nodes of the decision tree. In fact, the decision tree takes the form:

$$\mathcal{T} = \langle\langle X(s, n)\rangle_{s \in N(n)}, S(n), N(n)\rangle_{n \in N}.$$

Here N denotes the set of nodes of the decision tree. Each node is either a decision node at which the agent or decision-maker has a choice to make, or it is a chance move node at which "nature" makes a choice. The choices which nature makes serve to determine the state of the world s. $S(n)$ denotes the set of states of the world which are still possible at node n; it is the set of possible states of the world which are consistent with the chance moves which helped to bring about node n of the tree $\mathcal{T}$. $N(n)$ denotes the set of nodes of the tree $\mathcal{T}$ which succeed n, including n itself.

The objects of choice for the agent at each node n take the form of contingent acts $x_{S(n)} \in \Pi_{s \in S(n)} X(s)$, where $X(s)$ is the space of possible acts should s be the state of the world. At each node $n \in N$, there is a set $X(s, n)$ of contingent actions in state s which are consistent with the earlier decisions of the agent which helped to bring node n about.

Suppose that $n' \in N(n)$, which means that n' is a node which succeeds n. Then naturally $N(n') \subseteq N(n)$ because any node which succeeds n' must also succeed n. In addition, I shall assume perfect recall which implies that $S(n') \subseteq S(n)$ because if $s \in S(n')$ is a possible state of the world at node n', then it must also be possible at the earlier node n when fewer chance moves have occurred. Similarly, for each $s \in S(n')$ it must be true that $X(s, n') \subseteq X(s, n)$ because any contingent act $x(s) \in X(s, n')$ which is feasible at node n' must also be feasible at the earlier node n when the agent has committed himself to fewer decisions.

Formally, a *decision tree* $\mathcal{T}$ is a collection of sets of the form:

$$\langle\!\langle X(s, n)\rangle\!\rangle_{s \in S(n)}, S(n), N(n)\rangle\!\rangle_{n \in N},$$

which satisfies the following three properties:

(a)   There exists an *initial node* $n_0 \in N$ such that $N(n_0) = N$ (i.e. every node succeeds n_0).

(b)   The sets $\langle\!\langle X(s, n)\rangle\!\rangle_{s \in S(n)}, S(n), N(n)\rangle\!\rangle_{n \in N}$ satisfy the following three *nesting properties*, whenever $n' \in N(n)$: (i) $N(n') \subseteq N(n)$; (ii) $S(n') \subseteq S(n)$; and (iii) $X(s, n') \subseteq X(s, n)$ for all $s \in S(n')$.

(c)   Each node $n \in N$ is either a *decision node* at which $S(n') = S(n)$ for all $n' \in N_{+1}(n)$, or a *chance move node* at which $X(s, n') = X(s, n)$ for all $n' \in N_{+1}(n)$ and all $s \in S(n')$, or a *trivial node* at which both $S(n') = S(n)$ and $X(s, n') = X(s, n)$ for all $n' \in N_{+1}(n)$ and all $s \in S(n')$.

Here $N_{+1}(n)$ denotes the set of nodes of the tree $\mathcal{T}$ which immediately succeed node n.

Because of information constraints, not every contingent act $x_{S(n)}$ of the product set $\Pi_{s \in S(n)} X(s, n)$ is feasible at a given node n of the tree $\mathcal{T}$. In fact, the contingent act $x_{S(n)}$ is *information compatible at node n* if, whenever $n' \in N(n)$ is a succeeding node at which $x(\bar{s}) \in X(\bar{s}, n')$ for some $\bar{s} \in S(n')$, then $x(s) \in X(s, n')$ for all $s \in S(n')$. The rationale for this definition is as follows. If $x(\bar{s}) \in X(\bar{s}, n')$, then the contingent act $x_{S(n)}$ leads to node n' if the state of the world is $\bar{s} \in S(n')$. But the agent is unable to distinguish between the different states of the set $S(n')$ until after node n', so if the contingent act is information compatible, it must also lead to node n' in every other state of the world of the set $S(n')$. This means precisely that $x(s) \in X(s, n')$ for all $s \in S(n')$.

In what follows, $X(n)$ will denote the set of information compatible contingent acts at node n. N^* will denote the set of decision nodes of the tree $\mathcal{T}$, and $N^*(n) = N^* \cap N(n)$ the set of decision nodes which succeed n, including n itself if n is a decision node.

2.2. Individualistic consequentialism

Following Hammond (1982b) I am going to assume that the choice of any act depends on the consequences of that act. Only now there are many individuals in the society, so the consequences of each act to each individual in each possible state become relevant. Let the set of individuals i be the fixed finite set I. For each state $s \in S$, suppose there is a set $Y^i(s)$ of possible consequences to individual i in state s.[5] For any event $E \subseteq S$, let $Y^i_E := \Pi_{s \in E} Y^i(s)$. Assume that there is a mapping $\gamma^i_S : X \to Y^i_S$ from contingent acts $x \in X$ to contingent consequences for individual i, $y^i_S = \gamma^i_S(x) \in Y^i_S$. Thus, for each state $s \in S$, and each contingent act $x(s)$ in that state, $\gamma^i(s, x(s))$ is the consequence of $x(s)$ for individual i. γ^i_E will denote the restricted mapping from acts in X to Y^i_E, the space of E-contingent consequences for individual i.

The consequences for society as a whole are then specified by the product mappings $\gamma_E = \Pi_{i \in I} \gamma^i_E$ which map X into the space $Y_E := \Pi_{i \in I} Y^i_E$ of E-contingent consequences for all the individuals in society.

2.3. Von Neumann–Morgenstern Bergson social welfare functions

The main result of Hammond (1982b) is that, under some weak assumptions, if choice under uncertainty is consequentialist for all possible decision trees, then it must be dynamically consistent and maximize the expected value of a von Neumann–Morgenstern utility function defined on the space of consequences. In the present context the same result applies, and shows that there exists a *von Neumann–Morgenstern Bergson social welfare function* (NMBSWF) $W^*(s)$ defined on $Y(s)$ for each state of the world $s \in S$. In addition, there is a subjective probability measure π on S such that a contingent act $x_E \in X_E$ is chosen in order to maximize the expected level of social welfare:

$$W_E(x_E) \equiv \int_E W^*(s)[\gamma(s, x(s))] d\pi,$$

when the set of possible states of the world is E.

Such a social welfare function should not be imposed regardless of individuals' preferences or utilities. I shall now turn to consider individual utilities, and how social welfare can depend upon them through social welfare functionals.

---

[5] I want to allow consequences to be state dependent for reasons which are well discussed in Jones-Lee (1979).

3. Dynamic social welfare functionals

3.1. Consequentialist utility functions

I shall assume that for each individual $i \in I$ and each state $s \in S$ there is a *consequentialist utility function* $U^{*i}(s, \cdot)$ on $Y^i(s)$ which determines i's utility in state s as a function of the contingent consequence $y^i(s) \in Y^i(s)$. Notice that at this stage there is no presumption at all that the individual is concerned with any measure of expected utility on Y^i_E such as $\int_E U^{*i}(s, y^i(s))d\pi^i$. This will be considered further in section 5. For the moment, it is as though the same individual in each state is being treated as a separate individual.

3.2. Consequentialist social welfare functionals

Let $U^*_E := \langle\langle U^{*i}(s, \cdot)\rangle_{i \in I}\rangle_{s \in E}$ denote a profile of individual state-dependent consequentialist utility functions. For each $y_E \in Y_E$, U^*_E serves to determine the pattern of utility levels $\langle\langle U^{*i}(s, y^i(s))_{i \in I}\rangle_{s \in E}$ in each state s of the event E.

A *social welfare functional* (SWFL) is a mapping from profiles of individual utility *functions* to social (preference) orderings.

I shall assume that, for each event $E \subseteq S$, there is a *consequentialist SWFL* F^*_E such that

$$R^*_E = F^*_E(U^*_E)$$

determines the consequentialist social preference ordering R^*_E on Y_E as a function of the profile of individual state-dependent consequentialist utility functions.

3.3. Dynamic social welfare functionals

Let $\mathcal{T} = \langle\langle X(s, n)\rangle_{s \in S(n)}, S(n), N(n)\rangle_{n \in N}$ be any decision tree. At each decision node $n \in N^*$ of the tree $\mathcal{T}$, there is a consequentialist ordering of information compatible contingent acts in the set $X(n)$. This ordering $R(n)$ is given by:

$$x_{S(n)} R(n) x'_{S(n)} \iff \gamma_{S(n)}[x_{S(n)}] R^*_{S(n)} \gamma_{S(n)}[x'_S(n)].$$

In other words, contingent acts are ordered according to their consequences.

For each possible state $s \in S(n)$ at node n the individuals $i \in I$ have consequentialist utility functions $U^i(n)(s, \cdot)$ defined on the space $X(s, n)$ of contingent acts by

$$U^i(n)(s, x(s)) := U^{*i}(s, \gamma^i[s, x(s)]) \text{ (all } i \in I, x(s) \in X(s, n)).$$

Let $U(n) := \langle\!\langle U^i(n)(s, \cdot) \rangle_{i \in I} \rangle_{s \in S(n)}$ denote the profile of all such state dependent utility functions on the sets of acts $\langle X(s, n) \rangle_{s \in S(n)}$.

Given the decision tree $\mathcal{T}$, a *dynamic social welfare functional* is a list $\langle F(n) \rangle_{n \in N^*}$ of SWFLs, one for each decision node of the tree. Given any profile $U(n)$ of individual utility functions at node n, the dynamic SWFL $\langle F(n) \rangle_{n \in N^*}$ serves to determine a dynamic social ordering $\langle R(n) \rangle_{n \in N^*}$ according to the equation

$$R(n) = F(n)[U(n)] \quad \text{(all } n \in N^*).$$

3.4. Independence of dynamically irrelevant consequences

The formulation of a dynamic social welfare functional in the previous section embodies an important assumption which I shall call *independence of dynamically irrelevant consequences*. At any decision node $n \in N^*$ of the tree $\mathcal{T}$, each individual's utility function $U^i(n)(s, \cdot)$ in each state $s \in S(n)$ is only meaningfully defined on the set $X(s, n)$ of acts which are feasible at node n in state s. Contingent acts which lie outside the set $X(s, n)$ are no longer feasible and so, I assume, no longer relevant. The associated consequences in the set $Y^i(s)\backslash\gamma^i(s)[X(s, n)]$ are also no longer relevant in this case and so are *dynamically irrelevant consequences* to individual i. If the utility function extended to such "dynamically irrelevant" alternatives were relevant, this would make historically counterfactual options relevant – it would be like embodying sunk costs or regrets into the social welfare function. If this is to be done, how far back should we go? Why can we ignore history at the initial node n_0, but not at later nodes? That is the argument for treating "dynamically irrelevant alternatives" as indeed irrelevant.

3.5. Von Neumann–Morgenstern Bergson social welfare functionals (NMBSWFLs)

As in subsection 3.2 a social welfare functional is a mapping which determines the social ordering as a function of a profile of individual utility functions. A *Bergson social welfare functional* (BSWFL) is a mapping $G(U)$ which determines a Bergson social welfare function $W(x)$ on X as a function $G(U)$ of the utility function profile U, so that

$$W(x) \equiv G(U)(x).$$

In subsection 2.3 we saw how there must exist a von Neumann–Morgenstern Bergson social welfare function $W^*(s)$ defined on the consequence space $Y(s)$ for each $s \in S$. Now I assume that there is a corresponding consequentialist *von Neumann–Morgenstern Bergson social welfare functional* (NMBSWFL) $G^*(s)$ $(U^*(s))$ such that, for each $Y(s) \in Y(s)$ and each $s \in S$:

$$W^*(s)(y(s)) \equiv G^*(s)[U^*(s)(y(s))],$$

where $U^*(s)$ is the profile of consequential individual utility functions $\langle U^{*i}(s)\rangle_{i \in I}$ for state s.

Thus, the consequentialist SWFL $R_E^* = F_E^*(U_E^*)$ of subsection 3.2 is such that, for each pair $y_E^1, y_E^2 \in Y_E$:

$$y_E^1 F_E^*(U_E^*)y_E^2 \Longleftrightarrow \int_E G^*(s)[U^*(s)(y^1(s))]\mathrm{d}\pi \geqslant \int_E G^*(s)[U^*(s)(y^2(s))]\mathrm{d}\pi.$$

4.   Independence of irrelevant alternatives and expected ex-post utilitarianism

4.1.   *Independence of irrelevant alternatives*

Individualistic consequentialism, together with the condition of independence of dynamically irrelevant consequences, implies independence of irrelevant alternatives, as will now be shown. The independence condition which is entailed is the natural adaptation to social welfare functionals of Arrow's independence condition for Arrow social welfare functions. Specifically, the consequentialist SWFL F_E^* for the event $E \subseteq S$ satisfies *independence of irrelevant alternatives* if, for any given set $Z \subseteq Y_E$, and any pair of utility function profiles $U_E^*, \bar{U}_E^*$ on Y_E which satisfies $U^{*i}(s, y^i(s)) = \bar{U}^{*i}(s, y^i(s))$ for all $i \in I$, $s \in E$, and $y_E \in Z$, it must be true that, for all $y_E^1, y_E^2 \in Z$:

$$y_E^1 F_E^*(U_E^*)y_E^2 \Longleftrightarrow y_E^1 F_E^*(\bar{U}_E^*)y_E^2.$$

Proposition 1 (Consequentialism implies independence).   Suppose that F_E^* is a consequentialist SWFL for the event $E \subseteq S$. Then F_E^* satisfies independence of irrelevant alternatives if social choice on any permissible decision tree is consequentialist and independent of dynamically irrelevant alternatives.

Proof. Suppose that $E \subseteq S$, $Z \subseteq Y_E$, and the two utility function profiles U_E^*, $\bar{U}_E^*$ on Y_E are such that $U_E^*(y_E) = \bar{U}_E^*(y_E)$ for all $y_E \in Z$.

Let $R_E^* := F_E^*(U_E^*)$, $\bar{R}_E^* := F_E^*(\bar{U}_E^*)$ be the associated social orderings on Y_E. Take any pair y_E^1, $y_E^2 \in Z$ and construct the decision tree $\mathscr{T} = \langle\!\langle X(s, n)\rangle\!\rangle_{s \in S(n)}$, $S(n), N(n)\rangle_{n \in N}$ as in fig. 10.1, with:

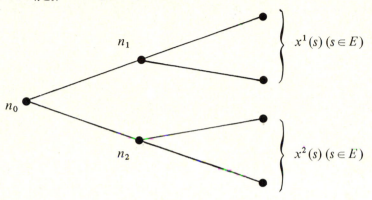

Figure 10.1

(i) $N(n_0) = \{n_0, n_1, n_2\} \cup \{x^1(s) \mid s \in E\} \cup \{x^2(s) \mid s \in E\}$,

   $N(n_1) = \{n_1\} \cup \{x^1(s) \mid s \in E\}$,

   $N(n_2) = \{n_2\} \cup \{x^2(s) \mid s \in E\}$, and

$$N(x^1(s)) = \{x^1(s)\}, N(x^2(s)) = \{x^2(s)\} \text{ (all } s \in E).$$

(ii) $S(n_0) = S(n_1) = S(n_2) = E$, and

$$S(x^1(s)) = S(x^2(s)) = \{s\} \text{ (all } s \in E).$$

(iii) $X(s, n_0) = \{x^1(s), x^2(s)\}$ (all $s \in E$),

   $X(s, n_1) = \{x^1(s)\}, X(s, n_2) = \{x^2(s)\}$ (all $s \in E$), and

$$X(s, x^1(s)) = \{x^1(s)\}, X(s, x^2(s)) = \{x^2(s)\} \text{ (all } s \in E).$$

Then $X(n_0) = \{x_E^1, x_E^2\}$, $X(n_1) = \{x_E^1\}$, $X(n_2) = \{x_E^2\}$ are the feasible sets of information compatible contingent acts as nodes n_0, n_1 and n_2, respectively.

Suppose that $\gamma^i(s, x^j(s)) = y^{\ddot{y}}(s)$ for all $i \in I, s \in E$, and $j = 1, 2$. Then $\mathscr{T}$ is a permissible decision tree with the mapping γ_E from acts to consequences.

Consider the two profiles $U(n_0)$, $\bar{U}(n_0)$ at node n_0 of $\mathscr{T}$, which are given by:

$$U^i(n_0)(s, x^j(s)) = U^{*i}(s, y^{ij}(s))$$
$$\left.\vphantom{\begin{matrix}a\\b\end{matrix}}\right\} \quad \text{all } s \in E, i \in I, \text{ and } j = 1, 2.$$
$$\bar{U}^i(n_0)(s, x^j(s)) = \bar{U}^{*i}(s, y^{ij}(s))$$

By hypothesis, $U^*_E(y^j_E) = \bar{U}^*_E(y^j_E)$, $(j = 1, 2)$ because $y^j_E \in Z$. Therefore $U(n_0)$ and $\bar{U}(n_0)$ are identical, and so, if

$$R(n_0) := F(n_0)(U(n_0)), \quad \bar{R}(n_0) := F(n_0)(\bar{U}(n_0))$$

it follows too that $R(n_0) = \bar{R}(n_0)$. But then:

$$y^1_E R^*_E y^2_E \iff x^1_E R(n_0) x^2_E \iff x^1_E \bar{R}(n_0) x^2_E \iff y^1_E \bar{R}^*_E y^2_E,$$

because $y^j_E = \gamma_E[x^j_E]$ $(j = 1, 2)$. Thus, F^*_E must indeed satisfy independence of irrelevant alternatives. ∎

4.2. *Expected ex-post utilitarianism*

I have just shown that, under individualistic consequentialism combined with independence of dynamically irrelevant consequences, the consequentialist SWFLs $\langle F^*_E \rangle_{E \subseteq S}$ for each event $E \subseteq S$ must satisfy independence of irrelevant alternatives. Suppose too that $F^*_E(U^*_E)$ is defined on an unrestricted domain of consequentialist utility function profiles U^*_E and that F^*_E also satisfies the following *ex-post Pareto indifference condition* (P^0):

If the pair $y^1_E, y^2_E \subseteq Y_E$ are such that $U^{*i}(s, y^{i1}(s)) = U^{*i}(s, y^{i2}(s))$ for all $s \in E$ and all $i \in I$, then $y^1_E I^*_E y^2_E$ (where I^* is the social indifference relation corresponding to $R^*_E = F^*_E(U^*_E)$).

Thus, if every individual $i \in I$ in every state $s \in E$ is indifferent ex-post between $y^{i1}(s)$ and $y^{i2}(s)$, then y^1_E and y^2_E should be indifferent.

Given these three conditions of unrestricted domain, independence or irrelevant alternatives, and Pareto indifference, it can be shown along the lines of d'Aspremont and Gevers (1977, lemmas 2 and 3) that in each single state $s \in S$ there is a *utilitarian social welfare functional* $\bar{R}^*(s)$ in the form of an ordering on the space E^I of utility vectors $u = \langle u^i \rangle_{i \in I}$ such that, for all $y^1(s), y^2(s) \in Y(s)$:

$$y^1(s) R^*(s) y^2(s) \iff U[s, y^1(s)] \bar{R}^*(s) U[s, y^2(s)],$$

where $R^*(s) = F^*(s)[U^*(s)]$ is the social ordering on $Y(s)$ which corresponds to the utility function profile $U^*(s)$, and where $U[s, y^j(s)]$ denotes $\langle U^i[s, y^{ij}(s)] \rangle_{i \in I}$ $(j = 1, 2)$.

Consider now the von Neumann–Morgenstern Bergson social welfare functional (NMBSWFL) $G^*(s)$ in each state $s \in S$, as discussed in subsection 3.5. This generates an NMBSWF $W^*(s)$ in each state $s \in E$ with:

$$W^*(s)(\boldsymbol{y}(s)) \equiv G^*(s)[\boldsymbol{U}^*(s)](\boldsymbol{y}(s)) \quad \text{(all } \boldsymbol{y}(s) \in \boldsymbol{Y}(s)).$$

But $W^*(s)(\cdot)$ must be a representation of the social ordering $R^*(s)$. Then, because $F^*(s)$ is utilitarian – i.e. $R^*(s) = F^*(s)(\boldsymbol{U}^*(s))$ corresponds to an ordering $\bar{R}^*(s)$ on utility space for each profile $\boldsymbol{U}^*(s)$ and each state $s \in S$ – it follows that there exists a function $w(s, \cdot)$ for each state $s \in S$ which determines social welfare $w(s, \boldsymbol{u}(s))$ as a function of the vector of individual utility levels $\boldsymbol{u}(s)$ in state s, and which satisfies:

$$W^*(s)(\boldsymbol{y}(s)) \equiv w(s, \boldsymbol{U}[s, \boldsymbol{y}(s)]) \quad \text{(all } s \in S, \boldsymbol{y}(s) \in \boldsymbol{Y}(s))$$
$$\equiv G^*(s)[\boldsymbol{U}^*(s)](\boldsymbol{y}(s)).$$

Such a function $w(s, \cdot)$ is a *von Neumann–Morgenstern utilitarian social welfare functional* (NMUSWFL).

The use of such an NMUSWFL can be called *ex-post utilitarianism*; $w(s, \cdot)$ is an ex-post (utilitarian) social welfare functional because it is based on the individual utilities of ex-post consequences. Before the state s is known, the appropriate criterion if the set of possible states of the world is the event E will be the following measure of conditionally expected ex-post welfare:

$$W_E^*[\boldsymbol{y}_E] \equiv \int\limits_{s \in E} w(s, \langle U^i(s, y^i(s)) \rangle_{i \in I}) \mathrm{d}\pi,$$

where π is the probability measure on S. This form of welfare function will be assumed from now on until the discussion of independence of dynamically irrelevant consequences is taken up again in section 7. The welfare function is precisely the ex-post welfare criterion which was discussed in the introduction.

The result of subsection 4.1, together with the discussion above, can be summarized in:

Proposition 2 (Consequentialism and collective Bayesian rationality together imply ex-post utilitarianism). If the consequentialist social welfare functionals $\langle F_E^* \rangle_{E \subseteq S}$ are defined on an unrestricted domain and satisfy ex-post Pareto indifference, and if the associated social orderings R_E^* correspond to the expected values of von Neumann–Morgenstern Bergson social welfare functions $W^*(s, \cdot)$ in each state $s \in S$, then for each $E \subseteq S$, F_E^* takes the *ex-post utilitarian* form in which R_E^* is represented on $\boldsymbol{Y}_E$ by:

$$W_E^*(y_E) \equiv \int\limits_E w(s, \langle U^{*i}[s, y^i(s)]\rangle_{i\in I}) \mathrm{d}\pi,$$

where $w(s, \cdot)$ is the (ex-post) *von Neumann–Morgenstern utilitarian social welfare functional* in each state $s \in S$.

5. Consistency between ex-ante and ex-post

5.1. *Ex-ante utilitarianism*

The ex-post approach to collective choice under uncertainty discussed in subsection 4.2 is in marked contrast to the ex-ante approach which will now be discussed. Under the ex-ante approach it is assumed that individuals are also Bayesian rational so that every individual $i \in I$ has a consequentialist expected utility function V_E^{*i} on Y_E^i, for each event $E \subseteq S$, with:

$$V_E^{*i}(y_E^i) = \int\limits_E U^{*i}[s, y^i(s)] \mathrm{d}\pi_E^i,$$

where π_E^i is i's conditional probability measure on E, given that E has occurred, and $U^{*i}[s, \cdot]$ is i's (state-dependent) von Neumann–Morgenstern utility function.

It is now assumed that the consequentialist social welfare functionals $\langle F_E^* \rangle_{E \subseteq S}$ on Y_E satisfy the following *ex-ante Pareto indifference condition*:

$$\text{if } V_E^{*i}(y_E^{i1}) = V_E^{*i}(y_E^{i2}) \text{ for all } i \in I, \quad \text{then } y_E^1 I_E^* y_E^2.$$

With this condition, it also follows, as in subsection 4.2, that if F_E^* is defined on an unrestricted domain of individual utility function profiles V_E^*, and if there is independence of dynamically irrelevant consequences – which implies independence of irrelevant alternatives – then F_E^* must take the *ex-ante utilitarian* form of corresponding to an ordering $\bar{R}_E^*$ on the space individual ex-ante utility levels, so that:

$$y_E^1 R_E^* y_E^2 \iff V_E^*(y_E^1)\bar{R}_E^* V_E^*(y_E^2),$$

where

$$V_E^*(y_E^i) = \langle V_E^{*i}(y_E^{ij})\rangle_{i\in I} \quad \text{for } j = 1, 2.$$

5.2. State-independent ex-post social welfare functionals: the Vickrey–Harsanyi case

As discussed by Diamond (1967a, 1967b) and Hammond (1981a), amongst others, the ex-ante and ex-post approaches to welfare economics under uncertainty are inconsistent except in a very special case. The special case occurs when all the following four conditions are satisfied. First, all individuals have their ex-ante expected utilities determined by coincident subjective probabilities. Secondly, these same probabilities are used to determine expected social welfare in the ex-post approach. Thirdly, ex-ante social welfare is a weighted sum of individuals' ex-ante expected utilities. And fourthly, ex-post social welfare is an identical weighted sum of the same utilities in each state.

This result is well known so I run the risk of being repetitive if I offer a proof, though the proof may be somewhat novel in using an argument due essentially to Gorman (1968). In addition, there is an extra implicit assumption that the ex-post SWFL is state independent which emerges in the course of the proof I now present.

Proposition 3. (Consistency between ex-ante and ex-post: case of state independent ex-post social welfare functionals). Suppose that all the conditions of proposition 2 are satisfied, and so there exists an ex-post NMUSWFL $w(s, \cdot)$ in each state $s \in S$ such that, for each profile U_E^* on Y_E, the ordering $R_E^* = F_E^*(U_E^*)$ on Y_E is represented by the Bergson social welfare function:

$$W_E^*(y_E) \equiv \sum_{s \in E} \pi_s w_s \langle U^{*i}[s, y^i(s)] \rangle_{i \in I})$$

(where it is being assumed that S is a *finite* set of possible states of the world: the extension to the case when S is an arbitrary measurable space is routine but unnecessarily technical for present purposes).

Suppose in addition that each individual $i \in I$ has an ex-ante expected utility function of the form:

$$V_E^{*i}(y_E^i) \equiv \sum_{s \in E} \pi_s^i U^{*i}[s, y^i(s)]$$

on Y_E^i, and that F_E^* satisfies the ex-ante Pareto indifference condition. Finally, suppose that each function $w_s(u_s)$ is independent of the state s and continuous in the utility vector u_s. Then

(i) $\pi_s^i = \pi_s$ for all $s \in S$ and all $i \in I$;

(ii) $w_s(\boldsymbol{u}_s) \equiv \Sigma_i \beta^i u_s^i$ for all $\boldsymbol{u}_s$ and all $s \in S$, where the weights $\beta^i (i \in I)$ are constant; and

(iii) $W_E^*(\boldsymbol{y}_E) \equiv \Sigma_i \beta^i V_E^{*i}(y_E^i)$ for all $\boldsymbol{y}_E \in Y_E$.

Proof.   Let u_s^i denote i's von Neumann–Morgenstern utility in each state s. Let π_s^i denote i's subjective probability in state s. Then i's ex-ante expected utility is $V_E^{*i} := \Sigma_{s \in E} \pi_s^i u_s^i$. According to the ex-ante approach, social welfare W^* is given by some function $W_E^a \equiv f(\langle V_E^{*i} \rangle_{i \in I})$ of the individuals' ex-ante expected utilities. On the other hand, according to the ex-post approach, social welfare in state s is given by some function $w_s \equiv w(\langle u_s^i \rangle_{i \in I})$ of the individuals' ex-post utilities in state s. (The key assumption here is that the interpersonal comparisons of von Neumann–Morgenstern utility functions which are embodied in the social welfare functional w are independent of the state of the world. The consequences of relaxing this assumption are discussed below in subsection 5.3.) Finally, according to the ex-post approach, social welfare W is given by the expected value $W_E^p \equiv \Sigma_{s \in E} \pi_s w_s$ of social welfare ex-post, where the probabilities π_s are "social" probabilities of some kind.

For the two approaches to be consistent, the functions W_E^a and W_E^p must give rise to the same social ordering in the double product space of contingent utility profiles $\langle\langle u_s^i \rangle_{i \in I} \rangle_{s \in E}$. By choosing the function f appropriately, we can arrange that the two approaches are consistent if and only if:

$$W^* \equiv f \left(\left\langle \sum_{s \in E} \pi_s^i u_s^i \right\rangle_{i \in I} \right) \equiv \sum_{s \in E} \pi_s w(\langle u_s^i \rangle_{i \in I}),$$

so that $W^* \equiv W^a \equiv W^p$. But now, in particular:

$$W^* \equiv f(\langle U^i(\langle u_s^i \rangle_{s \in E}) \rangle_{i \in I}) \equiv \phi(\langle w_s(\langle u_s^i \rangle_{i \in I}) \rangle_{s \in E}).$$

Thus, in the terminology of Gorman (1968), preferences over each of the sets $\{i\} \times E$ (all $i \in I$) and $I \times \{s\}$ (all $s \in E$) are separable. Provided that both I and E are sets with at least two members, $\{i\} \times E$ and $I \times \{s\}$ overlap (for each $i \in I$ and $s \in E$) and so, provided also that W^* is continuous over a connected domain with a non-empty interior, it follows that W^* must be additively separable. Thus, there exist continuous functions $\psi_s^i (i \in I, s \in E)$ such that after a suitable increasing transformation g has been applied:

$$\sum_{i \in I} \sum_{s \in E} \psi_s^i(u_s^i) \equiv \tilde{f}\left(\left\langle \sum_{s \in E} \pi_s^i u_s^i \right\rangle_{i \in I} \right) \equiv g\left(\sum_{s \in E} \pi_s w(\langle u_s^i \rangle_{i \in I}) \right).$$

From the first identity it follows that $\tilde{f}$ must be a linear function of $\langle U_i \rangle_{i \in I}$ and so there exists a constant α and positive constants $\beta^i (i \in I)$ such that:

$$\tilde{f}(\langle V_E^{*i} \rangle_{i \in I}) \equiv \alpha + \sum_{i \in I} \beta^i V_E^{*i}$$

$$\equiv \alpha + \sum_{i \in I} \beta^i \sum_{s \in E} \pi_s^i u_s^i.$$

Therefore:

$$\psi_s^i(u_s^i) \equiv \alpha_s^i + \beta^i \pi_s^i u_s^i \quad (\text{all } i \in I, s \in E),$$

where $\alpha_s^i (i \in I, s \in S)$ are constants satisfying $\sum_{i \in I} \sum_{s \in S} \alpha_s^i = \alpha$. But then g must also be linear, and the equation can be further transformed so g is the identity and:

$$\pi_s w(\langle u_s^i \rangle_{i \in I}) \equiv \sum_{i \in I} \psi_s^i(u_s^i) \quad (\text{all } s \in E),$$

so that (assuming $\pi_s > 0$, all $s \in E$):

$$w(\langle u_s^i \rangle_{i \in I}) \equiv \pi_s^{-1} \sum_{i \in I} \alpha_s^i + \sum_{i \in I} \pi_s^{-1} \beta^i \pi_s^i u_s^i.$$

Since w is independent of s, it follows that there are positive constants $\lambda^i (i \in I)$ such that:

$$\pi_s^{-1} \beta^i \pi_s^i = \lambda^i \quad (\text{all } s \in E, i \in I).$$

Because $E \subseteq S$ is arbitrary, this must be true in particular when $E = S$. But then, $\beta^i \pi_s^i = \lambda^i \pi_s$ (all $s \in S, i \in I$) and so, because $\sum_{s \in S} \pi_s^i = 1$ (all $i \in I$) and $\sum_{s \in S} \pi_s = 1$, it follows that $\lambda^i = \beta^i$ and $\pi_s^i = \pi_s$ (all $i \in I, s \in S$). This represents the first consequence of consistency. The third consequence is that $f(\langle U^i \rangle_{i \in I}) \equiv \sum_{i \in I} \beta^i U^i$ and the second is that $w(\langle u_s^i \rangle_{i \in I}) \equiv \sum_{i \in I} \beta^i u_s^i$ (all $s \in S$) (ignoring the additive constants α_s^i). Of course, these three conditions are sufficient for consistency because they imply:

$$W_S^* \equiv \sum_{i \in I} \beta^i \left(\sum_{s \in S} \pi_s^i u_s^i \right) \equiv \sum_{s \in S} \pi_s \left(\sum_{i \in I} \beta^i u_s^i \right). \quad \blacksquare$$

This is exactly the case advocated by Vickrey (1945) and Harsanyi (1955, 1975, 1978) and criticized by Diamond (1967a).

5.3. *Consistency with state-dependent social welfare functionals*

Let me drop the key assumption that the NMUSWFL $w_s(\cdot)$ is independent of s. Without it, we can still conclude that W_s^* is doubly additive and that $\tilde{f}$ is linear so that:

$$\psi_s^i(u_s^i) \equiv \alpha_s^i + \beta^i \pi_s^i u_s^i \quad \text{(all } i \in I, s \in S),$$

where $\Sigma_{i \in I} \Sigma_{s \in S} \alpha_s^i = \alpha$. With w_s dependent on s, however, after applying the further transformation which converts the linear function g into the identity

$$\pi_s w_s(\langle u_s^i \rangle_{i \in I}) \equiv \sum_{i \in I} \psi_s^i(u_s^i),$$

and so

$$w_s(\langle u_s^i \rangle_{i \in I}) \triangleq \pi_s^{-1} \sum_{i \in I} \alpha_s^i + \sum_{i \in I} \pi_s^{-1} \beta^i \pi_s^i u_s^i$$

$$\equiv \alpha_s + \sum_{i \in I} \beta_s^i u_s^i,$$

where $\Sigma_{s \in S} \alpha_s = \alpha$, and $\pi_s \beta_s^i = \pi_s^i \beta^i$ (all $i \in I, s \in S$). These equalities are sufficient, of course, because then:

$$W \equiv \sum_{i \in I} \beta^i \left(\sum_{s \in S} \pi_s^i u_s^i \right) \equiv \sum_{s \in S} \pi_s \left(\sum_{i \in I} \beta_s^i u_s^i \right)$$

(again ignoring the irrelevant additive constants α_s^i ($i \in I, s \in S$)). Thus, it is no longer necessary to have coincident individual probabilities, so the first of the four conditions can be dispensed with. The second condition is also modified, because the weights β_s^i attached to individuals' ex-post utilities in state s differ from the weights β^i attached to their ex-ante expected utilities. Notice that the relative weights β_s^i/β_s^j attached to the ex-post utilities in state s of two individuals i, j differ from the relative weights β^i/β^j attached to their ex-ante utilities in proportion to their relative assessments of the likelihood of state s, since

$$\frac{\beta_s^i}{\beta_s^j} = \left(\frac{\beta^i}{\beta^j}\right)\left(\frac{\pi_s^i}{\pi_s^j}\right).$$

For consistency, therefore, interpersonal comparisons ex-post in each state s must give relatively higher weights to individuals who were fortunate enough to regard state s as relatively more likely. While one may wish therefore to reward individuals who make somewhat better predictions of the future in order to improve the total information there is available, such rewards should be regarded as (incentive) *constraints* and the need for such incentives carefully assessed. Such incentives should *not* be allowed to colour what we regard as an ethical *objective* of the society. Thus, being forced to give undue weight ex-post to individuals who were fortunate in their probability assessments, or their information, in order to maintain consistency, is an uncomfortable procedure. In fact, it is a special case of the general method of achieving consistency between the ex-ante and the ex-post approaches by letting one's value judgements be dictated by the ex-ante approach and by the requirement of consistency between the two approaches. This is in general an uncomfortable procedure, as I shall now argue.

5.4. *Criticisms of consistency: value judgements and risk aversion*

Let me now consider in more detail what exactly is involved in making ex-post welfare judgements so that consistency with the ex-ante approach to collective choice is assured. The ex-ante welfare function W must be the weighted sum $\Sigma_{i \in I} \beta^i (\Sigma_{s \in S} \pi_s^i u_s^i)$, and the ex-post welfare function in each state s is $w_s \equiv \Sigma_{i \in I} \beta_s^i u_s^i$. We have already seen at the end of subsection 5.3 how the weights β_s^i depend positively on π_s^i, the probability i attaches to state s, and this is far from comfortable. Suppose, however, that individuals' probabilities are coincident, and that $\pi_s^i = \pi_s$ (all $i \in I$, $s \in S$) so that this source of discomfort disappears, and $w_s \equiv \Sigma_{i \in I} \beta^i u_s^i$ (all $s \in S$), where the utility weights β^i are independent of the state s. Even in this special case the discomfort is not entirely over.

The new source of discomfort is the use of von Neumann–Morgenstern utility functions to represent interpersonal comparisons of utility units, as reflected in the weighted utility sum $\Sigma_{i \in I} \beta^i u_s^i$. Of course, this is precisely the procedure which Harsanyi (1955, 1975), among others, has strongly advocated. Harsanyi's advocacy, however, rests crucially on what he believes an individual would choose were he placed in a version of what Rawls would call the "original position", behind "the veil of ignorance" in which the individual is uncertain who he will be among the various members of society. Rawls, however, has shown that there is more than one possible view of how an individual would choose in such a situation (see also Barry, 1973). Diamond (1967a) was also uncomfortable with Harsanyi's ex-ante welfare function, but for rather different reasons, as I shall discuss below in section 6.

To illustrate why this use of von Neumann–Morgenstern utility functions may be uncomfortable, consider the problem of allocating a contingent total income Y_s among the n individuals in the set I. Let y_s^i denote i's income in state s. Then we must have $\Sigma_{i \in I} y_s^i = Y_s$ (all $s \in S$). Suppose each individual i has a von Neumann–Morgenstern utility function of income of the constant relative risk aversion form:

$$u^i(y^i) = \frac{(y^i)^{1-\rho^i}}{1 - \rho^i} \quad (\rho^i > 0; \rho^i \neq 1).$$

Then the ex-ante welfare function is of the form:

$$W \equiv \sum_{i \in I} \sum_{s \in S} \pi_s \beta^i \, \frac{(y_s^i)^{1-\rho^i}}{1 - \rho^i}$$

(assuming that $\pi_s^i = \pi_s$, all $i \in I$, $s \in S$) and the corresponding ex-post welfare function in state s is:

$$w_s \equiv \sum_{i \in I} \frac{\beta^i (y_s^i)^{1-\rho^i}}{1 - \rho^i}.$$

Notice that this is not symmetric if the ρ^i's do indeed differ between individuals. Thus, ex-post, the welfare judgements imposed by the ex-ante approach show some preference for an unequal distribution of income. In fact, define $\bar{y}_s := n^{-1} Y_s$, the mean income per head in state s. Suppose income were distributed equally in state s, so that $y_s^i = \bar{y}_s$ (all $i \in I$). Then $\partial w_s / \partial y_s^i = \beta^i (\bar{y}_s)^{-\rho^i}$. Because w_s is strictly concave, it follows that, for an optimal ex-post distribution of income:

$$y_s^i > \bar{y}_s \Longleftrightarrow \beta^i (\bar{y}_s)^{-\rho^i} > n^{-1} \sum_{i \in I} \beta^i (\bar{y}_s)^{-\rho^i}$$

Thus the most risk-averse individuals, with high ρ^i, are likely to get about average incomes when mean income $\bar{y}_s$ is low, and below average incomes when mean income $\bar{y}_s$ is high. Naturally this is precisely what one expects of an ex-ante Pareto efficient allocation of risk-bearing. But the dependence of an optimal income distribution on attitudes to risk ex-ante and on whether the economy as a whole has performed well or badly ex-post is not something we have been accustomed to in the welfare economics of income distribution. This may be thought a consequence of modern welfare economists paying too little need to the views of Friedman (1962) who saw conflict between social values which, ex-ante, respect individuals' tastes for risk-taking, and, ex-post, show a preference for income inequality.[6] But it may also be because attitudes to risk really do have no place in the right attitude to inequality, in which case it is wrong to impose consistency between the ex-ante and ex-post approaches.

Even where individuals' attitudes to risk are identical, there is still a source of discomfort when it comes to deciding the trade-off between equity and efficiency. For suppose that:

$$u^i(y^i) = \frac{(y^i)^{1-\rho}}{1-\rho} \quad (\rho > 0; \rho = 1),$$

so that individuals have identical constant relative degrees of risk aversion. Then, if one also assumes symmetry so that $\beta^i = 1$ (all $i \in I$), consistency between ex-ante and ex-post requires an ex-ante welfare function of the form:

$$W \equiv \sum_{i \in I} \sum_{s \in S} \frac{\pi_s(y^i_s)^{1-\rho}}{1-\rho} \quad ,$$

and an ex-post welfare function in state s of the form:

$$w_s \equiv \sum_{i \in I} \frac{(y^i_s)^{1-\rho}}{1-\rho} \quad .$$

---

[6]   Kanbur (1979a, 1979b) has shown that the tempting inference that measures to reduce inequality will discourage risk-taking is not necessarily correct. Nor is it always true that more risk-taking leads to greater income inequality ex-post. His analysis, however, appears to rest on there being incomplete markets so that the distribution of risk-bearing is not fully optimal. This seems to be fair criticism of Friedman's original claim that a desire for risk leads to greater inequality, but it is possible that neither Friedman nor Kanbur have really captured the essence of the conflict between risk-taking and equality. Were there complete insurance markets, and a fully ex-ante Pareto efficient allocation of risk-bearing, then we would expect to see more income inequality ex-post if individuals had widely different degrees of risk aversion, but this is quite different from the claim Friedman made and Kanbur discussed. More to the point, perhaps, is the claim by Friedman and Savage (1948, p. 283, note 11) in connection with von Neumann–Morgenstern utility and individual attitudes to risk and its relationship to diminishing marginal utility of income, that "it is entirely unnecessary to identify the quantity that individuals are to be interpreted as maximizing with a quantity that should be given special importance in public policy". Thus, it is not at all clear that, in the end, Friedman would really want to advocate that individuals' attitudes to risk should determine the social attitude to income inequality. (See also Hammond, 1982a.)

If follows that ρ, the common degree of relative risk aversion, must also be equal to Atkinson's (1970) measure of relative inequality aversion. Thus, even though an ex-post optimal distribution of income is now an equal distribution, without regard to individuals' attitudes to risk, the willingness to sacrifice "efficiency" (total income) for "equity", as represented by the measure ρ, is pre-determined by the individuals' common attitude to risk.

In fact, this point illustrates the essence of the pure ex-ante approach. Ex-post welfare judgements regarding the distribution of income are no longer just a matter of ethical opinion – they become intimately connected with individuals' attitudes to risk. Harsanyi, among others, sees this as an advantage; among those who saw it as a disadvantage, perhaps one may cite and indeed quote from Arrow (1963, p. 10):[7]

> This theorem [of von Neumann and Morgenstern] does not, as far as I can see, give any special ethical significance to the particular utility scale found. For instead of using the utility scale found by von Neumann and Morgenstern we could use the square of that scale; then behavior is described by saying that the individual seeks to maximize the expected value of the square root of his utility ... [the von Neumann and Morgenstern theorem] has nothing to do with welfare considerations, particularly if we are interested primarily in making a social choice among policies in which no random elements enter. To say otherwise would be to assert that the distribution of the social income is to be governed by the tastes of individuals for gambling.

Of course, I am specifically considering policies in which "random elements" *do* enter ex-ante, but they do not enter ex-post. And why should the ex-post social welfare be "governed by the tastes of individuals for gambling"? Let us recognize, at least, that it is uncomfortable to have ex-post welfare determined in this way.

5.5. *Ex-post collective choice*

Section 4 showed that if collective choice is Bayesian rational, consequentialist, and independent of dynamically irrelevant consequences, then, given that it is also based on a social welfare functional which is defined for an unrestricted domain of utility function profiles and satisfies ex-post Pareto indifference, collec-

---

[7]   Sen (1970, p. 86) and Rawls (1971, p. 323) have also cited the same argument in criticizing the use of von Neumann–Morgenstern utility functions as appropriate cardinal utility functions for making interpersonal comparisons.

tive choice must be of the ex-post utilitarian form. In this section the implications of imposing the stronger condition of ex-ante Pareto indifference were explored, and found to be rather uncomfortable. This suggests that we should be content with ex-post utilitarianism. There are, however, some reservations that need to be discussed.

6. Ex-post collective choice: some reservations

6.1. Individual risk-taking

Unless the socially expected value of the ex-post welfare function happens to be an increasing function of individuals' ex-ante utilities, it is fairly evident that individuals' insurance decisions, in a competitive insurance market, can never be ex-post welfare optimal, even given appropriate lump-sum transfers. The point is that insurance market decisions reflect private ex-ante values, which are not the same as social ex-post values. This is explored more fully in Hammond (1981a). Even worse, however, is the fact that, even if all insurance and capital markets were closed down and replaced by optimal contingent intertemporal lump-sum transfers of purchasing power, the remaining spot markets for current commodities would still fail to achieve an ex-post welfare optimal allocation, except in a very special case. The special case is when intertemporal preferences are backwardly separable, so that an optimal decision on current spot markets is always independent of the future, though it may depend on the past. This effectively rules out durable goods, for instance. Yet, outside this special case, the fact that individuals' attitudes to risk are inconsistent with the ex-post welfare function can lead them to decisions such as an under- or overinvestment in risky durable goods.

This divergence between social and private values in the face of risk is a considerable inconvenience, but it is only really uncomfortable for more extreme proponents of laissez faire or consumer sovereignty. After all, we are surely accustomed to the view that not all consumers have tastes which should be fully respected; the only new feature which arises when there is uncertainty is that the inappropriateness of consumers' tastes may be rather more pervasive. No, the real source of discomfort with the ex-post approach to welfare economics is rather the difficulty there seems to be in paying adequate attention or even any attention at all to individuals' attitudes to risk. Let us illustrate this with a thoroughly ex-post approach to the problem of inequality under uncertainty.

Suppose ϵ is the degree of relative inequality aversion in each state s, ex-post, so that:

$$w_s \equiv \sum_{i \in I} \frac{(y_s^i)^{1-\epsilon}}{1-\epsilon} \quad (\epsilon > 0; \epsilon \neq 1).$$

Then a money measure of welfare in each state s is Atkinson's (1970) equally distributed equivalent income y_s^E defined by the identity:

$$w_s \equiv \frac{n(y_s^E)^{1-\epsilon}}{1-\epsilon} = \sum_{i \in I} \frac{(y_s^i)^{1-\epsilon}}{1-\epsilon} \,,$$

where n is the number of individuals in the set I.

Now consider an expected welfare function of the form:

$$W = \sum_s \pi_s u(y_s^E),$$

where $u(\cdot)$ is a social von Neumann–Morgenstern utility function which is intended to capture the social attitude to risk in the distribution of the welfare measure y_s^E. For example, suppose $u(y_s^E) = (y_s^E)^{1-\rho}/(1-\rho)$, where ρ is the constant relative degree of social risk aversion. Then

$$W \equiv \sum_s \frac{\pi_s}{1-\rho} \left\{ \sum_i (y_s^i)^{1-\epsilon} \right\}^{(1-\rho)/(1-\epsilon)}$$

(neglecting an irrelevant multiplicative constant). On the face of it, this pays no attention at all to individuals' attitudes to risk. Of course, ρ could be chosen with individuals' degrees of risk aversion in mind, but how this should be done is not clear. Indeed, even if all individuals have identical von Neumann–Morgenstern utility functions with constant relative risk aversion, it is by no means clear that ρ should be chosen equal to this common constant relative degree of risk aversion, for the reasons given in section 5. This is hardly comfortable: the discomfort arises, just as one would expect, from the failure to have an explicitly ex-ante welfare function, yet I would not advocate a return to the ex-ante approach.

6.2. Gambling

An objection to the ex-post approach and the goal of ex-post income equality is that it leads one effectively to nullify any gambling activities an individual may wish to undertake. This objection may actually be illusory, however. Where not very large gambles are involved, which individuals undertake because they enjoy gambling, then gambling itself is included as a "good" in each gambler's utility function and so should be taken account of in the collective choice rule. One takes account of the fact that trying to impose too much equality ex-post removes most of the enjoyment from gambling. Then it becomes a question of finding the optimal trade-off between ex-post equality and gambling: this is unlikely to involve having no effective gambling at the optimum.

There is also the point that, in an economy with serious non-convexities, an optimal allocation may well involve lotteries in any case. Then as good a way as any of bringing about such lotteries may be to allow gambles or lotteries with large prizes. For example, a former colleague of mine at work rationalized participating in British football pools by the desire to undertake a round-the-world cruise: participating in football pools presented an unfair lottery, but a small probability of winning enough to afford such a cruise, and was clearly better than not participating in them, even according to an ex-post view of welfare economics.

6.3. Individual expectations and information

There is another source of discomfort in the ex-post approach when one comes to consider the social probabilities π_s and the individual probabilities $\pi_s^i (i \in I)$ attached to any state $s \in S$. It is simply not clear how π_s should depend upon π_s^i. Of course, if there are "objective" probabilities and individuals' perceived probabilities differ from these only because of misinformation, then it is certainly tempting to make π_s equal to the objective probability of s. This seems ideal, and I am certainly making use myself of a welfare criterion like this in Hammond (1981b). And yet even this has a drawback. Suppose that giving an individual some extra information in the form of bad news has a very small positive effect on the allocation of resources, in any ex-post state of the world s which can occur. Then, since objective probabilities are unaffected by the extra information which is revealed to the individual, any ex-post welfare function with social probabilities equal to objective probabilities would favour a change of this kind. Yet, if the bad news spoils that individuals' enjoyment of life over a considerable period before he would otherwise have found out what was going to happen, his ex-ante utility may be much lower and one may wish to argue that the small gain in welfare ex-post is not worth the disappointment or misery which is now inflicted on the individual ex-ante. Issues of this kind have been discussed by Atkinson (1974) in the special context of whether it is really worth making somebody who is unlikely ever to give up smoking fully aware of all the health risks. Of course, we are on rather slippery ground here because if we admit that it is sometimes worth withholding bad news, it is easy to go from that position into wanting to create false good news. Yet this kind of argument is impermissible in the pure ex-post approach, and this in itself is a source of unease and discomfort (see also Hammond, 1982a).

6.4.   *The value of life and limb*

Using the ex-post approach on its own is peculiarly uncomfortable somehow when it comes to issues such as the costs of accidents and the value of a life. Ex-post, it may seem that no sum of money is too large to spend in order to save the life of an individual who can be saved if he would otherwise certainly die. Yet ex-ante we all take decisions without great thought which increase the risk of death barely perceptibly, and of course some of us eventually run out of luck. Decisions of this kind seem much more comfortable if we approach them from the ex-ante point of view, and look at the value of a reduction in the probability of death, rather than the value of a life. This approach has been extensively discussed by Jones-Lee (1974, 1976, 1980) as well as by Drèze (1962) and Mishan (1971, 1972). There has been a recent criticism of this approach by Broome (1978) who essentially points out that the ex-ante approach is inconsistent with the kind of ex-post view with which one is comfortable. The topic no doubt deserves much more discussion, but for the moment it suffices to notice that this is another instance where the pure ex-post approach is certainly uncomfortable as indeed may be the pure ex-ante approach. In this case, however, it seems that the discomfort arises from our willingness to face up to some very unpleasant decisions. At least the ex-post approach *does* face up to them squarely, and force us to think honestly of how much a life is worth to society as a whole. Moreover, if one really does believe that the right approach to questions of this kind is by looking at how individuals value reductions in the probability of death, injury, or sickness, one can still use the ex-ante approach provided it is consistent with the ex-post approach. Alternatively, some modification of the ex-ante approach might be appropriate, in which one there is an ex-post welfare function which depends also on ex-ante utilities, as will be considered in section 7.

6.5.   *Ex-ante fairness*[8]

Diamond (1967a) criticized Harsanyi (1955) by appealing to a specific example with two individuals, A and B, two equiprobable states, which I shall call s_1 and s_2, and two different social options, which I shall call a and b. The utility outcomes are:

[8]   This section owes much to Amartya Sen.

$$u^A(a, s_1) = u^A(a, s_2) = u^A(b, s_1) = u^B(b, s_2) = 1,$$
$$u^B(a, s_1) = u^B(a, s_2) = u^B(b, s_1) = u^A(b, s_2) = 0.$$

As Diamond argues, if one follows Harsanyi and maximizes the expected value of total utility, then a and b are socially indifferent. Moreover, the ex-post distribution of utilities is the same in each state, so a and b are indifferent whenever the ex-post social welfare functional takes the form:

$$w_s = w_s(u_s^A, u_s^B),$$

where $w_s(\cdot)$ is symmetric in individual utilities and state-dependent. Yet, as Diamond suggests, b does indeed seem superior to a, because it gives B some chance of the higher utility level, whereas a gives him none at all. A similar example has been presented recently by Myerson (1981). This consideration of ex-ante fairness cannot be captured in any purely ex-post welfare function. As Diamond also points out, such a consideration violates the sure-thing principle for collective choice. Yet in Hammond (1982b) it was proved that the sure-thing principle is necessary if consequentialist choice is to be dynamically consistent for any decision tree. The only way of accommodating ex-ante fairness within the ex-post welfare criterion is to relax the postulate of consequentialism or else the postulate of dynamically irrelevant consequences. It may be possible to do this so that the distribution of individuals' ex-ante expected utilities affects social welfare. It is now time to consider such a possibility.

7. Ex-post collective choice including ex-ante utilities

7.1. Dependence on dynamically irrelevant consequences

One of the assumptions which was shown in subsection 4.1 to lead to independence of irrelevant alternatives and so to ex-post utilitarianism was that of independence of dynamically irrelevant consequences. This implied that, given any decision tree $\mathscr{T} = \langle\!\langle X(s, n)\rangle_{s \in S(n)}, S(n), N(n)\rangle_{n \in N}$ and any decision node $n \in N^*$, the SWFL $F(n)$ at node n had to be a function $F(n)(U(n))$ of the profile of utility functions at the node n of $\mathscr{T}$. In particular, since the profile $U(n)$ is only defined on $\Pi_{s \in S(n)} X(s, n)$, this means that acts outside this set and their associated consequences are ignored at node n. But it is worth recalling the argument of subsection 3.4: in the absence of this crucial assumption, the whole collective choice procedure at any node n depends upon the past history of what might have been. Then, why should decisions at node n and not the initial node

n_0 depend on what has gone before? And if decisions at n_0 also depend on what might have been, how far back do we go, and how do we bring such considerations in? I believe such questions have no satisfactory answers and will retain the assumption of independence of dynamically irrelevant consequences. Instead, I shall look elsewhere for a way to include ex-ante utilities of individuals in the social welfare functional.

7.2. Intermediate consequentialism

If we retain the postulate of dynamically irrelevant consequences, and if we also stay clear of the Vickrey–Harsanyi case which was covered in section 5, the only other plausible way of abandoning purely ex-post utilitarianism and of introducing some dependence on ex-ante utilities is to relax the postulate of consequentialism. This, it should be recalled, involves evaluating each contingent act x_E by the (individualistic) consequences $\gamma^i[s, x(s)]$ which the act produces in each state $s \in E$ and for each individual $i \in I$. It seems an entirely natural assumption which, indeed, economists nearly always make as a matter of routine, and which underlies Savage's sure-thing principle which is the key assumption behind expected utility maximization. Yet, as is discussed in Hammond (1982b), consequentialism in this pure form is unreasonably restrictive in some decision problems. I believe that Diamond's (1967a) comment on Harsanyi, discussed in subsection 6.5 above, is a good illustration of this. The consequences of the two alternatives a and b in that example are an identical distribution of ex-post utilities — $u^A = 1$ and $u^B = 0$, or $u^A = 0$ and $u^B = 1$ — in each state. It is precisely *consequentialism* then which forces us to consider only these ex-post utilities and to declare a and b as indifferent, when instead b may seem preferable to a because the distribution of ex-ante utilities is equal with b and unequal with a.

Rather than remain within this narrow consequentialist framework, I propose instead to consider an extended form of consequentialism which I shall call *intermediate consequentialism*. The consequences of a contingent act x in event E are not only the terminal consequences $\gamma[s, x(s)]$ for $s \in E$ but also the whole pattern of contingent consequences:

$$\gamma_{E_1}[x_{E_1}], \gamma_{E_2}[x_{E_2}], \gamma_{E_3}[x_{E_3}], ...,$$

which are possible at various successive nodes $n_1, n_2, n_3, ...$ of the decision tree, where $S(n_1) = E_1$, $S(n_2) = E_2$, $S(n_3) = E_3$, ... The consequences $\gamma_{E_t}[x_{E_t}]$ ($t = 1, 2, ...$) are *intermediate consequences*, whereas $\gamma[s, x(s)]$ is a terminal consequence: that is why I use the term *intermediate consequentialism*. Then, when each individual evaluates $\gamma^i_{E_t}[x_{E_t}]$ on the basis of the expected value of his von Neumann—Morgenstern utility function, an intermediate consequentialist approach to collective choice permits social welfare to depend on ex-ante expected utility. This remains to be explored in later work, however.

8. Conclusions

The main message of this chapter is that if we are to persist in the habit of ignoring the tree structure of dynamic collective choice problems under uncertainty and to adopt what I have here called the "consequentialist" approach, then one is forced to use the ex-post approach to collective choice under uncertainty. More particularly, collective choice must be ordinal and satisfy independence of irrelevant alternatives — as I showed earlier in Hammond (1977) for the case of certainty — and it must also satisfy the sure-thing principle.

While it is possible to maximize the expected value of a weighted sum of individuals' von Neumann—Morgenstern utility functions, and so be consistent with the ex-ante approach to collective choice under uncertainty, this Vickrey—Harsanyi approach involves value judgements and interpersonal comparisons of utility which are not always ethically appealing. Moreover, it deals with only one of the two objections to the ex-post approach which seem really serious — namely, the objection that individuals' rights to take risks are not being respected.[9] The second, more fundamental, objection that Diamond (1967a) raised, concerning ex-ante fairness, cannot really be met at all in a purely consequentialist approach. On balance, however, I am not sure that this objection is altogether fatal. Indeed, perhaps both objections serve only to show that the usual consequentialist utilitarian approach to collective choice needs to be supplemented somewhat by non-utilitarian ideas such as liberty and equality of opportunity.

References

Arrow, K.J. (1963) *Social Choice and Individual Values*, 2nd edn. (Yale University Press, New Haven).
Arrow, K.J. (1971) *Essays in the Theory of Risk-Bearing* (North-Holland, Amsterdam).

[9] Harsanyi (1975) also relaxes his earlier "individualism" assumption, arrives at a criterion somewhere between ex-ante and ex-post, and finds the result "objectionable" for reasons similar to this. On the other hand, Friedman (1962) appears to base his defence of ex-ante Pareto efficiency as a welfare criterion on wanting to respect the right of individuals to take risks.

d'Aspremont, C. and L. Gevers (1977) "Equity and the Informational Basis of Collective Choice", *Review of Economic Studies*, 44, 199–209.

Atkinson, A.B. (1970) "On the Measurement of Inequality", *Journal of Economic Theory*, 2, 244–263.

Atkinson, A.B. (1974) "Smoking and the Economics of Government Intervention", in: M. Perlman, ed., *The Economics of Health and Medical Care*, Proceedings of a Conference held by the International Economic Association (Macmillan, London, and Halsted, New York), pp. 428–441.

Barry, B.M. (1973) *The Liberal Theory of Justice* (Clarendon Press, Oxford).

Broome, J. (1978) "Trying to Value a Life", *Journal of Public Economics*, 9, 91–100.

Dasgupta, P.A. and G.M. Heal (1979) *Economic Theory and Exhaustible Resources* (Cambridge Economic Handbooks).

Diamond, P.A. (1967a) "Cardinal Welfare, Individualistic Ethics and Interpersonal Comparisons of Utility: A Comment", *Journal of Political Economy*, 75, 765–766.

Diamond, P.A. (1967b) "The Role of a Stock Market in a General Equilibrium Model with Technological Uncertainty", *American Economic Review*, 57, 759–776.

Drèze, J.H. (1962) "L'utilité social d'une vie humaine", *Revue Française de Recherche Operationalle*.

Drèze, J.H. (1970) "Market Allocation Under Uncertainty", *European Economic Review*, 2, 133–165.

Friedman, M. (1962) *Capitalism and Freedom* (University of Chicago Press: Chicago).

Friedman, M. and L.J. Savage (1948) "The Utility Analysis of Choices Involving Risk", *Journal of Political Economy*, 56, 279–304.

Gorman, W.M. (1968) "The Structure of Utility Functions", *Review of Economic Studies*, 35, 367–390.

Guesnerie, R. and T. de Montbrial (1974) "Allocation Under Uncertainty: A Survey", in: J. Drèze, ed., *Allocation Under Uncertainty*, pp. 53–70.

Hakansson, N.H., J.G. Kunkel and J.A. Ohlson (1980), "Sufficient and Necessary Conditions for Information to Have Social Value in Pure Exchange", School of Business Administration, University of California, Berkeley, mimeo.

Hammond, P.J. (1976) "Changing Tastes and Coherent Dynamic Choice", *Review of Economic Studies*, 43, 159–173.

Hammond, P.J. (1977) "Dynamic Restrictions on Metastatic Choice", *Economica*, 44, 337–350.

Hammond, P.J. (1981a) "Ex-Ante and Ex-Post Welfare Optimality Under Uncertainty", *Economica*, 48, 235–250.

Hammond, P.J. (1981b) "On Welfare Economics with Incomplete Information and the Social Value of Public Information", Stanford University, Institute for Mathematical Studies in the Social Sciences, Economics Technical Report No. 332.

Hammond, P.J. (1982a) "Utilitarianism, Uncertainty and Information", in: A.K. Sen and B. Williams, eds., *Utilitarianism and Beyond* (Cambridge University Press).

Hammond, P.J. (1982b) "Consequentialism and Rationality in Dynamic Choice Under Uncertainty", Stanford University, Institute for Mathematical Studies in the Social Sciences, Economics Technical Report No. 387.

Harris, R.G. (1978) "Ex-Post Efficiency and Resource Allocation Under Uncertainty", *Review of Economic Studies*, 45, 427–436.

Harris, R.G. and N. Olewiler (1979) "The Welfare Economics of Ex-post Optimality", *Economica*, 46, 137–147.

Harsanyi, J.C. (1955) "Cardinal Welfare, Individualistic Ethics, and Interpersonal Comparisons", *Journal of Political Economy*, 63, 309–321.

Harsanyi, J.C. (1975) "Nonlinear Social Welfare Functions: Do Welfare Economists Have a Special Exemption from Bayesian Rationality?", *Theory and Decision*, 6, 311–332.

Harsanyi, J.C. (1978) "Bayesian Decision Theory and Utilitarian Ethics", *American Economic Review (Papers and Proceedings)*, 68, 223–228.

Hirshleifer, J. (1971) "The Private and Social Value of Information and the Reward to Inventive Activity", *American Economic Review*, 61, 561–574.

Jones-Lee, M.W. (1974) "The Value of Changes in the Probability of Death or Injury", *Journal of Political Economy*, 82, 835–849.

Jones-Lee, M.W. (1976) *The Value of Life: An Economic Analysis* (Martin Robertson, London, and University of Chicago Press).

Jones-Lee, M.W. (1979) "The Expected Conditional Utility Theorem for the Case of Personal Probabilities and State Conditional Utility Functions: A Proof and Some Notes", *Economic Journal*, 89, 834–849.

Jones-Lee, M.W. (1980) "Human Capital, Risk-Aversion and the Value of Life", in: D.A. Currie and W. Peters, eds., *Contemporary Economic Analysis*, vol. 2 (Croom-Helm, London), pp. 285–321.

Kanbur, S.M. (1979a) "Of Risk Taking and the Personal Distribution of Income", *Journal of Political Economy*, 87, 769–797.

Kanbur, S.M. (1979b) "Entrepreneurial Risk Taking, Inequality and Public Policy: An Application of Inequality Decomposition Analysis to the General Equilibrium Effects of Progressive Taxation", Economic Theory Discussion Paper No. 24, University of Cambridge.

Koopmans, T.C. (1964) "On Flexibility of Future Preference", in: Shelly and Bryan, eds., *Human Judgments and Optimality* (Wiley, New York), pp. 243–254.

Kreps, D.M. and E.L. Porteus (1978) "Temporal Resolution of Uncertainty and Dynamic Choice Theory", *Econometrica*, 46, 185–200.

Marshall, J.M. (1974) "Private Incentives and Public Information", *American Economic Review*, 64, 373–390.

Mirrlees, J.A. (1974) "Notes on Welfare Economics, Information and Uncertainty", in: M. Balch, D. McFadden and S. Wu, eds., *Essays on Economic Behavior Under Uncertainty* (North-Holland, Amsterdam), pp. 243–258.

Mishan, E.J. (1971) "Evaluation of Life and Limb: A Theoretical Approach", *Journal of Political Economy*, 79, 687–705.

Mishan, E.J. (1972) *Elements of Cost Benefit Analysis* (Allen and Unwin, London).

Myerson, R. (1981) "Utilitarianism, Egalitarianism, and the Timing Effect in Social Choice Problems", *Econometrica*, 49, 883–897.

Ng, D.S. (1975) "Information Accuracy and Social Welfare under Homogeneous Beliefs", *Journal of Financial Economics*, 2, 53–70.

Rawls, J. (1971) *A Theory of Justice* (Clarendon Press, Oxford).

Savage, L.J. (1954) *The Foundations of Statistics*, 2nd rev. edn. 1972 (John Wiley, Dover).

Sen, A.K. (1970) *Collective Choice and Social Welfare* (Holden-Day, San Francisco).

Starr, R.M. (1973) "Optimal Production and Allocation under Uncertainty", *Quarterly Journal of Economics*, 87, 81–95.

Strotz, R.H. (1956) "Myopia and Inconsistency in Dynamic Utility Maximization", *Review of Economic Studies*, 23, 165–180.

Vickrey, W.S. (1945) "Measuring Marginal Utility by Reactions to Risk", *Econometrica*, 13, 319–333.

Weller, P.A. (1978) "Consistent Intertemporal Decision-Making Under Uncertainty", *Review of Economic Studies*, 45, 263–266.

CHAPTER 11

Welfare aspects of naive and sophisticated decision-making

PAUL GROUT

University of Birmingham

1. Introduction

If preferences are changing over time, it is well known (see Strotz, 1956) that in many cases the plans instituted to maximise utility in period t will not be consistent with those plans that maximise utility at period $t + 1$, thus the plans instituted in period t will be overthrown at $t + 1$ and a new plan instituted. Plans made in one period without regard to the fact that tastes will change in the future are labelled naive or myopic, such plans being intertemporally inconsistent and Pareto inefficient. Each generation institutes plans which ex ante it believes will generate a certain level of utility but due to intertemporal inconsistency their actual utility derived is always less than anticipated. Three methods have been suggested to avoid this problem   the introduction of sophisticated planning, pre-commitment and intergenerational altruism. Hammond (1976) has pointed out that precommitment amounts to sophistication in a specially structured decision tree. This chapter will be mostly concerned with the comparison of naive and sophisticated planning. Basically, a sophisticated plan is one which explicitly takes into account that society's preferences are changing and is chosen solely from the set of plans which will not be overthrown in future periods.

If one poses the question whether sophisticated planning is superior to naive planning the sheer persuasiveness of the definitions alone would suggest a definite yes. Furthermore, the view that sophisticated planning is superior to naive planning appears frequently in the consistency literature. For example, Peleg and Yaari (1973) when discussing the Pareto inefficiency of sophisticated plans: "This

Social Choice and Welfare, edited by P.K. Pattanaik and M. Salles
© *North-Holland Publishing Company, 1983*

fact may be viewed by some readers as a serious drawback of the concept of an equilibrium consumption plan. However, we feel that the consistency property that characterises equilibrium plans is a minimal property. A consumption plan that does not have this property cannot be advocated seriously as a reasonable course of action for an agent with changing tastes". (Peleg and Yaari are actually discussing equilibrium consumption plans but, as will be seen below in the basic model, this coincides with sophisticated planning.) Similarly, Blackorby et al. (1973) discussing naive plans: "The present portion of the plan is executed and then revised in each period. Planning appears to make little sense in this context. The consumption programme generated by the behaviour is not optimal from any point of view. Hence it has been suggested that such a society follows a sophisticated optimum path". Obviously, sophistication removes the necessity to scrap unfinished plans which must bring benefits and by definition one may feel if a generation makes plans taking into account the future actions of others (which they cannot control) then surely they must be better off than when ignoring others actions. However, this does not in itself imply sophisticated planning is superior to naive planning except when viewed by one generation given that all other generations are acting in a sophisticated fashion. This type of argument seems to lie at the base of the view that sophistication is better, for example, again quoting Blackorby et al.: "The sophisticated solution (if it exists) would appear to be an improvement over naive planning. By explicitly considering the future preferences each generation realises a level of utility greater than that which is possible under inconsistent naive planning". However, it seems reasonable to suggest that either society will be sophisticated in each period or naive in each period and thus the true comparison should be between plans which are always naive or always sophisticated. If all generations are acting in a naive fashion, then looking at any one generation the losses that they receive due to the fact that their plans will be scrapped can be offset by the gains in overthrowing previous inconsistent plans and by the fact that the following generation will be acting in a naive fashion. This chapter will compare naive and sophisticated plans in conventional welfare economic terms, i.e. utilising Pareto efficiency and social welfare functions with each generation's inconsistent preferences as the welfare base. Adopting this approach the following sections argue that to use consistency as a proxy for such basic welfare judgements would be misleading. Moving from naive, inconsistent planning to sophisticated consistent planning does not guarantee any basic welfare improvement, this being a typical second-best result. Although consistency may be required in a full efficient allocation its introduction need bring no improvement when moving from one inefficient allocation to another. Of course, if consistency is valued in its own right and not as a proxy for efficiency then by definition sophisticated planning must be better than naive planning. But such an approach would in its turn beg questions about the role of consumer sovereignty and the concept of social welfare.

The discussion of myopic versus sophisticated equilibria is of further importance given the attitudes in recent years concerning the speed with which it is felt individuals learn the structure of the economy and thus have correct rather than incorrect expectations of their actions. If individuals are sophisticated then their expectations will be "rational", they are able to predict with certainty the outcome of any action they choose. The sophisticated equilibrium has been used to describe the rational expectations equilibrium in certain models (see Kydland and Prescott, 1977). The following section begins by using a decision tree format but most of the following section and section 3 concentrates on a simple growth model. Section 4 discusses the results and the appendix contains a proof of a result in the decision tree framework.

2.

This section will begin by considering a decision tree approach similar to that used by Hammond (1976). The model will be set in discrete time and in order to keep within the general interpretation of the rest of the chapter let each time period be a generation. A decision tree consists of a set of branches (or plans) and each generation has a strict preference order over the whole set of branches. We can say that plan x (Pareto) dominates[1] plan y if x is preferred to y at each time period. It is easy to show that in all decision trees there will exist a set of preferences such that the sophisticated plan Pareto dominates the myopic plan. However, it can also be shown (see appendix) that there will always exist preferences (many in fact) which have the property that the myopic plan is Pareto superior to the sophisticated plan in all decision trees where there is at least one plan with three or more nodes.[2] The problem with the decision tree approach is that in general Pareto dominance will give no answer between naive and sophisticated plans and in these cases one will wish to use a social welfare comparison. This will require a more specific model and the rest of the chapter will utilise what is probably the simplest model which generates the intertemporal problems.

The model is essentially that of Arrow (1973) with further restrictions. Each generation lives (or has power) for one period but also cares about consumption

---

[1] The terms "dominance" and "incomparable" are clearly related to concepts of Pareto dominance and Pareto incomparability. However, with models of changing tastes one has to be very careful how the concepts is interpreted (see Harsanyi, 1954). Therefore to avoid any confusion the terminology Pareto will be dropped.

[2] These results also generalise to less extreme forms of myopia (see Grout, 1982).

in the next period. Every individual is identical, thus we can act as if each generation consisted of one person, with utility, V,

$$V = U(C_t) + \delta\, U(C_{t+1}), \quad 0 < \delta < 1, \tag{1a}$$

with specific utility function:

$$U(cK_t) = \frac{1}{1-\rho}\,(cK_t)^{1-\rho}, \quad 0 < \rho < \infty, \rho \neq 1;$$

production function:

$$K_{t+1} = \alpha(1 - c_t)\,K_t;$$

and using the notation:

$$v(c; t) = U(cK_t) + \delta\, U((1-c)\,c\alpha K_t).$$

Before considering this model[3] it is perhaps worthwhile discussing this utility

---

[3] The model being used here is a frequently used one of non-overlapping generations
with altruism limited to their immediate successors. A feature of this model is that naive behaviour will be extremely naive and sophisticated behaviour will result in each individual
doing the best possible for themselves when they know everyone else's strategy and therefore have perfect foresight. Thus, a comparison between naive and sophisticated planning
is really comparing two extremes.
   There is another interpretation of the model which has been suggested to me. This is the
case where there is a single individual who considers, at time t, current consumption c_t and
a permanent consumption stream $c_{t+1} = c_{t+2} = \ldots$ thereafter. His utility is

$$U(c_t) + \sum_{s=t+1}^{\infty} \beta^{t-s} U(c_s),$$

which reduces to

$$U(c_t) + \delta\, U(c_{t+1}). \tag{10}$$

Notice that in this interpretation δ cannot be restricted to be less than one (since $\delta = \beta$
$(1 - \beta)$). The naive individual maximises (10) but a sophisticated consumer anticipates his
future savings behaviour (but assumes incorrectly that $c_{t+1} = c_{t+1} = \ldots$). The difference between the models is more than one of interpretation since the latter model implies all (Pareto)
dominance comparisons are irrelevant and the only relevant question becomes: Which type
of planning gives a higher value to the individual's true preferences?
   This may be an interesting way of looking at the problem but does have certain draw-
backs and will not be pursued here. First, the individual's preferences are not changing over
time. He has mistaken expectations of the future but the model does not explain why these
expectations arise; they are certainly not consistent with his true preferences at *any* time

function in more detail. It is often argued (e.g. see Phelps and Riley, 1978) that the correct interpretation of V should be

$$V_t = U_t + \delta V_{t+1},\tag{1b}$$

which gives

$$V_t = \sum_t \delta^{\bar{\imath}-t} U(C_{\bar{\imath}}),\tag{1c}$$

which exhibits intergenerational altruism (see Heal, 1973), thus there is no inconsistency in myopic planning. However, if one feels that dynamic inconsistency of myopic plans is likely it is not because one feels (1a) is an exact representation of preferences but simply that (1c) may not be. As long as the discounting process is truncated at some point or does not follow the form δ^t throughout, then time inconsistency can arise. There are many other functions which cause problems; (1a) is chosen basically because it is a particularly easy form to deal with. However, if one believes that people care for future utility and not consumption then just as (1a) is the simplest case of many possibilities then similarly (1b) is the simplest case of many others where utility is the relevant variable. However, to get to (1c) (the final objective of the latter approach) then the specific form (1b) is crucial – any other form does not lead to (1c). Thus, the argument in favour of intergenerational altruism is not simply that people care for future generations' utility rather than consumption but moreover that this must take the form given in (1b). This latter assumption is, of course, not easy to accept. Thus, the use of functions other than (1c) is plausible and (1a) is simply the most basic form.

If a generation determined the optimal consumption rate on the understanding that whatever rate they choose the following generation would be forced to follow suit, i.e.

$$\max_{c_t} \{U(c_t K_t) + \delta U((1 - c_t) c_{t+1} \alpha K_t) \mid c_{t+1} = c_t, \ c_t \in [0,1]\},$$

---

period. Secondly, a sophisticated individual is making mistakes every period in this latter framework. One of the attractions of the results given in this chapter is that one is considering a comparison of the most naive action an individual can adopt with the best he can do with perfect foresight. In this latter interpretation one is clearly not comparing the naive action with the best the individual is capable of doing acting independently. The motivation for a comparison of this type is far less clear.

the solution would be given by

$$Z_{\max} = (cK_t)^{-\rho}K_t - ((1-c)\,c\alpha K_t)^{-\rho}[cK_t\alpha\delta - (1-c)\,K_t\alpha\delta] = 0. \quad (2)$$

Given the form of the utility function each generation would choose the same c, call this $c_{\max}$. If the generation had to take the consumption rate of the following generation as given, then (2) would be inappropriate. In this case the generation would

$$\max_{c_t}\{U(c_t K_t) + \delta\, U((1-c_t)\,c_{t+1}\alpha K_t)\,|\,c_{t+1} = \bar{c}, c_t \in [0,1]\},$$

giving

$$Z_S = (c_t K_t)^{-\rho}K_t - ((1-c_t)\,c_{t+1}\alpha K_t)^{-\rho}[c_{t+1}K_t\alpha\delta] = 0. \quad (3)$$

For each c_{t+1} (3) defines c_t but one can go further and look for stationary points that solve (3), i.e. solutions with $c_t = c_{t+1}$. If we only look at positive c, then the stationary point of (3) will always be unique and will clearly be a Nash equilibrium: Peleg and Yaari's Equilibrium Consumption Plan. The Equilibrium Consumption Plan is defined somewhat differently from a sophisticated plan as defined by Strotz (1956) and Pollak (1968). However, in this case, since each generation's preferences do not pay regard to the past and the choice of consumption function is independent of the level of capital stock, the Strotz–Pollak sophisticated plan and the Equilibrium Consumption Plan coincide (see Peleg and Yaari, 1973). Thus, the sophisticated choice of c will be identical for each generation and will be the positive solution to (3), call this c_S. If generation t is naive they will

$$\max_{c_t, c_{t+1}}\{U(c_t K_t) + \delta\, U((1-c_t)\,c_{t+1}\alpha K_t)\,|\,c_t, c_{t+1} \in [0,1]\}.$$

They will set $c_{t+1} = 1$ and the solution will be given by

$$Z_n = (c_t K_t)^{-\rho}K_t - ((1-c_t)\,\alpha K_t)^{-\rho}\alpha\delta K_t = 0, \quad (4)$$

call this c_n. Although generation t acts as if $c_{t+1} = 1$, c_{t+1} will, in fact, be equal to c_n since the plan instituted at t will be overthrown at $t + 1$. Thus, their true ex post utility will be $v(c_n; t)$ and not the level they believe to receive ex ante, call this latter level naive expected utility.

Equations (2), (3) and (4) reduce to

$$\alpha\delta\,(2\,c_{max} - 1) = [\alpha(1 - c_{max})]^\rho, \tag{2'}$$

$$\alpha\delta\,c_{S} = [\alpha(1 - c_{S})]^\rho, \tag{3'}$$

$$c_{n} = \frac{\alpha}{\alpha + (\alpha\delta\,(1/\rho))}. \tag{4'}$$

Note that from (2') $c_{max} > \frac{1}{2}$, the reason being the symmetric nature of $(1 - c)c$. $v(c, t)$ as defined above is concave in c and also the naive expected utility is concave in c_{n}. Differentiation of Z_{S} with $c_{t} = c_{t+1} = c$ shows that this derivative is not always uniquely signed; however, if $c > \frac{1}{2}$ the derivative of Z_{S} must be negative and Z_{S} must be negative as c tends to one. Solving for c_{S} and substituting this c_{S} into (2) gives $Z_{max} > 0$, thus concavity of $v(c; t)$ implies $c_{max} > c_{S}$ for all ρ. If $\rho \in (0,1)$ and c_{S} is substituted into (4), then $Z_{n} < 0$ and concavity of the naive expected utility implies $c_{n} < c_{S} < c_{max}$. Thus, if $\rho \in (0,1)$

$$v(c_{S}; 0) > v(c_{n}; 0).$$

For a given c:

$$v(c; t) = \frac{A_t^{1-\rho}}{1-\rho}\,(1 + \delta B^{1-\rho}),$$

where

$$A_t = cK_0\,\alpha^t(1 - c_t)^t$$

and

$$B = \alpha(1 - c),$$

giving

$$\frac{dv}{dc} = A_t^{-\rho}\left[\frac{A_{t-1}}{c}\,(B - ct)\right] - A^{1-\rho}\delta B^{-\rho},$$

which will be negative at any c for large enough t. Thus, there exists a T such that

$$v(c_{n}; t) > v(c_{S}; t) \quad \text{for all} \quad t > T,$$

showing $\langle v(c_{n}; t)\rangle_{t=0}^{\infty}$ and $\langle v(c_{S}; t)\rangle_{t=0}^{\infty}$ are incomparable if $\rho \in (0, 1)$.

If $\rho \in (1, \infty)$, then substituting c_S into (4) gives $Z_n > 0$ and concavity of naive expected utility implies $c_n > c_S$. Now either

$$c_{max} \geqslant c_n > c_S \tag{5}$$

or

$$c_n > c_{max} > c_S \tag{6}$$

is possible. If (5) holds, then we have

$$v(c_n; 0) > v(c_S; 0)$$

and a T such that

$$v(c_S; t) > v(c_n; t) \quad \text{for all} \quad t \geqslant T.$$

Thus, if (5) holds $\langle v(c_S; t) \rangle_{t=0}^{\infty}$ cannot dominate $\langle v(c_n; t) \rangle_{t=0}^{\infty}$. Since $\rho \in (1, \infty)$ implies $c_n > c_S$, then

$$K_t(S) > K_t(n) \quad \text{for all} \quad t > 0, \tag{7}$$

which in conjunction with (8) below would imply

$$v(c_S; t) \geqslant v(c_n; t)$$

with a strict inequality at least for all positive t. Thus if $1 < \rho < \infty$, (8) is a necessary condition for $\langle v(c_S; t) \rangle_{t=0}^{\infty}$ to dominate $\langle v(c_n; t) \rangle_{t=0}^{\infty}$. Note, however, that when (6) holds this does not automatically imply

$$v(c_n; 0) \leqslant v(c_S; 0). \tag{8}$$

It can be shown that (5) must hold for values of $1 < \rho < 2$; thus one would expect (8) is most likely to happen when ρ is large.

Proposition 1. If ρ is "large" there exist $v(c_S; t)$ which dominate $v(c_n; t)$.

Setting $\alpha\delta - \delta = 1$. Proposition 1 of Grout (1977) shows $c_S = (1 - 1/\alpha)$ for all ρ, thus if we choose $\alpha = 2, \delta = 1$, then $c_S = \frac{1}{2}$ for all ρ. From (4') and (2') the following must hold:

$$\lim_{\rho \to \infty} c_n = \tfrac{2}{3},$$

$$\lim_{\rho \to \infty} c_{max} = \tfrac{1}{2},$$

thus

$$c_{max} = c_S < c_n.$$

c_{max} equal to c_S tells us (8) holds with strict inequality which, given $1 < \rho < \infty$, is the necessary condition for $\langle v(c_S;t)\rangle_{t=0}^{\infty}$ to Pareto dominate $\langle v(c_n;t)\rangle_{t=0}^{\infty}$.

However, this is not an argument for sophisticated planning even when ρ is known to be large since for "large" ρ there exist examples of incomparability, e.g. from (2'), (3'), and (4') we see that

$$\lim_{\alpha \to 1 \ \rho \to \infty} c_{max} = \tfrac{1}{2}$$

$$\lim_{\alpha \to 1 \ \rho \to \infty} c_n = \tfrac{1}{2}$$

and

$$\lim_{\alpha \to 1 \ \rho \to \infty} c_S = 0.$$

Thus,

$$v(c_n;0) > v(c_S;0)$$

and the necessary condition for dominance is violated.

Notice that if $1 < \rho < \infty$, then $c_n > c_S$. Thus, $v(c_S;t)$ must eventually overtake $v(c_n;t)$ and if $0 < \rho < 1$ all plans are incomparable. Thus:

Proposition 2. There are no α, δ, and ρ such that $\langle v(c_n;t)\rangle_{t=0}^{\infty}$ dominates $\langle v(c_S; t)\rangle_{t=0}^{\infty}$.

This result is not really surprising when one considers the strong restrictions this model places on the way in which each period's preferences differ. Since the model is essentially being used to consider social welfare comparisons this "apparent bias" of the model in favour of sophistication will only strengthen the results.

3.

We now come to the main aim of the chapter which is to compare $\langle v(c_n; t)\rangle_{t=0}^{\infty}$ and $\langle v(c_S; t)\rangle_{t=0}^{\infty}$ using social welfare functions; the two that will be used are the utilitarian and maximin welfare functions. $\langle v(c; t)\rangle$ will be preferred to $\langle v(\overline{c}; t)\rangle$ given the utilitarian approach if there exists a T such that

$$\sum_{i=0}^{t} (v(c; i) - v(\overline{c}; i)) > 0 \quad \text{for all} \quad t \geq T.$$

Note that maximisation of the sum of $v(c; t)$ is not the same as maximisation of the sum of $U(c_t K_t)$, since the first generation has a weight of one while all other generations have a weight of $(1 + \delta)$. If the first generation were also weighted at $(1 + \delta)$, then the optimum choice of c if $1 < \rho < \infty$ would be

$$c_u = 1 - \alpha^{(1-\rho)/\rho}.$$

If $0 < \rho < 1$, then for any comparison between c_i and c_j the smaller would always give a larger utility sum for a large t.

Proposition 3. Given the utilitarian welfare function:
    (i) $\langle v(c_n; t)\rangle$ is preferred to $\langle v(c_S; t)\rangle$ if $\rho \in (0,1)$, and
    (ii) $\langle v(c_S; t)\rangle$ is preferred to $\langle v(c_n; t)\rangle$ if $\rho \in (1, \infty)$.

For $0 < \rho < 1$ since $c_n < c_S$ there will exist a T such that

$$\sum_{i=0}^{t} U(c_n K_i) > \sum_{i=0}^{t} U(c_S K_i) \quad \text{for all} \quad t > T.$$

Equivalently,

$$\sum_{i=0}^{t} [v(c_n; i) - v(c_S; i)] + \delta [U(c_n K_0) - U(c_S K_0)]$$

$$- \delta [U(c_n K_{t+1}) - U(c_S K_{t+1})] > 0,$$

which together with the fact that

$$\delta [U(c_n K_0) - U(c_S K_0)] < 0$$

and

$$\delta [U(c_n K_{t+1}) - U(c_S K_{t+1})] > 0$$

implies that $\langle v(c_n; t)\rangle$ is preferred to $\langle v(c_S; t)\rangle$ if $\rho \in (0,1)$.

Substituting c_u into the right-hand side of (3') gives

$$\alpha\delta c < \alpha,$$

which implies $c_u < c_S$ giving, for $1 < \rho < \infty$,

$$c_u < c_S < c_n. \tag{9}$$

Generation 0 receive a weight of one, whereas all other generations receive a weight of $(1 + \delta)$ in the utilitarian sum. Thus, for a utility sum up to t the optimal constant cinsumption rate will be less than or equal to c_u (since a lower weight on the first generation will encourage greater growth) converging to c_u as t tends to infinity. Consequently (9) is sufficient (since the sum of concave functions is concave) for there to exist a T such that

$$\sum_{i=0}^{t} v(c_S; i) - v(c_n; i) > 0 \quad \text{for all} \quad t \geqslant T.$$

Thus, the optimality of naive or sophisticated plans turns neatly on the value of ρ, but there is again no presumption in favour of sophisticated planning.

Define $\langle v(c_1; t)\rangle$ as being preferred to $\langle v(c_2; t)\rangle$ given the maximin welfare function if there exists a T_0 such that

$$\min \langle v(c_1; t)\rangle_{t=0}^{T} > \min \langle v(c_2; t)\rangle_{t=0}^{T} \quad \text{for all} \quad T \geqslant T_0.$$

Proposition 4. Given the maximin welfare function, if $0 < \rho < 1$ and (i) $\alpha\delta - \delta \geqslant 1$, then $\langle v(c_S; t)\rangle$ is preferred to $\langle v(c_n; t)\rangle$, (ii) $\alpha\delta - \delta < 1$, then $\langle v(c_n; t)\rangle$ is preferred to $\langle v(c_S; t)\rangle$.

If $\alpha\delta - \delta \geqslant 1$, then $\langle v(c_S; t)\rangle_{t=0}^{\infty}$ is a constant or monotonic increasing sequence, hence

$$v(c_S; 0) \leqslant v(c_S; t) \quad \text{for all} \quad t.$$

The fact that $c_n < c_S$ and $\langle v(c_n; t)\rangle_{t=0}^{\infty}$ does not Pareto dominate $\langle v(c_S; t)\rangle_{t=0}^{\infty}$ implies

$$v(c_n; 0) < v(c_S; 0),$$

hence (i). If $\alpha\delta - \delta < 1$ then $\langle v(c_S; t)\rangle_{t=0}^{\infty}$ is a decreasing monotonic sequence, thus

$$\lim_{t\to\infty} v(c_S; t) = \min \langle v(c_S; t)\rangle_{t=0}^{\infty}$$

$\langle v(c_n; t)\rangle_{t=0}^{\infty}$ may be increasing, constant or decreasing. In each of these cases there exists a T_0 such that

$$v(c_S; t) < v(c_n; t) \quad \text{for all} \quad t \geqslant T_0,$$

hence (ii).

Thus, here the parameters of the economy will affect our decision as to which is preferable. Given the difficulty in determining dominance when $1 < \rho < \infty$ one would expect to be able to make less precise statements about the choice under maximin of the optimal sequence. This is in fact true:

Proposition 5. $1 < \rho < \infty$ and (i) $(\alpha\delta)^{1/\rho} (1 - 1/\alpha) < 1$ implies $\langle v(c_S; t)\rangle_{t=0}^{\infty}$ maximin dominates $\langle v(c_n; t)\rangle_{t=0}^{\infty}$; (ii) $(\alpha\delta)^{1/\rho} (1 - 1/\alpha) \geqslant 1$ implies $\langle v(c_S; t)\rangle_{t=0}^{\infty}$ maximin dominates $\langle v(c_n; t)\rangle_{t=0}^{\infty}$ if and only if $\langle v(c_S; t)\rangle_{t=0}^{\infty}$ dominates $\langle v(c_n; t)\rangle_{t=0}^{\infty}$.

Given (4′) and the fact that $c = 1 - 1/\alpha$ generates constant consumption per period, then

$$(\alpha\delta)^{1/\rho} \left(1 - \frac{1}{\alpha}\right) < 1 \quad \text{implies} \quad c_n > \left(1 - \frac{1}{\alpha}\right);$$

thus, $\langle v(c_n; t)\rangle_{t=0}^{\infty}$ is a monotonic decreasing function with

$$\lim_{t\to\infty} v(c_n; t) = \min \langle v(c_n; t)\rangle_{t=0}^{\infty}.$$

Since $c_n > c_S$ one can use a similar argument to the sketch proof of proposition 3(ii) to show (i) above. $(\alpha\delta)^{1/\rho} (1 - 1/\alpha) \geqslant 1$ implies

$$\min \langle v(c_n; t)\rangle_{t=0}^{\infty} = v(c_n; 0)$$

and $c_n > c_S$ implies

$$\min \langle v(c_S; t)\rangle_{t=0}^{\infty} = v(c_S; 0)$$

also. Since $\langle v(c_S; t)\rangle_{t=0}^{\infty}$ is increasing faster than $\langle v(c_n; t)\rangle_{t=0}^{\infty}$, then clearly

$$v(c_S; 0) \geqslant v(c_n; 0)$$

if and only if $\langle v(c_S; t)\rangle_{t=0}^{\infty}$ Pareto dominates $\langle v(c_n; t)\rangle_{t=0}^{\infty}$. For given values of δ, figs. 11.1 and 11.2 show the results of Propositions 3, 4, and 5.

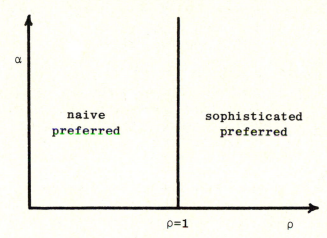

Figure 11.1

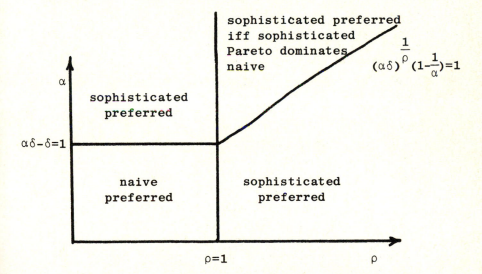

Figure 11.2

4.

It is clear from the discussion of naive plans that the ability of the first generation to pre-commit future behaviour would result in $c_0 = c_n, c_1 = 1$, and the end of the economy at this point. While such an approach is efficient the social welfare implications are fairly clear and basically unfavourable. If each generation accepted its successor's evaluation of the future as its own, i.e. exhibited intergenerational altruism, then it can be shown there would be no intertemporal inconsistency in the optimal plan since plans made by the first generation to give them maximum utility would coincide from period 1 onwards with those made by generation 1 at period 1, etc. However, it seems unreasonable to expect each generation's selfish preferences to exhibit this feature although their ethical preferences as represented by the social welfare function will almost certainly have this property. The chapter has adopted the approach of having a social welfare function defined over the selfish preferences of each generation. This approach is based on the concept that if each generation's preferences are dynamically inconsistent then this must be accepted and social welfare should be based on those preferences. There seems no reason to insist that selfish preferences should exhibit intergenerational altruism, although there is every reason to expect ethical preferences to have this property. If planners are free to maximise the social welfare function without constraints, then the problem of intertemporal inconsistency disappears since the sole maximand exhibits intergenerational altruism. However, a planner may believe in intergenerational liberty and decide that each generation has the right to determine their own level of consumption and, particularly, should not be forced to alter their behaviour to correspond to the wishes of a previous generation. If the planner's preferences are lexicographic, satisfying first intergenerational liberty and secondly a social welfare function, the issue of intertemporal inconsistency will be a real one. The planner may well be restricted to social welfare comparisons of naive and sophisticated choice even though neither maximise the social welfare function.

The results of this chapter show unequivocally that it is misleading to use consistency as a proxy for basic welfare judgements. Sophisticated planning is only better than naive planning in general terms if consistency is itself the final objective. One can argue that each generation can obtain a higher utility by being sophisticated given the actions of others, but this is the very definition of a Nash equilibrium which, in this model, is how one determines the sophisticated plan. Belonging to a society of sophisticated agents does not guarantee a higher utility than if one belonged to a society of naive agents and it was argued in the introduction that this is the true comparison. This case would be particularly clear if the model was one of an individual having different preferences over his lifetime.

It would be meaningless to expect him to adopt sophisticated actions for one time period of his life and act naively for the remainder.[4] Sophistication or naivety describe his actions period after period; he would be one or the other and in this context comparison of utility changes in one time period when the individual acts in a sophisticated way in that period but naively in others is a meaningless comparison. Therefore, one cannot conclude that sophisticated plans are superior. This may seem strange since naive plans are inefficient and by knowing the structure of the model and incorporating this knowledge to determine one's actions it seems reasonable to assume that it will always be possible to follow a plan which makes everyone better off. In one sense this is true in that knowing the structure of the model will enable society to achieve a more efficient plan if it is possible to pre-commit future actions. It has been shown that in the absence of pre-commitment it is straightforward to construct economic examples where all the plans that are Pareto superior to the naive plan are inconsistent with individuals knowing the structure of the model and using that information.

However, if pre-commitment is available this will be chosen by the first generation; hence, with pre-commitment there is no interest in a comparison of naive and sophisticated planning. It can be concluded that whenever one is interested in a comparison of sophisticated and naive plans the constraints on choices are such that it is impossible to justify the view that a society of sophisticated agents must be able to do better than a society of naive agents, even though naive actions imply inefficient plans. The interpretation of the results which is most clear is that consistency via sophisticated planning has no great welfare consequences, although consistency is to be preferred if possible. In this respect Hammond's (1976) conclusion (naive and sophisticated choice are questionable ways of achieving consistency) is given further backing. Clearly, if naive/myopic behaviour is unacceptable, then from a welfare standpoint so must sophistication; it cannot guarantee a better outcome. However, without pre-commitment the sophisticated plan is the natural equilibrium concept (in game theory terms it is the perfect equilibrium; see Goldman, 1980). This would suggest that changing the structure of the model, e.g. to introduce or try to bring about some form of pre-commitment, would help but in this model pre-commitment has unpleasant features. The problem stems from the liberal attitudes of the planner and it is perhaps the desire of the planner to impose a lexicographical preference for liberty over his other preferences that is unacceptable.

---

[4] Note, however, that it is feasible for an individual to begin life acting naively and to become sophisticated at some date. In this case the naive/sophisticated mix can never dominate the naive plan.

Appendix

This appendix shows that if there exists a plan with at least three nodes there
will always be preferences such that the naive plan dominates the sophisticated
one. The notation of the decision tree follows from Hammond (1976). $x\,p(t)\,y$
refers to the preference at t over plans x and y and $Z(t)$ refers to the set of plans
feasible at t if all future generations behave in a sophisticated fashion. The sophisticated plan is s such that $s\,p(0)\,x$ for all $x \in Z(0)$, $x \neq s$. To see the result choose
a branch with at least three nodes. Call this branch a and consider the first three
nodes of a; call these $n(0)$, $n(t_1)$, and $n(t_2)$. Choose three other plans with the
following property:

$$b \in \{X(n(t_2)) \setminus a\},$$

$$c \in \{X(n(t_1)) \setminus X(n(t_2))\},$$

$$d \in \{X \setminus X(n(t_1))\}.$$

Choose preferences such that the following hold:

(i) $a\,p(t)\,d$ for all t,

(ii) $d, c \in Z(t_1)$,

(iii) $a\,p(t)\,q$ for all $q \in \{X(n(t)) \setminus a\}$ for all $t \geq t_2$,

(iv) $a\,p(t_2)\,b\,p(t_2)\,d\,p(t_2)\,c\,p(t_2)\,x$ for all $x \in \{X \setminus a, b, c, d\}$,

(v) $b\,p(t_1)\,c\,p(t_1)\,a\,p(t_1)\,d\,p(t_1)\,x$ for all $x \in \{X \setminus a, b, c, d\}$,

(vi) $a\,p(0)\,d\,p(0)\,c\,p(0)\,b\,p(0)\,x$ for all $x \in \{X \setminus a, b, c, d\}$.

It can be shown that a is the naive plan. From (vi):

$$a\,p(0)\,x \quad \text{for all} \quad x \in \{X \setminus a\}.$$

From (v):

$$b\,p(t_1)\,x \quad \text{for all} \quad x \in \{X(n(t_1)) \setminus b\}.$$

From (iv):

$$a\,p(t_2)\,x \quad \text{for all} \quad x \in \{X(n(t_2)) \setminus a\}.$$

And from (iii):

$$a\,p(t)\,x \quad \text{for all} \quad x \in \{X(n(t)) \setminus a\}.$$

Thus, from the definition of a naive plan, a is the naive plan. It can also be shown that d is the sophisticated plan. From (ii), (iii), and (iv):

$$a, c, d \in Z(t_1).$$

From (v):

$$d\,p(t_1)\,x \quad \text{for all} \quad x \in X(d \setminus (t_1)), \quad x \neq d$$

and

$$c\,p(t_1)\,x \quad \text{for all} \quad x \in \{X(c(t_1) \cap Z(t_1), \quad x \neq c\}.$$

Therefore $c, d \in Z(0)$ and of principle importance $a \notin Z(0)$. From (vi):

$$d\,p(0)\,c\,p(0)\,x \quad \text{for all} \quad x \in \{Z(0) \setminus d, c\},$$

thus d is the sophisticated plan. From (i):

$$a\,p(t)\,d \quad \text{for all} \quad t;$$

thus, whenever there exists a plan with at least three nodes there exist preferences with the desired properties.

References

Arrow, K.J. (1973) "Rawls Principle of Just Saving", *Swedish Journal of Economics*, 75.

Blackorby, C., D. Nissen, D. Primont and R.R. Russell (1973) "Consistent Intertemporal Decision Making", *Review of Economic Studies*, 40.

Goldman, S.M. (1980) "Consistent Plans", *Review of Economic Studies*, 47.

Grout, P.A. (1977) "A Rawlsian Intertemporal Consumption Rule", *Review of Economic Studies*, 44.

Grout, P.A. (1982) "Welfare Economics of Decision Making with Changing Preferences", *Review of Economic Studies*, 49.

Hammond, P.J. (1976) "Changing Tastes and Coherent Dynamic Choice", *Review of Economic Studies*, 43.

Harsanyi, J.C. (1954) "Welfare Economics of Variable Tastes", *Review of Economic Studies*, 21.

Heal, G.M. (1973) *The Theory of Economic Planning* (North-Holland, Amsterdam).

Kydland, F.E. and E.C. Prescott (1977) "Rules Rather than Discretion: The Inconsistency of Optimal Plans", *Journal of Political Economy*, 85.
Peleg, B. and M.E. Yaari (1973) "On the Existence of a Consistent Course of Action when Tastes are Changing", *Review of Economic Studies*, 40.
Phelps, E.S. and E.A. Pollak (1968) "On Second-Best National Savings and Game Equilibrium Growth", *Review of Economic Studies*, 35.
Phelps, E.S. and J.G. Riley (1978) "Rawlsian Growth: Dynamic Programming of Capital and Wealth for Intergeneration 'Maximin' Justice", *Review of Economic Studies*, 45.
Pollak, R.A. (1968) "Consistent Planning", *Review of Economic Studies*.
Strotz, R.H. (1956) "Myopia and Inconsistency in Dynamic Utility Maximisation", *Review of Economic Studies*, 23.

PART II

THE POSITIVE ASPECTS OF SOCIAL CHOICE

Strategic voting for weakly binary group decision functions: The case of linear individual orderings

TARADAS BANDYOPADHYAY
University of Hull

and

RAJAT DEB
Southern Methodist University

1. Introduction

Until recently the fundamental results dealing with manipulability of group decision functions have used one or more of the following strong assumptions: univalence (Gibbard, 1973), binariness (Barberá, 1977a), neutrality (Gardenfors, 1976; Pattanaik, 1978), strong monotonicity (Barberá, 1977b), and cardinal individual utility together with expected utility maximization (Gibbard, 1977, 1978). The recent paper by MacIntyre and Pattanaik (1981) is a remarkable exception in that its main result relies on none of the above assumptions. MacIntyre and Pattanaik have shown that if the sure-thing rule is adopted, all group decision functions which are minimally binary and satisfy limited sovereignty for coalitions of $(n - 1)$ individuals[1] are manipulable. The version of the sure-thing rule used is eminently acceptable, the notion of minimal binariness very wide, and the limited sovereignty condition very weak. All this combines to make the results cover a very broad class of democratic non-binary (and binary) group decision functions. However, MacIntyre and Pattanaik (1979) go on to show that if individual preferences are restricted to be strict (linear), this result fails to hold!

---

[1] MacIntyre and Pattanaik also assumed that the number of alternatives is greater than 4.

Social Choice and Welfare, edited by P.K. Pattanaik and M. Salles
© *North-Holland Publishing Company, 1983*

In this chapter we show that if one strengthens one or more of MacIntyre and Pattanaik's original assumptions it is possible to get manipulability results which are valid whether or not the individual orderings are restricted to be strict. Furthermore, our results, like the main result of MacIntyre and Pattanaik, do not depend on univalence, neutrality, monotonicity, or on cardinal utility of individuals.[2]

2. Notation and results

Let X be the set of alternatives and $N = \{1, 2, 3, ..., n - 1, n\}$ be the set of individuals. We assume that $|N| = n \geqslant 2$ and $|X| \geqslant 3$. Let Π be the set of all orderings on X. Any $(R_1, R_2, ..., R_{n-1}, R_n) \in \Pi^n$ is called a *preference profile*. Preference profiles $(R_1, R_2, ..., R_n)$, $(R'_1, R'_2, ..., R'_n)$, etc. will be denoted by s, s', etc. Each R_i in a profile is the (weak) preference ordering of individual i. P_i is used to denote the asymmetric (strict preference) component of R_i and I_i the symmetric (indifference) component. We will call any non-empty subset of X an *issue*.

Definition 1. A *group decision function* (GDF) is a function f, which for every issue A and every preference profile s specifies exactly one non-empty subset of A: $f(A, s)$. The ordered pair (A, s) is called the *situation* and $f(A, s)$ the *outcome*.

For any given profile s a GDF f generates a *social preference relation R on X* as follows: for all $x, y \in X$, xRy iff $x \in f(\{x, y\}, s)$. Social strict preference is denoted by P (xRy and not yRx) and social indifference by I (xRy and yRx). For different profiles s, s', s^2, etc. we will denote corresponding social (weak) preference relations by $R, R', \underline{R}^2$, etc., strict preference relations by $P, P', \underline{P}^2$, etc., and the indifference relations by $I, I', \underline{I}^2$, etc.

A preference profile s represents the preferences expressed by individuals $i = 1, 2, ..., n$ for the purpose of social decision-making. The expressed preferences R_i in s may not represent individual i's true or sincere preference since i may well have concealed his true preference for strategic reasons. We will denote the *sincere preference profile* by $\bar{s} = (\bar{R}_1, \bar{R}_2, ..., \bar{R}_n)$, with $\bar{R}_i$ representing individual i's *sincere preference*. We assume that $\bar{s}$ may be any arbitrary element of Π^n. Furthermore, each individual i is assumed to have a binary relation $>_i$ defined on

---

[2]   MacIntyre and Pattanaik (1979) also provide such a result, but it is based on the violation of LRS which (they point out) is an unacceptable assumption in the context of linear individual orderings.

the set of all non-empty subsets of X; $>_i$ is interpreted as i's preference over alternative outcomes. Thus, if for all $i \in L$, if $E >_i E'$, we will say that the individuals in L *rank* the outcome E over the outcome E'. Clearly, it is reasonable to expect that $>_i$ (the way in which i ranks outcomes) is closely related to $\bar{R}_i$ (individual i's sincere preference on X). In definition 2 below we give a number of alternative assumptions about this relationship.

Definition 2. For all $i \in N$ and all non-empty subsets E, E' of X, if the restriction of $\bar{R}_i$ to $(E \cup E')$ is a linear (strict) ordering, $E \neq E'$ and $|E \cup E'| \leqslant 3$, then

(2.1) $A1$ is satisfied iff $E >_i E'$ if (for all $x \in E$ and all $y \in E', x\bar{R}_i y$) and (for some $x \in E$ and some $y \in E', x\bar{P}_i y$).

(2.2) $A2$ is satisfied iff $E >_i E'$ if one of the following is true:

(a) $E \subset E'$; for all $x \in E$ and all $y \in (E' - E), x\bar{R}_i y$ and for some $x \in E$ and some $y \in (E' - E), x\bar{P}_i y$.

(b) $E' \subset E$; for all $x \in (E - E')$ and all $y \in E', x\bar{R}_i y$ and for some $x \in (E-E')$ and some $y \in E', x\bar{P}_i y$.

(c) Neither $E \subset E'$ nor $E' \subset E$; for all $x \in (E-E')$ and all $y \in (E'-E), x\bar{R}_i y$ and for some $x \in (E-E')$ and some $y \in (E'-E), x\bar{P}_i y$.

(2.3) For all issues A, let $W(A, \bar{R}_i) = \{x \mid x \in A$ and for all $y, y \in A$ implies $y\bar{R}_i x\}$. Then $A3$ is satisfied iff $E >_i E'$ if one of the following is true for all $x, y \in X$:

(a) $x \in W(E, \bar{R}_i)$ and $y \in W(E', \bar{R}_i)$ implies $x\bar{P}_i y$.

(b) $W(E, \bar{R}_i) = W(E', \bar{R}_i) = K$, $W(E-K, \bar{R}_i) \neq \emptyset$ and $(x \in W(E-K, \bar{R}_i)$ and $y \in W(E'-K, \bar{R}_i)$ implies $x\bar{P}_i y)$.

(c) $W(E, \bar{R}_i) = W(E', \bar{R}_i) = K$, $W(E-K, \bar{R}_i) = W(E'-K, \bar{R}_i)$ and $|E| = 3$.

It is easy to check that $A3$ implies $A2$ and $A2$ implies $A1$. All the three assumptions, $A1, A2$, and $A3$, are weaker versions of standard assumptions in the literature. $A1$ is a weak form of the "sure-thing rule" due to Kelly (1977); $A2$ a weak form of the "sure-thing principle" due to Gardenfors (1976); and $A3$ is a weak variant of the standard maxi-min rule.[3] The "weakening" involved in all three cases consists of restricting the assumptions to "linear individual sincere preferences" and to comparison of "small" outcomes ($|E \cup E'| \leqslant 3$). The first restriction is important since it is used to ensure that the proofs of our results *remain valid even if the individual preferences are restricted to be strict*. The second restriction is equally important; it guarantees by a lemma[4] of Pattanaik that all three assumptions, $A1, A2$, and $A3$, are weaker than the standard assumption

---

[3] For instance, see Pattanaik (1978).
[4] See Pattanaik (1978), p. 17, lemma 2.2.

of "expected utility maximization". Hence, *any proof using one of these assumptions would remain valid even if the assumption were replaced by the assumption of "expected utility maximization".*

In the next definition we introduce the standard concept of manipulability.

Definition 3.

(3.1)   For all non-empty subsets L of N and all preference profiles s and s', s and s' are *L-variant* iff for all $i \in L, R_i \neq R_i'$ and for all $i \notin L, R_i = R_i'$.

(3.2)   A GDF f is *manipulable* iff there exists some $k \in N$, two $\{k\}$-variant profiles $\bar{s}$, s and some issue A such that the outcome $f(A, s)$ is ranked by $\{k\}$ over the outcome $f(A, \bar{s})$.[5]

For all preference profiles s we will use $s(xRy)$, $s(xPy)$, and $s(xIy)$ to denote the sets $\{i \mid i \in N \text{ and } xR_iy\}$, $\{i \mid i \in N \text{ and } xP_iy\}$ and $\{i \mid i \in N \text{ and } xI_iy\}$, respectively. Using this notation we introduce some properties of GDFs.

Definition 4.   Let f be a GDF.

(4.1)   For all preference profiles s and all issues A, the *choice set* on A, $C(A, R)$, is given by: $C(A, R) = \{x \mid x \in A \text{ and for all } y, y \in A \text{ implies } xRy\}$.

(4.2) f is *binary* iff for all preference profiles s and all issues A, $C(A, R) = f(A, s)$.

(4.3) f is *weakly binary* (WB) iff for all preference profiles s and all issues A either $C(A, R) = \varnothing$ or $f(A, s) = C(A, R)$.

(4.4) f is *minimally binary* (MB) iff for all preference profiles s and all issues A, *either* $C(A, R) = \varnothing$ or $C(A, R) \subseteq f(A, s) \subseteq \{y \mid y \in A \text{ and for all } x, x \in C(A, R) \text{ implies } yRx\}$.

(4.5) f satisfies *strict reward for pairwise optimality* (SRPO) iff for all profiles s and all issues A: (i) $C(A, R) \subseteq f(A, s)$ and (ii) whenever $C(A, R)$ contains only one element $C(A, R) = f(A, s)$.

(4.6) f satisfies *pairwise rejection* (P.Rej.) iff for all profiles s and all issues A, $(A - C(A, R)) \subseteq (A - f(A, s))$.

(4.7) f satisfies *minimal rejection* (MR) iff for all profiles s and all issues A, $(A - C(A, R)) \neq \varnothing$ implies $(A - f(A, s)) \neq \varnothing$.

(4.8) f satisfies *non-reversal* (NR) iff for all profiles s, and all $x, y \in X$, $(xPy$ and $x, y \in A)$ implies that if $x \notin f(A, s)$ then $y \notin f(A, s)$.

(4.9) f satisfies *absence of veto* (AV) iff for all preference profiles s, all $x, y \in A$ and all issues A, $\mid s(xPy) \mid = n - 1$ implies $y \notin f(A, s)$.

---

[5]   Notice that in this definition we implicitly assume that every possible profile is a possible sincere profile.

(4.10) f satisfies *limited sovereignty of coalitions with $n - 1$ members* (LSOV$_{n-1}$) iff for all $x, y \in X$ and all subsets L of N such that $|L| \geqslant n - 1$, there exist preference orderings R_i^* for $i \in L$ such that for all preference profiles s if $R_i = R_i^*$ for all $i \in L$, then xPy.

(4.11) f satisfies *limited absence of veto* (LAV) iff for all $x, y \in X$ and all preference profiles s, $|s(xPy)| = n - 1$ implies xPy.

(4.12) f satisfies *LIND** iff for all preference profiles s, s' and all $x, y \in X$ if $R_i = R_i'$ for all $i \in s(xIy)$ and $s(xRy) = s'(xR'y)$ and $s(yRx) = s'(yR'x)$, then $((xRy$ iff $xR'y)$ and $(yRx$ iff $yR'x))$.

(4.13) f satisfies *limited resoluteness* (LRS) iff for all preference profiles s and all $x, y \in X$ xPy or yPx.

(4.14) f satisfies the *Pareto criterion* iff for all profiles s, all issues A and all $x, y \in X$, $(s(xPy) = N$ and $x \in A)$ implies $y \notin f(A, s)$.

(4.1) gives the usual definition of a choice set. (4.2)–(4.8) give alternative ways in which the outcome may be said to be based on pairwise choice (i.e. alternative relations between the choice set and the set of outcomes). WB, MB, and SRPO require that "some elements" in the "choice set" be picked;[6] P. Rej., MR, and NR consider the elements rejected in the choice set, they require that "some" of these elements be rejected by the GDF. The relationship between the various "binariness" concepts is shown in fig. 12.1.

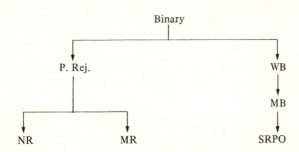

Figure 12.1

The concepts of AV, LAV, and the Pareto criterion in (4.9), (4.11), (4.13), and (4.14) are standard and require no discussion. LSOV$_{n-1}$ and LIND* defined in (4.10) and (4.12) were conditions introduced by MacIntyre and Pattanaik

[6] For an extensive discussion of B, WB, and MB the reader can consult MacIntyre and Pattanaik (1981).

(1979). LIND* is a weak version of Arrow's independence of irrelevant alternatives and $LSOV_{n-1}$ a stronger form of Arrow's citizen's sovereignty.[7] Clearly, AV implies LAV, and LAV implies $LSOV_{n-1}$.

Using definitions $1-4$ the main results of this chapter can be stated as follows:

Theorem 1. Let A1 be satisfied. If f is a GDF satisfying AV and SRPO, then f is manipulable.[8]

Theorem 2. Let A1 be satisfied and $|X| \geqslant 4$. If f is a GDF satisfying $LSOV_{n-1}$, MB, and NR then either f is manipulable or f violates the Pareto criterion.

Theorem 3. Let A2 be satisfied. If f is a GDF satisfying $LSOV_{n-1}$, WB, and MR, then f is manipulable.

Theorem 4. Let A3 be satisfied. If f is a GDF satisfying $LSOV_{n-1}$ and MB, then f is manipulable.

The results are arranged in increasing order of the strength of the behavioral assumption involved: theorems 1 and 2 use A1, theorem 3 uses A2, and theorem 4 employs the strongest assumption A4. These theorems are closely related to the main result of MacIntyre and Pattanaik (1981). Letting $A1'$ be A1 without the restrictions "$|E \cup E'| \leqslant 3$" and "the restriction of $\bar{R}_i$ to $(E \cup E')$ is a linear ordering" (see definition 2) the MacIntyre and Pattanaik theorem can be stated as follows:

Theorem A (MacIntyre and Pattanaik). Let $A1'$ be satisfied and $|X| \geqslant 4$. If f is a GDF satisfying $LSOV_{n-1}$ and MB, then f is manipulable.

It is interesting to compare the hypothesis of theorem A to those of theorems $1-4$. Theorem 1 weakens the MB assumption in theorem A to SRPO and strengthens $LSOV_{n-1}$ to AV. Theorem 2 *adds* NR and the Pareto criterion to the hypothesis of theorem A. Theorem 4 "strengthens" the behavioral assumption $A1'$ to A3 and theorem 3 "strengthens" slightly both the behavioral assumption ($A1'$ to A2) and the binariness condition (MB to WB and MR). However, unlike theorem A, the conclusion of theorems $1-4$ is *valid whether or not individual preferences permit indifference*. Thus, theorems $1-4$ may usefully be viewed as versions of

---

[7] See Arrow (1963).

[8] Note that the hypothesis of the theorem would be non-trivially satisfied only if $|X| < n$. It is well known that "voting paradoxes" can be constructed when $|X| \geqslant n$; in a sense this theorem looks at the other side of the question and asks what happens when $|X| < n$.

theorem A where the hypothesis of theorem A is "strengthened" in various ways so that the conclusion may be extended to the case of linear individual orderings. Such an extension is of interest because MacIntyre and Pattanaik have shown that their result is not valid in the case of linear individual orderings.[9] This raises the possibility that the MacIntyre Pattanaik "type" of manipulability result is fundamentally dependent on the presence of individual indifference. Theorems 1—4 dispel this possibility by showing that by strengthening slightly the hypothesis of theorem A in alternative ways its conclusion can be extended to the case of linear orderings.

3. Proofs

In proving theorems 1—4 we will make repeated use of a process of transforming one preference profile to another by changing individual preferences "one at a time." We introduce this process in the next definition.

Definition 5. Let f be a GDF and A a given issue.

(5.1) For all profiles s, s' and for all $0 \leqslant k \leqslant n$, let the preference profile $\psi(s, s', k) = (R_1', R_2', ..., R_k', R_{k+1}, R_{k+2}, ..., R_n)$.

(5.2) For all preference profiles s, s' let $k^*(s, s')$ be an integer between 1 and n such that $f(A, \psi(s, s', k)) = f(A, s)$ for all $0 \leqslant k \leqslant k^* - 1$ and $f(A, \psi(s, s', k^*)) \neq f(A, s)$.

(5.3) A *critical switch from s to s'* is a change of the preference profile from $\psi(s, s', k^* - 1)$ to $\psi(s, s', k^*)$. $f(A, \psi(s, s', k^* - 1))$ is called the *initial outcome* and $f(A, \psi(s, s', k^*))$ the *new outcome*.

$\psi(s, s', k)$ is a preference profile obtained from s by replacing the orderings of the first k individuals in s by their orderings in s'. Clearly, $\psi(s, s', 0) = s$ and $\psi(s, s', n) = s'$. From the definitions of $k^*(s, s')$ and critical switch it is immediate that either $f(A, \psi(s, s', k))$ is the same for all $0 \leqslant k \leqslant n$ or a critical switch exists. In particular we have the following lemma.

Lemma 1 (MacIntyre and Pattanaik). Let f be a GDF and A a given issue. If s, s' are preference profiles such that $f(A, s) \neq f(A, s')$, then there exists a critical switch from s to s'.

To prove theorems we need the following preliminary results.

[9] See MacIntyre and Pattanaik (1981).

Lemma 2 (MacIntyre and Pattanaik).   Let A1 be satisfied. If f violates LIND*, then f is manipulable.

For a proof of this result see MacIntyre and Pattanaik (1981).

Lemma 3.   For $r = 1$ or 2 or 3 let Ar be true. Let f be a GDF, A be a given issue, and s and s' two L-variant preference profiles such that a critical switch from s to s' exists. Then,

(3.1)   If using Ar with $\bar{s} = s$ the new outcome can be ranked over the initial outcome by all the individuals in L, f is manipulable.

(3.2)   If using Ar with $\bar{s} = s'$ the initial outcome can be ranked over the new outcome by all the individuals in L, f is manipulable.

Proof.

(3.1)   Consider the critical switch from s to s'. $\psi(s, s', k* - 1)$ and $\psi(s, s', k*)$ are $\{k*\}$-variant. Let $\bar{s} = \psi(s, s', k* - 1)$. Note that $k* \in L$ and $\bar{R}_{k*} = R_{k*}$; by the hypothesis of (3.1), using Ar, $f(A, \psi(s, s', k*))$ is ranked over $f(A, \psi(s, s', k* - 1)$ by $\{k*\}$. Therefore, f is manipulable.

(3.2)   The proof is similar to (3.1) and is therefore omitted.

Lemma 4.   Let A1 be true. If f is a GDF which satisfies LSOV_{n-1} and violates LAV, then f is manipulable.

Proof.   Since LAV is violated, there exists $x, y \in X, L \subseteq N$ such that $|L| \geqslant n - 1$, and some situation s' such that $L \subseteq s'(xP'y)$ and $yR'x$. By LSOV_{n-1} for all $i \in L$ there exists R_i^* such that for all $s, R_i = R_i^*$ for $i \in L$ implies xPy. Let $\hat{s}$ be such that for all $i \in L, \hat{R}_i = R_i^*$ and for $j \notin L$: $\hat{R}_j = R_j'$. Clearly, by LSOV_{n-1}, $\{x\} = f(\{x, y\}, \hat{s}) \neq f(\{x, y\}, s')$; since (by $yR'x$) $f(\{x, y\}, s')$ is either $\{y\}$ or $\{x, y\}$. By lemma 1 there exists a critical switch from $\hat{s}$ to s'. The initial outcome is $\{x\}$ and the new outcome is either $\{y\}$ or $\{x, y\}$. In either case, if $\bar{s} = s'$ by A1 and $L \subseteq s'(xPy)$, the initial outcome is ranked over the new outcome by all the members of L. By lemma 3.2, f is manipulable.

The proofs of theorems 1—4 consist of considering critical switches between four preference profiles. To avoid repetition we define these four distinguished profiles. In the definition (given below), we denote individual preference orderings as columns with better elements on top. Thus, if for $i \in L, xP_iyP_iz$, we write:

$$\frac{L}{x}$$

$$y$$

$$z$$

Definition 6. Let f be a GDF satisfying LAV.

(6.1) L is *decisive for x against y* iff for all preference profiles s, $L \subseteq s(xPy)$ and $(N - L) \subseteq s(yPx)$ implies xPy.

(6.2) $D_f = \{L \mid L$ is decisive for x against y for some $x, y \in X\}$.

(6.3) $\bar{D}_f = \{L \mid L \in D_f$ such that for all L', subset of N, $L' \in D_f$ implies $\mid L' \mid \geqslant \mid L \mid\}$. A member of $\bar{D}_f$ is called a *smallest decisive set*.[10]

(6.4) Let L^* be a smallest decisive set, decisive for x against y for some $x, y \in X$. If $k_1, k_2 \in L^*$ such that $k_1 \neq k_2$, then $\underline{s}'$, $\underline{s}^2$, $\underline{s}^3$, and $\underline{s}^4$ are defined over $\{x, y, z\}$ as follows:[11]

$\underline{s}'$:	$L^* - \{k_1\}$	$N - L^*$	$\{k_1\}$	$\underline{s}^2$:	$L^* - \{k_1\}$	$N - L^*$	$\{k_1\}$
	x	y	z		x	z	z
	y	z	x		y	y	x
	z	x	y		z	x	y

$\underline{s}^3$:	$L^* - \{k_1\}$	$N - L^*$	$\{k_1\}$
	x	y	z
	y	x	x
	z	z	y

$\underline{s}^4$:	$L^* - \{k_1\} - \{k_2\}$	$N - L^*$	$\{k_1\}$	$\{k_2\}$
	x	y	z	y
	y	z	x	x
	z	x	y	z

Proof of theorem 1. By lemma 2 it is sufficient to show that if f does not satisfy LIND*, then it is manipulable. Therefore, henceforth we assume LIND* is true. Let $A = \{x, y, z\}$ and let $\underline{s}'$ be the restriction of any profile to A. By LIND* and AV, $f(A, \underline{s}')$ is either $\{x\}$ or $\{y\}$ or $\{x, y\}$.[12] In each of these three cases we show that f is manipulable.

[10] LAV ensures that D_f (and hence $\bar{D}_f$) are non-empty.
[11] By LAV, such an L^* exists and $\mid L^* \mid \geqslant 2$.
[12] Henceforth we use LIND* in exactly the same way without explicitly mentioning it.

Case 1. $f(A, \underline{s}') = \{x\}$. Consider the profile $\underline{s}^2$. Since L^* is decisive for x against y, $x\underline{P}^2 y$. As L^* is a smallest decisive set, $z\underline{R}^2 y$ and $z\underline{R}^2 x$. By SRPO $f(A, \underline{s}^2)$ is either $\{z\}$ or $\{x, z\}$ or $\{y, z\}$ or $\{x, y, z\}$. In any case, $f(A, \underline{s}^2) \neq f(A, \underline{s}') = \{x\}$. By lemma 1 there exists a critical switch from $\underline{s}'$ to $\underline{s}^2$. Consider the critical switch from $\underline{s}'$ to $\underline{s}^2$. Note that $\underline{s}'$ and $\underline{s}^2$ are $(N-L^*)$-variant and if $\bar{s} = \underline{s}'$ then using A1 the initial outcome is ranked by $(N-L^*)$ below the new outcome (in fact the initial outcome is ranked "lowest"). By lemma (3.1), f is manipulable.

Case 2. $f(A, \underline{s}') = \{y\}$. Consider the profile $\underline{s}^3$. Since L^* is decisive for x against y, $x\underline{P}^3 y$. By LAV, $x\underline{P}^3 z$ and $y\underline{P}^3 z$. By SRPO, $f(A, \underline{s}^3) = \{x\}$. Hence, $f(A, \underline{s}^3) \neq f(A, \underline{s}') = \{y\}$. By lemma 1 there exists a critical switch from $\underline{s}'$ to $\underline{s}^3$. Consider the critical switch from $\underline{s}'$ to $\underline{s}^3$. $\underline{s}'$ and $\underline{s}^3$ are $(N - L^*)$-variant and that if $\bar{s} = \underline{s}^3$ then using A1 the initial outcome $\{y\}$ is ranked over all other non-empty subsets of A; in particular, $\{y\}$ is ranked over the new outcome. By lemma (3.2), f is manipulable.

Case 3. $f(A, \underline{s}') = \{x, y\}$. Consider the profile $\underline{s}^3$. Following the argument in case 2 above, $f(A, \underline{s}^3) = \{x\} \neq f(A, s')$. By lemma 1 there exists a critical switch from $\underline{s}'$ to $\underline{s}^3$. By AV there are two possibilities: (a) the new outcome is $\{x\}$ and (b) the new outcome is $\{y\}$.

   (a) If the new outcome is $\{x\}$, then using A1 if $\bar{s} = \underline{s}^3$ then the initial outcome $\{x, y\}$ is ranked over the new outcome $\{x\}$ by all the members of $(N - L^*)$. Since $\underline{s}'$ and $\underline{s}^3$ are $(N - L^*)$-variant by lemma (3.2), f is manipulable.

   (b) If the new outcome is $\{y\}$, then if $\underline{s} = \underline{s}'$ using A1, the new outcome $\{y\}$ is ranked above the initial outcome $\{x, y\}$ by all individuals in $(N - L^*)$. Since $\underline{s}'$ and $\underline{s}^3$ are $(N - L^*)$-variant by lemma (3.1), f is manipulable. ∎

Proof of theorem 2. Consider a preference profile on $\{x, y, z, w\}$:

s^*:	$L^* - \{k_1\}$	$N - L^*$	$\{k_1\}$
	x	y	w
	y	w	z
	w	z	x
	z	x	y

Since L^* is decisive for x against y, xP^*y. By lemma 4 using LAV, yP^*z. Since L^* is the smallest decisive set, either zP^*x or zI^*x. We will show that zI^*x is impossible. If $A = \{x, y, z\}$ and zI^*x, MB implies $y \notin f(A, s^*)$. By NR $z \notin f(A, s^*)$. Hence, $\{x\} = f(A, s^*)$. Following the argument in case 1 in theorem 1, this is manipulable. Hence, zP^*x. So, using the Pareto criterion and LAV we have: xP^*y, yP^*w (by LAV), wP^*z (Pareto), and zP^*x. By NR, if $\hat{A} = \{x, y, z, w\} f(\hat{A}, s^*) = \hat{A}$. Since $z \in \hat{A}$, this violates the Pareto criterion. ∎

Proof of theorem 3. By lemmas 2 and 4 it is sufficient to show that if A2 is true and f satisfies LIND*, LAV, WB, and MR, then f is manipulable. Let $A = \{x, y, z\}$ and consider the profile $\underline{s}'$ on A. $f(A, \underline{s}')$ is either $\{x\}$ or $\{y\}$ or $\{x, y\}$ or $\{x, z\}$ or $\{z\}$ or $\{y, z\}$ or $\{x, y, z\}$. We call these cases $1-7$, respectively, and show that in each of cases $1-6$ f is manipulable and that case 7 is impossible.

Cases 1 and 2. $f(A, \underline{s}') = \{x\}$ or $\{y\}$. These cases have already been discussed in the proof of theorem 1. Noting that A1 is weaker than A2, SRPO is weaker than WB and that in the proof of these cases in theorem 1, LAV rather than much stronger AV is needed, it is clear that for these two cases the same proof remains valid.

Case 3.[13] $f(A, \underline{s}') = \{x, y\}$. Consider the profile $\underline{s}^3$. Using the same argument as in case 2 of theorem 1, $f(A, \underline{s}^3) = \{x\} \neq f(A, \underline{s}') = \{x, y\}$. By lemma 1 there exists a critical switch from $\underline{s}'$ to $\underline{s}^3$. There are two possibilities: (a) the new outcome is $\{y\}$ and (b) the new outcome is not $\{y\}$.

(a) If the new outcome is $\{y\}$, then if $\bar{s} = \underline{s}'$ using A2, $\{y\}$ is ranked over $\{x, y\}$ by the individuals in $(N - L^*)$. Since $\underline{s}'$ and $\underline{s}^3$ are $(N - L^*)$-variant by lemma (3.1), f is manipulable.

(b) If the new outcome is other than $\{y\}$ (i.e. any other non-empty subset of A) and if $\bar{s} = \underline{s}^3$, then by A2 the initial outcome $\{x, y\}$ is ranked above the new outcome by the individuals in $(N - L^*)$. Since $\underline{s}'$ and $\underline{s}^3$ are $(N - L^*)$-variant, by lemma (3.2), f is manipulable.

Case 4. $f(A, \underline{s}') = \{x, z\}$. Consider the profile $\underline{s}'$. Since L^* is decisive for x against y, $xP'y$. By LAV, $yP'z$. Since L^* is the smallest decisive set either $zP'x$ or $zI'x$. If $zI'x$, then by WB, $f(A, \underline{s}') = \{x\}$. This contradicts $f(A, \underline{s}') = \{x, z\}$. Therefore, $xP'y$, $yP'z$, and $zP'x$. Consider the profile $\underline{s}^2$. By LIND* (comparing $\underline{s}'$ and $\underline{s}^2$), $xP^2 y$ and $zP^2 x$. Since L^* is the smallest decisive set, $zR^2 y$. By WB, $f(A, \underline{s}^2)$, $= \{z\} \neq f(A, \underline{s}') = \{x, z\}$. By lemma 1 there is a critical switch from $\underline{s}'$ to $\underline{s}^2$. There are two possibilities: (a) the new outcome is $\{x\}$ and (b) the new outcome is other than $\{x\}$.

(a) If the new outcome is $\{x\}$, then by A2 if $\bar{s} = \underline{s}^2$, $\{x\}$ is ranked below the initial outcome $\{x, z\}$ by $(N - L^*)$. Noting that $\underline{s}'$ and $\underline{s}^2$ are $(N - L^*)$-variant, by lemma (3.2), f is manipulable.

(b) If the new outcome is any non-empty subset of A other than $\{x\}$, then using A2 and letting $\bar{s} = \underline{s}'$, the new outcome will be ranked above the initial outcome $\{x, z\}$ by the individuals in $(N - L^*)$. Since $\underline{s}'$ and $\underline{s}^2$ are $(N - L^*)$-variant by lemma (3.1), f is manipulable.

Cases 5 and 6. $f(A, \underline{s}') = \{z\}$ or $\{y, z\}$. Exactly as in case 4 above we have

---

[13] Even though this case has been considered in the proof of theorem 1, the proof makes use of AV and would fail under A1 if AV were replaced by LAV.

$x\underline{P}'y$, $y\underline{P}'z$, and $z\underline{P}'x$. Comparing $\underline{s}'$ and $\underline{s}^4$ and using LIND*, $y\underline{P}^4z$ and $z\underline{P}^4x$. Since L^* is the smallest decisive set, $y\underline{R}^4x$. By WB, $f(A,\underline{s}^4) = \{y\}$. Hence, there exists a critical switch from $\underline{s}'$ to $\underline{s}^4$. The initial outcome is $\{z\}$ or $\{y, z\}$ *and the new outcome is* $\{y\}$. In either case, by A2 setting $\overline{s} = \underline{s}'$ the new outcome is ranked over the initial outcome by the member of $\{k_2\}$. Since $\underline{s}'$ and $\underline{s}^4$ are $\{k_2\}$-variant, by lemma (3.1), f is manipulable.

Case 7. $f(A, \underline{s}') = \{x, y, z\}$. Following the proof in case 4 above, $x\underline{P}'y$, $y\underline{P}'z$, and $z\underline{P}'x$. By MR, $f(A,\underline{s}') \neq \{x,y,z\}$, a contradiction. ∎

Proof of theorem 4. By lemma 2 and 4 it is sufficient to show that if A3 is true, then all GDFs, f, satisfying LIND*, LAV, and MB are manipulable. Let $A = \{x, y, z\}$. Consider the profile $\underline{s}'$ on A. $f(A,\underline{s}')$ is either $\{x\}$ or $\{y\}$ or $\{x, y\}$ or $\{x, z\}$ or $\{z\}$ or $\{y, z\}$ or $\{x, y, z\}$. We call these cases $1-7$ respectively.

Cases 1, 2, and 3. For cases 1 and 2 notice that the proof for these cases in theorem 1 remains valid here (since LAV rather than AV is used in the proofs SRPO is weaker than MB and since A1 is weaker than A3). For case 3, noting that A3 is stronger than A2, it is easy to check that WB can be replaced by MB in the proof of case 3 of theorem 3 without impairing its validity.

Cases 4, 5, 6, and 7. $f(A,\underline{s}') = \{x, z\}$ or $\{z\}$ or $\{y, z\}$ or $\{x, y, z\}$. Consider the profile $\underline{s}^4$. Since L^* is the smallest decisive coalition $y\underline{R}^4x$ and $z\underline{R}^4x$. By LAV, $y\underline{P}^4z$. By MB, $f(A, \underline{s}^4)$ is either $\{y\}$ or $\{x, y\}$. Hence, there exists a critical switch from $\underline{s}'$ to $\underline{s}^4$. The initial outcome is either $\{x, z\}$ or $\{z\}$ or $\{y, z\}$ or $\{x, y, z\}$ and the new outcome is either $\{y\}$ or $\{x, y\}$. In any case, if $\overline{s} = \underline{s}'$, by A3, the new outcome is ranked over the initial outcome by the individual in $\{k_2\}$. Noting that $\underline{s}'$ and $\underline{s}^4$ are $\{k_2\}$-variant, by lemma (3.1), f is manipulable. ∎

References

Arrow, K.J. (1963) *Social Choice and Individual Values*, 2nd edn. (Wiley, New York).

Barberá, S. (1977a) "Manipulation of Social Decision Functions", *Journal of Economic Theory*.

Barberá, S. (1977b) "The Manipulation of Social Choice Mechanisms That Do Not Leave 'Too Much' to Chance", *Econometrica*.

Gardenfors, P. (1976) "Manipulation of Social Choice Functions", *Journal of Economic Theory*.

Gibbard, A. (1973) "Manipulation of Voting Schemes: A General Result", *Econometrica*.

Gibbard, A. (1977) "Manipulation of Schemes that Mix Voting with Chance", *Econometrica*.

Gibbard, A. (1978) "Straightforwardness of Game Forms with Lotteries as Outcomes", *Econometrica*, 46.

Kelly, J.S. (1977) "Strategy-Proofness and Social Choice Functions Without Single-Valuedness", *Econometrica*.

MacIntyre, I. and Prasanta K. Pattanaik (1981) "The Sure-Thing Rule and Strategic Voting Under Minimally Binary Group Decision Functions", *Journal of Economic Theory*.

Pattanaik, P.K. (1978) *Strategy and Group Choice* (North-Holland, Amsterdam).

CHAPTER 13

Further results on voting with veto

BHASKAR DUTTA*
Indian Statistical Institute

1. Introduction

Given the Gibbard–Satterthwaite impossibility result on the possibility of constructing strategy-proof decision rules, much of the recent literature on strategic
voting attempts to formulate conditions which are weaker than strategy-proofness,
and then examines whether one can construct decision rules which satisfy these
weaker concepts. For instance, Pattanaik (1976) introduced concepts of equilibrium which are weaker than Nash equilibrium by permitting individuals to take
into account the possibility of counter-threats, and then inquired whether one
could construct group decision rules under which every possible true preference
profile would constitute an equilibrium under the weaker concept of equilibrium.
In a seminal paper, Peleg (1978) introduced the concept of *exact and strong consistency*, under which there must exist at least one strong equilibrium giving the
same outcome as the sincere preference profile. A related concept of *implementability* was introduced by Maskin (1979).

Although these concepts are weaker than the Gibbard–Satterthwaite notion
of strategy-proofness, there does not seem to be a large number of existence results.
For instance, Pattanaik (1976) shows that most non-dictatorial rules violate the
weaker notion of strategy-proofness introduced by him. Maskin (1979) shows
that the only single-valued decision rule implementable via strong equilibria is
the dictatorial one. The existing results on exact, strong consistency are some-

* I am grateful to Hervé Moulin and Bezalel Peleg for comments on earlier drafts of this
chapter.

Social Choice and Welfare, edited by *P.K. Pattanaik and M. Salles*
© *North-Holland Publishing Company, 1983*

what different. It would appear from the results of Dutta and Pattanaik (1978) and Peleg (1978) that some decision rules which endow individuals with *veto power* over at least one alternative are, in fact, exactly and strongly consistent.

The present chapter extends this analysis. First, using a concept of equilibrium which is weaker than the one used by Pattanaik (1976), we show that under some decision rules which endow individuals with veto power, the sincere preference profile is always an equilibrium. Secondly, we also construct a *neutral* and exact and strongly consistent decision rule — this rule also endows individuals with veto power. Our last result is negative. We extend Maskin's result by showing that even if the concept of strong equilibrium incorporates a particular type of counter-threat, only dictatorial decision rules can be implemented.

In section 2 we describe the framework. Section 3 introduces the various concepts of manipulability, and also contains a brief summary of existing results. Section 4 discusses the decision rules to be used in the proofs of the existence results, while section 5 contains our results.

2. The framework

Let $N = \{1, 2, ..., n\}$ be the set of agents with $n \geq 2$. Although we will denote by n both the cardinality of N as well as the individual "n", this will cause no ambiguity since the context will make the meaning clear. A denotes the set of feasible alternatives, fixed throughout the chapter. The cardinality of A is m. Every individual i has a *sincere* or *true* preference ordering $\bar{P}_i$ over A. The preferences actually *expressed* by i are denoted by P_i, P_i', etc. We assume that both expressed as well as sincere preferences, are *strict* or *linear* orderings over A. Let π be the set of strict orderings over A. Thus, any element of π^n will be a preference profile. Preference profiles will be indicated by P, P', etc. The sincere preference profile is represented by $\bar{P}$.

Definition 1. A *social choice function* (scf) is a function $f: \pi^n \to A$.

In order to be "acceptable", a scf has to satisfy some ethical properties. Some of the conditions which have been proposed in the literature are described below.

Definition 2. Let f be any scf, and $P, P' \in \pi^n$.

(2.1) *Anonymity* (AN): Let ρ be a permutation of N. If for all $i \in N, P_i = P'_{\rho(i)}$, then $f(P) = f(P')$.

(2.2) *Neutrality* (NT): Let μ be a permutation of A. If for all $i \in N$, for all $x, y \in A, xP_iy$ iff $\mu(x)P'_i \mu(y)$, then $f(P) = \mu f(P')$.

(2.3) *Monotonicity* (M): Let $f(P) = a$. If for all $i \in N$, [(for all $b \in A$, $aP_i b \to aP_i' b$) and (for all $x, y \in A - \{a\}$, $xP_i y$ iff $xP_i' y$)], then $f(P') = a$.

(2.4) *Strong positive association* (SPA): Let $f(P) = a$. If for all $i \in N$, $(aP_i b \to aP_i' b$ for all $b \in A)$, then $f(P') = a$.

(2.5) *Absence of veto power* (AVP): For all $a \in A$, if $|\{i \in N \mid aP_i b$ for all $b \in A - \{a\}\}| \geq n - 1$, then $f(P) = a$.

(2.6) *Non-dictatorship* (ND): There does not exist any $i \in N$ such that for all $P \in \pi^n$, $f(P)$ is the P_i-maximal element in A.

Most of these conditions are all familiar in the literature and hardly need any explanation. SPA was introduced by Muller and Satterthwaite (1977), who showed that SPA was necessary and sufficient for the Gibbard–Satterthwaite concept of strategy-proofness. It therefore follows directly that only dictatorial scfs can satisfy SPA.

AVP means that no single individual can override the preferences of the rest of the society. A dictatorial scf or the scheme of choosing the "status quo" if it is Pareto-optimal are rules violating AVP. While AVP may at first sight look like an extremely desirable ethical property, there are instances where AVP may conflict with other norms which are also considered ethically desirable – Sen's condition of liberalism and the Rawlsian concept of justice are two well-known examples. Moulin (1982) also argues convincingly that some veto power may be desirable in order to prevent exploitation of minorities. Moreover, judging by the nature of the results on the weaker concepts of strategy-proofness, it seems worthwhile to analyse scfs not satisfying AVP.

3. Some weaker conditions of strategy-proofness

As we have remarked above, the Gibbard–Satterthwaite impossibility theorem has led to the search for weaker concepts which serve almost the same intuitive purposes as strategy-proofness. In this section we discuss some of these weaker concepts.

Underlying all these concepts is the notion of equilibrium behaviour of agents. We first introduce some notions of equilibrium which will be used below. For any $T \subset N$ and any $P \in \pi^n$, we say that P' is T-*variant* from P iff $P_i = P_i'$ for all $i \in N - T$, and $P_i \neq P_i'$ for some $i \in T$.

Definition 3. Let f be any scf, $P \in \pi^n$, and $S \subset N$.

(3.1) A *threat* to P is an ordered pair (P', S) such that P' is S-variant from P, and $f(P') \bar{P}_i f(P)$ for all $i \in S$.

(3.2)   Let (P', S) be a threat to P. A *counter-threat* is an ordered pair (P'', S') such that P'' and P' are S'-variant profiles with $S' \subset N - S$ and for some $i \in S$, $f(P) \bar{P}_i f(P'')$.

(3.3) P is a *strong equilibrium* (type 1) iff there is no threat to P. P is a *strong equilibrium* (type 2) iff for every threat to P there is a counter-threat.[1,2]

Note that in the above definition, if we restrict the coalition S to be a singleton, then we get the familiar concept of *Nash equilibrium* (type α). Under equilibrium (type 1), the coalition S will disrupt the initial situation P if the member(s) of S can become better-off, the coalition S implicity assuming that the individuals in $N - S$ do not retaliate. Clearly, this implies a very optimistic behavioural assumption. Equilibrium (type 2), on the other hand, implies far more conservative behaviour — the initial situation will be disrupted only if the rest of society cannot retaliate and punish at least one member of S. The intuitive rationale underlying Equilibrium (type 2) is the same as the solution concept to cooperative games without side payments proposed by Luce and Raiffa (1957, p. 174), who remark:

> ... it is surely not reasonable to suppose that the remaining groups of players will carry on as if the change had not occurred. ... if the players in S are conservative they will expect the worst — they will expect all the remaining players, $- S$, to form a coalition against S. Furthermore, the most effective way that $- S$ could go after the coalition S would be to seek out the weakest member of S and to attack him with unrelenting pressure.

Given the scf f, and the sincere profile $\bar{P}$, let $SE(f, \bar{P})$ be the set of strong equilibria (type α). Obviously, $SE_1(f, \bar{P}) \subset SE_2(f, \bar{P})$.

Definition 4.   For $\alpha = 1, 2$, an scf is:

(1)   *strategy-proof* (type α) iff every possible sincere $\bar{P}$ is a Nash equilibrium (type α);

(2)   *strictly strategy-proof* (type α) iff every $\bar{P} \in SE_\alpha(f, \bar{P})$, and

(3)   *exactly and strongly consistent* (type α) iff for every possible sincere $\bar{P}$, there exists $P \in SE_\alpha(f, \bar{P})$ such that $f(P) = f(\bar{P})$.

In the present terminology, Gibbard (1973) and Satterthwaite (1975) showed that no non-dictatorial scf is strategy-proof (type 1). This result was extended by

---

[1]   Pattanaik (1976) introduces a weaker notion of equilibrium by permitting only those counter-threats under which members in S' do not become worse-off.

[2]   Note that if a preference profile P is a strong equilibrium (type 2) then it is also in the *core*, although the converse is not true.

Pattanaik (1976), who showed that all non-imposed scfs satisfying M violate strategy-proofness according to his notion of equilibrium. In this chapter we present two existence results on strategy-proofness – there exists (i) a strictly strategy-proof (type 2) scf satisfying ND, AN, and M; and (ii) there exists a strategy-proof (type 2) scf satisfying ND, NT, and M.

The notion of exactly and strongly consistent (type 1) voting schemes was introduced by Peleg (1978). All that this notion demands is that there should be *some* strong equilibrium profile giving the same outcome as the sincere profile. Note that exactly and strongly consistent scf's are perfectly adequate substitutes for strictly strategy-proof voting schemes provided $SE(f, \overline{P})$ is always a singleton set. However, equilibrium need not be unique, and there may be $P \in SE(f, \overline{P})$ giving an outcome which is different from $f(\overline{P})$. In such cases, exact and strong consistency may be viewed as a "necessary" condition for reaching the same outcome as the sincere situation. We show that there exists a neutral scf satisfying this necessary condition since it is exactly and strongly consistent (type 1). Incidentally, it may be noted that this is the first example of a neutral and non-dictatorial scf satisfying exact strong consistency.

The notion of exact and strong consistency is significant because it departs from the earlier writers' myopic concern with equilibrium of the sincere profile alone. Presumably, we are interested in the *outcome* corresponding to the sincere profile and not in the sincere profile per se, and exact consistency guarantees that this outcome will be achieved if equilibrium is unique. Thus, the earlier impossibility results on strategy-proofness provide an important motivation for studying the possibility of decision rules satisfying conditions like exact consistency.

Note that like the concept of strategy-proofness, exact consistency is also related to the strategic properties of the voting scheme f itself. In an important paper, Maskin (1981) proposed the notion of *implementability*. The intuitive rationale of implementability is that the ethical concerns of society are embodied in the scf f, while the strategic interactions of the agents are represented through some arbitrary *game form g*. Hence, the aggregation procedure *actually used* is the game form g, but the equilibrium behaviour of the agents facing g leads to the outcome which would have been reached if the aggregation process had been f, *and* individuals had revealed their preferences sincerely. In other words, although f is not actually used for aggregation, the strategic interaction of the agents is equivalent to f being used and individuals voting sincerely.

In order to introduce the notion of implementability more formally, we need some further notation. First, note that under game forms which are not necessarily social choice functions, an individual's strategy set need not be the set of preference orderings over A. Let S_i denote the arbitrary strategy set or message space of individual i, and let $S = S_1 \times S_2 \times ... \times S_n$. A *game form* is a function $g: S \to A$. Secondly, in order to make the notion of implementability precise, we have to explicitly state the equilibrium concept used. Let B be an equilibrium concept, and let $E(B, g)$ be the set of B-equilibrium strategy n-tuples under game form g.

Definition 5. An scf f is *B-implementable* iff for all sincere preference profiles $\bar{P}$, there exists some game form g such that for all $s \in E(B, g), g(s) = f(\bar{P})$.

Maskin (1981) has shown that all *social choice correspondences* (i.e. decision rules selecting a subset of alternatives, and not necessarily a single alternative) satisfying M and AVP are Nash-implementable. An important corollary was that social choice functions were not Nash-implementable. Again, in the non-cooperative context Moulin (1980) proved an important result showing that "voting with proportional veto power" was implementable if "dominance solvability" is the equilibrium concept. In this chapter we study the notion of implementability in a cooperative framework, and use concepts of strong equilibrium (type α) for $\alpha = 1, 2$. To save notation, we merely write implementability (type α) instead of strong implementability (type α). Maskin (1979) has already shown that no non-dictatorial scf can be implementable (type 1). An interesting question is whether this impossibility result can be extended to the case of implementability (type 2). We prove that this is indeed true by showing that SPA in a necessary condition for implementability (type 2).

4. Voting with veto social choice functions

In this section we describe the social choice functions which will be used in the proofs of the existence results.

The first scf was initially proposed by Dutta and Pattanaik (1978). Let σ be a given function from $\{1, 2, ..., m\}$ to A, and let $a^1 = \sigma(1)$. Then, for any $P \in \pi^n$,

$$f_1(P) = a^m,$$

where for all $k(1 < k < m)$, if $a^k P_i \sigma(k + 1)$ for some $i \in N$, then $a^k = a^{k+1}$ and if $\sigma(k + 1) P_i a^k$ for all $i \in N$, then $a^{k+1} = \sigma(k + 1)$.

f_1 has a simple interpretation. Let the alternatives in A be arranged as $A = \{a_1, a_2, ..., a_m\}$. The final outcome is reached after $(m - 1)$ stages of voting. In the first stage, voting takes place between a_1 and a_2. If at least one i prefers a_1 to a_2, a_2 is eliminated and a_1 is pitted against a_3. If someone prefers a_1 to a_3, then a_3 is now eliminated. The process continues to the $(m - 1)$ stage, when a^{m-1} (the alternative not eliminated in the earlier rounds) is pitted against a_m, and the winner is declared to be the final outcome. Readers can check that f_1 has the alternative formulation: if $\sigma(1)$ is Pareto-optimal, then it is to be chosen; if, on the other hand, $\sigma(1)$ is not Pareto-optimal, then the σ-greatest element among those Pareto-optimal alternatives which are also Pareto-superior to $\sigma(1)$ is to be chosen.

The second social choice function is closely related to Moulin's (1982) "voting with proportional veto power". In defining this scf, to be denoted by f_2, we distinguish between two possible cases:

Case (1): $m > n$.
Case (2): $m \leqslant n$.

In case (1), let $r = (r_1, ..., r_n)$ be an n-tuple of positive integers satisfying:
  (i) $\Sigma r_i = m - 1$, and
  (ii) $\max(r_i) - \min(r_i) \leqslant 1$.
In case (2), notice that we can write $n = qm + \ell$, where $q \geqslant 1$, $\ell = 0, 1, ..., m - 1$. Let $k = (q + 1)$, and select the n-dimensional vector r such that:
  (i) $\Sigma r_i = k m - 1$, and
  (ii) $\max(r_i) - \min(r_i) \leqslant 1$.

Then in case (1), f_2 is the scf obtained when individual i "vetoes" r_1 alternatives in A; next, individual 2 vetoes r_2 alternatives among the $(m - r_1)$ remaining alternatives in A, and so on. Given that $\Sigma r_i = m - 1$, only one alternative will remain non-vetoed, and this is declared the final outcome. In case (2), again each individual i has r_i vetoes, but now k vetoes are required to eliminate any alternative (i.e. the alternatives in A are "replicated" k times). Again, given that $\Sigma r_i = km - 1$, only one alternative will remain uneliminated.

More formally,

$$f_2(P) = kA - (B_1 \cup B_2 \cup \ldots \cup B_n),$$

where

B_1 = the r_i least preferred alternatives of P_i in kA,
.
.
.
B_i = the r_i least preferred alternatives of P_i
    in $kA - (B_1 \cup B_2 \cup \ldots \cup B_{i-1})$.[3]

[3] We will represent by B_i the alternatives vetoed by i under profile p; $\bar{B}_i$ will correspond to $\bar{P}, B_i'$ to P_i' and so on.

Both f_1 and f_2 satisfy M. f_1 satisfies AN, but violates NT since the order of voting on the alternatives is fixed. On the other hand, f_2 satisfies NT, but not AN since the individuals veto alternatives in a given order. f_1 also satisfies the property of *individual rationality* – if some distinguished alternative is the "status quo", then every individual can secure an outcome at least as good as the status quo (by choosing σ such that $\sigma(1)$ is the status quo). However, if $n \geqslant m$, then for some $i, r_i < k$, so that f_2 violates individual rationality.

It is also interesting to compare the distribution of veto power amongst various scfs. Moulin (1982) introduced the notion of *veto power function* of a social choice function. Let T be any coalition, and $\pi^{|T|}$ denote the strategy sets of members of T, so that $\pi^n = \pi^{|T|} \times \pi^{|N-T|}$. An element of $\pi^{|T|}$ is represented by $P^{|T|}$.

Definition 6. Let $T \subset N$. The veto power of T in the scf f is the maximal integer q such that for all $B \subset A[|B| \leqslant q] \Rightarrow$ [there exists P^T such that for all P^{N-T}; $f(P^T, P^{N-T}) \in A - B]$.

The veto power of T is denoted by $v_f(T)$. Obviously, $v_f(N) = m - 1$ for any f. The veto power function of f is said to be (i) *maximal* iff for all T, $v_f(T) + v_f(N - T) = m - 1$; (ii) *veto anonymous* iff $v_f(T) = v_f(T')$ for all T, T' such that $|T| = |T'|$; and (iii) *proportional* iff for all T, $v_f(T) = m[|T|/n] - 1$, where $[x]$ is the smallest integer greater than or equal to x.

Note that v_{f_1} is veto anonymous since it satisfies AN, and the latter implies veto anonymity. However, v_{f_1} violates maximality and proportionality. To see this, note that under f_1, if $T \neq N$, then T cannot veto $\sigma(1)$ under f_1. Hence, for all coalitions, T, if $T \neq N$, then $v_{f_1}(T) = 0$.

It is easily shown that v_{f_2} satisfies maximality. Moreover, although v_{f_2} is not veto anonymous, it has the property that for all $i, j \in N$, $v_{f_2}(\{i\}) - v_{f_2}(\{j\}) \leqslant 1$. Thus, the distribution of veto power is not very unequal. v_{f_2} is not proportional either, but the distribution of veto power under f_2 is much "smoother" than under f_1.

5. Possibility theorems

In this section we first show that f_1 and f_2 do satisfy some of the non-manipulability properties discussed above.

In order to prove our results, we need some additional notation. Let Q be the Pareto-dominance relation defined over A as follows: for all $x, y \in A$, xQy iff xP_iy for all $i \in N$. $\bar{Q}$ corresponds to profile $\bar{P}$, Q' to profile P', and so on. The set of Pareto-optimal alternatives is given by $Q(P) = \{x \in A$ for no $y \in A: yQx\}$. $Q(\bar{P})$ and $Q(P')$ are defined in an analogous manner.

Theorem 1.

(1.1) There exists a non-dictatorial and non-imposed scf satisfying AN, M, and strict strategy-proofness (type 2).

(1.2) There exists a non-dictatorial and non-imposed scf satisfying NT, M, and strategy-proofness (type 2).

Proof.

(1.1) We show that f_1 is strictly strategy-proof (type 2). It is obvious that f_1 satisfies all the other properties listed above.

Consider any $\bar{P}$, and let $f_1(\bar{P}) = x$. Suppose (P, T) is a threat to $\bar{P}$, and $f_1(P) = y$, so that $y\bar{P}_i x$ for all $i \in T$. We first show that $x \neq \sigma(1)$. For suppose $x = \sigma(1)$. Hence $y\bar{P}_i \sigma(1)$ for all $i \in T$. Since f_1 is Paretian and $f_1(\bar{P}) = \sigma(1)$, $\sigma(1) \in Q(\bar{P})$. Therefore, there exists $j \in N$ such that $\sigma(1)\bar{P}_j y$ and $P_j = \bar{P}_j$. This implies that $\sim yQ \sigma(1)$. By construction of f_1, if $\sim yQ \sigma(1)$, then $f_1(P) \neq y$.

Hence, $f_1(\bar{P}) = x \neq \sigma(1)$. For analogous reasons, we must have $x\bar{Q} \sigma(1)$. Therefore, $x\bar{P}_i \sigma(1)$ for all $i \in T$.

Consider P' such that for all $i \in T$, $P'_i = P_i$, and $\sigma(1) P_j a$ for all $a \in \{A - \sigma(1)\}$ for some $j \in N - T$. Note that $N - T$ is non-empty since $x \in Q(\bar{P})$. Obviously, $f_1(P') = \sigma(1)$ since $\sigma(1) \in Q(P')$. Since $x\bar{P}_i \sigma(1)$ for all $i \in T$, $(P', \{j\})$ is a counterthreat and $\bar{P} \in SE_2(f_1, \bar{P})$.

Hence, f_1 is strictly strategy-proof (type 2).

(1.2) We show that f_2 is strategy-proof (type 2). It is clear that f_2 satisfies the other conditions specified above.

Let $f_2(\bar{P}) = x$, and $(P, \{i\})$ be a threat to $\bar{P}$. Suppose $f_2(P) = y$, so that $y\bar{P}_i x$ holds.

Case (1): $m > n$. Since $f_2(P) \neq x$, either $x \in B_i$ or $x \in B_k$ for some $k > i$. Since $x \notin \bar{B}_j$ for any $j \in N$, in either case we must have $z \in \bar{B}_i - B_i$. Also, for all $a \in \bar{B}_i, x\bar{P}_i a$. In particular, $x\bar{P}_i z$.

Since $z \notin B_i$, clearly one can construct P' which is $N - (i)$ variant from P, and $f_2(P') = z$. Then $(P, L - \{i\})$ is a counter-threat, and $\bar{P}$ is a Nash equilibrium (type 2).

Case (2): $m \leq n$. In this case note that $v_{f_2}(i) \leq 1$. Also, there exists $a \in A$ such that $x\bar{P}_i a$. For suppose that x is the $\bar{P}_i$-worst element in A. Then, if $v_{f_2}(\{i\}) = 1$, $f_2(\bar{P}) \neq x$. And, if $v_{f_2}(\{i\}) < 1$, then given that P and P' are $\{i\}$-variant and f_2 is monotonic, we cannot have $f_2(P) \neq x$.

Clearly, since $v_{f_2}(\{i\}) \leq 1$, one can construct P', which is $L - \{i\}$-variant from P such that $f_2(P') = a$. Since $x\bar{P}_i a$ holds, $(P', L - \{i\})$ is a counter-threat.

Hence, f_2 is strategy-proof (type 2).

Remark 1. f_2 is *not* strictly strategy-proof (type 2). This is shown by the following example.

Let $N = \{1, 2, 3, 4\}$, $A = \{a_1, a_2, a_3, a_4, a_5\}$, and $r = (1, 1, 1, 1)$. Consider $\bar{P}$ and P such that

$$
\begin{aligned}
\bar{P}_1 &: (a_1\ a_2\ a_3\ a_4\ a_5) \quad \text{and} \quad P_1 : (a_1\ a_2\ a_3\ a_5\ a_4), \\
\bar{P}_2 &: (a_1\ a_4\ a_3\ a_2\ a_5) \quad \text{and} \quad P_2 : (a_1\ a_4\ a_3\ a_2\ a_5), \\
\bar{P}_3 &: (a_2\ a_5\ a_3\ a_4\ a_1) \quad \text{and} \quad P_3 : (a_2\ a_5\ a_3\ a_4\ a_1), \\
\bar{P}_4 &: (a_2\ a_5\ a_3\ a_4\ a_1) \quad \text{and} \quad P_4 : (a_2\ a_1\ a_4\ a_3\ a_5).
\end{aligned}
$$

[Here, P_i: $(a\ b\ c)$ refers to $aP_i b\, P_i c$ and so on.]

Check that $f_2(\bar{P}) = a_3$, $f_2(P) = a_2$, so that $(P, \{1, 3, 4\})$ is a threat to $\bar{P}$. There cannot be any counter-threat to this threat. For, suppose that P' is 2-variant from P. Either $B_2' = \{a_2\}$, in which case $f_2(P') = a_3$, or $B_2' \neq \{a_2\}$, in which case $f_2(P') = a_2$. Hence, $\bar{P} \notin SE_2(f_2, \bar{P})$.[4]

In the next theorem we show that f_2 is exactly and strongly consistent (type 1). Of course, Dutta and Pattanaik (1978) have already shown that f_1 satisfies this property.

Theorem 2. There exists a non-dictatorial and non-imposed scf satisfying NT, M and exact and strong consistency (type 1).

Proof. We prove this result only for the case of $m > n$. The proof for the case $m \leqslant n$ is left to the reader.

Let $f_2(\bar{P}) = x$. Consider P such that for all $i \in N$:

(i) $x P_i a$ for all $a \in A - \{x\}$, and

(ii) for all $a \in \bar{B}_i$, and all $b \in A - \bar{B}_i$, $b P_i a$.

Suppose P' is such that $P_i = P_i'$ for some $i \in N$. Let $a \in \bar{B}_i$. From condition (ii), a is amongst the r_i-worst elements in P_i'. Hence the following statement is true.

(i)   for all $P' \in \pi^n$, $[P_i = P_i'$ and $a \in \bar{B}_i] \to [(a \in B_i')$ or $(a \in B_j'$ for some $j < i.)]$.

Suppose $P \notin SE_1(f_2, \bar{P})$. Let (P', T) be a threat to P. There are two possibilities:

Case (i): $n \in T$.

Case (ii): $n \notin T$.

For any coalition C, let $P(C) = \{a \in A \,|\, a\bar{P}_i x$ for all $i \in C\}$. In case (i), $y \in P(\{n\})$ where $y = f_2(P)$. Since $f_2(\bar{P}) = x \neq y$, $y \in \bar{B}_i \cup \bar{B}_2 \ldots \cup \bar{B}_{n-1}$. Hence, there exists $i \in N$ such that $y \in \bar{B}_i$, but $y \notin B_1' \cup B_2' \ldots \cup B_i'$. From statement

---

[4]   In a private communication, H. Moulin has pointed out that under f_2 every sincere profile $\bar{P}$ belongs to the *core* of f_2.

(i), this is not possible if $P_i = P_i'$. Hence, $i \in T$, so that $y\bar{P}_i x$. But $P(\{i\}) \cap \bar{B}_i = \varnothing$ for all $i \in N$. Hence, $n \notin T$.

Suppose case (ii) occurs, so that $n \notin T$. Since $y \neq f_2(\bar{P})$, $y \in \bar{B}_i$ for some $i \in N$. Also, note that since $B_j = \bar{B}_j$ for all $j \in N$, and $P(\{j\}) \cap \bar{B}_j = \varnothing$, $i \in N - T$. But, if $i \in N - T$, then $P_i = P_i'$. From (1), $y \in \bigcup_{i \in N} B_i'$, so that $f_2(P') \neq y$.

Hence, f_2 is exactly and strongly consistent (type 1).

Remark 2. f_2 is the first example of a *neutral and exactly and strong consistent scf*.

Theorems 1 and 2 would seem to indicate that many of the impossibility results on strategy-proofness can be avoided if we search for scfs giving individuals some veto power. A natural question to ask is whether such scfs are implementable. However, Maskin (1979) has already shown that only dictatorial scfs are implementable (type 1). In the next result, we extend Maskin's result by showing that only dictatorial scfs can be implementable (type 2).

Theorem 3. An scf is implementable (type 2) only if f satisfies SPA.

Proof. Suppose f violates SPA. Then there exist $P, P' \in \pi^n$ such that $f(P) = x$, for all $i \in N$, for all $a \in A - \{x\}$, $xP_i a \to xP_i' a$, but $f(P') = y \neq x$.

Let $\bar{P}^0 = P$ and $\bar{P}^1 = P'$. If f is implementable (type 2), then there exists a game form g, and $s \in SE_2(g, \bar{P}^0)$ such that $g(s) = x = f(\bar{P}^0)$.

If $s \in SE_1(g, \bar{P}^1)$, then f is not implementable (type 2), since $SE_1(g, \bar{P}^1) \subset SE_2(g, \bar{P}^1)$, and $g(s) = x \neq f(\bar{P}^1)$. So, let $(\hat{s}, T)$ be a threat to s when the sincere profile is $\bar{P}^1$. Let $g(\hat{s}) = z$, so that $z\bar{P}_i^1 x$ for all $i \in T$. But, by construction, $z\bar{P}_i^1 x \to z\bar{P}_i^0 x$. Hence $(\hat{s}, T)$ is also a threat to s under $\bar{P}^0$. Therefore, $SE_1(g, \bar{P}^0) \subset SE_1(g, \bar{P}^1)$.

So there exists s such that $s \notin SE_1(g, \bar{P}^0)$, but $s \in SE_2(g, \bar{P}^0)$ and $g(s) = x$.

Since $s \notin SE_1(g, \bar{P}^0)$, there exists a threat $(\hat{s}, T)$ to s. Let $g(\hat{s}) = a$, so that $a\bar{P}_i^0 x$ for all $i \in T$.

Since $s \in SE_2(g, \bar{P}^0)$ there exists a counter-threat to this threat. Let (s^*, T') be the counter-threat. Suppose $g(s^*) = b$, so that for some $i \in T$, $x\bar{P}_i^0 b$. But, $x\bar{P}_i^0 b \to x\bar{P}_i^1 b$. Hence, (s^*, T') is also a counter-threat (type 2) when the sincere profile is $\bar{P}^1$.

Therefore, $SE_2(g, \bar{P}^0) \subset SE_2(g, \bar{P}^1)$. Hence, f is not implementable (type 2) since $g(s) = x \neq f(\bar{P}^1)$ and $s \in SE_2(g, \bar{P}^1)$.

References

Dutta, B. and P.K. Pattanaik (1978) "On Nicely Consistent Voting Schemes", *Econometrica*, 46, 163–170.

Gibbard, A. (1973) "Manipulation of Voting Schemes: A General Result", *Econometrica*, 41, 587–601.

Luce, R.D. and H. Raiffa (1957) *Games and Decision* (Wiley, New York).

Maskin, E. (1979) "Implementation and Strong Nash Equilibrium", in: J.J. Laffont, ed., *Aggregation and Revolation of Preferences* (North-Holland, Amsterdam).

Maskin, E. (1981) "Nash Equilibrium and Welfare Optimality", *Mathematics of Operations Research*.

Moulin, H. (1980) "Implementing Efficient, Anonymous and Neutral Social Choice Functions", *Journal of Mathematical Economics*, 7, 249–270.

Moulin, H. (1982) "Voting with Proportional Veto Power", *Econometrica*, 50, 145–162.

Mueller, D.C. (1978) "Voting by Veto", *Journal of Public Economics*, 10, 57–75.

Muller, E. and M.A. Satterthwaite (1977) "The Equivalence of Strong Positive Association and Strategyproofness", *Journal of Economic Theory*, 14, 412–418.

Pattanaik, P.K. (1976) "Counter-threats and Strategic Manipulation Under Voting Schemes", *Review of Economic Studies*, 42,

Peleg, B. (1978) "Consistent Voting Systems", *Econometrica*, 46, 53–161.

Satterthwaite, M.A. (1975) "Strategyproofness and Arrow's Conditions: Existence and Correspondence Theorems for Voting Procedures and Social Welfare Functions", *Journal of Economic Theory*, 10, 187–217.

CHAPTER 14

On simple games and social choice correspondences

BEZALEL PELEG
The Hebrew University

1. Introduction

This chapter consists of a detailed investigation of the relationship between simple games and social choice correspondences. Section 2 contains the necessary definitions. We begin our investigation in section 3 by associating three simple games, which are derived from three different notions of effectiveness, with every social choice correspondence. We proceed with a study of the properties of, and the interrelations between, the three simple games. Then we consider several examples, including the Borda rule. A social choice correspondence is *tight* if our three notions of effectiveness coincide for it. We conclude section 3 by demonstrating that certain conditions are sufficient for tightness. In section 4 we consider the converse problem, namely that of representing simple games by social choice correspondences. We find sufficient conditions for tightness of representations, and prove, by constructing suitable examples, the existence of tight and "nice" representations. We also have the following interesting result which ties our representation theory with the core. Let $G = (N, W)$ be a simple game and let A be a finite set of m alternatives, $m \geqslant 2$. Then, there exists a strongly monotonic representation of G of order m, if and only if for every profile of preferences (on A) R^N the core of G, with respect to A and R^N, is not empty.

2. Preliminaries

Let A be a finite set of *alternatives*. We assume that A contains at least two alternatives. A *linear order* on A is a complete, reflexive, transitive and antisymmetric

Social Choice and Welfare, edited by P.K. Pattanaik and M. Salles
© *North-Holland Publishing Company, 1983*

binary relation on A. We denote by L the set of all linear orders on A. Also, the set of all *non*-empty subsets of A is denoted by 2^A.

Let N be a finite set with n members. N is called a *society*, members of N are called *voters*, or *players*, and non-empty subsets of N are called *coalitions*. For a coalition S we denote by L^S the set of all functions from S to L.

Definition 2.1. A *social choice correspondence* (SCC) is a function from L^N to 2^A.

We shall be interested in the following properties of SCCs. Let $H: L^N \to 2^A$ be a SCC.

Definition 2.2. H is *Paretian* if it satisfies:

(P) If $R^N \in L^N$, $x, y \in A$, $x \neq y$ and $xR^i y$, for all $i \in N$, then $y \notin H(R^N)$.

Definition 2.3. A permutation π of N is a *symmetry* of H if for all $R^N = (R^1, ..., R^n)$ in L^N $H(R^N) = H(R^{\pi(1)}, ..., R^{\pi(n)})$. The group of all symmetries of H will be denoted by SYM(H).

Definition 2.4. H is *anonymous* if SYM(H) = S_n, the group of all permutations of N.

Let σ be a permutation of A and let $R \in L$. We denote by $\sigma(R)$ the linear order defined by the following condition: for all $x, y \in A$, $\sigma(x)\sigma(R)\sigma(y)$ if and only if xRy.

Definition 2.5. H is *neutral* if for every permutation σ of A, and for every $R^N = (R^1, ..., R^n)$ in L^N, $H(\sigma(R^1), ..., \sigma(R^n)) = \sigma(H(R^N))$. [Here $\sigma(H(R^N))$ is the image of $H(R^N)$ under σ.]

Definition 2.6. Let $R^N \in L^N$ and let $x \in A$. $R_1^N \in L^N$ *is obtained from* R^N *by an improvement of the position of* x *if:*

$$\text{for all } a, b \in A - \{x\}, \text{ and for all } i \in N, aR^i b \Longleftrightarrow aR_1^i b, \tag{1}$$

and

$$\text{for all } a \in A, \text{ and for all } i \in N, xR^i a \Rightarrow xR_1^i a. \tag{2}$$

Definition 2.7. *H* is *monotonic* if it satisfies:

If $R^N \in L^N$, $x \in H(R^N)$ and R_1^N is obtained from R^N by an improvement of the position of x (see definition 2.6), then $x \in H(R_1^N)$ and $H(R_1^N) \subset H(R^N)$. $\quad(3)$

Definition 2.8. *H* is *strongly monotonic* if it satisfies:

If $R^N \in L^N$, $x \in A$ and R_1^N is obtained from R^N by an improvement of the position of x (see definition 2.6), then $H(R_1^N) \subset \{x\} \cup H(R^N)$. $\quad(4)$

Remark 2.9. It can be shown that a strongly monotonic SCC is monotonic.

Definition 2.10. *H* has the *strong positive association property* if it satisfies:

Let $R^N \in L^N$ and $x \in H(R^N)$. If $R_1^N \in L^N$ and for all $i \in N$ and $y \in A$, xR^iy implies xR_1^iy, then $x \in H(R_1^N)$. $\quad(5)$

Remark 2.11. It can be shown that *H* has the strong positive association property if and only if it is strongly monotonic. However, it is convenient to work with both concepts together.

Definition 2.12. *A simple game* is an ordered pair $G = (N, W)$, where *N* is a society and *W*, the set of *winning coalitions*, satisfies:

$$[S \in W \text{ and } T \supset S] \Rightarrow T \in W(\text{monotonicity}).\quad(6)$$

We now define some basic properties of simple games. (For a comprehensive study of simple games the reader is referred to Shapley, 1962.)

Definition 2.13. Let $G = (N, W)$ be a simple game. *G* is *proper* if:

$$S \in W \Rightarrow N - S \notin W.\quad(7)$$

G is *strong* if:

$$S \notin W \Rightarrow N - S \in W.\quad(8)$$

G is *weak* if:

$$V = \cap \{S \mid S \in W\} \neq \emptyset. \tag{9}$$

G is *symmetric* if:

$$[S \in W, T \subset N \text{ and } |T| = |S|] \Rightarrow T \in W, \tag{10}$$

where, here and in the sequel, if B is a finite set, then $|B|$ denotes the number of members of B. Finally, G is *non-null* if:

$$W \neq \emptyset.$$

Remark 2.14. Let N be a society with n members and let $0 \leqslant k \leqslant n$. By (n, k) we denote the simple game (N, W), where

$$W = \{S \mid S \subset N \text{ and } |S| \geqslant k\}. \tag{11}$$

Clearly, a simple game $G = (N, W)$ is symmetric if and only if there exists $0 \leqslant k \leqslant n$ such that $G = (n, k)$.

Definition 2.15. Let $G = (N, W)$ be a simple game. A permutation π of N is a *symmetry* of G if for every $S \in W$, $\pi(S) = \{\pi(i) \mid i \in S\} \in W$. The group of all symmetries of G will be denoted by SYM(G).

Remark 2.16. Clearly, a simple game $G = (N, W)$ is symmetric if and only if SYM$(G) = S_n$, the group of permutations of N.

Remark 2.17. A simple game $G = (N, W)$ is non-null (see definition 2.13) if and only if $N \in W$.

Remark 2.18. If $G = (N, W)$ is weak [see eq. (9)], then the members of V are called *veto players*.

3. The simple games associated with a SCC

In the beginning of this section we associate three simple games with every SCC. Our approach consists of a (straightforward) generalization of that in Peleg (1980).

Let A be a finite set of m alternatives, $m \geqslant 2$, and let N be a society.

Notation 3.1. Let $H: L^N \to 2^A$ be a SCC and let $R^N \in L^N$. If $H(R^N) = \{x\}$, then we shall also write $H(R^N) = x$.

Definition 3.2. Let $H: L^N \to 2^A$ be a SCC and let $x \in A$. A coalition S is *winning for x* (with respect to H), if

$$[R^N \in L^N \text{ and } xR^i y \text{ for all } i \in S \text{ and all } y \in A] \Rightarrow H(R^N) = x$$

(see notation 3.1). The set of all winning coalitions for x is denoted by $W(H, x)$ or $W(x)$.

Remark 3.3. Let $H: L^N \to 2^A$ be a SCC and let $x \in A$. If $S \in W(x)$, then S can enforce x *without* knowing the preferences declared (or possessed) by the members of $N - S$.

Definition 3.4. Let $H: L^N \to 2^A$ be a SCC. A coalition S is *winning* (with respect to H) if $S \in W(H, x)$ for all $x \in A$ (see definition 3.2). The *first simple game associated with H* is the game $G^*(H) = (N, W)$, where $W = W(H)$ is the set of all winning coalitions with respect to H.

Remark 3.5. Let $H: L^N \to 2^A$ be a SCC. Clearly, $G^*(H)$ satisfies the monotonicity property (6). Also, since $|A| \geqslant 2$, $G^*(H)$ is proper [see (7)].

Definition 3.6. Let $H: L^N \to 2^A$ be a SCC and let $x \in A$. A coalition S is *α-effective for x* (with respect to H) if there exists $Q^S \in L^S$ such that for all $P^{N-S} \in L^{N-S}$ $H(Q^S, P^{N-S}) = x$. The set of all α-effective coalitions for x is denoted by $W_\alpha(H, x)$ or $W_\alpha(x)$.

Remark 3.7. Let $H: L^N \to 2^A$ be a SCC and let $x \in A$. If $S \in W_\alpha(x)$ then, again, S can enforce x *without* knowing the preferences declared (or possessed) by the members of $N - S$. However, the computational effort needed in order to check whether a coalition T belongs to $W_\alpha(x)$ is much higher than that needed in order to check whether $T \in W(x)$ (see definition 3.2). On the other hand, coalitions in $W_\alpha(x) - W(x)$ can hardly be qualified as "ineffective."

Definition 3.8. Let $H: L^N \to 2^A$ be a SCC. A coalition S is *α-winning* (with respect to H), if $S \in W_\alpha(H, x)$ for all $x \in A$ (see definition 3.6). The *second simple game associated with H* is the game $G_\alpha(H) = (N, W_\alpha)$, where $W_\alpha = W_\alpha(H)$ is the set of all α-winning coalitions.

Remark 3.9. Let $H: L^N \to 2^A$ be a SCC. $G_\alpha(H)$ satisfies the monotonicity property (6). Also, since $|A| \geqslant 2$, $G_\alpha(H)$ is proper [see (7)]. Furthermore, $W_\alpha(H) \supset W(H)$ (see definitions 3.4 and 3.8).

We now introduce the notion of β-effectivity in order to define the third game.

Definition 3.10. Let $H: L^N \to 2^A$ be a SCC and let $x \in A$. A coalition S is *β-effective for x* (with respect to H) if for every $P^{N-S} \in L^{N-S}$ there exists $Q^S \in L^S$ such that $H(Q^S, P^{N-S}) = x$. The set of all β-effective coalitions for x denoted by $W_\beta(H, x)$ or $W_\beta(x)$.

Remark 3.11. Let $H: L^N \to 2^A$ be a SCC and let $x \in A$. Let further $S \in W_\beta(x)$ (see definition 3.10). We observe that S may be unable to obtain x without knowing the preferences declared by the members of $N - S$. Thus, if the choice of a profile $R^N \in L^N$ is done by a *secret* ballot, then β-effectivity considerations are inappropriate. However, in open voting processes β-effectivity arguments may be valid. Another situation in which β-effectivity considerations may appear is the following. Let T be a coalition. When T contemplates what can be achieved by $N - T$, it might happen that it cannot rule out the possibility that $N - T$ will attain an alternative for which it is only β-effective. (Since, even if T decides to keep its action secret, it may not be completely sure that its choice is not discovered by the members of $N - T$.)

Definition 3.12. Let $H: L^N \to 2^A$ be a SCC. A coalition S is *β-winning* (with respect to H) if $S \in W_\beta(H, x)$ for all $x \in A$ (see definition 3.10). The *third simple game associated with H* is the game $G_\beta(H) = (N, W_\beta)$, where $W_\beta = W_\beta(H)$ is the set of all β-winning coalitions.

Remark 3.13. Let $H: L^N \to 2^A$ be a SCC. $G_\beta(H) = (N, W_\beta)$ is monotonic [see (6)], and $W_\beta \supset W_\alpha$ (see definition 3.8). However, G_β may *not* be proper [see (7)], as is shown by example 3.17 below.

The following notation is needed in the sequel.

Notation 3.14. Let $R^N \in L^N$. For $a \in A$ we denote

$$v(R^N, a) = |\{i \,|\, i \in N \text{ and } aR^i x \text{ for all } x \in A\}|. \tag{12}$$

Notation 3.15. Let $R \in L$. We denote by $t_i(R)$ the ith alternative in the order R. Thus, $t_1(R)$ is the best alternative according to R, $t_2(R)$ is the second alternative, and so on.

We also introduce the following definition.

Definition 3.16. A *social choice function* (SCF) is a single-valued SCC (see definition 2.1). (Thus, a SCF is, essentially, a function from L^N to A.)

Example 3.17. Let $A = \{x_1, x_2, x_3, x_4\}$ and let $N = \{1, 2, 3, 4\}$. We define a SCF $F: L^N \to A$ by the following rules. For $R^N \in L^N$ we denote

$$B(R^N) = \{h \mid v(R^N, x_h) \geqslant v(R^N, x_t) \text{ for } t = 1, 2, 3, 4\} \tag{13}$$

[see (12)]. If $|B(R^N)| = 1$ then we define $F(R^N) = x_h$, where $B(R^N) = \{h\}$. If $|B(R^N)| \geqslant 2$, let (i, j) be the first pair, in the lexicographic order, of members of $B(R^N)$. Let further (u, v) be the remaining (ordered) pair in $\{1, 2, 3, 4\}$. We consider now the set

$$S(R^N) = \{h \mid h \in N \text{ and } x_u R^h x_v\}, \tag{14}$$

and define $F(R^N) = x_i$ if $|S(R^N)|$ is odd, and $F(R^N) = x_j$ if $|S(R^N)|$ is even. Before we proceed to investigate the properties of F, we illustrate its definition by computing its value for the following profile:

R^1	R^2	R^3	R^4
x_3	x_3	x_4	x_4
x_1	x_1	x_2	x_2
x_2	x_2	x_1	x_1
x_4	x_4	x_3	x_3

$B(R^N) = \{3, 4\}$. Hence $(i, j) = (3, 4)$, $(u, v) = (1, 2)$ and

$$S(R^N) = \{h \mid h \in N \text{ and } x_1 R^h x_2\} = \{1, 2\}.$$

Thus, $|S(R^N)|$ is even and therefore $F(R^N) = x_4$.

We now turn to examine the properties of F. It is clear that F is Paretian and anonymous (see definitions 2.2 and 2.4, respectively). We claim that F is also monotonic (see definition 2.7). Indeed, let $R^N \in L^N$ and let $F(R^N) = x_i$. If $R_1^N \in L^N$ is obtained from R^N by an improvement of the position of x_i (see definition 2.6), we have to show that $F(R_1^N) = x_i$. If $B(R_1^N) = \{i\}$ [see (13)], then $F(R_1^N) = x_i$. Otherwise (i.e. when $|B(R_1^N)| \geqslant 2$) $B(R_1^N) = B(R^N)$. Also, $S(R^N) = S(R_1^N)$ [see (14)]. Hence, again, $F(R^N) = F(R_1^N)$.

We conclude by showing that $G_\beta(F) = (4, 2)$ (see remark 2.14 and definition 3.12). It is enough to show that $T = \{1, 2\}$ is β-effective (see definition 3.10) for x_4. Let $R^{N-T} \in L^{N-T}$. As the reader can easily verify there exists $R^T \in L^T$ such that $F(R^T, R^{N-T}) = x_4$.

In order to make a further observation on example 3.17 we need the following definition.

Definition 3.18. Let $F: L^N \to A$ be a SCF (see definition 3.16), and let $R^N \in L^N$. The *game associated with F and R^N* is the *n*-person game in normal form $g(F, R^N)$ where

$$L \text{ is the set of strategies for each player } i \in N, \tag{15}$$

$$F \text{ is the outcome function}, \tag{16}$$

$$R^i \text{ is the preference relation of player } i \in N \text{ on the outcome space } A. \tag{17}$$

Remark 3.19. Let F be the SCF of example 3.17 and let $R^N \in L^N$ satisfy $t_1(R^1) = t_1(R^2) = x_1$, and $t_1(R^3) = t_1(R^4) = x_2$ (see notation 3.15). Denote $T_1 = \{1, 2\}$ and $T_2 = \{3, 4\}$. Then, clearly, $T_1 \cap T_2 = \varnothing$. However, in the game $g(F, R^N)$ (see definition 3.18), there exists *no* pair of strategies (Q^{T_1}, Q^{T_2}), where $Q^{T_i} \in L^{T_i}$, $i = 1, 2$, such that Q^{T_1} is a best reply to Q^{T_2} and vice versa. This peculiar phenomenon is due entirely to the discrete character of our model. Indeed, Aumann (1961, section 9) proves that the above phenomenon is impossible in a cooperative game (in normal form) which is the *mixed* extension of a finite game.

Remark 3.20. Let $H: L^N \to 2^A$ be a SCC. If H is anonymous (see definition 2.4) then $G^*(H)$, $G_\alpha(H)$ and $G_\beta(H)$ (see definitions 3.4, 3.8 and 3.12, respectively) are symmetric [see (10)]. If H is neutral (see definition 2.5) then $W(H) = W(H, x)$, $W_\alpha(H) = W_\alpha(H, x)$ and $W_\beta(H) = W_\beta(H, x)$ for all $x \in A$. Also, if H is Paretian (see definition 2.2) then $N \in W(H)$.

We now compute the simple games associated with two well-known SCCs.

Example 3.21. For $R^N \in L^N$ let $M(R^N) = \{a \mid a \in A$ and $v(R^N, a) \geqslant v(R^N, x)$ for all $x \in A\}$ (see notation 3.14). Then $M = M(m, n)$ (where $m = |A|$ and $n = |N|$) is the rule of choice by plurality voting. Clearly, M is Paretian, anonymous, neutral and monotonic (see definition 2.7). By remark 3.20 all the games associated with M are symmetric. Moreover, as the reader can easily verify, $G^*(M) = G_\alpha(M) = G_\beta(M) = (n, [n/2] + 1)$ (see remark 2.14) for all n and all $m \geqslant 2$.

Example 3.22. Let $w: L \times A \to \{0, 1, ..., m-1\}$ be defined by $w(R, x) = m - i$ if $t_i(R) = x$ (see notation 3.15). For $R^N \in L^N$ and $x \in A$ we denote

$$w(R^N, x) = \sum_{i=1}^{n} w(R^i, x). \tag{18}$$

Now, for $R^N \in L^N$ let

$$B(R^N) = \{a \mid a \in A \text{ and } w(R^N, a) \geqslant w(R^N, x) \text{ for all } x \in A\} \tag{19}$$

[see (18)]. Then $B = B(m, n)$ is the well-known Borda rule. Again, B is Paretian, anonymous, neutral and monotonic. By remark 3.20 all the games associated with B are symmetric. We show first:

Claim 3.23. $G^*(B(m, n)) = (n, k(m, n))$, where $k(m, n) = [n(m-1)/m] + 1$.

Indeed, let $S \subset N$ with $|S| = k$. Then $S \in W(B(m, n))$ (see definition 3.4) if and only if

$$k(m - 1) > k(m - 2) + (n - k)(m - 1) \tag{20}$$

(see definition 3.2, remark 3.20 and eq. (19)). Clearly, (20) is satisfied if and only if $k \geqslant k(m, n)$, which proves our claim.

Next, we show

Claim 3.24. $G_\alpha(B(m, n)) = (n, k_\alpha(m, n))$, where $k_\alpha(m, n) = [(2(m - 1)n + 1)/(3m - 2)] + 1$.

Let $S \in W_\alpha$ with $|S| = k$, let $T = N - S$ and let $x \in A$. There exists $P^S \in L^S$ such that for all $Q^T \in L^T B(P^S, Q^T) = x$ (see notation 3.1). We may assume that $t_1(P^i) = x$ for all $i \in S$ (see notation 3.15). The remaining $m - 1$ alternatives get together $k(m - 1)(m - 2)/2$ points. Hence, there exists $y \in A, y \neq x$, such that $w(P^S, y) \geqslant [(k(m - 2) - 1)/2] + 1$ [see (18)]. Since k is an integer the inequalities

$$w(P^S, x) > w(P^S, y) + w(Q^T, y) \quad \text{for all } Q^T \in L^T,$$

imply that

$$k(m - 1) > k(m - 2)/2 + 1/2 + (n - k)(m - 1). \tag{21}$$

Expression (21) implies that $k \geqslant [(2(m - 1)n + 1)/(3m - 2)] + 1$. Thus, $k_\alpha(m, n) \geqslant [(2(m - 1)n + 1)/(3m - 2)] + 1$. We shall now prove the reverse inequality. We start with the following observations.

Remark 3.25. Let $A = \{x_1, ..., x_m\}$ and let $Q_1 = (x_m, x_1, x_2, ..., x_{m-1})$ and $Q_2 = (x_m, x_{m-1}, x_{m-2}, ..., x_1)$. Then for each $i = 1, ..., m - 1$, $w(Q_1, x_i) + w(Q_2, x_i) = m - 2$.

Remark 3.26. Let m be even. If

$$Q_3 = (x_m, x_{m-1}, x_{m-3}, ..., x_1, x_{m-2}, x_{m-4}, ..., x_2)$$

and

$$Q_4 = (x_m, x_{m-2}, x_{m-4}, ..., x_2, x_{m-1}, x_{m-3}, ..., x_1),$$

then $w(Q_1, x_i) + w(Q_3, x_i) + w(Q_4, x_i) = 3(m - 2)/2$ for $i = 1, ..., m - 1$. Indeed, for $i = m - 2t - 1$ (where $0 \leqslant t \leqslant m/2 - 1$):

$$w(Q_1, x_i) + w(Q_3, x_i) + w(Q_4, x_i) = m - 1 - (m - 2t - 1) + m - 1 - (t + 1) + m - m/2 - (t + 1) = 3(m - 2)/2.$$

If $i = m - 2t$ (where $1 \leqslant t \leqslant m/2 - 1$), then

$$w(Q_1, x_i) + w(Q_3, x_i) + w(Q_4, x_i) = m - 1 - (m - 2t) + m/2 - 1 - t + m - 1 - t = 3(m - 2)/2.$$

Remark 3.27. Let m be odd. If

$$Q_5 = (x_m, x_{m-1}, x_{m-3}, ..., x_2, x_{m-2}, x_{m-4}, ..., x_1)$$

and

$$Q_6 = (x_m, x_{m-2}, x_{m-4}, ..., x_1, x_{m-1}, x_{m-3}, ..., x_2)$$

then $w(Q_1, x_i) + w(Q_5, x_i) + w(Q_6, x_i) \leqslant 3(m-2)/2 + 1/2$ for $i = 1, ..., m-1$. (The proof of our last claim is left to the reader).

We now complete the proof of claim 3.24 in the following way. Let $k = [(2(m-1)n+1)/(3m-2)] + 1$. Let further $S = \{1, ..., k\}$ and $T = N - S$. It is sufficient to prove that there exists $P^S \in L^S$ such that for all $R^T \in L^T$ $B(P^S, R^T) = x_m$ (see remark 3.20). We distinguish the following possibilities.

(a) k is even. Let $P^i = Q_1$ if $1 \leqslant i \leqslant k/2$, and $P^i = Q_2$ if $k/2 < i \leqslant k$ (see remark 3.25). Now, $w(P^S, x_i) = k(m-2)/2$ for $i = 1, ..., m-1$. Hence, by the choice of k, $B(P^S, R^T) = x_m$ for all $R^T \in L^T$ [see (21)].

(b) k is odd. Without loss of generality $k \geqslant 3$. We further distinguish the following subcases.

(b.1) m is even. Let $k = 3 + 2h$, where $h \geqslant 0$. Let now $P^1 = Q_1$, $P^2 = Q_3$, $P^3 = Q_4$, $P^i = Q_1$ for $3 < i \leqslant 3 + h$, and $P^i = Q_2$ for $3 + h < i \leqslant 3 + 2h$ (see remarks 3.25 and 3.26). Again, if $1 \leqslant i < m$, then $w(P^S, x_i) = k(m-2)/2$. Hence, as in case (a) $B(P^S, R^T) = x_m$ for all $R^T \in L^T$.

(b.2) m is odd. The proof in this case follows from remarks 3.25 and 3.27. Since it is similar to the proof of (b.1), it is omitted.

Remark 3.28. It is interesting to note that $\lim_{n, m \to \infty} k_\alpha(m, n)/n = 2/3$.

We conclude the discussion of example 3.22 by computing $G_\beta(B(m, n))$ (see definition 3.12). First we introduce the following notation.

Notation 3.29. Let $R \in L$. By $_*R$ we denote the reverse order to R. (Thus, for $x, y \in A$, $x_* R y$ if and only if yRx.)

Claim 3.30. $G_\beta(B(m, n)) = (n, [n/2] + 1)$.

Let $G_\beta(B(m, n)) = (n, k_\beta)$. Clearly, $k_\beta \geqslant [n/2] + 1$. Thus, we have to show the reverse inequality. Assume first that n is odd. Let $n = 2k + 1$, $S = \{1, ..., k+1\}$ and $T = N - S$. Let $R^T \in L^T$. We have to show that there exists $Q^S \in L^S$ such that $B(Q^S, R^T) = x_m$ (see remark 3.20). For $i = 2, ..., k+1$ let $Q^i = _*R^{k+i}$ (see notation 3.29) and let $Q^1 \in L$ satisfy $t_1(Q^1) = x_m$. As the reader can easily verify, $B(Q^S, R^T) = x_m$. The proof when n is even is similar.

Remark 3.31. A similar investigation of the strategical properties of Borda's rule is contained in Moulin (1982) and Gardner (1977).

Let $H: L^N \to 2^A$ be a SCC. It follows from remarks 3.3, 3.7 and 3.11 that if the three notions of effectiveness which we have discussed coincide for H, then the analysis of H, from a strategic and informational points of view, is greatly simplified. This observation leads to the following investigation.

Definition 3.32. Let $H: L^N \to 2^A$ be a SCC. H is *tight* if for every $x \in A$ $W_\beta(x) = W(x)$ (see definitions 3.2 and 3.10).

Remark 3.33. If a SCC H is tight, then $G^*(H) = G_\beta(H)$ (see definitions 3.4 and 3.12). Hence, in particular, $G_\beta(H)$ is proper (see remark 3.13). The converse is not true, as is shown by the following example.

Example 3.34. Let $A = \{x_1, x_2, x_3\}$ and let $N = \{1, 2\}$. We define a SCF F: $L^N \to A$ (see definition 3.16) by the following rule. For $R^N \in L^N$ $F(R^N)$ is the first alternative in $\dot{B}(R^N)$ [see (19)]. As the reader can easily verify $G^*(F) = G_\beta(F) = (2,2)$. However, $\{1\} \in W_\beta(x_1)$, while $\{1\} \notin W(x_1)$.

The following simple result is true.

Theorem 3.35. Let $H: L^N \to 2^A$ be a SCC. If $G^*(H)$ is strong [see (8)] then H is tight.

Proof. Let $x \in A$ and let S be coalition. If $S \notin W(x)$, then we have to show that $S \notin W_\beta(x)$. Let $T = N - S$. Since $G^*(H)$ is strong and $S \notin W(H)$ (see definition 3.4), $T \in W(H)$. Let $a \in A - \{x\}$ (recall that $|A| \geqslant 2$), and let $P^T \in L^T$ satisfy $t_1(P^i) = a$ for all $i \in T$ (see notation 3.15). Then $H(P^T, Q^S) = a$ for all $Q^S \in L^S$. Thus, $S \notin W_\beta(x)$. ∎

We conclude this section with the following lemma and corollary.

Lemma 3.36. Let $H: L^N \to 2^A$ be a monotonic SCC. If H depends only on top alternatives, i.e. there exists a function $h: A^N \to 2^A$ such that $H(R^N) = h(t_1(R^1), ..., t_1(R^n))$ for every $R^N = (R^1, ..., R^n)$ in L^N, then H is tight.

Proof. Let $x \in A$ and let $S \notin W(x)$. We have to show that $S \notin W_\beta(x)$. Assume, on the contrary, that $S \in W_\beta(x)$. Since $S \notin W(x)$ there exists $R^N \in L^N$ such that $xR^i y$ for all $i \in S$ and $y \in A$, while $H(R^N) \neq x$. Now, since $S \in W_\beta(x)$ there exists $Q^S \in L^S$ such that $H(Q^S, R^T) = x$, where $T = N - S$. Since H is monotonic we may assume that $t_1(Q^i) = x$ for all $i \in S$ (see definition 2.7). Hence, by assumption, $H(R^N) = H(Q^S, R^T) = x$, which is the desired contradiction.

Corollary 3.37. Choice by plurality voting (see example 3.21) is tight.

4. Representations of simple games by SCCs

Definition 4.1. Let $G = (N, W)$ be a proper simple game [see (7)] and let A be a set of m alternatives, $m \geqslant 2$. A SCC $H: L^N \to 2^A$ is a *representation of G of order m* if $G^*(H) = G$ (see definition 3.4).

Intuitively, if $G = (N, W)$ is a committee which has to choose a (non-empty) subset of a set A of alternatives, then a representation $H: L^N \to 2^A$ is a feasible choice procedure which reflects "faithfully" the distribution of "power" in G. We shall now investigate the problem of existence of representations. It turns out that the solution of this problem is closely related to the investigation of cores of simple games. We start with the following definitions.

Definition 4.2. Let $G = (N, W)$ be a simple game and let A be a finite set of alternatives. Let further $R^N \in L^N$, $x, y \in A$, $x \neq y$ *and* $S \in W$. *x dominates y* (with respect to R^N) via S, written x dom $(R^N, S)y$, if $xR^i y$ for all $i \in S$. *x dominates y* (with respect to R^N), written x dom $(R^N)y$, if there exists $T \in W$ such that x dom $(R^N, T)y$. The *core* of A (with respect to G and R^N) is the set of all undominated alternatives in A, and is denoted by $C(N, W, A, R^N) = C(R^N)$.

Definition 4.3. Let $G = (N, W)$ be a simple game and let A be a finite set of alternatives. Let further $R^N \in L^N$. An alternative $c \in A$ is a *Condorcet alternative* (with respect to R^N), if c dom $(R^N)x$ for all $x \in A - \{c\}$ (see definition 4.2).

Let $G = (N, W)$ be a proper simple game and let A be a finite set of m alternatives, $m \geqslant 2$.

Definition 4.4. A SCC $H: L^N \to 2^A$ satisfies the *Condorcet condition* if for every $R^N \in L^N$: if c is a Condorcet alternative with respect to R^N (see definition 4.3), then $H(R^N) = c$ (see notation 3.1).

Definition 4.5. A SCC $H: L^N \to 2^A$ is *core-inclusive* if for every $R^N \in L^N$ $H(R^N) \supset C(N, W, A, R^N)$ (see definition 4.2).

The following interesting result is true.

Theorem 4.6. Let $H: L^N \to 2^A$ be a SCC. If H satisfies the Condorcet condition and is core-inclusive (see definitions 4.4 and 4.5, respectively), then H is a tight representation of G (see definitions 4.1 and 3.32).

Proof. Let $G^*(H) = (N, W(H))$ (see definition 3.4). We shall prove first that $W \subset W(H)$. Let $S \in W$. If $R^N \in L^N$, $x \in A$ and $xR^i y$ for all $i \in S$ and all $y \in A$, then x is a Condorcet alternative with respect to R^N (see definition 4.3). Since H satisfies the Condorcet condition, $H(R^N) = x$. Hence, $S \in W(H, x)$ (see definition 3.2). Since x is arbitrary, $S \in W(H)$. We shall complete the proof by showing that $W_\beta(H, x) \subset W$ for every $x \in A$ (see definition 3.10). Indeed, let $x \in A$. If $S \notin W$ then $T = N - S$ is (by definition) blocking. Let $y \in A - \{x\}$ and let $R^T \in L^T$ satisfy $t_1(R^i) = y$ for all $i \in T$ (see notation 3.15). Then, for every $Q^S \in L^S$ $y \in C(Q^S, R^T)$ (see definition 4.2). Since H is core-inclusive, $y \in H(Q^S, R^T)$ for all $Q^S \in L^S$. Hence, $S \notin W_\beta(H, x)$.

We shall now examine the possibility that the core consists of a representation of G. First we need the following definition.

Definition 4.7. Let the SCC $H: L^N \to 2^A$ be a representation of G (see definition 4.1). H is a *faithful* representation of G if $\mathrm{SYM}(H) = \mathrm{SYM}(G)$ (see definitions 2.3 and 2.15).

Corollary 4.8. Assume that for every $R^N \in L^N$ $C(N, W, A, R^N) = C(R^N) \neq \varnothing$. Then $C(\cdot)$ is a tight and faithful (see definition 4.7) representation of G. Furthermore, $C(\cdot)$ is Paretian, neutral and has the strong positive association property (see definitions 2.2, 2.5 and 2.10, respectively).

Proof. Definition 4.2 and theorem 4.6.

Remark 4.9. If G is weak [see (9)] then $C(N, W, A, R^N) \neq \varnothing$ for all $R^N \in L^N$. If G has no veto players (see remark 2.18), then $C(N, W, A, R^N) \neq \varnothing$ for all $R^N \in L^N$ if and only if $|A| < v(G)$, where

$$v(G) = \min \{ |\sigma| \mid \sigma \subset W \text{ and } \cap \{S \mid S \in \sigma\} = \varnothing\} \tag{22}$$

(see Nakamura, 1979).

Let $G = (N, W)$ be a proper simple game without veto players. Before we proceed to construct representations of G of every order (see definition 4.1), we prove an impossibility theorem for representations. Our theorem is a corollary of the following lemma.

Lemma 4.10. Let $G = (N, W)$ be a proper simple game and let A be a set of m alternatives, $m \geqslant 2$. Let further $H: L^N \to 2^A$ be a strongly monotonic SCC (see definition 2.8). If H is a representation of G then $H(R^N) \subset C(N, W, A, R^N)$ for all $R^N \in L^N$.

The following notation is needed for the proof of lemma 4.10.

Notation 4.11. Let $R \in L$ and $B \subset A$. $R(B)$ denotes the following linear order: if $x, y \in B$ or $x, y \notin B$, then $xR(B)y$ if and only if xRy. If $x \in B$ and $y \in A - B$, then $xR(B)y$. Also, if $R^N \in L^N$ and $B \subset A$, then $R^N(B) = (R^1(B), ..., R^n(B))$.

Proof of lemma 4.10. Let $R^N \in L^N$ and let $y \notin C(R^N)$. There exist $x \in A$, $x \neq y$ and $S \in W$ such that xR^iy for all $i \in S$. Let $B = \{x, y\}$ and let $Q_0^N = R^N(B)$ (see notation 4.11). Clearly, xQ_0^iz for all $i \in S$ and for all $z \in A$. Since H is a representation of G, $S \in G^*(H)$ (see definition 3.4). Hence, $H(R^N(B)) = x$. Let $A - B = \{a_1, ..., a_{m-2}\}$ and let

$$B_j = B \cup \{a_h \mid 1 \leqslant h \leqslant j\}, \quad j = 0, 1, ..., m - 2.$$

(Thus, $B_0 = B$ and $B_{m-2} = A$.) Let $Q_j^N = R^N(B_j)$, $j = 0, 1 ..., m - 2$. Then Q_j^N is obtained from Q_{j-1}^N by an improvement of the position of $a_j, j = 1, ..., m - 2$ (see definition 2.6). Hence

$$H(Q_j^N) \subset \{a_j\} \cup H(Q_{j-1}^N), \quad j = 1, ..., m - 2 \tag{23}$$

(see definition 2.8). It follows from (23) that $H(R^N) = H(Q_{m-2}^N) \subset A - \{y\}$. Thus, $y \notin H(R^N)$ and the proof is complete.

Theorem 4.12. Let $G = (N, W)$ be a proper simple game without veto players. If $m \geqslant v(G)$ [see (22)], then G has no strongly monotonic representation of order m.

Proof. Remark 4.9 and lemma 4.10.

We now present three extensions of the core which are defined for every simple game and any number of alternatives. These extensions will yield tight and "nice" representations of simple games.

Let $G = (N, W)$ be a non-null (see remark 2.17) proper simple game and let A be a set of m alternatives, $m \geqslant 2$. Our first example is due to Gillies (1959).

Example 4.13. Let $R^N \in L^N$ and let $x, y \in A, x \neq y$. x *majorizes* y (with respect to R^N), written x maj$(R^N)y$, if (a) x dom$(R^N)y$ (see definition 4.2), and (b) if z dom$(R^N)x$, then z dom$(R^N)y$. The set of unmajorized alternatives is denoted by GIL(R^N) = GIL(N, W, A, R^N). Since maj(R^N) is transitive GIL(R^N) $\neq \varnothing$ for all $R^N \in L^N$. Thus, GIL$(\cdot)$ is a SCC. Clearly, GIL$(\cdot)$ satisfies the Condorcet condition and is core-inclusive (see definitions 4.4 and 4.5). Hence, by theorem 4.6 GIL$(\cdot)$ is a tight representation of G. Since G is non-null, GIL$(\cdot)$ is Paretian (see definition 2.2). Also, GIL$(\cdot)$ is neutral but not monotonic (see definitions 2.5 and 2.7). Finally, it can be verified that GIL$(\cdot)$ is a faithful representation (see definition 4.7).

Remark 4.14. Let $R^N \in L^N$ and suppose that alternatives are eliminated from A by a sequence of binary comparisons which are based solely on dom(R^N). Then, if $x, y \in A$ and x maj$(R^N)y$ then, obviously, y should be rejected in favor of x. Thus, we are led to GIL$(\cdot)$.

Remark 4.15. We may have GIL$(R^N) \neq C(R^N)$ even if $m < v(G)$. Indeed, let $G = (4,3)$ (see remark 2.14) and let $A = \{a, b, c\}$. Since $v(G) = 4$ $|A| < v(G)$. Consider the situation:

R^1	R^2	R^3	R^4
a	a	c	b
b	b	a	c
c	c	b	a

Then $C(R^N) = \{a\}$ while GIL$(R^N) = \{a, c\}$.

Our next two examples are ad hoc constructions.

Example 4.16. Let $R^N \in L^N$ and let $x \in A$. We denote

$$\text{dom}^{-1}(x) = \text{dom}^{-1}(x, R^N) = \{y \,|\, y \in A \text{ and } y \text{ dom}(R^N)x\}. \tag{24}$$

We define

$$\theta(R^N) = \{x \in A \mid | \text{dom}^{-1}(x) | \leqslant | \text{dom}^{-1}(y) | \text{ for all } y \in A\}$$

[see (24)]. Clearly, $\theta(R^N) = C(R^N)$ if $C(R^N) \neq \varnothing$. Hence $\theta(\cdot)$ satisfies the Condorcet condition and is core-inclusive. Thus, $\theta(\cdot)$ is a tight representation of G. Furthermore, it can be verified that $\theta(\cdot)$ is Paretian, neutral, monotonic and faithful. Also, $\theta(R^N) \subset \text{GIL}(R^N)$ for all $R^N \in L^N$ (see example 4.13).

Example 4.17. For $1 \leqslant k \leqslant n$ we denote

$$W_k = \{S \mid S \in W \text{ and } |S| \geqslant k\}.$$

Let now $R^N \in L^N$. We define

$$C_k(R^N) = C(N, W_k, A, R^N) \quad \text{(see definition 4.2)}.$$

Let further

$$h = h(R^N) = \min\{k \mid C_k(R^N) \neq \varnothing\}. \tag{25}$$

Clearly, $C_n(R^N) \neq \varnothing$. Hence, $h(R^N)$ is well defined. Let $\sigma(R^N) = C_h(R^N)$, where $h = h(R^N)$ [see (25)]. Then $\sigma(\cdot)$ is a tight and faithful representation of G. Furthermore, $\sigma(\cdot)$ is Paretian, neutral and monotonic.

While the Condorcet condition (see definition 4.4) is well known, core-inclusion (see definition 4.5) is a new condition. We conclude with the following example which illuminates the role of core-inclusion.

Example 4.18. Let $G = (8,7)$ (see remark 2.14) and let $A = \{a, b, c\}$. By remark 4.9 $C(R^N) \neq \varnothing$ for all $R^N \in L^N$. We define a SCC $H: L^N \to 2^A$ by the following rule. Let $R^N \in L^N$. An alternative $x \in A$ is *blocked* (relative to R^N) if

$$| \{i \mid i \in N \text{ and } t_3(R^i) = x\} | \geqslant 3 \quad \text{(see notation 3.15)}.$$

We define now $H(R^N)$ to be the set of unblocked alternatives in $C(R^N)$. As the reader can easily verify, $H(R^N) \neq \varnothing$ for all $R^N \in L^N$. Thus, H satisfies the Condorcet condition. Also, H is Paretian, anonymous and neutral and $G^*(H) = G$ (see definition 3.4). Thus, H is a faithful representation of G. Furthermore, one can show that H has the strong positive association property (see definition 2.10) and $G_\alpha(H) = (8,6)$ (see definition 3.8). Thus, H consists of a representation of G which has all the "desirable" properties except tightness (see definition 3.32). Clearly, H violates core-inclusion.

References

Aumann, R.J. (1961) "The Core of a Cooperative Game Without Side Payments", *Transactions of the American Mathematical Society*, 98, 539–552.

Gardner, R. (1977) "The Borda Game", *Public Choice*, 30, 43–50.

Gillies, D.B. (1959) "Solutions to General Non-zero-Sum Games", in: A.W. Tucker and R.D. Luce, eds., *Contributions to the Theory of Games*, vol. IV, Annals of Mathematics Studies, no. 40 (Princeton University Press, Princeton, N.J.), pp. 47–85.

Moulin, H. (1982) "Voting with Proportional Veto Power", *Econometrica*, 50, 145-162.

Nakamura, K. (1979) "The Vetoers in a Simple Game with Ordinal Preferences", *International Journal of Game Theory*, 8, 55–61.

Peleg, B. (1980) "A Theory of Coalition Formation in Committees", *Journal of Mathematical Economics*, 7, 115–134.

Shapley, L.S. (1962) "Simple Games: An Outline of the Descriptive Theory", *Behavioral Science*, 7, 59–66.

CHAPTER 15

Equilibria in simple dynamic games

NORMAN SCHOFIELD*

University of Essex and University of Manchester

1. Introduction

It is well known that general voting games may be badly behaved, in the sense of generating cycles, when either the number of alternatives or the nature of preferences is unrestricted. However, if the set of alternatives is one-dimensional and preference is reasonably well behaved, then a core, or set of unbeaten outcomes, may exist. This formed the basis of Downs' (1957) suggestion that there might be a convergence of party platforms in the one-dimensional case. Even when preference is non-convex, but satisfies a regularity condition, then a "local" core will exist (Kramer and Klevorick, 1974; Salles and Wendell, 1977) in a large class of voting games. Even in this case voting cycles may exist.

On the other hand, in two dimensions the analysis of Plott (1967) suggested that a majority rule core would be unlikely to exist. A result by McKelvey (1976) showed that with no core, if the policy space W was the entire two-dimensional plane, then *discontinuous* voting trajectories could cover the whole of W. In contrast to this result Tullock (1967) argued that *continuous* voting cycles would be constrained to the Pareto set, and that these "Paretian cycles" would become less significant as the number of voters increases.

Here we examine a set called IC which consists precisely of those points which support continuous local voting cycles. We show that for any voting game σ there

* This material is based upon work undertaken under the SSRC/CNRS research exchange scheme. I am grateful to Herve Moulin, Maurice Salles and George Bordes for stimulating discussions.

Social Choice and Welfare, edited by P.K. Pattanaik and M. Salles
© *North-Holland Publishing Company, 1983*

is an integer $v^*(\sigma)$ such that when the dimension of the policy space W is no greater than $v^*(\sigma)$, then local cycles cannot exist, while if dimension $(W) = v^*(\sigma) + 1$, then local cycles, if they exist, will be constrained to the Pareto set. The integer $v^*(\sigma)$ can be readily calculated from the Nakamura (1978) number of the game. For example, with majority rule, for a society of odd size, $v^*(\sigma) = 1$. Thus, we obtain a proof of Tullock's conjecture that continuous voting cycles will be Paretian in two dimensions.

It is also known from previous work that any voting games without a collegium of vetoers has an *unstable* dimension $w^*(\sigma)$. If the dimension of the policy space is at least $w^*(\sigma)$, then a core can almost never exist (Schofield, 1980). Indeed, for majority rule $w^*(\sigma)$ will be either two or three (Schofield, 1981a). In higher dimensions the cycle set, IC, will be open dense in W. Even in three dimensions, therefore, majority rule procedure may be badly behaved.

However, when W is a convex compact Euclidean space and IC is empty, then a set, IO, of voting optima will be non-empty. Moreover, if individual preference is convex then IO coincides with the usual notion of the core (Schofield, 1981b).

Of particular interest is the q-majority game, where any coalition containing at least q players, out of the society of n players, is winning. When $q = n$, then define $v^*(\sigma)$ to be infinity. If $q < n$, then $v^*(\sigma)$ is the largest integer which is strictly less than $q/(n - q)$.

Greenberg (1979) has previously shown that when dimension $(W) < q/(n - q)$ and preference is convex, then the q-majority core is non-empty. The results presented here extend Greenberg's theorem to general voting games and also clarify the role played by the convexity and compactness assumptions of his theorem.

In the conclusion it is suggested that it is precisely when the cycle set IC is non-empty that preference and agenda manipulation may be possible.

In section 2 the basic definitions and statements of the main theorem are presented. Section 3 gives the proof of the theorem, while section 4 computes the Nakamura number for various voting games. The conclusion gives some examples and discusses the relationship between the results on voting in discrete and spatial alternative sets.

2. Optima and cycles

We assume that the policy space W is a smooth locally Euclidean topological manifold of dimension w. More conveniently, W may be regarded as a w-dimensional Euclidean space. At each point x in W, let $T_x W$ be the tangent space at x. For x in the interior of W, $T_x W$ may be identified with a copy of R^w, and this induces a unique linear structure on $T_x W$. For x in the boundary of W, $T_x W$ is identified with a closed half space in R^w. Let $TW = \cup \{T_x W : x \in W\}$.

A preference for an individual i is represented by a correspondence or preference field $h_i : W \to TW$, where for each $x \in W$, $h_i(x)$ is a cone in $T_x W$.

The cone $h_i(x)$ may be regarded as the set of directions at x that individual i prefers.

For example, if preference of individual i is represented by a smooth utility function $u_i : W \to R$, then $h_i(x) = \{v \in T_x W : du_i(x)(v) > 0\}$, where $du_i(x)$ is the direction gradient of the utility function at x.

A *profile* for a society N of size n is a family of preference fields $h = (h_1, ..., h_n)$. We assume for each i and for each $x \in W$ that

(a) $h_i(x)$ is open in $T_x W$, and

(b) there exists a linear map $d_i(x) : T_x W \to R$ such that $d_i(x)(v) > 0$ for all $v \in h_i(x)$.

Note that (a) and (b) are analogues of the continuity and convexity assumptions A.2 and A.3 of Greenberg (1979).

The class of profiles satisfying assumptions (a) and (b) we shall write as $\mathscr{C}(W)^N$; a profile in $\mathscr{C}(W)^N$ we shall call continuous. When individual preference can be represented by a smooth utility function, we shall call it *smooth* and let $P(W)^N$ represent the class of smooth profiles. Clearly, $P(W)^N$ is a subset of $\mathscr{C}(W)^N$.

For a continuous preference field $h_i \in \mathscr{C}(W)$, define a preference ρ_i on W as follows. Write $x \rho_i y$ if and only if there is a smooth integral path $c : (-1, 1) \to W$ for h_i such that $c(0) = y$ and $\lim_{t \to 1} c(t) = x$ such that for each $t \in [0, 1)$ the direction gradient of c at $z = c(t)$ belongs to $h_i(z)$. For example, if preference is represented by smooth utility, then $x \rho_i y$ if and only if there is a smooth path from y to x along which utility increases.

For $h \in \mathscr{C}(W)^N$ define the critical optima set for i to be

$$IO(W, i, h) = \{x : h_i(x) = \varnothing\}.$$

Clearly, if $y \in IO(W, i, h)$, then $x \rho_i y$ for no x in W.

For a coalition M in N, define the M-preference field $h_M : W \to TW$ by $h_M(x) = \cap \{h_i(x) : i \in M\}$.

When each h_i satisfies assumptions (a) and (b) above, then so does h_M. Define $x \rho_M y$, as above, when there is an integral path for h_M from y to x, and let

$$IO(W, M, h) = \{x : h_M(x) = \varnothing\}$$

be the *critical optima set* for coalition M. For a cone A in $T_x W$, define the dual cone A^* in $T_x W$ by

$$A^* = \{b \in T_x W : (a \cdot b) > 0 \quad \text{for all} \quad a \in A\},$$

where $(\cdot)$ is the scalar product induced on $T_x W$. In particular, if $h_i \in \mathscr{C}(W)$, then we shall write $p_i(x)$ for the dual cone $h_i(x)^*$ at x. When $h_i \in P(W)$, then $p_i(x)$ may be regarded as the direction of most preferred change at x. If $h_i(x) = \varnothing$, then for convenience define $p_i(x) = T_x W$. For coalition M, define $p_M(x)$ to be the convex hull of $\{p_i(x): i \in M\}$. Since we assume each $h_i(x)$ is open in $T_x W$, the dual $p_i(x)$ is closed in $T_x W$ (Schofield, 1981c) and therefore so is $p_M(x)$. Moreover, if $h_M(x)$ is non-empty, then $p_M(x) = [h_M(x)]^*$.

On the other hand, if x is an interior point of W, then $h_M(x) = \varnothing$ iff $\{p_i(x), i \in M\}$ are semipositively dependent, i.e. $0 \in p_M(x)$ (Smale, 1973).

We consider an arbitrary voting game σ which is characterized by a family of winning coalitions $\mathscr{D}$. Let h be a profile. Then at a point x the set of directions which are *socially preferred* is defined to be $h_\sigma(x) = \cup \{h_M(x): M \in \mathscr{D}\}$. Call h_σ: $W \to TW$ the *social preference* field. Clearly, $h_\sigma(x)$ will be open in $T_x W$ for each x in W.

The social preference relation defined by σ on the profile h is $\sigma(h) = \rho_\sigma = \cup \{\rho_M: M \in \mathscr{D}\}$. Thus, $x\rho_\sigma y$ iff $x\rho_M y$ for some $M \in \mathscr{D}$. If x_0 belongs to W, and U is an open neighbourhood of x_0 say, there is a ρ_σ-cycle in U through x_0 iff there is a finite sequence of points $\{x_1, ..., x_r\}$ all in U such that $x_0 \rho_\sigma x_r \rho_\sigma x_{r-1}$ ... $\rho_\sigma x_1 \rho_\sigma x_0$, where as before $y\rho_\sigma z$ iff $y\rho_M z$ for some $M \in \mathscr{D}$ and each smooth path from x_{j-1} to x_j, for $j = 1, ..., r$, and the path from x_r to x_0 stays within U.

Definition 1. Let σ be a voting game and h a continuous profile on a smooth policy space. Define

(i)   the *infinitesimal optima set*:

$$IO(W, \sigma, h) = \{x: h_\sigma(x) = \varnothing\};$$

(ii)   the *infinitesimal cycle set*:

$$IC(W, \sigma, h) = \{x: [h_\sigma(x)]^* = \varnothing\};$$

(iii)   the *local cycle set* $LC(W, \sigma, h)$ by $x \in LC(W, \sigma, h)$ iff for any neighbourhood U of x there exists a ρ_σ-cycle in U through x.

From results in Schofield (1981c) it is known that when $h \in \mathscr{C}(W)^N$, then

$$LC(W, \sigma, h) \subset \overline{IC}(W, \sigma, h),$$

where $\overline{A}$ stands for the closure of a set A in W.

If, moreover, each individual preference field satisfies a natural integrability property, then $IC(W, \sigma, h)$ will be open, and

$$IC(W, \sigma, h) \subset LC(W, \sigma, h).$$

In particular, this will be true if $h \in P(W)^N$ (see Schofield, 1978a, 1978b).

The main theorem we prove in this chapter is that for a voting game σ there is an integer $v^*(\sigma)$ such that dimension $(W) \leqslant v^*(\sigma)$ implies that $IC(W, \sigma, h)$ must be empty for all $h \in \mathscr{C}(W)^N$.

To define $v^*(\sigma)$ we introduce the Nakamura number for σ.

Let $\mathscr{D}$ be an arbitrary collection of subsets of N, and define the $\mathscr{D}$-collegium $C(\mathscr{D})$ by

$$C(\mathscr{D}) = \cap \{M : M \in \mathscr{D}\}.$$

For a voting game σ, with its collection $\mathscr{D}$ of winning coalitions, call σ *collegial* if $C(\mathscr{D})$ is non-empty. Define $v(\sigma)$ to be infinity in this case. If $C(\mathscr{D})$ is empty call σ *non-collegial*. In this case define the Nakamura (1978) number by

$$v(\sigma) = \min \{|\mathscr{D}'| : \mathscr{D}' \subset \mathscr{D} \text{ and } C(\mathscr{D}') = \varnothing\}.$$

Define the *stability dimension* $v^*(\sigma)$ of σ by $v^*(\sigma) = v(\sigma) - 2$.

Theorem 1. Let σ be a voting game on a smooth manifold W of dimension w.
 (i) If $w \leqslant v^*(\sigma)$, then $IC(W, \sigma, h)$ is empty for all $h \in \mathscr{C}(W)^N$.
 (ii) If $w = v^*(\sigma) + 1$, then $IC(W, \sigma, h)$ if non-empty, belongs to $IO(W, N, h)$, the infinitesimal optima set for the society.
 (iii) If $w \geqslant v^*(\sigma) + 1$, then it is possible to find a profile $h \in \mathscr{C}(W)^N$ such that $IC(W, \sigma, h)$ is non-empty, and $IO(W, \sigma, h)$ is empty. ∎

The significance of part (i) of this theorem is that when W has nice properties, then the emptiness of $IC(W, \sigma, h)$ implies the non-emptiness of $IO(W, \sigma, h)$. When the state space W is a compact convex w-dimensional subset of Euclidean space, then call W *admissible*.

Theorem 2 (Schofield, 1981b). If σ is a voting game on an admissible state space W, and $h \in \mathscr{C}(W)^N$ is such that $IC(W, \sigma, h)$ is empty, then $IO(w, \sigma, h)$ is non-empty. ∎

Suppose now that for each individual i preference is represented by a discrete preference relation P_i. For the voting game σ with a discrete profile $P = (P_1, ..., P_n)$ the *global optima set* is

$$GO(W, \sigma, P) = \{x: \text{ there exists no } M \in \mathscr{D} \text{ and no } y \in W \text{ st.}$$

$$yP_i x \text{ for all } i \in M\}.$$

Kramer and Klevorick (1974) have also examined the *local optima set* when W is a topological space:

$$LO(W, \sigma, P) = \{x: \text{ there exists a nbd. } U \text{ of } x \text{ in } W \text{ such that for no } M \in \mathscr{D}$$

$$\text{and for no } y \in U \text{ is } yP_i x \text{ for all } i \in M\}.$$

For a discrete profile $P = (P_1, ..., P_n)$ it is possible to construct a profile of preference fields $h = (h_1, ..., h_n)$ such that

$$GO(W, \sigma, P) \subset IO(W, \sigma, h).$$

Indeed, if each discrete individual preference is convex, in the sense that for all $y \in W$, the set $\{x \in W: xP_i y\}$ is a convex set in W, then

$$GO(W, \sigma, P) = IO(W, \sigma, h).$$

Consequently, when W is admissible of dimension no greater than $v^*(\sigma)$, and preference is convex, then a global optima set, or core, must exist.

The set $IO(W, \sigma, h)$ is the analogue for a social preference relation of the set of critical points of a single utility function. The analysis of Smale (1974) suggests that it is possible to define a generalized Hessian at points in $IO(W, \sigma, h)$ to determine their stability properties. Indeed, the result of Kramer and Klevorick (1974) on the existence of local optima suggests that $IO(W, \sigma, h)$ will always contain local optima when W is compact.

3.   Cycles in low dimensions

We seek to show that $IC(W, \sigma, h)$ must be empty in dimension less than $v^*(\sigma)$, and to do this we examine $[h_\sigma(x)]^*$ at any point $x \in W$. At x, and for profile h, let $\mathscr{D}(x) = \{M \in \mathscr{D} : h_M(x) \neq \varnothing\}$. From Schofield (1978a, lemma 2.1):

$$[h_\sigma(x)]^* \ = \ [\cup\{h_M(x): M \in \mathcal{D}(x)\}]^*$$
$$= \ \cap\{[h_M(x)]^*: M \in \mathcal{D}(x)\}$$
$$= \ \cap\{p_M(x): M \in \mathcal{D}(x)\}.$$
$$= \ p_\sigma(x).$$

For coalition M and profile h, let

$$IC(W, M, h) = \{x: [h_M(x)]^* = \varnothing\}.$$

Note that when $h \in \mathscr{C}(W)^N$, then by assumption (b) $[h_M(x)]^* \neq \varnothing$ for all $x \in W$. Thus, assumption (b) guarantees that individual and coalition preference is locally acyclic, and that $p_M(x) \neq \varnothing$ for all x in W.

Lemma 1. Let $\mathcal{D}'$ be any subset of $\mathcal{D}$, and h a profile. Then if $C(\mathcal{D}') \neq \varnothing$:
   (i) $\cap\{p_M(x): M \in \mathcal{D}'\} \neq \varnothing$ at any x in W, and
   (ii) $IO(W, C(\mathcal{D}'), h) \subset \cap\{IO(W, M, h): M \in \mathcal{D}'\}$.

Proof.
   (i)   For any $i \in C(\mathcal{D}')$ and any $x \in W$, $p_i(x) \in p_M(x)$ for $M \in \mathcal{D}'$. (Note here that we define $p_M(x) = T_x W$ when $h_M(x) = \varnothing$.) Thus, $p_i(x) \in \cap\{p_M(x): M \in \mathcal{D}'\} \neq \varnothing$.
   (ii)   If $x \in IO(W, C(\mathcal{D}'), h)$ then

$$\cap\{h_i(x): i \in C(\mathcal{D}')\} = \varnothing.$$

But since $C(\mathcal{D}') \subset M$ for each $M \in \mathcal{D}'$.

$$\cap\{h_i(x): i \in M\} = \varnothing \ \text{ for } \ M \in \mathcal{D}'. \quad \blacksquare$$

Lemma 2. If σ is a collegial voting game, then for any $h \in \mathscr{C}(W)^N$, $IC(W, \sigma, h) = \varnothing$. If W is admissible, then $IO(W, \sigma, h) \neq \varnothing$.

Proof.
By lemma 1, since $C(\mathcal{D}) \neq \varnothing$, $[h_\sigma(x)]^* \neq \varnothing$ at any $x \in W$. Thus, $IC(W, \sigma, h) = \varnothing$. Moreover, when W is admissible, then by proposition 1, $IO(W, C(\mathcal{D}), h)$, and thus $IO(W, \sigma, h)$ are both non-empty. $\quad \blacksquare$

Note that this lemma proves theorem 1 in the case when σ is collegial. We now consider the case of a non-collegial voting game.

To prove theorem 1 in this case, let W be a smooth manifold, let h be an arbitrary profile in $\mathscr{C}(W)^N$, and let x be any point in W. For each $i, p_i(x)$ is a "closed" cone in $T_x W$, not containing the origin. Let $\theta : T_x W \overset{\sim}{\approx} R^w$ be the linear isomorphism between $T_x W$ and Euclidean space of dimension $(W) = w$, and let $p_i'(x)$ be the image of $p_i(x)$ under θ. For each i, select a unit vector $q_i(x)$ in R^w belonging to $p_i'(x)$. For each coalition $M \in \mathscr{D}(x)$, let $q_M(x)$ be the convex hull of $\{q_i(x): i \in M\}$. Note that $q_M(x)$ is convex, compact, and that $q_M(x) \subset \theta(p_M(x))$.

Helly's theorem (Berge, 1963). Let $C_1, ..., C_{w+k}$ $(k > 0)$ be a family of compact, convex sets in R^w. If the intersection of any subfamily of cardinality $(w + 1)$ is non-empty, then the intersection of the family is non-empty.

Lemma 3. Let σ be a voting game with Nakamura number $v(\sigma)$. If dim $(W) \leqslant v(\sigma) - 2$, then $IC(W, \sigma, h) = \varnothing$ for all $h \in \mathscr{C}(W)^N$.

Proof. Let h be any profile, x be any point in W, and

$$\mathscr{D}(x) = \{M \in \mathscr{D} : h_M(x) \neq \varnothing\}.$$

Let $\mathscr{D}'$ be any subfamily of $\mathscr{D}(x)$ with cardinality $|\mathscr{D}'| \leqslant v(\sigma) - 1$. By the definition of the Nakamura number $C(\mathscr{D}') \neq \varnothing$. Consider $q(\mathscr{D}') = \cap \{q_M(x): M \in \mathscr{D}'\}$. As in lemma 1(i), for any $i \in C(\mathscr{D}'), q_i(x) \in q(\mathscr{D}')$. But since each $q_M(x)$ is a compact convex set in R^w, and $w \leqslant v(\sigma) - 2$, by Helly's theorem

$$q(\mathscr{D}) = \cap \{q_M(x): M \in \mathscr{D}(x)\} \text{ is non-empty.}$$

But $q(\mathscr{D}) \subset p'(\mathscr{D}) = \cap \{p_M'(x): M \in \mathscr{D}(x)\}$. Moreover, $\theta^{-1}(q'(\mathscr{D})) \subset p_\sigma(x)$. Thus, $p_\sigma(x)$ is non-empty. Since this is true at every point in $W, IC(W, \sigma, h)$ is empty for all $h \in \mathscr{C}(W)^N$. ∎

This proves theorem 1(i). To prove the second part, consider a point x *outside* the Pareto set $IO(W, N, h)$. This implies that the sets $\{p_i(x): i \in N\}$ are not semipositively dependent. Thus, there exists an open half-space Z in $T_x W$ defined by

$$Z = \{z \in T_x W: (z \cdot p) > 0\} \quad \text{for some} \quad p \in T_x W,$$

such that $p_i(x) \in Z$, for each $i \in N$.

Now let $p^\perp = \{v \in T_x W: (v \cdot p) = 0\}$, and V be the image of $p^\perp$ under the chart $\theta : T_x W = R^w$. Note that V will be a linear subspace of R^w of dimension $(w - 1)$.

Lemma 4. If σ is a voting game with Nakamura number $v(\sigma)$, and dimension $(W) \leqslant v(\sigma) - 1$, then

$$LC(W, \sigma, h) \subset IO(W, N, h) \quad \text{for all} \quad h \in \mathscr{C}(W)^N.$$

Proof. Assume $x \notin IO(W, N, h)$. For each $M \in \mathscr{D}(x)$, $p_M(x)$ belongs to the open half-space Z in $T_x W$. Thus, $q_M(x)$ will belong to the open half-space $\theta(Z)$ in R^w. Now let

$$s: \theta(Z) \subset R^w \rightarrow V \subset R^{w-1}$$

be the cononical projection of $\theta(Z)$ onto the equatorial plane V in R^{w-1}.

As in the proof of theorem 1(i), any subfamily $\mathscr{D}'$ of $\mathscr{D}(x)$ of cardinality at most $v(\sigma) - 1$ has non-empty intersection.

But each set $s(q_M(x))$ is a compact convex set in V in R^{w-1}. Moreover $q(\mathscr{D}')$ $= \cap \{q_M(x): M \in \mathscr{D}'\}$ is non-empty. Thus, $s(q(\mathscr{D}')) = \cap \{s(q_M(x)): M \in \mathscr{D}'\}$ is non-empty. Since $w \leqslant v(\sigma) - 1$, dimension $(V) \leqslant v(\sigma) - 2$. Again by Helly's theorem:

$$s(q(\mathscr{D})) = \cap \{s(q_M(x)): M \in \mathscr{D}(x)\} \quad \text{must be non-empty.}$$

But as before, $s(q(\mathscr{D})) \subset s(p'(\mathscr{D}))$ and so $p_\sigma(x)$ must be non-empty, and thus $x \notin IC(W, \sigma, h)$. Hence, $IC(W, \sigma, h) \subset IO(W, N, h)$. But when $h \in \mathscr{C}(W)^N$, $IO(W, N, h)$ is a closed set (since it is given by semipositive dependencies). Moreover, $LC(W, \sigma, h)$ belongs to the closure of $IC(W, \sigma, h)$. Thus, $LC(W, \sigma, h) \subset \overline{IC}(W, \sigma, h) \subset IO(W, N, h)$ and this proves the lemma. ∎

Note that this proves theorem 1(ii). To prove the third part of the theorem we introduce the following notion.

Definition 2. Let h be a profile in $\mathscr{C}(W)^N$, and $\mathscr{D}$ the class of σ-winning coalitions. At $x \in W$, let $\mathscr{D}(x) = \{M \subset N: h_M(x) \neq \varnothing\}$ as before. Say that h *covers the tangent space at* x with respect to σ iff for any *non-zero* vector $v \in T_x W$, there is some $M \in \mathscr{D}(x)$ such that $v \in p_M(x)$.

Lemma 5. If h covers the tangent space at x w.r.t. σ, then $x \in IC(W, \sigma, h)$.

Proof. Suppose that h covers the tangent space, but that $x \notin IC(W, \sigma, h)$. Then $p_\sigma(x) \neq \varnothing$. Let p be a tangent vector in $p_\sigma(x)$. By definition $p \in p_M(x)$ for every $M \in \mathscr{D}(x)$. But since $(-p)$ is a non-zero tangent vector, by assumption there is some $M \in \mathscr{D}(x)$ such that both $(-p)$ and (p) belong to $p_M(x)$. But $(-p)$ and (p) are semipositively dependent, which implies $h_M(x) = \varnothing$, contrary to the assumption that $M \in \mathscr{D}(x)$. Hence, $x \in IC(W, \sigma, h)$. ∎

Corollary 6. If σ is a voting game with Nakamura number $v(\sigma)$ and W is a smooth manifold of dimension $\geqslant v(\sigma) - 1$, then there is a profile $h \in P(W)^N$ such that $LC(W, \sigma, h) = W$ and $IO(W, \sigma, h)$ is empty.

Proof. Choose unit vectors $\{q_i : i \in N\}$ in R^w such that there exists a subfamily $\mathscr{D}'$ of $v(\sigma)$ distinct coalitions such that for each $M \in \mathscr{D}'$, $\{q_i : i \in M\}$ are semipositively independent. By the definition of $v(\sigma)$ it is possible to choose $\mathscr{D}'$ such that $C(\mathscr{D}') = \varnothing$. Moreover, $\{q_i : i \in N\}$ can be chosen such that for any non-zero vector $p \in R^w$ there exists some $M \in \mathscr{D}'$ and $\lambda > 0$ such that $\lambda p \in q_M$.

Construct a profile h for N on W as follows. For each open set U chart θ and $x \in U$, and $i \in N$. Let $\theta(p_i(x)) = (q_i)$. By the construction $\mathscr{D}' \subset \mathscr{D}(x)$, and h covers the tangent space at x. Thus, $IC(W, \sigma, h)$ includes the interior of the manifold W.

By the construction $W = LC(W, \sigma, h)$, and so $IO(W, \sigma, h)$ is empty. ∎

The idea of corollary 6 is that in dimension $v(\sigma) - 1$ it is always possible to find direction gradients at a particular point so that the directions satisfy the pointwise property of "infinitesimal cyclicity". The profile $h \in P(W)^N$ is then constructed so that preferences at each point are "locally cyclic". As a consequence $IO(W, N, h)$ must be empty. Clearly, corollary 6 gives the proof of theorem 1(iii).

Lemmas 3 and 5 together imply that in dimension $v(\sigma) - 2$, at no point may a profile cover the tangent space.

4. Classification of voting games

Consider a q-majority game, σ_q, whose winning coalitions are defined by $\mathscr{D} = \{M \subset N : |M| \geqslant q\}$, and suppose $q < n$. Define $v(n, q)$ to be the largest integer which is strictly less than $q/(n - q)$.

Lemma 7. For a non-collegial q-game, σ_q, $v(\sigma_q) = v(n, q) + 2$.

Proof. Greenberg (1979, lemma 1) has shown that a necessary and sufficient condition for every subfamily $\mathscr{D}'$, of cardinality $|\mathscr{D}'| = r$, to have non-empty intersection is $q > [(r-1)/r] n$. This inequality can be written $r < [q/(n-q)] + 1$.

Thus, $|\mathscr{D}'| \leqslant 1 + v(n, q)$ implies that $C(\mathscr{D}') \neq \varnothing$. Hence, $1 + v(n, q) < v(\sigma_q)$. On the other hand, if $r \geqslant [q/(n-q)] + 1$, then it is possible to find a subfamily $\mathscr{D}'$ of $\mathscr{D}$ with cardinality r such that $C(\mathscr{D}')$ is empty. But $1 + v(n, q) < 1 + [q/(n-q)] \leqslant 2 + v(n, q)$. Hence, there exists a subfamily $\mathscr{D}'$ of $\mathscr{D}$ of cardinality $|\mathscr{D}'| = 2 + v(n, q)$ such that $C(\mathscr{D})$ is empty.

Thus, the Nakamura number $v(\sigma_q)$ of the q-game is $v(\sigma_q) = 2 + v(n, q)$. ∎

Note that the *stability* dimension $v^*(\sigma_q)$ of a q-game is precisely $v(n, q)$.

As an example consider the q-majority game given by $(n, q) = (4, 3)$. Clearly, $v(n, q) = 2$. For a two-dimensional manifold local cycles for such a game cannot exist. When W is admissible, then by proposition 1 an infinitesimal optima set must exist. Indeed, proposition 1 can be extended to the case where W is a smooth topologically complete manifold with non-zero Euler characteristic (Schofield, 1981d). Thus, for example, the optima set must be non-empty for this voting game on a two-dimensional sphere.

In general, however, for simple majority rule the stability dimension $v^*(\sigma) = 1$.

Lemma 8. If σ is simple majority rule (other than the case $(n, q) = (4, 3)$), then $v^*(\sigma) = 1$.

Proof. Majority rule is a q-rule, where $q = k + 1$ when $n = 2k$ or $2k + 1$. Thus, $q/(n-q) = (k + 1)/k$ or $(k + 1)/(k - 1)$ depending on whether n is odd or even. For n odd, $k \geqslant 1$ and so $1 + 1/k > v^*(\sigma)$, or $v^*(\sigma) = 1$. For n even, $k \geqslant 3$ and so $1 + 2/k > v^*(\sigma)$ or $v^*(\sigma) = 1$. ∎

A voting game σ is called *proper* iff any two winning coalitions have non-empty intersection. The game is called *strong* iff whenever M is not winning then its complement $N - M$ is winning.

Lemma 9.

(i) If σ is proper, then $v(\sigma) \geqslant 3$.

(ii) If σ is proper, strong, and there exist two distinct minimal winning coalitions, then $v(\sigma) = 3$.

(iii) For any non-collegial voting game $v(\sigma) \leqslant n$.

Proof.

(i) Suppose σ is proper and there exist $M_1, M_2 \in \mathscr{D}$. Since $M_1 \cap M_2 \neq \varnothing$ it is clear that $v(\sigma) - 1 \geqslant 2$.

(ii) Suppose M_1, M_2 are distinct minimal winning coalitions. Then $M_1 \cap M_2$ will be non-empty and non-winning. Thus, $M_3 = N - (M_1 \cap M_2) \in \mathscr{D}$. But then $M_1 \cap M_2 \cap M_3 = \varnothing$. Hence, $v(\sigma) = 3$.

(iii) For a non-collegial voting game $C(\mathscr{D}) = \varnothing$. Consequently, for each coalition $M \in \mathscr{D}$ there exists some distinct individual $i_M \in M$ such that $i_M \notin \cup \{L \in \mathscr{D} : L \neq M\}$.

It is therefore always possible to find a subfamily $\mathscr{D}'$ of $\mathscr{D}$, where $|\mathscr{D}'| \leqslant n$ such that $C(\mathscr{D}') = \varnothing$. Hence, $v(\sigma) \leqslant n$. ∎

It is known that for any non-collegial voting game there is an instability dimension $w^*(\sigma)$ such that dimension $(W) \geqslant w^*(\sigma)$ implies that for nearly all $h \in P(W)^N$, $IO(W, \sigma, h)$ is either empty or contained in the boundary of W. By the contrapositive of proposition 1 this implies that $IC(W, \sigma, h)$ is "often" non-empty. In dimension at least $w^*(\sigma) + 1$, the set $IC(W, \sigma, h)$ will be dense in W. From the results in Schofield (1980, 1981a) the instability dimensions for majority rule are known to be two or three depending on whether n is odd or even. Note that it is necessary that $v^*(\sigma) < w^*(\sigma)$ for any voting game.

For example, for a non-collegial q-majority game, σ_q, we have $v^*(\sigma_q) = v(n, q) < q/(n-q) < q$, and $w^*(\sigma_q) \leqslant q$.

For a general non-collegial voting game, σ, $v^*(\sigma) \leqslant n-2$, while $w^*(\sigma) \leqslant n-1$ (see table 15.1).

Table 15.1
Classification of voting games

Dimension (W)	W a manifold	W admissible
$v^*(\sigma)$	$IC(W, \sigma, h) = \phi$	$IO(W, \sigma, h) \neq \phi$
$v^*(\sigma) + 1$	$IC(W, \sigma, h) \subset IO(W, N, h)$	
$w^*(\sigma)$	$IO(W, \sigma, h)$ in ∂W or empty for nearly all $h \in P(W)^N$	$IC(W, \sigma, h)$ often non-empty
$w^*(\sigma) + 1$	$IC(W, \sigma, h)$ nearly always dense	

Voting game	$v^*(\sigma)$	$w^*(\sigma)$
Majority rule:		
n odd	1	2
$(n, q) = (4, 3)$	2	3
n even otherwise	1	3
General q-game	$< \dfrac{q}{n-q} \leqslant q$	$\leqslant q$
Non-collegial game	$\leqslant n-2$	$\leqslant n-1$

5. Conclusion: example and discussion

As an example consider simple majority rule with n odd. When W is a one-dimensional subset of the real line, and preference is convex, then a global core $GO(W, \sigma, h)$ is non-empty. When preference h is non-convex then, as Kramer and Klevorick (1974) have shown, the discrete preference relation $\sigma(h)$ may contain cycles, although there will exist a local optima set. Theorem 1 shows, however, that no continuous cycles exist in one dimension. If we consider an incremental model of political change in one dimension, then policy-makers will change position continuously to increase votes and eventually come to the optima set.

It is known from McKelvey's work that, when the state space is R^2, there can exist discrete voting cycles throughout the space. Experimental results by Fiorina and Plott (1978) and Laing and Olmstead (1978) have found that voting outcomes are not in general scattered throughout the state space, but are restricted to the Pareto set, and typically belong to the local cycle set (Schofield, 1978b).

Consider fig. 15.1 which represents the game $(n, q) = (3,2)$ with Euclidean preferences (McKelvey, 1976) in two dimensions. The optima sets for the three individuals are marked $IO(i)$. At a point x in the interior of the Pareto set $IO(\{1, 2, 3\})$, the tangent space is covered by $\{p_{12}(x), p_{13}(x), p_{23}(x)\}$ and so x belongs to $IC(W, \sigma, h)$.

Indeed, $LC(W, \sigma, h)$ is identical to the Pareto set $IO(W, N, h)$: see Kramer (1973) and Schofield (1977). At point y outside $IO(W, N, h)$ the "social direction gradient" $p_\sigma(y)$ "points towards" $IC(W, \sigma, h)$. If we imagine a myopic voting process occurring, then at a point such as y it is possible to implement coherent vote-maximizing policies which lead to the Pareto set.

This phenomenon was observed by Tullock (1967) who argued that voting cycles, when they occurred, would be restricted to the Pareto set. Moreover, if we consider the family of majority rules $(k + 1, 2k + 1)$ as $k \to \infty$, then the cycle set IC becomes less significant in relation to the Pareto set (Schofield, 1981b).

However, in the case with n odd in three dimensions the cycle set IC will not belong to the Pareto set. In particular this means that a myopic voting process will not necessarily lead towards the Pareto set.

For a q-majority game, σ_q, on a finite set of alternatives, W, of cardinality r it is known that when $q > [(r-1)/r]\, n$, then the voting game is acyclic (Ferejohn and Grether, 1974) and thus has a core. When this inequality is satisfied, the game is consistent in the sense of being insensitive to preference manipulation (Peleg, 1978). We may also write this inequality as $r = |W| \leqslant 1 + v^*(\sigma_q)$. For a discrete voting game, σ, Nakamura (1978) has shown that when $|W| \leqslant 1 + v^*(\sigma)$, then a core to the voting game exists.

On the other hand, if $|W| \geqslant n$, then there is no non-collegial voting game on

W which is acyclic (Brown, 1975) and non-manipulable (Ferejohn and Grether, 1979).

Since the instability dimension, $w^*(\sigma)$, for a non-collegial spatial voting game is bounded above by $(n - 1)$, this strongly suggests that, for a general non-colle-

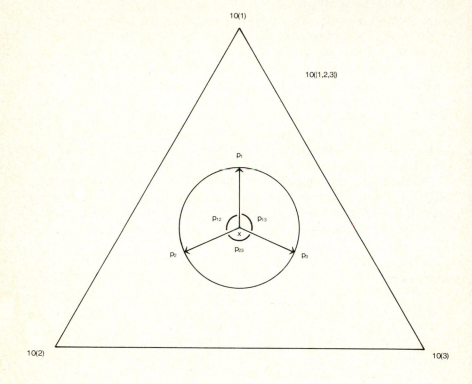

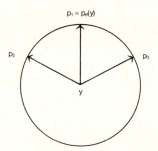

Figure 15.1. The game $(n, q) = (3,2)$ in two dimensions showing a locally cyclic point (x) and a locally acyclic point (y).

gial voting games, σ on a discrete alternative set W, when $|W| \geqslant 1 + w^*(\sigma)$, then σ may be both cyclic and manipulable.

Finally, Ferejohn, Grether and McKelvey (1982) have examined the question of manipulation of voting rules in the spatial context. They show that for a voting rule, σ, on a topological space, W, that

   (i)   if σ is a majority rule and dim $(W) \geqslant 2$, then σ is manipulable, and

   (ii)   if σ is a general non-collegial rule and dim $(W) \geqslant n$, then σ is manipulable.

Indeed, their analysis indicates that it is precisely when $IC(W, \sigma, h)$ is non-empty that the voting rule is susceptible to preference manipulation. Thus, we suggest the generalization that when dimension $(W) > v^*(\sigma)$ there exists a profile h on W such that $\sigma(h)$ is preference-manipulable.

Moreover, the results of Slutsky (1979) indicate that when a point, x, belongs to $IC(W, \sigma, h)$, then it is possible to construct an institutional arrangement such that x becomes a structure induced equilibrium (Shepsle, 1979). In particular, when $IC(W, \sigma, h)$ is not constrained to the Pareto set $IO(W, N, h)$, then institutional arrangements (or agenda manipulation) may lead to non-Paretian outcomes.

There appears, therefore, to be a close correspondence between the characterization of voting games by the cardinality of the alternative set, W, in the discrete case, and the dimensionality of the space, W, in the topological case.

References

Berge, C. (1963) *Topological Spaces* (Oliver and Boyd, London).

Brown, D.J. (1975) "Aggregation of Preferences", *Quarterly Journal of Economics*, 89, 456–469.

Downs, A. (1957) *Economic Theory of Democracy* (Harper and Row, New York).

Ferejohn, J.A. and D.M. Grether (1974) "On a Class of Rational Social Decision Procedures", *Journal of Economic Theory*, 8, 471–482.

Ferejohn, J.A. and D.M. Grether (1979) "Stable Voting Procedures and the Theory of Social Choice", Cal. Tech. Social Science Working Paper No. 210.

Ferejohn, J.A., D.M. Grether and R.D. McKelvey (1982) "Implementation of Democratic Social Choice Functions", *Review of Economic Studies*, 49, 439–446.

Fiorina, M.P. and C.R. Plott (1978) "Committee Decisions under Majority Rule: An Experimental Study", *American Political Science Review*, 72, 575–598.

Greenberg, J. (1979) "Consistent Majority Rules over Compact Sets of Alternatives", *Econometrica*, 47, 627–636.

Kramer, G.H. (1973) "On a Class of Equilibrium Conditions for Majority Rule", *Econometrica*, 41, 285–297.

Kramer, G.H. and A.K. Klevorick (1974) "Existence of a 'Local' Cooperative Equilibrium in a Class of Voting Games", *Review of Economic Studies*, 41, 539–548.

Laing, J.D. and S. Olmstead (1978) "An Experimental and Game Theoretic Study of Committees", in: P. Ordeshook, ed., *Game Theory and Political Science* (New York University Press), pp. 215–281.

McKelvey, R.D. (1976) "Intransitivities in Multidimensional Voting Models and Some Implications for Agenda Control", *Journal of Economic Theory*, 12, 472–482.

Nakamura, K. (1978) "The Vetoers in a Simple Game with Ordinal Preferences", *International Journal of Game Theory*, 8, 55–61.

Peleg, B. (1978) "Consistent Voting Systems", *Econometrica*, 46, 153–161.

Plott, C.R. (1967) "A Notion of Equilibrium and its Possibility under Majority Rule", *American Economic Review*, 57, 787–806.

Salles, M. and R.E. Wendell (1977) "A Further Result on the Core of Voting Games", *International Journal of Game Theory*, 6, 35–40.

Schofield, N. (1977) "Transitivity of Preferences on a Smooth Manifold of Alternatives", *Journal of Economic Theory*, 14, 149–171.

Schofield, N. (1978a) "Instability of Simple Dynamic Games", *Review of Economic Studies*, 45, 575–594.

Schofield, N. (1978b) "The Theory of Dynamic Games", in: P.C. Ordeshook, ed., *Game Theory and Political Science* (New York University Press), pp. 113–164.

Schofield, N. (1980) "Generic Properties of Simple Bergson Samuelson Welfare Functions", *Journal of Mathematical Economics*, 7, 175–192.

Schofield, N. (1981a) "Generic Instability of Simple Majority Rule", Essex Economic Paper No. 174.

Schofield, N. (1981b) "Equilibrium and Cycles in Voting on Compacta: On the Relevance of the General Impossibility Theorem", Essex Economic Paper No. 173.

Schofield, N. (1981c) *Social Choice and Democracy* (University of Essex).

Schofield, N. (1981d) "Political And Economic Equilibrium on a Manifold", Essex Economic Paper No. 177.

Shepsle, K.A. (1979) "Institutional Arrangements and Equilibrium in Multidimensional Voting Models", *Journal of Political Science*, 23, 27–59.

Slutsky, S. (1979) "Agenda Manipulability and Other Properties of a Restricted Multidimensional Voting Equilibrium", Presented at the Public Choice Meeting, Charleston, South Carolina, March 1979.

Smale, S. (1973) "Global Analysis and Economics I: Pareto Optimum and a Generalization of Morse Theory", in: M. Peixoto, ed., *Dynamical Systems* (Academic Press, New York), pp. 531–544.

Smale, S. (1974) "Sufficient Conditions for an Optimum", in: A. Manning, ed., *Dynamical Systems – Warwick* (Springer-Verlag, Berlin), pp. 287–292.

Tullock, G. (1967) "The General Irrelevance of the General Impossibility Theorem", in: *Towards a Mathematics of Politics* (University of Michigan Press, Ann Arbor), pp. 37–49.

CHAPTER 16

Directional and local electoral equilibria with probabilistic voting

PETER COUGHLIN*
University of Maryland at College Park

and

SHMUEL NITZAN
Hebrew University

1. Introduction

Electoral competitions and simple voting games in which each of the candidates and/or the society is restricted to choosing among "local" options (namely directions of motion away from the status quo or policies within a small neighborhood of the status quo) have been studied by Plott (1967), Kramer and Klevorick (1974), Schofield (1978), Matthews (1979), Cohen and Matthews (1980), and others. Such social choice situations are of interest for a number of reasons. For example, the expense of acquiring information may restrict candidates to learning about voter behavior only near the status quo. Alternatively, institutional restrictions may rule out large changes. These and other reasons have been carefully discussed by the above authors.

The existing results on this problem have been derived for societies with full participation electorates and deterministic voting. These results have established

* This paper previously appeared in the *Journal of Economic Theory*, 24(1981), pp. 226–239. We would like to thank Academic Press for giving us permission to include it in this volume. It should be noted that this version includes a small number of changes and corrections which were originally sent to Academic Press, but which arrived too late to be included in the original version.

Social Choice and Welfare, edited by *P.K. Pattanaik and M. Salles*
© *North-Holland Publishing Company, 1983*

that there are usually directional, stationary and local electoral equilibria when the society's policy space is one-dimensional. However, they have also established that such equilibria rarely exist when there are two or more dimensions. Local cycles have therefore been studied for societies with such multi-dimensional policy spaces.

Other recent work on the theory of economic policy formation through elections has been concerned with the consequences of random voting behavior. Full participation electorates have been studied in Comaner (1976), Hinich (1977, 1978), Kramer (1978) and Coughlin and Nitzan (1981). Related studies of electorates with abstentions are due to Hinich et al. (1972, 1973), McKelvey (1975) and Denzau and Kats (1977).

This chapter extends the foundations of spatial models of electoral competition with probabilistic voting from those established in Comaner (1976). Hinich (1977), Kramer (1978) and Coughlin and Nitzan (1981) (section 2). From these foundations, we first derive (in section 3) a necessary and sufficient condition for two directions from a given status quo to constitute an equilibrium strategy pair for candidates in an electoral competition (theorem 1). This condition implies that there is such an equilibrium pair at every status quo (corollary 1). We then derive a necessary and sufficient condition for a status quo to have equilibrium directions which are "no change," (i.e. to have a stationary electoral equilibrium) (theorem 2). This condition implies the existence of a status quo with a stationary electoral equilibrium (corollary 2).

In section 4, we are concerned with local electoral equilibria. We analyze this problem under conditions which are standard in micro-economic analyses. For these societies we derive necessary and sufficient conditions for a status quo to have a local electoral equilibrium (theorem 3). This condition implies the existence of a status quo with a local electoral equilibrium (corollary 3).

The results derived in this chapter hold for any multi-dimensional policy space and do not use any special symmetry requirements on the distribution of voters' preferences. The general existence results established in corollaries 1–3 are, therefore, in sharp contrast to the conclusion of Plott (1967) and others (for deterministic voting) that directional and stationary electoral equilibria rarely exist when the society's policy space has at least two dimensions. They also do not use any of the special concavity conditions in Hinich et al. (1972, 1973) and Denzau and Kats (1977).

Theorems 2 and 3 also establish the equivalence between status quos which have stationary equilibria (respectively, status quos which have local equilibria) and the stationary outcomes (respectively, local maxima) for the society's mean (or social) log-likelihood function. They, therefore, reveal a close connection between certain electoral choices and those from alternative social choice mechanisms which are based on such functions. This also provides a method for finding the status quos which have electoral equilibria.

Section 5 concludes. The proofs are given in the appendix.

2. Probabilistic voting and electoral competitions

Empirical studies of voting behavior as a function of proposed policies and existing economic conditions leave a significant amount of unexplained variation (e.g. Kramer, 1971; Stigler, 1973; and Fair, 1978). This has led to the conclusion that uncertainty and non-policy considerations result in random (or indeterminate) voting behavior when this behavior is viewed as a function of existing and proposed policies. Intriligator (1973), Fishburn (1975) and others have formulated indeterminateness in voter behavior with individual choice probabilities. For a non-empty Euclidean space of social alternatives, $X \subset R^n$, these individual choice probabilities can be summarized by a density function on X (e.g. Nitzan, 1975). One possible interpretation (which is suggested by these articles) is that at any given $x \in X$, the probabilistic voting density function for an individual expresses the likelihood of him choosing that alternative when (1) he can choose any $x \in X$, and (2) his choice becomes the social choice. For an alternative interpretation, see McFadden (1974).

Learning the behavior of every individual is impossible. Therefore, political entrepreneurs (or candidates) have to estimate voter behavior. Since the candidates usually have access to the same information (polls, past election data, etc.), we will assume that candidates obtain a common *probabilistic voting estimator* which estimates the proportions of the population that are described by particular probabilistic voting density functions. To be precise, let $\Theta \subseteq R^l$ denote an index set of parameters for a class of density functions. Then we are assuming that the candidates obtain a *probabilistic voting estimator, $\hat{g}(\theta)$*, which is a bounded (Lebesgue) measurable function on Θ such that the Lebesgue integral $\int_\Theta \hat{g}(\theta) \cdot d\theta$ equals one (e.g. $\hat{g}(\theta)$ may be a continuous probability density function or a discrete probability function on Θ).

For instance, candidates may be willing to use normal probabilistic voting estimators. In this case, the candidates can estimate the proportions of the population that correspond to certain combinations of possible means and variances.

$f(x; \theta)$ will denote a real-valued density function on X which has the parameter $\theta \in \Theta$. Since these density functions are only estimates of individual behavior, we will make three regularity assumptions. Specifically,

(i)   Each $f(x; \theta)$ is a positive and continuously differentiable function of x.

(ii) $f(x; \theta)$ is a bounded, (Lebesgue) measurable function of θ whose lower bound is strictly positive.

(iii) $\partial f(x; \theta)/\partial x_h$ $(h = 1, ..., n)$, is a bounded, (Lebesgue) measurable function of θ.

In an election, each voter must choose from a pair of policy-proposing candidates. Therefore, we must learn the consequences of probabilistic voting for pairwise choices. We will let ψ_1 and ψ_2 denote policies which have been proposed by candidates who are labelled 1 and 2, respectively. Additionally, we will let $P_\theta^j(\psi_1, \psi_2)$ denote the probability that an individual, whose behavior is described by $f(x; \theta)$, votes for candidate $j, j = 1, 2$.

The following two assumptions provide the basis for calculating individual binary choice probabilities from probabilistic voting behavior on X.

First, we assume that the candidates estimate the behavior of concerned citizens who vote. This is especially plausible in a local equilibrium analysis where only alternatives near the currently proposed positions are of interest. This means that we are concerned with a *full participation electorate* where

$$P_\theta^1(\psi_1, \psi_2) + P_\theta^2(\psi_1, \psi_2) = 1 \tag{1}$$

for every $\theta \in \Theta$ and $(\psi_1, \psi_2) \in X \times X$. This assumption is repeatedly made in the literature on local equilibria.

Second, we want to relate random voting behavior on a Euclidean policy space to behavior on binary choices, i.e. choices between two proposed policies. We therefore assume that each individual's choice probabilities satisfy (in the terminology of Luce) *independence from irrelevant alternatives*, i.e.

$$\frac{P_\theta^1(\psi_1, \psi_2)}{P_\theta^2(\psi_1, \psi_2)} = \frac{f(\psi_1; \theta)}{f(\psi_2; \theta)} \tag{2}$$

for each $\theta \in \Theta, (\psi_1, \psi_2) \in X \times X$.

This is a "separability" condition which merely states that the relative likelihoods of choosing ψ_1 and ψ_2 from X are preserved when choosing from the set $\{\psi_1, \psi_2\}$. This is the continuous version of the independence from irrelevant alternatives which follows from the basic choice axioms in Luce (1959, axiom 1 and lemma 3) (also in Luce and Suppes, 1965; Ray, 1973; McFadden, 1974; and elsewhere).

Finally, since vote totals are random, a candidate could concern himself with his expected plurality or with his probability of winning. However, Hinich (1977, pp. 212–213) has proven that, for many large electorates with a reasonably large amount of indeterminateness, these two objectives are equivalent. Therefore, we will consider the more tractable objective function, and assume that each candidate is concerned with his expected plurality. We will denote the expected plurality for candidate 1 at the pair of proposed policies $(\psi_1, \psi_2) \in X \times X$ by $Pl(\psi_1, \psi_2)$. In the appendix, we prove that this function exists at every possible pair of proposed strategies.

$S \subset X$ will be used to denote the set of policies which are feasible for the society when the candidates' strategic decisions are to be made. We will assume throughout that S is non-empty, compact and contained in the interior of X. When candidates have complete mobility within this set of feasible alternatives, electoral competitions are two-person, zero-sum games where the common strategy set for the two candidates is S and $Pl(\psi_1, \psi_2)$ and $-Pl(\psi_1, \psi_2)$ are the payoff functions for candidates 1 and 2, respectively. This chapter analyzes the directional and local electoral competitions that arise within this framework when both candidates start at a (common) status quo and then only evaluate their positions on the margin or in comparison with local alternatives. In these games the payoffs will be either expected pluralities very close to the status quo or marginal variations in expected pluralities.

3. Directional and stationary equilibria

A society always has some current state (or status quo). In this section, we analyze situations in which (i) candidates can, at most, marginally vary their positions from the status quo, and (ii) the status quo is associated with a candidate if he does not choose a direction which varies his position away from it.

The possible directions in which a candidate can move his position from the status quo, together with the choice of "no change," define the candidates' strategy space. The marginal gains in expected plurality from simultaneous variations in positions define the candidates' payoffs. The formal definitions are as follows.

A feasible direction u at a status quo, $\psi \in S$, is a vector in R^n of unit length for which there exists a $\lambda_1 > 0$ such that $\psi + \lambda \cdot u \in S$ for every $\lambda \in (0, \lambda_1)$ or, if ψ is on the boundary of S, which is in the tangent cone of S at ψ (as defined in Cohen and Matthews (1980, pp. 978–979)). The common strategy set, $T(\psi)$, at a status quo $\psi \in S$, consists of all the feasible directions at ψ together with the zero vector in R^n (i.e. together with "no change"). $u \in T(\psi)$ and $v \in T(\psi)$ will denote directions selected by candidates 1 and 2, respectively.

The payoff functions at ψ are defined by the net effects of the simultaneous variations u and v. In symbols, the payoff function for candidate 1, $P(u, v)$ on $T(\psi) \times T(\psi)$, is

$$P(u, v) = D_{(u,v)} Pl(\psi_1, \psi_2) = \sum_{h=1}^{n} \frac{\partial Pl}{\partial \psi_{1h}} u_h + \sum_{h=1}^{n} \frac{\partial Pl}{\partial \psi_{2h}} v_h \qquad (3)$$

at $\psi_1 = \psi_2 = \psi$. The payoff function for candidate 2 is given by $-P(u, v)$. $(u^*, v^*) \in T(\psi) \times T(\psi)$ is a *directional electoral equilibrium* (in pure strategies) at the status quo $\psi \in X$ if and only if

$$P(u, v^*) \leqslant P(u^*, v^*) \leqslant P(u^*, v) \quad \forall u, v \in T(\psi). \tag{4}$$

We can now characterize the directional electoral equilibria which occur at a given status quo.

Theorem 1. $(w^*, z^*) \in T(\psi) \times T(\psi)$ is a directional electoral equilibrium at the status quo ψ if and only if

$$D_{(w^*, 0)} Pl(\psi_1, \psi_2) = \max_{u \in T(\psi)} D_{(u, 0)} Pl(\psi_1, \psi_2),$$

and

$$D_{(0, z^*)} Pl(\psi_1, \psi_2) = \min_{v \in T(\psi)} D_{(0, v)} Pl(\psi_1, \psi_2)$$

at $\psi_1 = \psi_2 = \psi$.

This implies

Corollary 1. There exists a directional electoral equilibrium at every status quo in S.

In addition, (3) also implies that these equilibria are always dominant strategy equilibria.

If, in a directional electoral equilibrium, both candidates choose to remain at the status quo, then the society is in a stationary equilibrium. In our terminology, there is a *stationary electoral equilibrium* at a status quo ψ if and only if the zero vector in R^{2n} is a directional electoral equilibrium at ψ.

We should remark that there are many alternatives to the existing institution of political elections for making a social choice. Various suggestions for aggregating individual choice probabilities and then determining the social choices have been proposed (e.g. see Intriligator, 1973; Fishburn, 1975; and Nitzan, 1975). We present below one such possible aggregation rule which, it turns out, is closely related to electoral competitions.

Recall that individual choice probabilities are summarized in the density functions $f(x; \theta)$, or, equivalently, in the log-likelihood functions $\ln f(x; \theta)$. The society's *mean* (or *social*) *log-likelihood function* is given by

$$L(x) = \int_\Theta \ln(f(x; \theta)) \hat{g}(\theta) \, d\theta. \tag{5}$$

If a society is concerned with the marginal changes in $L(x)$ which result from variations in the status quo, then they will not vary a status quo $\psi \in X$ (i.e. will choose "no change") if and only if

$$D_u L(\psi) \leqslant 0, \quad \forall u \in T(\psi). \tag{6}$$

We will therefore refer to any such point in the society's policy space as a *stationary outcome* for the social (or mean) log-likelihood function.

Using this alternative social choice mechanism and theorem 1 we can now characterize the status quos at which stationary electoral equilibria occur.

Theorem 2. There is a stationary electoral equilibrium at a status quo $\psi \in X$ if and only if ψ is a stationary outcome for the society's mean log-likelihood function.

This, in turn, directly implies.

Corollary 2. There exists some status quo, $\psi \in X$, at which there is a stationary electoral equilibrium.

4. Local equilibria

Some stationary equilibria have the local instability property that, if the initial position of the candidates is perturbed slightly, we can find the candidates choosing an equilibrium direction which points away from the neighboring stationary equilibrium point. This is the case, for instance, when candidates are locally minimizing their expected pluralities (taking their rival's position as no change from the status quo). We therefore now consider existence and location questions for the stronger concept of a *local Nash equilibrium*.

We can consider the possible candidate strategies to be "small" neighborhoods of the status quo, and the payoffs to be the candidates' respective expected pluralities rather than marginal changes in their values. Given the expected plurality function, $Pl(\psi_1, \psi_2)$, the status quo $\psi \in X$ is a *local electoral equilibrium* if and only if

$$Pl(\psi_1, \psi) \leqslant Pl(\psi, \psi) = 0 \leqslant Pl(\psi, \psi_2) \tag{7}$$

for every $\psi_1 \in N_{\epsilon_1}(\psi)$ and $\psi_2 \in N_{\epsilon_2}(\psi)$ for some $\epsilon_1, \epsilon_2 > 0$.

We will study local electoral equilibria under assumptions on the "social opportunity set" S which are standard for such sets in microeconomic analyses. Specifically, we will assume that S is a compact subset of X which is defined by twice continuously differentiable equations of the form

$$g_k(x) = 0 \quad (k = 1, ..., m < n) \tag{8}$$

with the property that each $x \in S$ is a normal point (e.g. see Hestenes, 1975, p. 114).

This will mean that candidates (when they take their rival's position as given) and society will have Lagrangean maximization problems.

We will also strengthen our regularity conditions (see section 2) on the individuals' probabilistic voting estimators and additionally assume:

(1) Each $f(x; \theta)$ is twice continuously differentiable in x, and

(2) $\partial^2 f(x; \theta)/\partial x_h \partial x_l (h, l \in \{1, ..., n\})$ is a bounded, (Lebesgue) measurable function of θ.

Finally, in order to study this problem for C^2 payoff functions, we will analyze those situations in which $Pl(x, \psi)$ and $L(x)$ are non-degenerate functions with respect to the constraints given by (8) (see Hestenes, 1975, p. 153). It should be observed that this imposes essentially no further restriction on the class of electoral competitions we are analyzing since, generically, every C^2 function is non-degenerate (e.g. see Hirsch, 1976, theorem 6.1.2).

For this standard microeconomic decision-making context we can obtain a complete characterization of the status quos at which there are local electoral equilibria:

Theorem 3. There is a local electoral equilibrium at a status quo $\psi \in S$ if and only if ψ is a local maximum for the society's mean log-likelihood function.

This, again, gives us a general equilibrium result:

Corollary 3. There exists some status quo, $\psi \in S$ at which there is a local electoral equilibrium.

5. Conclusion

This chapter began by extending the foundations of spatial models of electoral competitions with probabilistic voting from those established in Comaner (1976), Hinich (1977, 1978), Kramer (1978) and Coughlin and Nitzan (1981). We then derived necessary and sufficient conditions for directional, stationary and local electoral equilibria. These conditions establish general existence results for such electoral equilibria. They also reveal the close relation between elections and certain social choice mechanisms which select stationary outcomes or local maxima of the society's mean log-likelihood function.

Appendix

We will begin by establishing that the candidates' expected plurality functions and all of their first partial derivatives exist at every $(\psi_1, \psi_2) \in X^2$. By (1) and (2),

$$P_\theta^1 (\psi_1, \psi_2) = \frac{f(\psi_1; \theta)}{f(\psi_1; \theta) + f(\psi_2; \theta)} \tag{9}$$

for every $\theta \in \Theta$ and $(\psi_1, \psi_2) \in X \times X$.

The expected plurality for candidate 1 from an individual with the probabilistic voting density function indexed by θ is

$$P_\theta (\psi_1, \psi_2) = P_\theta^1 (\psi_1, \psi_2) - P_\theta^2 (\psi_1, \psi_2) = 2P_\theta^1 (\psi_1, \psi_2) - 1.$$

Therefore, the expected plurality for candidate 1 from the entire population is the Lebesgue integral

$$Pl(\psi_1, \psi_2) = \int_\Theta P_\theta (\psi_1, \psi_2) \hat{g}(\theta) \, d\theta$$

$$= \int_\Theta \left\{ 2 \cdot \frac{f(\psi_1; \theta)}{f(\psi_1; \theta) + f(\psi_2; \theta)} - 1 \right\} \hat{g}(\theta) \, d\theta. \tag{10}$$

Since $f(x; \theta)$ is a measurable function of θ for any given $x \in X$, $f(x; \theta) + f(y; \theta)$ is measurable for any given $x, y \in X$. $f(x; \theta) > 0$ for every $x \in X$ and $\theta \in \Theta$. Therefore,

$$\left\{ \theta \in \Theta \ \middle| \ \frac{1}{f(x; \theta) + f(y; \theta)} < k \right\} = \left\{ \theta \in \Theta \ \middle| \ f(x; \theta) + f(y; \theta) > \frac{1}{k} \right\}$$

for any $k > 0$. Furthermore,

$$\left\{ \theta \in \Theta \ \middle| \ \frac{1}{f(x; \theta) + f(y; \theta)} < k \right\} = \varnothing$$

for any $k \leqslant 0$.

Hence, $1/[f(x; \theta) + f(y; \theta)]$ and, in turn, $P_\theta(\psi_1, \psi_2)$ are measurable functions of θ. Additionally, by (9), $P_\theta(\psi_1, \psi_2)$ is bounded by 0 and 1. Finally, since $\dot{g}(\theta)$ is a bounded and (Lebesgue) measurable function on Θ, the product $P_\theta(\psi_1, \psi_2) \cdot \dot{g}(\theta)$ is bounded and measurable and hence, Lebesgue integrable. Therefore, the integral $Pl(\psi_1, \psi_2) = \int_\Theta P_\theta(\psi_1, \psi_2) \dot{g}(\theta)\, d\theta$ exists.

By corollary 5.9 in Bartle (1966) and the regularity conditions on the $f(x; \theta)$, the gradient of $Pl(x, \psi)$ has as its terms the values given by

$$\frac{\partial Pl(x, \psi)}{\partial x_h} = \int_\Theta \frac{\partial}{\partial x_h} \left(\frac{2f(x;\theta)}{f(x;\theta) + f(\psi;\theta)} - 1 \right) \dot{g}(\theta)\, d\theta \tag{11}$$

for $h = 1, ..., n$. (The existence of each of these integrals follows directly from arguments analogous to the ones that we've just carried out for $Pl(\psi_1, \psi_2)$.)

Proof of theorem 1. By (10), $Pl(x, y) = -Pl(y, x)$. Therefore, (3) implies $P(w, z) = -P(w, z)$ and $P(z, z) = 0$ for all $w, z \in T(\psi)$. In other words, the candidates' directional game is symmetric and zero-sum. Consequently, $(w^*, z^*) \in T(\psi) \times T(\psi)$ is a directional electoral equilibrium if and only if both (w^*, w^*) and (z^*, z^*) are also directional electoral equilibria. Additionally, this implies that (w^*, w^*) is a directional electoral equilibrium at ψ if and only if

$$D_{(u, w^*)} Pl(\psi, \psi) \leqslant D_{(w^*, w^*)} Pl(\psi, \psi) = 0 \tag{12}$$

for every $u \in T(\psi)$.

By (3), (12) is equivalent to

$$\sum_{h=1}^{n} \frac{\partial Pl(\psi, \psi)}{\partial \psi_{1h}} u_h + \sum_{h=1}^{n} \frac{\partial Pl(\psi, \psi)}{\partial \psi_{2h}} w_h^* \leqslant 0 \tag{13}$$

for every $u \in T(\psi)$.

Now, $Pl(x, y) = -Pl(y, x)$ implies

$$\frac{\partial Pl(\psi, \psi)}{\partial \psi_{2h}} = \frac{-\partial Pl(\psi, \psi)}{\partial \psi_{1h}}.$$

Therefore, (13) is equivalent to

$$\sum_{h=1}^{n} \frac{\partial Pl(\psi, \psi)}{\partial \psi_{1h}} u_h - \sum_{h=1}^{n} \frac{\partial Pl(\psi, \psi)}{\partial \psi_{1h}} w_h^* \leqslant 0 \tag{14}$$

for every $u \in T(\psi)$.

Finally, (14) is equivalent to

$$D_{(u,0)} Pl(\psi, \psi) \leqslant D_{(w^*,0)} Pl(\psi, \psi) \tag{15}$$

for every $u \in T(\psi)$.

By a similar argument, (z^*, z^*) is a directional electoral equilibrium at ψ if and only if

$$D_{(0,v)} Pl(\psi, \psi) \geqslant D_{(0,z^*)} Pl(\psi, \psi) \tag{16}$$

for every $v \in T(\psi)$.

Hence the theorem follows. ∎

Proof of corollary 1.   At any $\psi \in X$,

$$D_u Pl(x, \psi) \mid_{x=\psi} = \sum_{h=1}^{n} \frac{\partial Pl(x, \psi)}{\partial \psi_{1h}} \bigg|_{x=\psi} \cdot u_h$$

is linear as a function of the vectors $u \in R^n$. Additionally, since S is compact, the set of feasible directions, at any $\psi \in S$, is a compact subset of R^n. Therefore, $D_u Pl(\psi, \psi)$ achieves a maximum over this set. Either a maximizing direction in this set or the zero vector must, therefore, maximize $D_u Pl(\psi, \psi)$. ∎

Proof of theorem 2.   First of all, $\ln f(x; \theta)$ is a bounded function of θ which is defined for every $x \in X$, since $f(x; \theta) > 0$ is a bounded function of θ whose lower bound is strictly positive, for any $x \in X$ (see section 2). Additionally, for any given x,

$$\{\theta \in \Theta \mid \ln f(x; \theta) > k\} = \{\theta \in \Theta \mid f(x; \theta) > e^k\}$$

for any $k \in R$. Therefore, since $f(x; \theta)$ is a measurable function of θ, $\ln f(x; \theta)$ is measurable. Consequently the integral defining $L(x)$ exists.

By corollary 5.9 in Bartle (1966) and the regularity conditions on the $f(x; \theta)$, for $h = 1, ..., n$,

$$\frac{\partial L(x)}{\partial x_h} = \int_{\Theta} \frac{\dfrac{\partial f(x; \theta)}{\partial x_h}}{f(x; \theta)} \, \hat{g}(\theta) \, d\theta. \tag{17}$$

As stated in (11),

$$\frac{\partial Pl(x, \psi)}{\partial x_h} = \int_\Theta \frac{\partial}{\partial x_h} \left(\frac{2f(x;\theta)}{f(x;\theta) + f(\psi;\theta)} - 1 \right) \hat{g}(\theta) \, d\theta. \tag{18}$$

Therefore,

$$\frac{\partial Pl(x, \psi)}{\partial x_h}\bigg|_{x=\psi} = 2 \cdot \int_\Theta \frac{f(\psi;\theta) \cdot \dfrac{\partial f(x;\theta)}{\partial x_h}}{(f(x;\theta) + f(\psi;\theta))^2}\bigg|_{x=\psi} \hat{g}(\theta) \, d\theta$$

$$= \int_\Theta \frac{\dfrac{\partial f(x;\theta)}{\partial x_h}\bigg|_{x=\psi}}{2f(\psi;\theta)} \hat{g}(\theta) \, d\theta.$$

Hence,

$$\frac{\partial Pl(x, \psi)}{\partial x_h}\bigg|_{x=\psi} = \frac{1}{2} \frac{\partial L(x)}{\partial x_h}\bigg|_{x=\psi} \tag{20}$$

Therefore, for any $u \in T(\psi)$,

$$D_{(u,0)} Pl(\psi, \psi) = \sum_{h=1}^n \frac{\partial Pl(\psi, \psi)}{\partial x_h} u_h = \frac{1}{2} \sum_{h=1}^n \frac{\partial L(\psi)}{\partial x_h} = \frac{1}{2} D_u L(\psi). \tag{21}$$

By theorem 1, $(0, 0) \in T(\psi) \times T(\psi)$ is an equilibrium strategy pair at ψ if and only if $D_{(u,0)} Pl(\psi, \psi) \leqslant 0$ for every feasible direction at ψ and, hence, if and only if $D_u L(\psi) \leqslant 0$ for every feasible direction at ψ. ∎

Proof of corollary 2. Consider any $\psi \in X$. Since $f(x;\theta)$ is a continuous function of x (by regularity condition (i)), $\ln f(x;\theta)$ is a continuous function of x. Therefore, $L(x)$ is continuous (by the Lebesgue Dominated Convergence Theorem). Hence, since S is compact, there is some $\psi \in S$ such that ψ is a critical point or a boundary maximum of $L(x)$. Any such point must satisfy (6). Therefore there is some stationary outcome for the social log-likelihood function. Hence, by theorem 1, there must be a stationary electoral equilibrium. ∎

Proof of theorem 3. First, at $x = \psi$.

$$
\frac{\partial^2 Pl(x, \psi)}{\partial x_h \, \partial x_l} = \int_\Theta \left\{ \frac{2(f(x;\theta) + f(\psi;\theta))^2 \, f(\psi;\theta) \, \dfrac{\partial^2 f(x;\theta)}{\partial x_h \, \partial x_l}}{(f(x;\theta) + f(\psi;\theta))^4} \right.
$$

$$
\left. - \frac{4f(\psi;\theta) \, (f(x;\theta) + f(\psi;\theta)) \, \dfrac{\partial f(x;\theta)}{\partial x_h} \cdot \dfrac{\partial f(x;\theta)}{\partial x_l}}{(f(x;\theta) + f(\psi;\theta))^4} \right\} \hat{g}(\theta) \, d\theta
$$

(22)

(by corollary 5.9 in Bartle, 1966, and the regularity conditions on the $f(x;\theta)$). Therefore,

$$
\frac{\partial^2 Pl(x, \psi)}{\partial x_h \, \partial x_l} \bigg|_{x=\psi} = \int_\Theta \left\{ \frac{\dfrac{\partial^2 f(x;\theta)}{\partial x_h \, \partial x_l} f(x;\theta) - \dfrac{\partial f(x;\theta)}{\partial x_h} \cdot \dfrac{\partial f(x;\theta)}{\partial x_l}}{2f(x;\theta)^2} \right\}_{x=\psi} \hat{g}(\theta) \, d\theta.
$$

(23)

But, at $x \in \psi$ we also have

$$
\frac{\partial^2 L(x)}{\partial x_h \, \partial x_l} = \int_\Theta \left\{ \frac{f(x;\theta) \, \dfrac{\partial^2 f(x;\theta)}{\partial x_h \, \partial x_l} - \dfrac{\partial f(x;\theta)}{\partial x_h} \cdot \dfrac{\partial f(x;\theta)}{\partial x_l}}{f(x;\theta)^2} \right\} \hat{g}(\theta) \, d\theta
$$

(24)

(by corollary 5.9 in Bartle, 1966, and the regularity conditions on the $f(x;\theta)$). Therefore,

$$
\frac{\partial^2 Pl(x, \psi)}{\partial x_h \, \partial x_l} = \frac{1}{2} \frac{\partial^2 L(x)}{\partial x_h \, \partial x_l} \quad \text{at} \quad x = \psi.
$$

(25)

Now, suppose that there is a local electoral equilibrium at $\psi \in S$. Then, since $\psi \in S$ is a normal point, there exists unique multiplier $\lambda_1, \ldots, \lambda_m$ such that, if we set $L_1(x) = Pl_1(x, \psi) + \lambda_1 g_1(x) + \ldots + \lambda_m g_m(x)$, then $\nabla L_1(\psi) = 0$ (e.g. see theorem 3.2.2 in Hestenes, 1975). Therefore, since $Pl(x, \psi)$ is non-degenerate with respect to the constraints given by (8),

$$
L_1''(\psi) = \sum_{l=1}^n \sum_{h=1}^n \frac{\partial L_1(\psi)}{\partial x_h \, \partial x_l} \cdot w_h \cdot w_l > 0
$$

for every non-zero vector $w \in R^n$ which satisfies the equation $\nabla g_k(\psi) \cdot w = 0$
$(k = 1, ..., m)$. (For example, see theorem 3.3.2 in Hesteness, 1975.)

Now consider $L(x)$. Since $\nabla L(\psi) = 2 \cdot \nabla Pl(x, \psi)$ at $x = \psi$, we must have
$L_2(x) = L(x) + 2 \cdot \lambda_1 g_1(x) + ... + 2 \cdot \lambda_m g_m(x)$ implies $\nabla L_2(\psi) = 0$. Additionally, since (25) implies

$$\frac{\partial^2 L(\psi)}{\partial x_h \, \partial x_l} = 2 \cdot \frac{\partial^2 Pl(x, \psi)}{\partial x_h \, \partial x_l} \quad \text{at} \quad x = \psi,$$

we must have

$$L_2''(\psi) = \sum_{l=1}^{n} \sum_{h=1}^{n} \frac{\partial L_2(\psi)}{\partial x_h \, \partial x_l} \cdot w_h \cdot w_l > 0$$

for every non-zero vector $w \in R^n$ which satisfies $\nabla g_k(\psi) \cdot w = 0$ $(k = 1, ..., m)$.
Therefore, since $L(x)$ is non-degenerate with respect to the constraints given by
(8), ψ must be a strict local maximum of $L(x)$ (e.g. see theorem 3.3.2 in Hestenes,
1975).

The converse follows similarly. ■

Proof of corollary 3. By the argument of corollary 2, $L(x)$ is a continuous function of x. Therefore, since S is compact there is some $\psi \in S$ such that ψ is a local
maximum of $L(x)$. By theorem 3, this ψ must also be a status quo at which there
is a local electoral equilibrium. ■

Acknowledgments

We would like to express our thanks for individual comments and suggestions
from Ken Arrow, Bob Aumann, Mel Hinich, Bezalel Peleg, Micha Perles, Ariel
Rubenstein and an anonymous referee.

References

Bartle, R. (1965) *The Elements of Integration* (Wiley, New York).
Cohen, L. and S. Matthews (1980) "Constrained Plott Equilibria, Directional Equilibria and
    Global Cycling Sets", *Review of Economic Studies*, 47, 975–986.
Comaner, W. (1976) "The Median Voter Rule and the Theory of Political Choice", *Journal of
    Public Economics*, 5, 169–178.
Coughlin, P. and S. Nitzan (1981) "Electoral Outcomes with Probabilistic Voting and Nash
    Social Welfare Maxima", *Journal of Public Economics*, 15, 113–122.

Denzau, A. and A. Kats (1977) "Expected Plurality Voting Equilibrium and Social Choice Functions", *Review of Economic Studies*, 44, 227–233.

Fair, R. (1978) "The Effect of Economic Events on Votes for President", *Review of Economics and Statistics*, 60, 159–173.

Fishburn, P. (1975) "A Probabilistic Model of Social Choice: Comment", *Review of Economic Studies*, 42, 197–301.

Hestenes, M. (1975) *Optimization Theory* (Wiley, New York).

Hinich, M. (1977) "Equilibrium in Spatial Voting: The Median Voter Result is an Artifact", *Journal of Economic Theory*, 16, 208–219.

Hinich, M. (1978) "The Mean Versus the Median in Spatial Voting Games", in: P. Ordeshook, ed., *Game Theory and Political Science* (New York University Press).

Hinich, M., J. Ledyard and P. Ordeshook (1972) "Nonvoting and the Existence of Equilibrium Under Majority Rule", *Journal of Economic Theory*, 4, 144–153.

Hinich, M., J. Ledyard and P. Ordeshook (1973) "A Theory of Electoral Equilibrium: A Spatial Analysis Based on the Theory of Games", *Journal of Politics*, 35, 154–193.

Hirsch, M. (1976) *Differential Topology* (Springer-Verlag, New York).

Intriligator, M. (1973) "A Probabilistic Model of Social Choice", *Review of Economic Studies*, 40, 553–560.

Kramer, G. (1971) "Short-term Fluctuation in U.S. Voting Behavior, 1896–1964", *American Political Science Review*, 65, 131–143.

Kramer, G. (1978) "Robustness of the Median Voter Result", *Journal of Economic Theory*, 19, 565–567.

Kramer, G. and A. Klevorick (1974) "Existence of a 'Local Cooperative Equilibrium' in a Class of Voting Games", *Review of Economic Studies*, 41, 539–547.

Luce, R. (1959) *Individual Choice Behavior* (Wiley, New York).

Luce, R. and P. Suppes (1965) "Preferences, Utility and Subjective Probability", in: *Handbook of Mathematical Psychology* (Wiley, New York).

Matthews, S. (1979) "A Simple Direction Model of Electoral Competition", *Public Choice*, 34, 141–156.

McFadden, D. (1974) "Conditional Logit Analysis of Qualitative Choice Behaviors", in: P. Zarembka, ed., *Frontiers in Econometrics* (Academic Press, New York).

McKelvey, R. (1975) "Policy Related Voting and Electoral Equilibria", *Econometrica*, 43, 815–844.

Nitzan, S. (1975) "Social Preference Ordering in a Probabilistic Voting Model", *Public Choice*, 24, 93–100.

Plott, C. (1967) "A Notion of Equilibrium and its Possibility Under Majority Rule", *American Economic Review*, 57, 787–806.

Ray, P. (1973) "Independence from Irrelevant Alternatives", *Econometrica*, 41, 987–991.

Schofield, N. (1978) "Instability of Simple Dynamic Games", *Review of Economic Studies*, 45, 575–594.

Stigler, G. (1973) "General Economic Conditions and National Elections", *American Economic Review*, 63, 160–167.

λ-transfer value and fixed-price equilibrium in two-sided markets

ROY GARDNER*
Iowa State University

1. Introduction

This chapter analyzes certain questions of disequilibrium economics from the standpoint of the theory of games. Following the logic of the fix-price method,[1] disequilibrium arises because prices are fixed during the trading period. Prices are environmental variables in the sense that they do not change during trading and, thus, form part of the trading environment. However, we shall suppose that prices can change between trading periods.

Two questions immediately arise in such a context. First, how is quantity demanded equal to quantity supplied when prices are not consistent with Walrasian equilibrium? Secondly, how does price change from period to period? In particular, is there any reason to expect Walrasian equilibrium prices to emerge from the adjustment process?

The first of these questions has received a great deal of attention recently. The three major equilibrium concepts due to Drèze (1975), Benassy (1975), and Younes (1975), show that a wide variety of rationing schemes are consistent with fixed-price equilibrium. The interested reader should consult the review by

* The author wishes to thank Y. Balasko, V. Böhm, F. Breyer, J.M. Grandmont, R. Guesnerie, and W. Hildenbrand for their comments. Research support from C.N.R.S. is gratefully acknowledged. Preliminary versions of this research were presented at the Conference on the Economics and Econometrics of Disequilibrium, Toulouse, and at the Alfred Weber Institute, University of Heidelberg.
[1]   Grandmont (1977a) describes this logic in detail.

Social Choice and Welfare, edited by P.K. Pattanaik and M. Salles
© *North-Holland Publishing Company, 1983*

Grandmont (1977a) for an introduction to this literature. The second question has only recently begun to be studied; here, one can cite the work by Laroque (1978a, 1978b) and Grandmont, Laroque and Younes (1978).

In contrast with the existing literature, which is general equilibrium in nature, these questions will be addressed here in an extremely partial equilibrium: Böhm-Bawerk's (1923) horse market and natural generalizations thereof. Following Shapley and Shubik (1972), I shall call such markets two-sided. As with any paradigm case, one hopes that results for two-sided markets will yield insights into more complicated situations.

Two-sided markets will be considered here as cooperative games without side-payments, and the solution game applied to them will be the Shapley value (λ-transfer value). From this standpoint, the answer to the first question is as follows: for almost all fixed-prices, the only rationing consistent with the Shapley value is uniform rationing (theorem 1). Indeed, when price is fixed at Walrasian levels, the value allocation is a Walrasian allocation. A small set of prices revealing Roth's paradox (Roth, 1977) is the content of theorem 2.

These results suggest the central role of uniform rationing in the dynamic adjustment of prices. Specifically, we shall suppose that agents currently trading in the market vote, at the close of trading, on next period's price. One has a majoritarian price dynamics when next period's price is the majority rule equilibrium of this period's traders. In Böhm-Bawerk's horse market, the majoritarian price dynamics lead to Walrasian equilibrium in, at most, two periods (theorem 3). A series of simple counterexamples shows that Walrasian equilibrium is not always stable relative to these dynamics. However, it is shown that in a large economy analogous to Böhm-Bawerk's, one observes the same two-period convergence to Walrasian equilibrium (theorem 4).

2. Two-sided markets

In two-sided markets, there are two kinds of agents, buyers and sellers, and two goods. Good 1, called money, is the medium of exchange. Good 2 is indivisible, and no agent has need of more than one unit of it. A buyer trades good 1 for 2; a seller trades in the opposite direction. The price p, at which any trades take place, is fixed in advance of trading.

The set of sellers M contains m members (m finite). Each seller i in M has a utility function $U_i(x_{i1}, x_{i2})$ and an endowment (e_{i1}, e_{i2}) with $e_{i2} = 1$.

Consider the maximization problem:

(I) max $U_i(x_{i1}, x_{i2})$
    s.t. $x_{i1} + px_{i2} = e_{i1} + pe_{i2}$
        $x_{i2} = 0$ or 1.

The asking price $a(i)$ of seller i is defined to be the minimum of all prices p such that $x_{i2} = 0$ is a solution of (I); it is the lowest price at which seller i is willing to sell. Clearly,

$$U_i(e_{i1} + a(i), 0) = U_i(e_{i1}, 1).$$

Taking U_i to be a von Neumann–Morgenstern utility, we normalize such that

$$U_i(e_{i1} + a(i), 0) = 0.$$

Denote by $x_{i1}^*(p), x_{i2}^*(p))$ the solution to (I). Then, the indirect utility function $V_i(p)$ is defined by $V_i(p) = U_i(x_{i1}^*(p), x_{i2}^*(p))$ and is given by

$$V_i(p) = \begin{cases} U_i(e_{i1} + p, 0), & \text{when } p \geqslant a(i), \\ 0, & \text{otherwise.} \end{cases}$$

The indirect utility $V_i(p)$ makes clear the role of p on seller i's utility and will play a central role throughout the chapter.

The set of buyers N contains n members, n not necessarily equal to m. Each buyer j in N has a utility function $U_j(x_{j1}, x_{j2})$ and an endowment (e_{j1}, e_{j2}) with $e_{j2} = 0$.

Consider the maximization problem:

(II) max $U_j(x_{j1}, x_{j2})$
    s.t. $x_{j1} + px_{j2} = e_{j1}$
        $x_{j2} = 0$ or 1.

The bid price $b(j)$ of buyer j is defined to be the maximum of all prices p such that $x_{j2} = 1$ is a solution of (II); it is the highest price at which buyer j is willing to buy. Clearly $b(j)$ satisfies

$$U_j(e_{j1}, 0) = U_j(e_{j1} - b(j), 1).$$

Again, utility is normalized so that $U_j(e_{j1}, 0) = 0$. The indirect utility for buyers, $V_j(p)$, analogous to that for sellers, satisfies

$$V_j(p) = \begin{cases} U_j(e_{j1} - p, 1), & p \leqslant b(j), \\ 0, & \text{otherwise.} \end{cases}$$

Example (Böhm-Bawerk).   Böhm-Bawerk considers the case where good 1 is the Austrian currency and good 2 is horses. $m = 8$ and $n = 10$. Agents are described directly in terms of bid and ask prices:

i	1	2	3	4	5	6	7	8		
$a(i)$	\$ 10	11	15	17	20	21.50	25	26		

j	1	2	3	4	5	6	7	8	9	10
$b(j)$	\$ 30	28	26	24	22	21	20	18	17	15

all prices being quoted in dollars hereafter. All agents are assumed to be risk neutral, hence, the indirect utility functions are linear in p.

Market demand and supply curves are depicted in fig. 17.1. The Walrasian equilibrium prices, $21 < p < 21.50$, follow from the marginal pair $i = 6, j = 6$ in

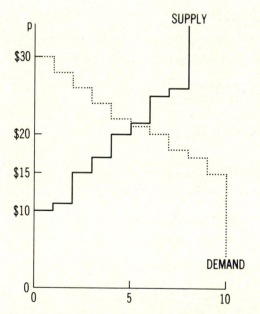

Figure 17.1.   Demand and supply, Böhm-Bawerk's horse market.

Böhm-Bawerk's analysis. For $p > 21.50$, the market is in excess supply; for $p < 21$, excess demand.

One can imagine various temporary equilibria with rationing for non-Walrasian p. Suppose $10 < p < 11$. Then, seller 1 sells to buyer 1, all other buyers facing the constraint $x_{j2} = 0$, is an equilibrium with rationing. Seller 1 selling to buyer 2, or selling with probability $1/2$ to buyer 3 and probability $1/2$ to buyer 6, are likewise equilibria with rationing.[2] We shall call rationing uniform[3] if, whenever rationing is present, each agent on the long side of the market has the same probability of making a trade, while each agent on the short side of the market is sure of trading. For two-sided markets, and for almost all prices, from the game-theoretic standpoint of the Shapley value, only uniform rationing turns out to be a game equilibrium.

3. The Shapley value

A cooperative game is a pair (T, v) consisting of the set of players T and characteristic function v. This section discusses a particular solution concept for transferable utility games, the Shapley value, and its extension to games without side-payments. The next section derives the characteristic function for two-sided market games, and shows that these are indeed games without side-payments.

For games with transferable utility, the Shapley value ψ is the unique operator on v satisfying the following axioms (Aumann and Shapley, 1974, appendix A):

Additivity: $\psi(v + w) = \psi v + \psi w$.
Symmetry: If θ is a permutation of T, $\psi(\theta v) = \theta \psi(v)$.
Efficiency: $\psi v(T) = v(T)$.
Null player: If $v(S/\{t\}) = v(S)$ for some player t and all coalitions S, then $\psi v(t) = 0$.

The Shapley value can be interpreted as a stable outcome of bargaining (Harsanyi, 1977, ch. 11) or as the expected utility of playing the game (Aumann and Shapley, 1974; Roth, 1977). The former interpretation makes the connection between the Shapley value and generalized Nash bargaining theory. The latter interpretation begins with the fact that ψ satisfies the formula

$$\psi v(t) = E[v(S_t^R/\{t\}) - v(S_t^R)].$$

[2] In the present model, all such temporary equilibria with rationing are K-equilibria as defined in Grandmont (1977b).
[3] I am grateful to J.M. Grandmont for suggesting this nomenclature.

Here S_t^R is the set of players preceding t in a random order R on the set of players, and E is the expectations operator when all orders on T are assigned equal
probability. In this way, the Shapley value of a player is the expected value of
his marginal contribution to society, given that he is equally likely to occupy
any place in a random order.

For games without side-payments, Shapley (1969) has proposed the following extension of the value, the λ-transfer value. For such games, $v(S)$ is a set. No
generality is lost by supposing $v(S)$ is convex, bounded above, closed, and contains 0. Let $(\lambda(t))$ be a vector of non-negative weights, one for each player t, and
define the λ-transfer characteristic function v_λ by

$$v_\lambda(S) = \max_{t \in S} \Sigma \; \lambda(t)u(t)$$
$$\text{s.t. } u(S) \in v(S).$$

Now treat v_λ as though it were a transferable utility game; then it has a value
ψv_λ. A λ-transfer value for the game v is a feasible outcome $u(t) \in v(T)$ such
that, for all players t,

$$\lambda(t)u(t) = \psi v_\lambda(t).$$

Shapley (1969) proves the existence of λ-transfer values. Roth (1977) raises
some difficulties in interpreting the λ-transfer value in the same way as the transferable utility value, especially on the boundary of $v(S)$. We will return to this
issue in the discussion of theorem 2 below.

4. Two-sided markets as cooperative games

In this section, two-sided markets are interpreted as cooperative games (T, v),
where $T = M \cup N$ is the set of all buyers and sellers, and v is the characteristic function to be derived. For coalition $S \subset T$, $v(S)$ shows the utility levels S can achieve
for its members. In the von Neumann–Morgenstern theory, the derivation of v
rests on two assumptions: fixed threat and unrestricted side-payments. Here, only
the first of these is satisfied, the fixed threat being refusal to trade. The assumption that price is fixed prevents the making of side-payments. If exchange of a
unit of good 2 involved a sum of money different from p, this would mean that
price was variable, not fixed.

It is clear from the normalization that for any agent t, $v(t) = 0$. It is equally
clear that for any two sellers, say i and i', $v(i, i') = \{(u_i, u_{i'}): u_i \leqslant 0, u_{i'} \leqslant 0\}$ and

likewise, for any two buyers. The only two-player coalitions able to achieve a positive result for their members must, therefore, consist of a buyer and a seller. Here, there are six cases to consider, depending on the relationship of $a(i), b(j)$, and p:

$$a(i) < p < b(j),$$
$$p < a(i) < b(j),$$
$$a(i) < b(j) < p,$$
$$p < b(j) < a(i),$$
$$b(j) < p < a(i),$$
$$b(j) < a(i) < p.$$

For $p < a(i)$, seller i is better off not selling; for $p > b(j)$, seller j is better off not buying. Therefore, the only positive gain is achieved in the case $a(i) < p < b(j)$. In this case:

$$v(\{i,j\}): \{(u_i, j_j): u_i \leq V_i(p), u_j \leq V_j(p)\}.$$

For fixed p, call a seller i *interested* if $a(i) \leq p$; likewise, a buyer j is interested if $p \leq b(j)$. An *interested pair* (i, j) consists of an interested buyer and interested seller. An interested seller i is *borderline* if $a(i) = p$; an interested seller j is *borderline* if $b(j) = p$. The above can be summarized by saying that an interested pair can achieve a positive result — a gain from trade — as long as neither member is borderline. This is the basic principle behind $v(S)$ for larger coalitions also.

Let $M(p)$ be the set of interested sellers and $N(p)$ be the set of interested buyers at price p; these sets have $m(p)$ and $n(p)$ members, respectively. For coalition S, $S \cap M(p)$ is the set of interested sellers in S; $S \cap N(p)$, the set of interested buyers in S. A trade is feasible for S if it involves no more than $k = \min$ $(|S \cap M(p)|, |S \cap N(p)|)$ traders of each type. Let $Z(S)$ be the set of all trades feasible for S, and $X(S)$ the set of corresponding utility vectors. Clearly, for any $z(S) \in Z(S), u(S) \in X(S)$ satisfies

$$u_i = \begin{cases} V_i(p), & \text{if } i \text{ trades in } z(S), \\ 0, & \text{otherwise;} \end{cases}$$

$$u_j = \begin{cases} V(p), & \text{if } j \text{ trades in } z(S), \\ 0, & \text{otherwise.} \end{cases}$$

Let conv $X(S)$ be the convex hull of $X(S)$; this corresponds to the randomization of the various feasible trades. Then

$$v(S) = \{u(S): u(S) \leqslant y(S) \text{ for some } y(S) \text{ in conv } X(S)\}.$$

Note that $v(S)$ is never empty, because the 0-vector, corresponding to no-trade, is always one of its members.

5. λ-Transfer values for two-sided markets

This section reports on the λ-transfer values for the fixed-price model. The first result is the following:

Theorem 1. Suppose there are no borderline agents at fixed price p. Then there is a λ-transfer value such that if $m(p) \geqslant n(p)$:

$$u_i = \begin{cases} \dfrac{n(p)}{m(p)} \, V_i(p), & \text{if } i \text{ is interested,} \\ 0, & \text{otherwise;} \end{cases}$$

$$u_j = \begin{cases} V_j(p), & \text{if } j \text{ is interested,} \\ 0, & \text{otherwise;} \end{cases}$$

and if $n(p) \geqslant m(p)$:

$$u_i = \begin{cases} V_i(p), & \text{if } i \text{ is interested,} \\ 0, & \text{otherwise;} \end{cases}$$

$$u_j = \begin{cases} \dfrac{m(p)}{n(p)} \, V_j(p), & \text{if } j \text{ is interested,} \\ 0, & \text{otherwise.} \end{cases}$$

Proof. For any non-negative vector $\lambda \in R^{m+n}$ and any uninterested agent t, it is clear that $v_\lambda(S/\{t\}) - v_\lambda(S) = 0$, i.e. that t is a dummy in the game v_λ. Hence, $\psi v_\lambda(t) = 0 = \lambda(t)u_t$. This is solved for any $\lambda(t) \geqslant 0$, since $u_t = 0$ is the utility of no-trade. Hence, it remains to consider the set of interested agents, $M(p) \cap N(p)$.

We will consider the case $m(p) \geqslant n(p)$; the argument for the opposite case is analogous.

For all i, j define

$$\lambda_i = [V_i(p)]^{-1} \frac{m(p)}{n(p)} \left[1/2 - \frac{m(p) - n(p)}{2m(p)} \sum_{\ell=0}^{n(p)} \frac{m(p)! \, n(p)!}{(m(p) + \ell)! \, (n(p) - \ell)!} \right],$$

$$\lambda_j = [V_j(p)]^{-1} \left[1/2 + \frac{m(p) - n(p)}{2m(p)} \sum_{\ell=1}^{n(p)} \frac{m(p)! \, n(p)!}{(m(p) + \ell)! \, (n(p) - \ell)!} \right]$$

A routine calculation shows that

$$\lambda_i V_i(p) + \lambda_j V_j(p) = 1 = v_\lambda(\{i, j\}) \quad \text{for all } (i, j).$$

Then, it follows that

$$v_\lambda(S) = \min \left(|S \cap M(p)|, |S \cap N(p)| \right) \quad \text{for any } S.$$

The value ψv_λ is shown in Shapley (1967) to be

$$\psi v_\lambda(i) = 1/2 - \frac{m(p) - n(p)}{2m(p)} \sum_{\ell=0}^{n(p)} \frac{m(p)! \, n(p)!}{(m(p) + \ell)! \, (n(p) - \ell)!} \, ,$$

$$\psi v_\lambda(j) = 1/2 + \frac{m(p) - n(p)}{2m(p)} \sum_{\ell=1}^{n(p)} \frac{m(p)! \, n(p)!}{(m(p) + \ell)! \, (n(p) - \ell)!} \, .$$

At a value allocation u:

$$\lambda_i u_i = \psi v_\lambda(i) \text{ implies } u_i = \frac{n(p)}{m(p)} V_i(p),$$

$$\lambda_j u_j = \psi v_\lambda(j) \text{ implies } u_j = V_j(p),$$

which was to be shown.

The terms of the form $m(p)/n(p)$ and $n(p)/m(p)$ in the statement of theorem 1 correspond to uniform rationing. Note that when $m(p) = n(p)$, the theorem states that the Walrasian equilibrium is a λ-transfer value allocation.

It is clear from symmetry considerations that the only value allocation with $\lambda(t) > 0$ for all interested agents is that of theorem 1. However, there also exist *trivial* λ-transfer values of the form $\lambda(t) = 0$ if t is interested, $\lambda(t) > 0$ for at least one uninterested t. Then, in the game $v_\lambda(S)$, every agent is a dummy. Hence, $\lambda(t)u(t) = \psi v_\lambda(t) = 0$ has a solution for any $u(t)$, such that $u(t) \geqslant 0$ all t; that is, any von Neumann–Morgenstern imputation is a λ-transfer value. What is more surprising, if there exists a borderline agent, there exist only trivial λ-transfer values.

Theorem 2. Suppose there is at least one borderline agent. Then, any imputation is a λ-transfer value.

Proof. Consider the case where seller i is borderline; the case for a borderline buyer is similar.

At a value allocation, for any buyer j, $\lambda_j = 0$. Suppose not. Then, $v_\lambda(i,j) > 0$. Since $v_\lambda(i) = 0$, i is not a dummy, so $\psi v_\lambda(i) > 0$. At a value allocation, since i is borderline, $\cup < \psi v_\lambda(i) = \lambda_i u_i = \lambda_i \cdot 0 = 0$, a contradiction. Hence, $\lambda_j = 0$ for any buyer j.

Next, for any interested buyer i, $\lambda_i = 0$. If not, $v_\lambda(i,j) = \lambda_i V_i(p) + 0 \cdot V_j(p) = \lambda_i V_i(p) > 0$. Then, $\psi v_\lambda(j) > 0$, which leads to a contradiction, as before.

Therefore, at any value allocation, $\lambda(t) = 0$ for all interested t. Then, the game $v_\lambda(S)$ is inessential, and any imputation is a λ-transfer value, as long as some $\lambda(t) > 0$ for uninterested t.

It is the aspect of things noted in theorem 2 which recalls the problem raised by Roth (1980). Namely, a rational player would not expect the presence of a borderline agent to make anything possible, including no trade whatsoever, but this is precisely what happens. On the other hand, the problem is not so serious if one considers that the set of all prices where there is a borderline agent is negligible in relation to the set of all prices. In the remainder of the chapter attention will be restricted to the set of prices, where there exist non-trivial λ-transfer values.

6. Böhm-Bawerk's horse market

This section considers Böhm-Bawerk's horse market, introduced in section 2, from the standpoint of theorem 1. Given the demand and supply curves of fig. 17.1, one can compute the individual buying and selling probabilities corresponding to uniform rationing. This is done in table 17.1. For an interested buyer, this probability is simply min $[m(p)/n(p), 1]$; for an interested seller, min $[n(p)/m(p), 1]$. We denote these functions by $f(p)$, and $g(p)$, respectively; they are computed in table 17.1.

Table 17.1
Individual buying and selling probabilities

Price interval ($)	Probability that interested buyer buys	Probability that interested seller sells
(0,10)	0	1
(10,11)	1/10	1
(11,15)	2/10	1
(15,17)	3/9	1
(17,18)	4/8	1
(18,20)	4/7	1
(20,21)	5/6	1
(21,21.50)	1	1
(21.50,22)	1	5/6
(22,24)	1	4/6
(24,25)	1	3/6
(25,26)	1	3/7
(26,28)	1	2/8
(28,30)	1	1/8
(30, ∞)	1	0

By the expected utility theorem, these probabilities readily lead to a calculation of expected utility as a function of fixed price p. We shall call these functions $E\,V_t(p)$, *appraisal functions*.

In general, a seller i's appraisal function is given by

$$E\,V_i(p) = g(p)\,V_i(p) + [1 - g(p)] \cdot 0$$
$$= \begin{cases} 0, & \text{if } p < a(i) \\ g(p)\,V_i(p), & \text{if } p > a(i), \end{cases}$$

and a buyer j's appraisal function is given by

$$E\,V_j(p) = f(p)\,V_j(p) + [1 - f(p)] \cdot 0$$
$$= \begin{cases} 0, & \text{if } p > b(j), \\ f(p)\,V_j(p), & \text{if } p < b(j). \end{cases}$$

Two such functions, one for seller 1 ($a(1) = 10$) and one for buyer, buyer 8 ($b(8) = 30$), are graphed in fig. 17.2. The two appraisal functions are chosen to depict the broadest possible range of agents' experience. The piecewise linearity is due to the hypothesis of risk neutrality; piecewise curvature would result from risk-aversion.

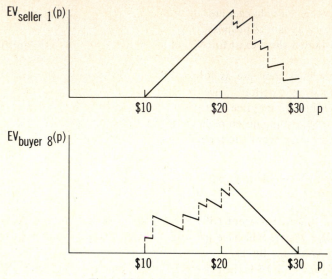

Figure 17.2. Appraisal functions.

Define a price regime as any interval on which both $f(p)$ and $g(p)$ are constant. Clearly, for any interested agent t, $E\,V_t(p)$ is continuous on any regime, but discontinuous at boundary points marking a change of regime. Furthermore, on any regime, $E\,V_i(p)$ is an increasing function of p if i is interested; $E\,V_j(p)$, a decreasing function of p if j is interested. This reveals an interesting phenomenon, first noted by Laroque (1978a) in another context:

> ... assuming local unicity, an increase of the price of one commodity near the competitive equilibrium is always to the advantage of the sellers and the disadvantage of the buyers. This suggests that the long run determination of prices should be the outcome of a struggle between buyers and sellers in each market.

The next section of the chapter proposes a price adjustment process for two-sided markets that incorporates the struggle aspect just noted.

7. Price dynamics in two-sided markets

At any given price, it is evident that some agents will desire a higher price next period, other agents a lower price. In the neighborhood of the current price, buyers' and sellers' interests are directly opposed. This need no longer be the case, however, when price changes are large enough to imply a change of regime. There-fore, the price dynamics proposed here will be regime dynamics, and interest will focus on whether there exist forces within the market that lead to a Walrasian re-gime, for instance.

The dynamics then are as follows. At current price p, all interested agents have a vote on next period's price. Next period's price regime is chosen by major-ity rule, with the exact price next period being drawn from a uniform probability distribution over the chosen regime's prices. Under this hypothesis,[4] regime (p_0, p_1) is preferred by agent t to regime (p_0', p_1') if and only if

$$\frac{1}{p_1 - p_0} \int_{p_0}^{p_1} E\, V_t(p)\, \mathrm{d}p > \frac{1}{p_1' - p_0'} \int_{p_0'}^{p_1'} E\, V_t(p)\, \mathrm{d}p.$$

Call a regime *ideal* for agent t if t prefers that regime to any other. For any sel-ler, the ideal regime will have prices at least as high as Walrasian levels, the re-verse holding for any buyer.

More formally, if p^t is the price at time t within the price regime (p_0^t, p_1^t) and $M(p^t) \cup N(p^t)$ is the set of interested agents at time t, then p^{t+1} in (p_0^{t+1}, p_1^{t+1}), where for any other regime (p_0^{-t+1}, p_1^{-t+1}), the number of interested agents pre-ferring (p_0^{t+1}, p_1^{t+1}) to (p_0^{-t+1}, p_1^{-t+1}) is greater than the number of interested agents with the opposite preference.

The intuitive meaning of these dynamics is as follows. At price p^t, only the interested agents have market power (positive Shapley value). This market power takes the form of a vote on next period's price regime. One can think of voting in this context as an exact description of the decision-making process, or simply as a stylization of something more complicated. In any event, a majority rule equilibrium, should one exist, will have very strong attractive properties as the group choice — for instance, as a strong Nash equilibrium of the associated voting game.

Under these dynamics, a Walrasian regime is a dynamic equilibrium and so the question immediately arises, is the Walrasian regime a stable dynamic equilibrium, starting from any given fixed price? For Böhm-Bawerk's horse market, one has a very satisfactory answer:

Theorem 3. For Böhm-Bawerk's horse market, the majority-rule price dynamics converge to the Walrasian regime in, at most, two periods, starting from any fixed price.

---

[4]   This is not the only set comparison imaginable. A variety of possible set comparisons are given in Gardenfors (1979). Expected utility comparison has the virtue of being complete.

Table 17.2
Sellers' table

Interval a(i)	10,11	11,15	15,17	17,18	18,20	20,21	21,21.5	21.5,22	22,24	24,25	25,26	26,28	28,30
$10	0,5	3	6	7,5	9	10,5	11,25	9,8	8,7	7,25	6,7	4,25	2,3
11	0	2	5	6,5	8	9,5	10,25	9,0	8,0	6,75	6,2	4,0	2,2
15	0	0	1	2,5	4	5,5	6,25	5,6	5,3	4,75	4,5	3	1,8
17	0	0	0	.5	2	3,5	4,25	4,0	4,0	3,75	3,6	2,5	1,5
20	0	0	0	0	0	.5	1,25	1,5	2,0	2,25	2,4	1,8	1,1
21,5	0	0	0	0	0	0	0	0,2	1,0	1,5	1,7	1,4	0,9
25	0	0	0	0	0	0	0	0	0	0	0,2	0,5	0,5
26	0	0	0	0	0	0	0	0	0	0	0	0,25	0,4

Table 17.3
Buyers' table

b(j)	Interval 10,11	11,15	15,17	17,18	18,20	20,21	21,21.5	21.5,22	22,24	24,25	25,26	26,28	28,30
30	2,0	3,4	4,8	6,25	6,3	7,9	8,75	8,25	7	5,5	4,5	3	1
28	1,8	3,0	4,0	5,25	5,1	6,25	6,75	6,25	5	3,5	2,5	1	0
26	1,6	2,6	3,3	4,25	4,0	4,6	4,75	4,25	3	1,5	0,5	0	0
24	1,4	2,2	2,6	3,25	2,9⁻	2,9⁺	2,25	2,25	1	0	0	0	0
22	1,2	1,8	2,0	2,6	2,0	1,25	0,75	0,25	0	0	0	0	0
21	1,0	1,4	1,7	1,75	1,1	0,4	0	0	0	0	0	0	0
20	1,0	1,4	1,3	1,25	0,6	0	0	0	0	0	0	0	0
18	0,8	1,0	0,7	0,25	0	0	0	0	0	0	0	0	0
17	0,6	0,8	0,3	0	0	0	0	0	0	0	0	0	0
15	0,4⁺	0,4	0	0	0	0	0	0	0	0	0	0	0

Table 17.4
Agents' characteristics

| | Buyers' characteristics | | | Sellers' characteristics | |
	Bid price ($)	Ideal interval		Ask price ($)	Ideal interval
1	30	(21,21.5)	1	10	(21,21.5)
2	28	(21,21.5)	2	11	(21,21.5)
3	26	(21,21.5)	3	15	(21,21.5)
4	24	(17,18)	4	17	(21,21.5)
5	22	(17,18)	5	20	(25,26)
6	21	(17,18)	6	21,5	(25,26)
7	20	(15,17)	7	25	(26,28)
8	18	(11,15)	8	26	(28,30)
9	17	(11,15)			
10	15	(10,11)			

Proof. In tables 17.2 and 17.3 are computed the average expected utilities by regime for sellers and buyers, respectively. This forms the basis for the ideal regimes noted in table 17.4. It is clear that agents' preferences are single-peaked[5] on the set of regimes, so that the median voter corresponds to a majority rule equilibrium.

The proof proceeds by inspection of cases.

Case 1. $p^t < \$ 10$. In this case, all interested agents are buyers. The majority rule equilibrium among buyers is the regime ($\$ 17, 18$). Therefore, $p^{t+1} \in (17, 18)$. In the regime $(17, 18)$, there are eight interested buyers, those with bid price above $\$ 17$, and four interested sellers, those with ask price below $\$ 18$. For this set of interested agents, seven have the Walrasian regime as ideal. This majority makes $p^{t+2} \in (21, 21.5)$, as was to be shown.

The cases $10 < p^t < 11$ and $11 < p^t < 15$ are exactly like this case.

Case 2. $15 < p^t < 17$. Here, there are nine interested buyers and four interested sellers. Of these, seven have ideal regime at Walrasian prices. Hence, $p^{t+1} \in (21, 21.5)$ is a majority rule equilibrium.

One can check that all cases $17 < p^t < 30$ behave like this one.

Case 3. $p^t > 30$. In this case, the only interested agents are the eight sellers, four of which favor the Walrasian regime. The median regime here is not unique, the median being the set $\{21, 21.5), (21.5, 22), (22, 24), (24, 25), (25, 26)\}$. However, whichever of these is chosen, one has $p^{t+2} \in (21, 21.5)$, as in case 2. This exhausts all the cases.

---

[5] See Black (1958) for a discussion of this concept.

One would like to know how general is the phenomenon noted in theorem 3. Although a complete answer to this question is not yet available, one can point out the following important features of the above demonstration. First and foremost is the single-peakedness of agents' preferences, which allows for the existence of a majority rule equilibrium at each step of the process. Secondly, one has a direct relationship between an agent's ask or bid price and their ideal regime. Sellers with higher asking prices tend to have higher-priced ideal regimes, as do buyers with higher bid prices. This gives a preponderant role in the process to the lowest asking-price sellers and highest bid-price buyers — just those agents most likely to have the Walrasian regime as their ideal. Indeed, for Böhm-Bawerk's data, one observes a concentration of seven agents' ideal regime at the Walrasian regime, which surely accounts for the rapid rate of convergence. Thirdly, the example has dealt solely with risk-neutral agents. It is obvious, however, that for a given distribution of agents' characteristics, the effect of risk-aversion is to make the Walrasian regime, with its attendant certain outcome, more attractive. The effect of risk-loving will be more problematic.

For a general convergence result, conditions of the following sort appear to be needed:

(1) all agents risk-neutral or risk-averse,

(2) bid prices and asking prices fairly evenly spread, and

(3) a fairly even number of potential buyers and sellers.

When such conditions on the distribution of agents' characteristics are not satisfied, it is easy to give counterexamples to the dynamic stability of the Walrasian regime.

To see the role of (2), suppose that in Böhm-Bawerk's example, buyer 1 bids $3,000 instead of $30. Obviously, every seller thinks the regime (28, 3,000) ideal, so for $p^t > 21.5$, one has one-step convergence to this regime.

The following example shows the role of (3). Suppose $a(1) = 1, b(1) = 8, b(2) = 7, b(3) = 3, b(4) = 2$. Potential buyers considerably outnumber sellers, but all are risk-neutral. For buyers 1 and 2, the ideal regime is (3,7); for 3 and 4, (2,3). Thus, for any price $p^t < 7$, the system converges in one step to the regime (3,7), instead of the Walrasian regime (7,8).

The final example shows the role of (1). Let $a(1) = 5, a(2) = 10, b(1) = 13, b(2) = 8$. The Walrasian interval is (8,10). All agents are risk-neutral except seller 1, who is risk-loving with $V_1(p) = (p - 5)^2$. A routine calculation shows that (10,13) is ideal for both sellers; hence, one has one-step convergence to (10,13) if $p^t > 10$.

Further insight into the convergence question can be gained by considering a large economy framework.[6] This will be pursued in the next section.

---

[6] See, for instance, Hildenbrand (1974).

8. Price dynamics in a large economy

In the large economy we shall consider, there will be a continuum of potential buyers and sellers with both sides of the market having equal measure. This captures condition (3) above. Bid and ask prices will be distributed uniformly over the respective intervals of agents. In particular, letting $M = N = [0,1]$, we suppose bid- and asking-price distributions of the following sort:

$$a(0) = a_0,$$

$$a(i) = a_0 + i, \qquad 0 \leqslant i \leqslant 1,$$

$$b(0) = b_0,$$

$$b(j) = b_0 - j, \qquad 0 \leqslant j \leqslant 1.$$

All agents are supposed to be potentially active at some positive price: $a_0 \geqslant 0$, $b_0 \geqslant 1$.

There is a unique Walrasian equilibrium price and a positive quantity transacted as long as

$$0 < b_0 - a_0 < 2.$$

In this case, the Walrasian equilibrium quantity transacted is $(b_0 - a_0)/2$, and the Walrasian equilibrium price is $(b_0 + a_0)/2$. For $b_0 - a_0 > 2$, all agents transact at Walrasian equilibrium and any price in the interval $[a_0 + 1, b_0 - 1]$ is an equilibrium price. For $b_0 - a_0 \leqslant 0$, the Walrasian equilibrium quantity transacted is 0, and any price in the interval $[b_0, a_0]$ is an equilibrium price. In this situation there will be a continuum of regimes. This completes the formalization of points (1)–(3) above.

We shall continue to assume that all agents are risk-neutral. What we can now show is the following:

Theorem 4. In the large economy, as long as $0 < b_0 - a_0 < 2$, there is convergence in a finite period of time to Walrasian equilibrium, when the majority price dynamics are in force.

Proof. We will consider the case $b_0 - a_0 = 1$; the other cases follow by a quite analogous argument.

We begin by deriving the appraisal function for seller $a(i)$. The selling probability function $g(p)$ is given by

$$g(p) = \begin{cases} 1, & \text{for } a_0 \leqslant p \leqslant p^*, \\ \dfrac{b_0 - p}{p - a_0}, & \text{for } p > p^* \geqslant b_0, \\ 0, & \text{for } p > b_0, \end{cases}$$

where p^* is the Walrasian price equilibrium. The appraisal function $E\, V_i(p)$, therefore, is

$$E\, V_i(p) = \begin{cases} 0, & \text{for } p < a(i), \\ p - a(i), & \text{for } 0(i) \leqslant p \leqslant p^*, \\ \dfrac{b_0 - p}{p - a_0}\,(p - a(i)), & \text{for } p^* < p, \\ 0, & \text{for } b_0 < p. \end{cases}$$

Of course, some of the above intervals may be empty for a given value of $a(i)$.

Given the appraisal function for seller i, one can determine the ideal price $p(i)$ for agent i. Here $p(i)$: $\max_p E\, V_i(p)$. Clearly, there are two cases of the maximization: at p^* or at a price above p^*.

It is easy to check that the dividing line between these two cases is precisely $a(i) = 3/4\, a_0 + 1/4\, b_0$, namely:

$$p(i) = \begin{cases} \dfrac{a_0 + b_0}{2}, & \text{for } a(i) \leqslant 3/4\, a_0 + 1/4\, b_0, \\ a_0 + \sqrt{(a(i) - a_0)}, & \text{for } a(i) > 3/4\, a_0 + 1/4\, b_0. \end{cases}$$

When all sellers are risk-neutral, the sellers with lower reservation prices are more likely to find the Walrasian price regime ideal.

Similarly for buyers, the buying probability function is:

$$f(p) = \begin{cases} 0, & \text{for } p < a, \\ \dfrac{p - a_0}{b_0 - p}, & \text{for } a_0 \leqslant p \leqslant p^*, \\ 1, & \text{for } p^* < p \leqslant b_0, \end{cases}$$

and the appraisal function $E\, V_j(p)$ is

$$\mathrm{E}\,V_j(p)=\begin{cases}0, & \text{for } p<a_0,\\[2mm]\dfrac{p-a_0}{a_0-p}\,(b(j)-p), & \text{for } a_0\leqslant p\leqslant p^*,\\[2mm]b(j)-p, & \text{for } p^*<p\leqslant b(i),\\[2mm]0, & \text{for } p>b(j).\end{cases}$$

The ideal prices for buyers $p(j)$ are then given by:

$$p(j)=\begin{cases}\dfrac{a_0+b_0}{2}, & \text{for } b(j)\geqslant a_{0/4}+3/4\,b_0,\\[2mm]b_0-\sqrt{b_0-b(j)}, & \text{for } b(j)<a_{0/4}+3/4\,b_0.\end{cases}$$

It is precisely the buyers with the highest reservation price whose ideal is a Walrasian price.

Now, one can define the price dynamics $p^{t+1}=F(p^t)$, where F is the majority price adjustment. F can be described as follows. Given p^t, the set of interested agents $I(p^t)$ is given as follows:

$$I(p^t)=M(p^t)\cup N(p^t),$$

where

$$M(p^t)=\{i:a(i)\leqslant p^t\},$$
$$N(p^t)=\{j:b(j)\geqslant p^t\}.$$

Clearly, the majority rule equilibrium of the set of interested agents will be the ideal price of the median interested agent. This majority rule equilibrium price will then be the price p^{t+1}.

To describe F explicitly, let b_{med} be the ideal price of the media seller, and a_{med} the ideal price of the median buyer. Then $F(p^t)$ is given by:

$$F(p^t)=\begin{cases}b_{\mathrm{med}}, & p^t<a_0,\\[2mm]b_0-\sqrt{b_0-(p^t+\tfrac{1}{2})}; & a_0\leqslant p^t<3\,\dfrac{a_0}{4}+\dfrac{b_0}{4},\\[2mm]\dfrac{a_0+b_0}{2}, & \text{if } 3\,\dfrac{a_0}{4}+\dfrac{b_0}{4}\leqslant p^t\leqslant\dfrac{a_0}{4}+3\,\dfrac{b_0}{4},\\[2mm]a_0+\sqrt{(p^t-\tfrac{1}{2})-a_0)}, & \dfrac{a}{4}+\dfrac{3}{4}\,b^0<p^t\leqslant b_0\\[2mm]a_{\mathrm{med}}; & b_0<p^t,\end{cases}$$

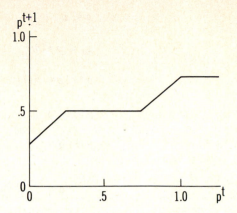

Figure 17.3. Majoritarian price adjustment function, $F(p^t)$ $\alpha_0 = 0; b_0 = 1; p^* = 0,5$.

where

$$b_{med} = b_0 - \sqrt{\tfrac{1}{2}},$$

$$a_{med} = a_0 + \sqrt{\tfrac{1}{2}}.$$

Fig. 17.3 illustrates $F(p^t)$ for the case $a_0 = 0_1$, $b_0 = 1$.

Now it is clear from $F(p^t)$ why p^t converges to p^* in a finite number of steps. For any p^t in the interval $[3a_0/4 + b_0/4, a_0/4 + 3(b_0/4)]$, one has one-step convergences. For p^t outside this interval, $F(p^t)$ represents a contraction of p^t towards this interval. Thus, for any p^t below a^0, $p^{t+1} = b_0 - \sqrt{\tfrac{1}{2}}$, which is already in this interval. The symmetry of the adjustment process yields a similar convergence in at most two steps for $p^t > a_0/4 + 3b_0/4$.

However, for general $b_0 - a_0$, one can only show finite convergence: the convergence slows down as $b_0 - a_0$ approaches 2.

What is interesting about this result is that one observes the same two-step convergence that one did in Böhm-Bawerk's example. Indeed, the latter looks very much like a random sample of size 18 drawn from the population of the large economy suitably normalized. This suggests the following line of argument.[7]

Consider a sequence E_n of economies approaching the large way E is the limit. Corresponding to each of the E_n will be a dynamic price adjustment equation F_{E_n}. Then it seems likely that for E_n close enough to E, F_{E_n} is close enough to F_E to have the same convergence properties. Thus, the finite convergence prop-

---

[7] I am grateful to Y. Balasko for pointing this out.

erty for two-sided markets would appear to be the rule rather than the exception.

9. Conclusion

It would be desirable to investigate the issues that concern this chapter in a more general setting, for instance one with many divisible goods. However, it is clear at the outset that certain generalizations will not hold. First, in a more general setting, the connection between value allocation and K equilibrium is sure to be lost, since a value allocation is a Pareto optimum relative to the fix price system p, while a K-equilibrium need not be.[8] Similarly, in a multi-dimensional model, majority rule equilibrium is unlikely to exist, and the majoritarian price dynamics must be redefined.

Nevertheless, one can sketch how such a theory would look. Given a fixed price p, one computes the value allocation relative to p. This value allocation will in general force both sides of the market off their demand and supply curves, when goods are divisible. One then computes the appraisal functions on the price space p, and introduces a collective choice mechanism as a basis for the price dynamics. Needless to say, the construction of such a theory is an effort for future research.

Yet I think it likely that, even in more complicated settings, something like the present dynamic theory will still go through. One has to admit though that the dynamic tendency to Walrasian equilibrium remains largely unexplored.

References

Aumann, R.J. and L.S. Shapley (1974) *Values for Non-Atomic Games* (Princeton University Press).

Benassy, J.P. (1975) "Neo-Keynesian Disequilibrium in a Monetary Economy", *Review of Economic Studies*, 42, 503–524.

Black, R.D. (1958) *The Theory of Committees and Elections* (Cambridge University Press, New York).

Böhm, V. and H. Muller (1977) "Two Examples of Equilibrium under Price Rigidities and Quantity Rationing", *Feitschrift fur National Okonomic*, 37, 165–173.

Böhm-Bawerk, E. Von (1923) *Positive Theory of Capital* (G.E. Steckert, New York).

Drèze, J.H. (1975) "Existence of an Exchange Equilibrium under Price Regidities", *International Economic Review*, 16, 301–320.

Gardenfors, P. (1979) "On Definitions of Manipulation of Social Choice Functions", in: J.J. Laffont, ed., *Aggregation and Revelation of Preferences* (North-Holland, Amsterdam).

---

[8] See Böhm and Muller (1977) for examples of this phenomenon.

Grandmont, J.M. (1977a) "The Logic of the Fix-Price Method", *Scandanavian Journal of Economics*, 79, 169–186.

Grandmont, J.M. (1977b) "Temporary General Equilibrium Theory", *Econometrica*, 45, 535–572.

Grandmont, J.M., G. Laroque, and Y. Younes (1978) "Equilibrium with Quantity Rationing and Recontracting", *Journal of Economic Theory*, 19, 34–102.

Harsanyi, J.C. (1977) *Rational Behavior and Bargaining Equilibrium in Games and Social Situations* (Cambridge University Press).

Hildenbrand, W. (1974) *Core and Equilibria of a Large Economy* (Princeton University Press).

Laroque, G. (1978a) "The Fixed-Price Equilibrium: Some Results in Local Comparative Statics", *Econometrica*, 46, 1127–1154.

Laroque, G. (1978b) "On the Dynamics of Disequilibrium: A Simple Remark", *Review of Economic Studies*, 45, 273–278.

Roth, A.E. (1977) "The Shapley Value as a von Neumann-Morgenstern Utility", *Econometrica*, 45, 657–664.

Roth, A.E. (1980) "Values for Games Without Sidepayments: Some Difficulties with Current Concepts", *Econometrica*, 48, 457–465.

Shapley, L.S. (1967) "The Value of the Game's a Tool in Theoretical Economics", P-3658 (The Rand Corporation, Santa Monica).

Shapley, L.S. (1969) "Utility Comparisons and the Theory of Games", in: Gh.T. Guilbaud, ed., *La Decision* (Editions du CNRS, Paris).

Shapley, L.S. and M. Shubik (1972) "The Assignment Game I: The Core", *International Journal of Game Theory*, 2, 111–130.

Younes, Y. (1975) "On the Role of Money in the Process of Exchange and the Existence of a Non-Walrasian Equilibrium", *Review of Economic Studies*, 42, 489–501.